Humanizing
the School

CURRICULUM DEVELOPMENT
AND THEORY

Ryland W. Crary

UNIVERSITY OF PITTSBURGH

HUMANIZING THE SCHOOL

CURRICULUM DEVELOPMENT AND THEORY

 Alfred A. Knopf   New York

LB
885
C7

To

Jane,
Gretchen,
Laura,
James,
Stephen,
and Nathan

Acknowledgments

To assess the weight of intellectual influence upon one's own work is probably impossible; yet it seems to me that my views of the school and society may have been most profoundly affected by Thorstein Veblen, Lester Frank Ward, Martin Luther King, Jr., Martin Buber, Albert Camus, Erich Fromm, Raymond O. Williams, Gardner Murphy, and surely—as so many others have acknowledged—George S. Counts and John Childs.

My view of the profession has been enriched immeasurably by men for whom I have worked, among them, Harry K. Newburn, Howard Anderson, John Haefner, Erling Hunt, Lyle Ashby—and by Brooks Courtright and Mac Crary, two of the most dedicated educators I have known.

The students who have sustained and challenged me are numbered in literal thousands. They must be unnamed, but hundreds of them are far from anonymous in my mind. Without a doubt, I have learned more from them than ever they did from me.

I can only try to express my appreciation for the unmistakable affection and confidence of my colleagues in the School of Education at the University of Pittsburgh. Among these, the late Maurice Thomas alone shall I single out to express an esteem which he well knew I held.

Some of the best assistance must no doubt go unacknowledged. But I must speak of the editorial encouragement and assistance of Robert Weiss and Ina Winer, and of the fine work of the lady who not only typed the manuscript from my illegible scrawl but spoke well of its substance, Edna Anish. And large credit for seeing to it that the work was brought to completion, I owe my wife, Penny.

Contents

PART THREE
LEARNING RESOURCES AND HUMAN POTENTIAL

Chapter VIII The Humanistic–Ethical Dimension 253

Chapter IX The Creative–Aesthetic Dimension 285

Chapter XIV   Since 1967—The Urban Effort
Reconsidered   441

xi

Humanizing the School

CURRICULUM DEVELOPMENT
AND THEORY

Introduction

The course of the American nation has been committed to democracy; key words of this commitment have been liberty, equality, freedom—to which, in our time, security has been added. Because these goals, while not mutually exclusive, are not altogether harmonious, the problems of balance and priority of objectives raise severe stresses and issues.

Thomas Jefferson saw the nation as a land of freeholders, independent in their decision-making, but such has not been the product of our history. American civilization has developed complex aggregates of big institutions with large power: big business, big government, big labor, big agriculture, and big education. It would be fatuous to assert that these institutional complexes have made easier the achievement of the American dream. Jefferson's ideal of the yeoman farmer and the contemporary complete company man are as far apart as 1776 and 1984.

The dream of America has posed the free man as the ultimate goal of democracy. The free man seeks his own interest—but if he does not seek it intelligently, he winds up unhappy; if he does not seek it ethically, he risks the loss of his own freedom. If he seeks it with spiritual understanding, he may search out his own interest through service to others.

The coercions and persuasions of the modern institutional

3

world tend toward a different effect; there is always the anthro-pomorphic, institutional image to be served: "The company comes first," "just one big happy family at Amalgamated, Inc.," "you're gonna like it in Successnikiana, 'cause all the folks like the same things and get along real well." Freedom here is in no peril of death from cannons and tanks as it might be in a totalitarian state, but it may be smothered under the pillows of materialism and conformity.

What is happening? It is possible to perceive trends toward greater concentrations of wealth and economic power, toward fewer men fully their own decision-makers, toward wrestling among the dinosaurs of organizational might, toward observable corruption of popular media. But also perceptible is a growing awareness of these hazardous trends and awakening critical appraisal and analysis.

This is where education enters. Education can bolster the will, knowledge, and understanding. If the survival of our nation is to be measured in the growth of our democratic institutions, then teachers must analyze the times, interpret them for our youth, and enable our youth to play willingly the joyful, hazardous role of free men.

The American school has been unique in its obligation to educate all the children of all the people. It is, of course, a dual institution: a center for intellectual development as well as a center for youth development. It has recently become the focus of reexami-nation and has received unfavorable evaluation from such nonedu-cators as Admiral Hyman Rickover, who rejected both its products and its premises, and critical vindication from such distinguished professionals as Dr. James B. Conant.

Few would quarrel with the obligation of education to be intellectual, and few would doubt that the intellectual quality of the American school can be improved. There *is* room, however, to doubt some of the prescriptions for intellectualizing the curricu-lum; the process is sometimes summarily equated with such devices as returning to the classical tradition, primarily emphasizing mathematics and science, "toughening up" the courses, following a European model of selectivity and discipline, or simply scuttling all aspects of program not related directly to college preparation.

"Life adjustment" has been a particular target for those critics

4

who refuse to admit the dual function of the high school. They rail at education for assuming functions that they claim more properly belong to such other institutions as the church and the home, and one might add, by implication, the workhouse, the pool hall, and the reformatory. The statistics on juvenile delinquency, mental illness, and family instability make it clear that for the school to assume any less obligation for life adjustment and youth development would be a cardinal error of social irresponsibility. These attitudes are axiomatic, even clichés, among teachers who live and work with the daily realities of students in curriculum and in life. When the armchair- or editorial-critics of education resolutely refuse to face the facts among which educators live, the best course is to ignore the nuisances they create as much as possible.

Of their own volition, educators will not destroy the basic concept of education that has made American civilization great. On the other hand, they should not defend the indefensible. They can afford to laugh at some of the curricular and extracurricular practices that have been adopted or forced upon them by vested interests or the common culture. But, simply because amateur critics do not know what such things are about, they have not scuttled some of the necessities of a first-rate school: a guidance program, a physical education and recreational program, an activities program, experience in the arts, and a student government.

When the critic speaks of the intellect, the educator will listen respectfully to him if the critic talks twentieth-century sense, but the educator may have a little trouble concealing his boredom if he is harangued with antique nonsense about mental discipline, faculty psychology, or doctrines of the elite. The educator will be forced to evaluate the perspective of special pleaders, however eloquently they argue the narrow case for more scientists, more typists who can spell better than the boss, more free-enterprise indoctrination, more neohumanists. It sounds a mite naïve, perhaps even chauvinistic, but the educator's commitment is to produce thinking, well-informed, healthy, happy, democratic American citizens.

No particular issue stands at this point; the student can work harder and learn more in school than he does now. If the community wants intellectuality in its schools, it can have it. It will have to be a deliberate choice. This choice will involve such matters as: a willing investment in school libraries and laboratories on a scale comparable to that spent on athletic plants; cutting off the support of anti-intellectual postures in the common culture; securing the position of the scholar–teacher with a decent teaching schedule and the bulwarks of true academic and intellectual freedom; supporting "the method of intelligence," which is not a retreat to the comforting illusions of tradition but a daring venture into exploration and experimentation.

If the critics of education and the supporting public want a school devoted both to intelligence and the welfare of youth, they can have it. And the first obligation is not to endorse a blank check for financial support; it is to find out what modern education is all about.

Modern education is what this book is about. Perhaps *post-modern* would be an even more appropriate term. The curriculum theory herein elaborated is set squarely amid the strange realities of a world invested with the capacity to destroy itself and as yet unsure whether or not to test that capacity. In this sense, the author heartily concurs with Norman Cousins that "modern man is obsolete."

The modern American curriculum theory is solidly rooted in progressive, educational experience, altered, criticized, and extended—*made* modern, as it were. Despite the historical and rhetorical epitaphs written for progressive education by Lawrence Cremin and Paul Woodring, among others, we are sure that the reports of its death (like Mark Twain's, once upon a time) have been greatly exaggerated. However, we are aware of the shortcomings and confusions of the progressive movement. We have long taken issue with erstwhile curriculum experts who, we thought, in the name of reforming the curriculum, made war upon it. We have seen maudlin sentiment and anti-intellectuality masquerade as progressive techniques. We have seen laissez faire confused with democratic methods. Perhaps progressive education labored in enough confusion to warrant the charge that it lacked an adequate philosophy. The likelier assumption is that it neglected to operate consistently on the profound insights available to it. John Dewey stated the issue clearly enough when he asserted:

> As far as school education is a part of the required practical means, educational theory or philosophy has the task and the opportunity of helping to break down the philosophy of fixation that bolsters external authority in opposition to free cooperation.[1]

This text is rooted in a quest for educational reality; the curriculum theory herein set forth is deeply philosophical. Every effort has been made in the writing of this text to create a *true book*. By this we mean that the work has its beginning in a set of clearly articulated premises, it explores them, it develops them, and it works toward a termination. The parts and chapters would not make their clearest sense if shuffled about. The sense is intended to be cumulative. What goes before is essential to the conceptualizing of what comes after. It is not possible to begin reading this book in the middle and make complete sense of it.

Conceptualized learning is the theoretical thesis to be explored in this book. Because the term has become fairly hackneyed of late, the text will precisely define, elaborate, clarify, and illustrate what is meant. In Part One, without attempting a capsulized review of American educational or curricular history, we establish foundations in a historical and social setting. Modern educational theory demands a philosophy, and a philosophy is herein both exposited and applied. This philosophy we have called *pragmatic existentialism*. The pervasive meaning of this is consistent throughout the work. Because curriculum goes into action only when planned learning takes place, we have asserted a new model for instruction, consonant both with the theory of conceptualized learning and with the broad philosophical umbrella encompassing it.

In Part Two the educational continuum is explored in its institutional terms. In both the elementary and secondary schools we acknowledge the necessity and worth of considerable current practice; because we are rooted in reality, we make no utopian assump-

---

[1] John Dewey, "Challenge to Liberal Thought," *Fortune* (August 1944), p. 190.

tions about starting over. As Albert Camus said in *The Rebel*, history has taught us the vainglory and grandiosity of revolutionary hopes. The intent of this book is to clarify purposes, to urge the necessity to study in perspective, and searchingly to reappraise every aspect of our educational institutions and their programs.

Part Three deals with the substance of learning under rubrics that have philosophical validity. Not to war upon the subjects, but to explore their substance more profoundly, we use four headings in our search for content: (1) the humanistic–ethical dimension; (2) the creative–aesthetic dimension; (3) the scientific–quantitative dimension; and (4) the vocational–utilitarian dimension. Perhaps the most surprising outcome of this pattern of analysis will be the student's discovery that practically any subject, be it American literature, physics, or vocational agriculture, may have substantive derivatives from or applications to all these areas.

This text also joins issue. Even though our philosophical umbrella is broad, even eclectic, we find it necessary to identify and repudiate curricular premises from philosophical sanctions as diverse as essentialism and social reconstructionism. The text uses authoritative documents critically. Superficial platitudes are not used for interpretive leverage, however austere the committee that repenned them most recently. Though we make sense of some of the causes promoted by specialized groups within education, our efforts are mainly directed toward dissuading educators from jumping aboard any of today's many bandwagons and encouraging those who are already on, to hop off. And while we rejoice at Dr. Conant's first-rate educational sense, and the prestige his name has given to good causes, we do not hesitate to utilize his recommendations critically, and none would applaud this in principle sooner than he.

Because our main preoccupation is with the substance, the stuff, the content of education, and our principal aim is to help humanize through education, we hold some devices in low esteem. Partly because so much time has been spent on gadgets and arrangements that have nothing to do with the substance of education, we have scant concern for instructional television, teaching machines, and team teaching. The opposition (for that is the tone of this text) to these devices is philosophical as well. Depersonalization is so great a hazard in contemporary society that we would hold devices suspect that further depersonalize the school, even if research bore out the grandiose claims of their proponents as to improved academic learning (and for the most part, it does not) .

If we have insisted that this text is both theoretical and philosophical, do not be misled. It is practical. This text makes precise definitions; then it holds to them, applies them, and uses them. It tells what and why; it also tells how. Its specifics are not the specifics of educational folklore or of easy words assigned by one committee or another. Its specifics are the realities and the hard sense of the school in a troubled world. The curriculum recommendations are made only when research and experience demonstrate that they can be carried out. The admonition "ought to be done" is used sparingly; the text does not urge education to essay the impossible or to try to work against the realities of social process. When it says "ought," it has first ascertained that it can be done; it is respectfully thoughtful in stating why and practical in telling how.

This, at any rate, is our intent. The text will make sense, we think, to a great many educators. To some it will not. But for those who do find it sensible, it can be more than reading. It can be a tool; it can be put to work.

PART ONE

FOUNDATIONS OF CURRICULUM

Chapter I

Key Concepts in Curriculum Development

In every child who is born, under no matter what circumstances, and of no matter what parents, the potentiality of the human race is born again: and in him, too, once more, and of each of us, our terrific responsibility towards human life; towards the utmost idea of goodness, of the horror of error, and of God.

Every breath his senses shall draw, every act and every shadow and thing in all creation, is a mortal poison, or is a drug, or is a signal or symptom, or is a teacher, or is a liberator, or is liberty itself, depending entirely upon his understanding: and understanding, and action proceeding from understanding and guided by it, is the one weapon against the world's bombardment, the one medicine, the one instrument by which liberty, health, and joy may be shaped or shaped towards, in the individual, and in the race.[1]

—*James Agee*

Curriculum is the program of intended learning devised by the school. However, in human affairs what is devised is seldom pre-

---

[1] James Agee and Walker Evans, *Let Us Now Praise Famous Men* (Boston: Houghton Mifflin, 1941), p. 269. Reprinted by permission of the publisher.

13

cisely what occurs, and the curriculum may be better understood as what goes on in the school that is more or less intentional. The stir and clamor of occurrences, of events, do not always reveal their meanings or foretell their outcomes. In a profound sense, therefore, the curriculum occurs within the student, and its outcomes are often in behaviors long deferred.

Apparently, curriculum itself is a concept of rather formidable depth. Intent, actuality, and psychic response are all relevant to the concept.

Intention of the Curriculum

Intention considerably defines the job to be done; the school cannot afford to be witless about its purposes. However, a school can devise a full program without any important deliberations as to intent. After all, common practices, authoritative guidelines, textbooks, syllabuses, and bandwagon appeals are abundant.

A curriculum can be looked upon as an empty schedule to be filled. To fill it without a second's reasoning as to why and wherefore is no trick at all. Salesmen, special pleaders, subject specialists, and reformers all have pretty packages to peddle, some well worth examining. Wise shopping, nevertheless, probably follows some appraisal of needs.

To determine intent is not easy. Certainly it is more difficult than to articulate high purposes. Writers of textbooks and courses of study have good memories (or good notebooks) ; never do they seem at a loss to recollect the rhetoric of official sanction—this authority, that committee of seven, seventeen, or thirty-seven, a gubernatorial conclave, or even a White House Conference. Often the words are good and the work behind them, impressive. Sometimes, however, either the textual material beyond the introduction or the content beyond the statement of objectives flatly fails to serve the purposes or at worst denies them.

The schools have a common obligation: to give all the children of all the people a good education. This premise may be presumed to be axiomatic; it is basically understood and reasonably well agreed upon in American education. Communities, whether stingily or generously, tax themselves with some sense of this obligation.

However, a fundamental problem resides in this circumstance; the schools have a common obligation but lack a common intent. This statement should not lead to impetuous conclusions. It does not argue for a centralization of authority, more plans for articulation, or national curricula. The common intent that is lacking in the American school is intent to carry out its obligation.

To make this obligation come alive in practice is what this book is about. So many educators and scholars have spent so much time seeking the answers, and much has been said. Much study, much research, much investment of careers for school and classroom have gone into what is currently known. The largest effort to communicate effective sense about curriculum is to sort, select, and mobilize knowledge to some central effect.

Presently, the intent of educators somewhat less than meets the obligation. This is understandably so because society has let the educator in for the most formidable undertaking in human experience. Intent is eroded in many ways: by allowing social-class perceptions of the student or of educational purpose to distort the obligation, by accepting the current school's image as good education, by measuring the student through his degree of conformity to unexamined standards, by letting some of a school population wander through the curriculum in default of learning, by deliberately running two or more schools under one roof with one of them better than another, or by conceiving of teaching in easy terms.

Much of the erosion of intent is inevitable slippage in the social process. However, the school must regard the human worth of each student as its full trust. Nothing less than full commitment to each child is its burden, and failure in this intent is betrayal.

To give all the children of all the people a good education is scarcely a simple matter, for these children come to school with diverse backgrounds, interests, and motivations. How, indeed, is it possible to give them all a good education? What *is* a good education? How can a good education be effected for all?

As workable instruments within this text, certain key concepts of curriculum development are set forth.

The Duality of the Institution—Key Concept 1

Such critics as Arthur Bestor have made a fair point when they have insisted that the school exists for intellectual development; they have been on solid ground when they have insisted that schools have too often taught shoddy and incompetent substance. The educator can accept the goal of intellectual development and recognize the defects of program and instruction with a view toward improvement. What the educator recognizes (and where the critic goes wrong) is that the American school is comprised of two institutions, inextricably related but clearly distinguishable.

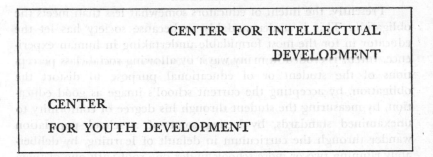

CENTER FOR INTELLECTUAL DEVELOPMENT

CENTER FOR YOUTH DEVELOPMENT

The American school is both a center for intellectual development and a center for youth development. This is not just another way of saying curricular and extracurricular or cocurricular, as the case may be. Nor does it connote an academic program or any activities program. However, the basic concept of duality clears up many contradictions about the school's complexity.

The duality concept does not split the school down the middle as does curricular and cocurricular activities. Neither does it split the student. On the contrary, it states that if a student is sent to a

16

school which is one institution and not the other, half that child is left awandering. But if he is sent to the school that is both a center for youth development and a center for intellectual development, he remains whole and intact the livelong day.

The dual functions of the school may be distinguished, but only at hazard to a complete educational development can they be separated. That a dichotomy of curricular and cocurricular activities may lead to absurdity is indicated by such questions as these:

1. Do algebra and geometry provide opportunity for intellectual development but not for practical mathematics or an astronomy club?

2. Are discussions of race bias and cultural antipathies in an English or history classroom conducive to healthy social development, while advancements of the principles of human acceptance on the athletic field are not?

3. Are communications arts and skills the tools of intellectual development when taught by an English teacher, while those used by boys in a vocational agriculture demonstration are not?

Our contention is that youth development and intellectual development go on in the same person in the same school at the same time. A school that risks working for intellectual development alone risks changing the meaning of *intellectual* to *academic,* which implies that there are no consequences beyond the school.

The schools in the Soviet Union recognize both functions of education but split them institutionally. Intellectual development takes place in school, essentially a European model; youth development is the task of the Pioneers, an extended version of the Boy Scouts and Girl Scouts. Thus, in school Ivan acquires academic learning and some aspects of intellectuality; in another institution he develops as a young, socialized, well-exercised being.

If the purpose of education is to rear people to use their heads when deemed appropriate and to behave in agreeable, well-disciplined conformity the rest of the time—in other words, to raise men to be human some of the time and well-trained, domestic animals at others—the Soviet system and some critics of the American school make sense. However, this is far from the idea of humanity that the American people are committed to developing in their schools.

How then are youth development and intellectual development to proceed together in the school? This text is based on belief in substantive learning, within a meaningful and useful content. (These terms are defined on pp. 107–108.) In Chapter VIII through Chapter XI the substance of the curriculum is categorized under four rubrics of human experience: the humanistic–ethical dimension, the creative–aesthetic dimension, the scientific–quantitative dimension, and the vocational–utilitarian dimension. Without exploring these dimensions at length but by applying the present problem within them, the interrelationships between youth development and intellectual development may be suggested.

In the scientific dimension, for example, youth is both at home and lost in the modern world. The young person is aware that science considerably shapes his world. He knows that much of what he enjoys or aspires to materially is the product of science and technology. That careers in science abound is not news to him; he has certainly heard of space adventures. The modern child will accept scientific content, procedures, and assumptions even in the elementary school. He comes to school partly shaped by the mass media and a common culture in which science is roughly established. If the scientific dimension is elaborately systematic, his secondary school may invade advanced areas in scientific content, bring down, as it were, college subjects to the high school.

Science subjects have sufficient reputation as "hard work" to qualify as intellectual development in the minds of the more severe critics. In a more thoughtful sense, the way of science *is* intellectual development; it is a mode of mind in process. Both as a way of thinking and as a body of knowledge increasingly beyond easy or ordinary perceptions, science has presented modern mankind with dilemmas. Beyond the discovery and ordering of a set of facts, science can deeply affect philosophies and value structures.

Science will not merely develop the mind of the young person; science will shake him up. The way of inquiry in areas from astronomy to sociology may set youth against parental views or set them at

18

odds with provincial and ethnic cultural biases. Evolutionary teaching still upsets some communities; what can be expected when larger implications of relativity come home to the student?

Science, then, affects youth development head on. It may cause emotional upheavals, not because it seeks to do so but because that is the way things are. Science can wash its hands of unreasonable consequences; *education* cannot. Scientific teaching in the schools will immeasurably clear the thinking of youth; it will considerably induct them into the world of reality. But the conflicts it may cause, conflicts in loyalties and in relation to other institutions of society, can bring the young person much emotional strain and mental anguish. Youth development, with the emotional and social dimensions of learning, is implicitly at the core of modern intellectual development.

To relate them, three areas must be recognized by the school:

1. Forums must exist, in science classes and clubs, where the subject matter is not science but the dilemmas, the emotions, the social issues posed by science.

2. Modern youth, like modern man, must have respite from his encounter with baffling reality; he must play and dance and run about. Perhaps as never before in history, modern man needs his games.

3. The school must be prepared to assist in rationalizing the dilemmas and resolving some of the tensions that affect youth.

A live curriculum in science will disturb the student even while it develops his intellect. That disturbance is real; it is a consequence of education and a concern for education. Thus, guidance and adjustment become implicit obligations.

An academic curriculum that is formalistic and meaningless will not dictate youth development, nor will it develop the intellect. The moment that the school really does begin to develop the mind it begins to affect the student's whole life. The chain reaction of intellectual development runs through the entire life of the student. It is not then a matter of choice; it is not to debate the desirability of relating the two roles of education. The apparent reality of intellectual and youth development is that you can't have one without the other. The dual function of the school is related to the other dimensions of fundamental content as well. In the humanistic–ethical dimension the school will find a place for history and for literature. If in history and literature the student can find no validation for civilized concepts of law and justice, or for rights, due process, and human respect, the subjects are strangely termed humanities. The humanities, however, have rewarded man and predictably will continue to do so. (The manner in which intellectual development proceeds from study in this dimension will be explored later.) It is important here to note that as students develop intellectually in the humanistic–ethical dimension, they will again be seriously affected. When students see law and good conduct and rights and rules meaningfully related, they will press to put these developed concepts to work. Arbitrary school policies, unreasonable discipline, second-class or nonparticipating school citizenship will be less likely to occur if this area is well taught.

Active and effective student government and school politics may be taken as indications of youth development in effective intellectual development. Such activities are erroneously tabbed as competitive with intellectual development; in point of fact, in a good school they are a *consequence* of it. Only if intelligence is neglected will it be inert. It follows that the school which lacks the programmatic attributes belonging to youth development first lacked a program which effectively stirred up the minds of its students.

The same dynamics apply in the other dimensions. The school cannot develop an intellectual program in the creative–aesthetic dimension without also providing avenues for expression. The dramatics program, assemblies, musicals, art exhibits, and little magazines will look like so-called activities. Students will work long and hard without extrinsic motivations and will have fun doing it. Leadership will shift as functions change. Teachers will move about in enterprises as peers with students. The attributes of creativity in action, unless creativity is denied a place in respectable intellectual development, will lead to school practices not merely reminiscent of progressive education but to practices that go far beyond those which most progressive schools ever put to practice.

The necessity for the dual function of the school is easiest to demonstrate in this creative–aesthetic dimension. At its best, classroom instruction is related to creativity and aesthetic realization about as much as a map of Africa is to the reality of that vast continent, to its resources and potentialities, to its problems and complexities, to its beauty and terror. Like a map, instruction may serve to point direction and describe landmarks, but it cannot determine the actual experiences and perceptions of the individual acting under its guidance.

Creativity, by its very nature, refuses academic confinement. Rigid structures can kill it in any area, from science and mathematics to music and sculpture. Creative–aesthetic experiences are experiences in perception of reality. In the best research-vindicated terms, therefore, they demand the whole child, which is the reality of the student. Treated only as intellectual exercises, these experiences become difficult games. Without the application of human intelligence, they lack form and substance and end where they begin. Any school that tries to institutionalize one of its roles in this dimension in preference to the other completely rules out creativity.

Because of the peculiar role that the vocational–utilitarian content has played in the schools, this area will be better understood when it is considered further on. Without too much difficulty, it can be rationalized within this relationship. But because it has been held suspect by academic critics as too remote from intellectual development, it cannot and should not be treated here as a parallel concern.

A school can well serve its students, its faculty, and society when it accepts its full responsibility for the child as a complex human being deeply involved in the process of discovering and maintaining his integrity of self and his participation in society. Such a school will build its curriculum in full awareness of the need for intellectual development and youth development and will be in accord with the best learning research of our time as well as with the experience and wisdom of good teachers throughout the centuries.

The Content–Method Nexus—Key Concept 2

Much acid has been spilled in the teacher-education dispute over the relative significance of content and method. The nature of that dispute is that no matter who wins, both lose. To resolve the impasse philosophically, it is necessary to distinguish between *subject matter* and *content*. In our context, subject matter is the raw material of occurrence, information, substance, or a body of knowledge. Content, in the educational sense, comes into being when a method is devised by which subject matter may be learned. Whether learning is conceived as experience, conceptualization, meaningful restructuring, codification, or analysis and synthesis, the distinction is useful and important.

Content and method, though distinguishable, are inseparable. Method is thus intrinsic in curriculum. To study the curriculum in a school is to observe instruction, not so much to see what teaching is being attempted, but to see what is in condition to be learned and what is being learned. What occurs and what is being experienced are thus distinguished. Experience is not exposure to occurrence or happenstance; it is the rendition of meaning to what takes place.

Subject matter is not always translatable into content. Statistical tables, encyclopedias, lexicons, and many textbooks are literally not teaching tools. On the other hand, method is not merely the reorganization of occurrence or neat arrangement of subject matter. Many barriers stand between the subject matter and the learner. The breaking or crossing of these barriers constitutes the method by which content is created.

Among the barriers with which method must contend are the following:

Dogmatic rejection. To enter the world of reality, where four is not simply two plus two, is to encounter the net resistance of all the errors of perception and the trite, easy formulas that the common culture has built up. Reality is more than a simple linear equation; the expression of it as such will lack validity at any level. The square root of minus one $(\sqrt{-1})$, is incomprehensible to the mind straitjacketed by dogmatic literalism. The certainties of absolutes are more comforting to this mind than the great likelihoods of the highest probabilities.

Sociologically rooted misperceptions. To those who think in terms of social class, all things may be possible except common human cause and effect. The aristocrat cannot perceive of Jefferson or Franklin D. Roosevelt except as traitors to a class. The Marxist rejects theology, then translates the devil into the bourgeois. The teacher is frequently hamstrung in developing content by his middle-class mores or his deliberate middle-class aspirations. The school itself may reflect or reinforce class structures that effectively stand between the learner and his chance to learn. (See Chapter III.)

Psychological hazards. The child instructed in being finicky and dreading blood and viscera will have difficulty translating biological subject matter into content. The anxieties and apprehensions of children constitute barriers to sensory perception. What one dreads seeing tends to be unseen, or it is seen in distorted and censored images. What one fears to hear is often unheard, or it is heard as what was not said or as a fearful reinforcement to the apprehension itself. The man worried about chronic dyspepsia often hurries to the radio to shut off the American Cancer Society's public-service announcements.

Physical disabilities. How much art appreciation will the color-blind achieve, or how much music appreciation the tone-deaf? To ask these questions is not to suggest an easy capitulation. Art, even the visual arts, is not all a matter of color. Some of the best classic cinema is in black and white. Line, light, form, composition, function are capable of meaning even to those who see green, red, and yellow in shades of gray. Sound is rich in rhythm, intensity, and volume even to those who lack a sense of pitch. In other words, the

23

test of method begins where the content takes professional competence to establish.

Every child has physical limitations. Acute sensory deprivations and physical handicaps are most often noted. However, compassionate exceptions are only the beginning of sound education; analysis of resources and the development of compensatory learnings make real professional demands on method. The bioneurological make-up of thirty students is composed of thirty unique sets of physical competences and limitations. This is one approach to demonstrating that attention to individual differences is a methodological necessity, not merely a sentimental democratic bias.

Cultural or experiential deprivation. Professor Erling Hunt of Columbia University always stressed in his methods classes that there were youngsters reared on Manhattan's East Side who had never seen the Hudson River (a country mile or two away). The cultural or experience bias in both intelligence and academic achievement tests has been apparent for some time. Projects for reconstructing the experience of the so-called culturally deprived are really vindications on a major scale of the necessity for method. The school that gives up on the inexperienced before developing compensatory experience. the school that writes off unready learners as stupid, or the one that glibly and irrevocably stereotypes its learners as slow, average, or gifted may be skirting if not abdicating its educational responsibilities.

Content is not, after all, so easy to come by. Most textbooks, courses of study, teachers' outlines, and study guides constitute subject matter. So too do most of the exercises, questions, quizzes, and, strangely enough, projects and activities. Too often the latter are irrelevant games, bearing only a marginal relation to turning occurrence into experience and verbalization into meaning. If content were easily come by, teaching could be entrusted to laymen, and for that matter, surgery to butchers. But method makes content. The very beginning of teaching methods means awarenesses that encompasses the social sciences; beyond this lies the demand of communication, understanding of the human group, and the rigors

24

of human encounter. Bringing a curriculum into being is a formidable enterprise, and teaching is quite a job.

Effective Learning as Concept Development— Key Concept 3

Learning is related to conceptual awareness and is particularly a process of conceptual criticism and a development of conceptual depth. *A concept may be defined as an intellectualized and behavioral codification of meaningful experience.* Therefore, in order to develop the concept, an articulate generalization must be devised to state it; a factor analysis must be made; its kinetic potential must be present and realized. Action is implicit in the concept. The experience must be internalized and personalized, and the action resulting must be willed and understood.

Stated extremely, this view of learning might imply that the curriculum for human development is basically the same at all stages, for the child and the adult alike. Curriculum for the mature person, which is life itself, is an extension of an intelligently conceived school program, not a supplement or a corrective, and certainly not a reversal of it. That is our assumption in this text.

An illustration may help to clarify the matter of conceptual development. A visitor in a nursery school or kindergarten will not be there long before he hears about sharing. The children *share,* even with a certain self-consciousness of virtue. Even against the grain of natural or acquired selfishness, the five-year-old may share to gain either adult or social approval. In the intermediate grades and the junior high school the term "community" occurs frequently, and courses in community study are not uncommon. In college, even in a graduate seminar, one may hear the phrases "the interdependence of man," "society," "human communities," or "nations."

Literally, in the kindergarten and in the seminar students are learning the same thing; throughout, it is a concept of formidable depth with a tremendous potential for action. Internalized and codified, it directs the child to wait his turn upon the slippery slide; it directs the adolescent to teamwork, consideration, and cooperation; it directs the adult to philanthropy, social legislation, missions, and institutions of world order. It is a concept rich in unexplored dimensions of both understanding and action. It is derived from a great civilized insight and observation on the fundamental recognition of the brotherhood of man.

Conceptual learning is both intellectual and emotional. This primary corollary further suggests the integrative quality in the school's dual function as a center for intellectual development and a center for youth development. Again, dualism is not the point of this stress. The noteworthy quality of human intelligence is not denied. In free choice, one must consider alternatives where the principles and consequences are unknown. Consciousness and the will are elevated in this nexus above instinct. The concept is advanced in awareness that man may be a brute or an automaton but denies that he must or should be. To avoid this, education must openly face the fact of man's complexity.

> Man is said to be a reasonable animal. I do not know why he has not been defined as an affective or a feeling animal. Perhaps that which differentiates him from other animals is feeling rather than reason. More often I have seen a cat reason than laugh or weep. Perhaps it weeps or laughs inwardly—but then perhaps, also inwardly, the crab resolves equations of the second degree.[2]

The mind is not all that must be schooled. Indeed, wisdom elevates and sustains man, but circumstances in life impose choice where wisdom fails; then courage or love must take over, or the man must flee. Said a man to a boy in the opening lines of Hugh Walpole's *Fortitude:* " 'Tisn't life that matters! / 'Tis the courage you bring to it."[3] The Persian poet in *The Rubáiyát of Omar Khayyám* found the doors of philosophy marked interchangeably

---

[2] Miguel de Unamuno, *The Tragic Sense of Life* (London: Macmillan, 1931), p. 3.

[3] Hugh Walpole, *Fortitude* (New York: Doran, 1913), p. 11.

"Exit" and "Entrance," and his flight was into hedonism. St. Augustine explored "the lust of the eye," the world of rational perception, the realm of humanistic scholarship. He did not find himself fully until he traveled far into the affective, into the spirit. The affective and the intelligence are not at war. Jesus taught with high regard for essential human intelligence. He reached out to teach sensibly to all, even to children, as though they might be instructed by sense. His parables were not so obvious that they did not tax the wit of his hearers. He argued but little from a priori; he made sense within the evident context of time-place circumstance. Yet, he knew how to teach with tears and anger and healing. He sought an extreme reasonableness in man, but the very extremity of the demand on reason, to turn the other cheek, is a demand for disciplined emotion. His greatest lessons were disquisitions on the rewards of affective achievement.

This is also true of Abraham Lincoln's "with malice toward none." He asked an extreme affective discipline of the nation that it did not muster, in the course of events. Meekness, purity of heart, freedom from malice, peacemaking are not unreasonable qualities to seek, but there is much in rational man that argues hard and effectively against as well as for them. They are scarcely to be mastered by the discipline of the mind alone.

"Perhaps," as Norman O. Brown puts it, "the time is now ripe when the mystic can break the glass through which he sees all things darkly, and the rationalist can break the glass through which he sees all things clearly, and both together can enter the kingdom of psychological reality."[4]

Important concepts, like the interdependence of man, strain both intellectual and affective attributes. The action potential of such a concept is great. A concept indeed travels around the world and through history. Furthermore, conceptual learning neither diminishes nor wears out. The cliché that one forgets 90 percent of what is learned may apply to formalistic exercise of categories of subject matter for its own sake or for purely academic purposes; it does not apply to the concept.

[4] Norman O. Brown, *Life Against Death* (New York: Random House, 1959), p. 34.

Deep in Western civilization, for example, are the conceptual roots of a genial tolerance for children and even an ultimate respect for them: "of such is the kingdom of heaven." Sooner or later, behavior in the Western world had to begin feeling the force of this concept; the school had to cease being an institution where children were punished for being born; love and respect had to enter the curriculum. And in time this concept richly infused Western civilization. The Madonna and Child lent it the affective weight of the genius of the Renaissance. In the nineteenth century anger at the abuse of children was the inspiration for Charles Kingsley's *The Water Babies* and for much of the work of Charles Dickens. John Steinbeck's tender episode of the penny candy in *The Grapes of Wrath* is also in this tradition. Albert Camus, a product of this heritage, is nowhere more moving than in *The Plague* where the protagonist reaches the deepest of human feelings at the meaningless suffering and death of a child.

In this context one may also note the necessity for conceptual criticism, for the concept can betray as well as liberate. The chaos of the child-centered school or the absurdity of the child-dictated home points up the hazard of the affective out of balance with reason or run to seed in sentimentality. The child too may be betrayed by emotion. The Children's Crusades were conceived in a spirit devoid of sense, and it is well to beware of the errands on which we send children—or humanity.

This concept illustrates the continuing task for curriculum. Children are still grievously abused. They cry in hunger in much of the world today. In Europe, after World War II, they ran in orphan packs amid the rubble that the war had made their legacy. On television we have seen some go to school in the face of threatening mobs of hate-filled adults. There is still much to learn and much to be done to make love of children an effective discipline of our society.

A second corollary, therefore, follows. *Conceptual continuity and consistency are essential to curriculum development.* The conceptual approach is most compatible with the idea of the educational continuum. A major implication is that concepts cannot be reversed in midstream. This dictate is ignored so often in formal education that it is surprising that students are not more confused than they are. A concept is meant to grow with a person through his lifetime. Obviously a child cannot be taught all there is to know about an automobile (which is a concept as well as an instrument), about love, about sex, or about loyalty. But the child must be instructed in the essence of the concept, or he will be the worse for it.

If the child is to be raised to drive a car with respect for life and self, he should not act in childhood as the rear-window sentinel to give warnings about the presence of a police officer. If he is to be taught to regard the amount of indulgence he receives as the measure of love, he cannot be expected to establish relationships in adulthood enriched by generous self-giving. If the child is nurtured on evasion and mythology about sex, his sexual behavior as an adult is not likely to be open, healthy, and responsible. And if the child gets his way by whining and cajolery and evades the consequences of his errors, he may become an adult characterized by infantile demands, buck-passing, and basic irresponsibility.

The curriculum is replete with instances of conceptual reversals. The need for vertical articulation should be seen at the basic substantive level; neat arrangements of units or topics in sequences to avoid overlap and repetition are not the answer. In fact, this cliché misses the point entirely, and it is rare that a school system's basic curricula are planned as a conceptual continuum from kindergarten through grade twelve.

Some conceptual reversals have been almost standardized in the schools over the years. For example, in first grade the child may study Indians and indeed may play at being an Indian for a time. Later, the same child may see the Indian as an antagonist, cruel and treacherous—a "dirty redskin" in the Hollywood tradition; subsequently he may sentimentalize the Indian as a "noble savage." Finally he may see him as a victim of a harsh, social process and of the white man. And all the while, he may see him on television in psychological horse operas as a tormented human being complete with complexes and traumas. If and when he ever meets a "real" Indian, he will be utterly confused by this maze of images and

29

seldom be able to perceive him in his reality. Indian life and culture was and is complex. It should be the concern of the school that the student at all levels be exposed to anthropological and historical consistency so that he may develop a sense of reality and a base for meaningful attitudes.

The first encounter with algebra in antique curricular designs often came as a shock because of conceptual reversal. A mathematics instructor recently said that on his first day in freshman algebra, the teacher announced that this was where we deal with the science of unknowns; that announcement floored him, he said, and he was so confused that he didn't know what was going on for a month.

After six years or more of arithmetic devoid of abstract or conceptual understanding, the simple linear equation, $x + 5 = 9$ may be formidable for a student in junior high school. However, at the University of Illinois Dr. Max Beberman had six- and seven-year-olds working out unknowns and embarking on algebraic vocabulary with ease and enthusiasm.

How can statistics and probabilities come naturally to students who have always considered mathematics to be the language of certainties? Will students readily grasp the nature and meaning of "sets," if early teaching has hammered home the fallacy that "you can't add apples and oranges"?

What will the consequence be in literary judgment or emotional reaction for a late adolescent when he encounters the earthy emotional quality and psychological profundity of the modern novel or modern drama, if the school has nurtured him on bowdlerized Shakespeare and heavy doses of Victorian prose and poetry with a little O. Henry thrown in for good measure? When travelers settle in a strange and alien community, they often encounter a paralyzing and upsetting phenomenon known as "culture shock"; when high schools conspire to make students lead sheltered lives intellectually and emotionally, the encounters with college or with the ways of the world are often as traumatic.

Significance and Relevance—Key Concept 4

The effort to devise programing demands rigorous attention to priorities and value scales.

In the course of a penetrating human study of a southern rural family, James Agee used telling words to describe the irrelevance of the school. Although he wrote during the Depression, his comments are relevant to our time:

> Or again on the curriculum: it was unnecessary to make even such search into this as I made to know that there is no setting before the students of "economic" or "social" or "political" "facts" and of their situation within these "facts," no attempt made to clarify or even slightly to relieve the situation between the white and negro races [*sic*], far less to explain the sources, no attempt to clarify psychological situations in the individual, in his family, or in his world, no attempt to get beneath and to revise those "ethical" and "social" pressures and beliefs in which even a young child is trapped, no attempt, beyond the most nominal, to interest a child in using or in discovering his senses and judgment, no attempt to counteract the paralytic quality inherent in "authority," no attempt beyond the most nominal and stifling to awaken, to protect, or to "guide" the sense of investigation, the sense of joy, the sense of beauty, no attempt to clarify spoken and written words whose power of deceit even at the simplest is vertiginous, no attempt, or very little, and ill taught, to teach even the earliest technique of improvement in occupation ("scientific farming," diet and cooking, skilled trades) , nor to "teach" a child in terms of his environment, no attempt, beyond the most suffocated, to awaken a student either to "religion" or to "irreligion," no attempt to develop in him either "skepticism" or "faith," nor "wonder," nor mental "honesty," nor mental "courage," nor any understanding of or delicateness in "the emotions" and in any of the uses and pleasure of the body save the athletic; no attempt either to relieve him of fear and of poison in sex or to release in him a free beginning of pleasure in it, nor to open within him the illimitable potentials of grief, of danger, and of goodness in sex and in sexual love, nor to give him the beginnings at very least of a knowledge, and

of an attitude, whereby he may hope to guard and increase himself and those whom he touches, no indication of the damages which society, money, law, fear, and quick belief have set upon these matters and upon all things in human life, nor of their causes, nor of the alternate ignorances and possibilities of ruin or of joy, no fear of doubtlessness, no fear of the illusions of knowledge, no fear of compromise:—and here again I have scarcely begun.[5]

Perhaps the schools in the late 1960s would have made Agee less discontent and perhaps not.

Today much discussion evolves around the "explosion of knowledge." So much to be learned makes selectivity essential to curriculum planning. The school often acts as though it had unlimited time to teach what ought to be learned. But when it takes such a big chunk of the child's life, the school must use relevance and significance as prime criteria for selection.

Beyond the basic outlines of knowledge that the school is teaching, there is much more being learned. This learning must be examined for its educational significance and relevance. In contrast, yet consonant with Agee's statement of values left unweeded if not destroyed, today's school often has an unspoken program for becoming a "successnik."

The successnik program is one engendered in the home, aided by the school, and too often rewarded by society. It has gone too long uncriticized and unexamined and is becoming the almost universally accepted direction and milieu in which to grow.

Raise a child to have nice manners; reward desired responses with smiles and candy; teach him to wipe his nose and to dread dirty hands; send him to school well scrubbed, well combed, and neatly dressed. Gently but consistently housebreak him to authority; never allow him to criticize the teacher or the school. Help him to routinize his young life; give him an attractive place to do his homework; reward desired responses with smiles and toys; help him to adjust to the inevitability of rules and institutional coercions; encourage him to take out his frustrations and aggressions on his smaller playmates and his pets.

[5] Agee, *op. cit.*, pp. 292–293.

Make sure that his toys are educational, his friends the right sort. See to it that he is assigned to ability group A (the right sort of friends may be an adequate qualification even if the I.Q. tests fail to measure his intelligence accurately). Steal a march on the school wherever possible with trips, encyclopedias, tutors. Instruct him that honesty is sound policy and that advantages are better than cheating. Reward correct responses; allowance bonuses for report card As are more sound psychologically than fines (or ear cuffing) — for Cs.

In high school watch his friends even more closely. It is important that some of them be girls (a potential hostess for the years ahead when established success involves tasteful entertaining); employ great vigilance where the girls are concerned. Maintain respect for the school and all established institutions, but guard against insidious notions, especially from social studies. The teacher must not be criticized for talking about rights and responsibilities, but make sure that the child is aware of his privileges.

Keep pressure on the school to keep pressure on students. See that more college subjects are offered in high school; get advanced-placement courses going. Put the heat on the guidance department to get him into the right college (check friends for influence; check bank account). Watch for a balance of interest in subjects; college boards cover a lot of ground. If grades sag, check reinforcements. The price may have gone up, or it may be a girl, or he may be going through an adolescent phase, or there may be something about a peer group perhaps. Consult your analyst, or maybe he needs a new car.

So goes the main line of the successnik program—RIGHT ATTITUDES, RIGHT MANNERS, RIGHT FAMILY, RIGHT SUBJECTS, RIGHT SCHOOL, RIGHT GROUP, RIGHT FRIENDS, RIGHT REWARDS, RIGHT PERSPECTIVE, RIGHT COLLEGE, RIGHT JOB, RIGHT FRIENDS, RIGHT HOUSE, RIGHT WIFE, RIGHT NEIGHBORS.

This appears to be a perception of reality supported by a significant segment of the American public, a perception upon which the school seems quite willing to build its program. The products of a curriculum constructed selectively to be relevant to such a view of life are as incapable of functioning as free and complete mature human beings as those subjected to the schools described by James Agee. Such a school will have betrayed its students; it will have ignored all the relevant issues of our time and all the meaningfulness of a real and valid education.

Joint Responsibility of School and Home— Key Concept 5

School and home do not have separate responsibilities; they do have differing subject matters, but they have the same child and their responsibility in every instance is complete. Solomon long ago gave the answer to those who would quarrel over what part of responsibility they have for a child. In this text we shall use this concept to delineate the responsibility of the school. Earl C. Kelley, *In Defense of Youth,* outlines a hard bill of particulars for the adult community with respect to youth; he includes an assertion of the school's large responsibility:

1. Our culture is in jeopardy unless we can adequately care for our young.

2. Our young people are all right when we get them. If all is not well with them, it is due to what has has happened to them in an adult-managed world.

3. If youth have not been too badly damaged by the life that has been thrust upon them, they enjoy and desire a good society as much as we do.

4. In urban society, our young live in much more difficult circumstances than they used to.

5. The measure of juvenile delinquency in any community is a measure of that community's lack of concern for its young.

6. There is really no valid, responsible place in our urban communities for youth. They are a displaced segment of our society.

7. A place must be made for them, and it seems to me that the only feasible place is the school.[6]

Thus, where youth go—and they go to school in ever-increasing numbers for ever-increasing durations—they bring the entire burden of youth with themselves. What can the school do other than rebuff them and evade its responsibility by assuming only a fraction of it?

The key to rational curriculum lies in giving attention *not to what can be taught but to what ought to be learned.*

Elementary-school children can learn French or Spanish (they could also be taught Latin, Swahili, or Hindi), but this does not determine whether such teaching is valid. Ten-year-olds can absorb a good deal of direct sex education, but this does not prove the value of leading them to the subject. The secondary-school program in mathematics can bring the student into calculus, but should it?

Education deals with only one child at a time. The responsibility implied is grave indeed. For that child, if education to any considerable degree is effective, it can truly make or break him. This child may or may not be the concern of loving and intelligent parents. The community may feel a stake and an involvement in his well being, but this is not always the case. Society often expresses considerable concern for children in general, but society calls no single child by name. The child may be the only one concerned with himself, and this subjectivity unguided may lead to a distorted image of self, and at worst, to a destruction of self.

Therefore, as an agency, the school is responsible for one child at a time. The American school culture accepts this as an obligation that derives from the classic democratic principle of respect for the individual. Attention to individual differences sometimes has been a discipline, sometimes merely a cliché of American educational practice. But it is not always fully and clearly recognized that to see each child complete and alone is an educational necessity. Although the school is an agency of society, the school is *not* society. The

6 Earl C. Kelley, *In Defense of Youth* (Englewood Cliffs, N.J.: Prentice-Hall, 1962) , p. 145.

school is a place to learn. The potential for learning lies in human intelligence, and the capacity for human intelligence is in the heads of the varied and separate persons who come to school. A school is simply an aggregate of people concerned with learning, and learning takes place within the human being.

School doors open and human beings enter; at all times these human beings are a charge upon the school. As Earl C. Kelley notes,[7] those who believe that the school should limit its function to the purely academic usually like neither the school nor youth.

Parents are human; they vary in quality. An educational analysis is no place either to slander or to sentimentalize the parent. A lot of American parents are ignorant and uneducated. Many children are unwanted and resented. In a confused culture *un*-love passes as a counterfeit for love, even as skim milk masquerades as cream. Out of *un*-love parents drive children into the rat race of social climbing and status seeking, vie for vicarious distinction through the competition of their offspring, coerce their every educational and social, even matrimonial, choice.

Probably there are more crimes by parents against children than any other category of injuries. Abundance of opportunity and of ignorance spell the major causes. Our jails are full of youth who have been put there directly by their parents. Our mental institutions are full not because of heredity but because of what parents have done to make their children suffer. Overconcern may spell one disaster, neglect another.

The fact of the matter is that the modern parent cannot get the job of child-rearing done without the school. Those parents who underrate the necessity of the school's social obligation to youth or who would blithely cast the burden elsewhere had better ponder on reality. In actuality, no conflict of interest exists; those parents who use the school most heavily for youth development are those who are the most responsible parents and do the most for youth development. The school and responsible parents are allies, not competitors. These parents understand that the school exists so that the best aspirations for youth may have some chance of realization. On the

---

[7] *Ibid.*, pp. 7–13.

other hand, those who have no such understanding in no way lessen the obligation of the school to the child.

Commentary: Toward the Modern Mind

Any program of intended learning (which is curriculum) must be realized in a dual dimension. Learning is both intellectual and emotional, and the two are naturally interrelated. This double emphasis warrants clarification.

The ancient humanist held that man has an endowment of reason. That reason and faith are not incompatible was the sum of the Thomistic synthesis of Aristotle and Augustine. Indeed, man is a rational being, contended the mentors of the Enlightenment. To the American pragmatist intelligence is the distinguishing characteristic of man. Infused with Rousseau's romantic optimism about the innate goodness of man's nature, much of our Western intellectual heritage has conduced toward great confidence in the human mind and the development of its capacity by education.

The view of man as predominantly rational has not been without challenge. Much theology refuses to accept man's intelligence as constituting the primary or exclusive basis for human distinctiveness. Newer fiats have challenged the view that man can be intelligent, that is, be self-determining, the master of choice, the maker of self. Adam Smith saw man subjected to the determinants of the market; Karl Marx saw him as the creature of materialistic, historical forces. Modern social science has tended toward a view of either environmental or societal determinism, to the degree to which it sanctions pure behaviorism or theories of social and cultural forces.

Other intellectual forces have pressed toward a diminution of man's stature. In turn, science has destroyed man's confidence in the centrality of his mortal abode within the universal scheme of things, has destroyed his idea of special creation in a divine image, and in our time has even destroyed belief that what man could make he could control. The naturalistic view of man taught the ramifica-

37

tions of man's animal nature, and the novelist, at least since Emile Zola, has not ceased to explore this dimension. Modern man, instructed in the naturalistic view of self, can see amazing complexities and exciting sensory manifestations of his creaturehood. However, he cannot easily gain a sense of human dignity by his view of himself as an ever-so-superior forager on a world-wide animal farm.

Least of all has the Freudian view enhanced modern man's self-esteem. It is not the seeking of help that is debilitating, for man in community does not necessarily lose dignity in seeking aid from his fellows; the basic premise of interdependence implies that a man may count on such help. In the Freudian scheme the man seeking help must look for the solution in the irrational and unconscious and thus must regard the willed dimension of intelligence as a lesser force in his life. However scientific it may be, the Freudian analysis has brought degradation to the rational image of man.

A basic premise in Western thought since antiquity enhanced man's self-esteem by building confidence in his reasonableness, and that, by force of reason, he could construct a satisfying life and community for himself. In the nineteenth century man had even begun to believe in a law of progress, but the nineteenth-century illusions have been shattered by the cataclysms of the twentieth. Other views of man have also diminished his view of self, sometimes to the point that the concepts of human dignity seemed imperiled. Thus, curriculum appears faced with a Hobson's choice here. Not one of three alternatives appears tenable.

> 1. Learning may be built exclusively on the intellectual pillar, on the historic precept that man is reasonable—that intelligence is his unique distinguishing characteristic. If a choice based on an illusion can be noble, this one is. From the humanistic standpoint there is no nobler illusion. The difficulty lies with the evidence and with experience. Auschwitz, Buchenwald, Budapest, Hiroshima, and Selma fail to support the precept.

> 2. Learning may be built upon a contrary assumption. It may follow a set of arbitrary and confident strictures regarding the nature of man and the world. In the event of such a priori conclusions dictating the educational pattern, the primary exercise of intelligence (in a Marxian setting, for instance) is to learn the rules and the

rationalizations that sustain them and to follow them in all the ramifications of personal and social behavior. Choice remains. The erectors of closed systems may call it "free," but it is the freedom to choose between fixed truth and error. To choose the latter becomes by definition an evidence of unregenerate character, a matter of heresy or treason.

3. Learning may even be built upon the structure of what Bertrand Russell calls "naked power." In the early stages of totalitarian systems there may be some effort to cloak the coercive use of education with the garments of philosophy. Alfredo Rocco and Giovanni Gentile attempted this masquerade for Italian fascist education, and the Soviet Union is not without sophistication in camouflaging the ultimate persuasion behind its teaching. The brutal assumption of brutish man that man is irrational, coercible, venal, and animalistic never paraded itself as candidly as in the years of the Nazis. The lesson was simply take and rule; the teacher had the gun. This is the ultimate hazard when man loses confidence both in his reason and in systems of historically vindicated patterns of social control.

A harder concept undergirds our philosophy of curriculum. It does not deny the noteworthy quality of human intelligence. It admits that free choice must consider alternatives where both the principles and consequences are unknown. It elevates consciousness and will above instinct in the arena of the mind. It includes the knowledge that man can be a brute but denies that he must or that he should be. And it faces his complexity honestly.

Curriculum occurs within. Effective learning reaches and develops the human quality of the whole person. Intelligence is a significant attribute of human distinctiveness, but it is not the whole of man. The affective quality is real and also the province of education. It is not apart from intelligence; there is but one person. Intelligence is a quality to be developed and integrated in the person, however. It is not the binder; the binder is "humanness." This human quality expresses itself in being and becoming, in acts of wisdom, love, and courage. It communicates. When the human acts, he behaves responsibly; he defines his meaning by what he does. The director and integrator of his actions is the willed intelligence.

Learning is the conceptualization of meaningful experience.

Man is capable of learning, but not all men learn, nor do all groups encourage learning. The creature whose potential is to be human also has a potential to be a brute; he is also prone to capture through conditioning and coercion; he is disposed toward ease and may become a robot, the automaton in society who moves by the conditioned and witless reflexes of the common culture. Education in any dimension must awaken the human to his potential and his responsibility.

The content of learning is composed of the skills, knowledges, experiences, and values that assist in realizing this goal. The method is intrinsic within the content. It consists of involving the person in meaningful, humane action. It imperils the goals when it is perceived as extrinsic either to the aims of education or to the nature of man. A content–method nexus conceived soundly does not diminish the person's esteem; it does not purchase his precious time with the spurious rewards of tinsel and sham.

Education may be served through many institutions, but it must serve a certain conceptual consistency. Education must respect, above all, the human's infinite potential. Its prescriptions must not be bound by its institutional limitations or its professional literal-mindedness.

Chapter II

The Curriculum and the Modern Mind

Old, complex, tradition-haunted societies find change as difficult to make as aged rheumatoid arthritics to move; old men,
however, die and are replaced, but in old societies young men
grow up, frustrated, crippled, distorted by them.[1]

—J. H. Plumb

Toward an Educational Philosophy

Curricular choice is rooted in philosophy, in value judgments.
Sometimes philosophical judgments dictate choice; more often they
merely weigh in the balance of choices made. The complexity of
circumstances in which American educational choices are made
tends toward a certain eclecticism in educational philosophy. This
eclecticism is a legitimate consequence of necessity rather than of
confusion or haphazardness. It is important, of course, to recognize
and to analyze the values and value sources that are drawn upon;

[1] J. H. Plumb (ed.), *Crisis in the Humanities* (Middlesex, England:
Penguin Books, 1964), p. 10.

41

otherwise we may be attempting to build on contradiction, simultaneously trying to homogenize the incompatible and developing irreconcilable concepts.

The American school functions in a culturally plural context. Many values are held, even as absolutes, by groups and subgroups within the culture. However, the consensus in which American political and educational institutions function is not a matter of absolutes; it is a matter of rather common agreement on modus vivendi, a pattern of ways of getting along without absolute definitions. In a single, private academy a particularist curriculum may be built upon the most dogmatic of philosophical premises. Such a curriculum represents a legitimate educational choice *within* the American consensus, a choice rather freely exercised. However, the largest American consensus with respect to education operates in favor of a common school functioning in general agreement for the advantage of all. The public school must not be built upon particularism, but upon a rationale sensitive to cultural complexities and sensible in advancing the best elements of the consensus.

The school as an institution with deep historical roots has built-in biases toward *essentialism*. To a degree, this includes both the weight of tradition and the force of institutional inertia, as well as institutional experience. Educational conservatism, as represented by William C. Bagley and William Brickman, plays as legitimate a role in our system as does liberalism. The school and society have strongly established notions concerning what is essential and fixed positions regarding the necessity of certain subject matters. Realities of social process are intrinsic in fixing the role of essentialism in educational choice; even if it were desirable, the educational system will not be reconstructed from scratch. The history of the most drastic revolutionary movements shows that social processes simply do not operate that way.

Essentialism is based on the fact that the school has always been somewhat rooted in human need. It errs in the perennialist direction when it misconstrues experience to mean that human need in all particulars has been and always will be the same everywhere. One function of education on which consensus is abundant is the necessity to transmit culture. Applying essentialism out of proportion tends to stack the educational cards toward conservatism, to discourage experimentation and progress, to obstruct development of other legitimate functions of the school, and thus to diminish the school's net utility and consequence to society. If educators were given a blank slate (and a blank check) for total curriculum redevelopment, it is likely that they would find it necessary (if not essential) to rebuild into the new much of the substance and intent of the old. This would be partly due to the fact that even the boldest imaginations are considerably culture bound; it would also be a vindication of a certain realism in essentialist arguments.

Reconstructionism is also implicit in the democratic consensus. Democracy must not fear the idea of a better society; it must indeed utilize its basic political instruments to achieve just that on a continuing basis. Democracy also distrusts fixed or long-term blueprints for social action, fearing the deterioration of flexible goals into party lines and strictures on subsequent choice. It particularly fears long-term grants of irrevocable power. It knows of the corruption of intent among the best men of good will when they start to slip; often they begin with apologies on the relation of means to ends and eventually arrive at the blunter assertion of all authoritarians.

Much of Theodore Brameld's intent for social achievement finds broad agreement:

> The world of the future should be a world which the common man rules not merely in theory but in fact. It should be a world in which the technological potentialities already discernible are released for the creation of health, abundance, security for the great masses of every color, every creed, every nationality. It should be a world in which national sovereignty is utterly subordinated to international authority. In short, it should be a world in which the dream of both ancient Christianity and modern democracy are fused with modern technology and art into a society under the control of the great majority of the people who are rightly the sovereign determiners of their own destiny. Reconstructionism is thus a philosophy of magnetic foresight—a philosophy of ends attainable through the development of powerful means possessed latently by the people. *To*

learn how to exercise that power for these ends is the first priority of education.[2]

The reconstructionist is, as Brameld says, "the radical."[3] Radicalism has a legitimate role in democratic thought; utopian dreams have on occasion become social reality. However, the reconstructionist plays his role in education by extending vision and challenging complacency. These are necessary and worthy critical functions. Utopians do this well, but to entrust utopians with political power does not necessarily work for the best interests of humanity.

Reconstructionism is vulnerable with respect to its own particularisms. To see education as a force whose first priority is in the exercise of power represents a minority view of the school and is fraught with intrinsic hazard. Pragmatic progressivism quarrels seriously with this assumption; it places confidence in the basic function of liberating the individual for free choice and trusts him to choose well. It also distrusts the willingness of the reconstructionist to flirt with shortcuts in method, for example, and to speak too well of indoctrination.

Reconstructionism errs oppositely and more than equally with what it accuses progressivism of doing—that is, focusing too much on means at the expense of ends. Reconstructionism overconfidently dwells on its ends. When accusing progressivism it joins the same dogmatists it spurns elsewhere and on the same grounds. Reconstructionism errs in a certain naïveté with respect to social process, where its revolutionary optimism may lead to no consequence for the reformers and meliorists of whom George Bernard Shaw spoke, and their "eternal ifs and ans which never become pots and pans."[4] It also shares the American optimist's error with its pragmatic cousins in failing to realize how profound is the human predicament, how enduring the hunger, the tyrannies, and the absurdities. Thus, both tend to overlook how essential it is to direct educational attention not to perennial answers but to perennial problems in

[2] Theodore Brameld, *Education for the Emerging Age* (New York: Harper & Row, 1961), p. 25. [Italics added.]

[3] *Ibid.*, p. 26.

[4] George Bernard Shaw, "The Revolutionist's Handbook," *Man and Superman* (Baltimore: Penguin, 1952), p. 241. (First published in 1903.)

order that perspective may bulwark man in his courage and spirit. The reconstructionist is a valuable philosophical gadfly, but he lacks profundity in his appraisal of the human condition. Moreover, for all its optimism, reconstructionism basically underrates the achievement of education; it sees a future when education "could at last demonstrate its capacity to play no longer a minor but a major role in the rebuilding of civilization."[5] Many others believe that education has been doing just that for some time.

Pragmatic Existentialism

We are not attempting to make a neat package of philosophical bases. The rationale is intended to be strong in constructive potential and responsive to the real needs of man in society. Its platform is consonant with the broad consensus of American democracy. The prospectus is intended to be capable of fulfillment. The scope of the philosophical rationale is most appropriately pragmatic existentialism and social humanism.

Considerable grounding in the pragmatic progressive tradition is too obvious and too pervasive in this philosophy to be missed. Much is owed in rich admixture to the pillars of tradition, with particular acknowledgments to such as Ralph Waldo Emerson for his sense of the necessity and efficacy of self-reliant individualism; to Henry Thoreau for his stubborn exercise of such individualism; to Lester Frank Ward for his bias toward the democratic and the utilitarian and for his Rabelaisian appetite for learning; to Henry George (whom John Dewey called the greatest American social philosopher) for a radical democratic sense of social justice; to John Dewey for the one great comprehensive treatise on the school in the democratic society—his life work; to John Childs for his exegesis on Dewey, his clarification of the essence of pragmatism, and his defense of Dewey before the uninformed and hostile; to George Counts for his insistence on the social function of education.

[5] Brameld, *op. cit.*, p. 27.

The frontiers of pragmatic philosophical insights have been extended; the existential is especially pertinent here. Existentialism holds that it is better to work together on the great fronts of human necessity than to divide on abstract issues or semantic hair-splitting. Its profound contemporary appeal is a product of awareness of the ills that have wracked the twentieth century. American pragmatism was born of both optimism and innocence, no mean characteristics for youth. But the latter twentieth century has offered us the harder reality of "blood and sweat, toil and tears." Existentialism affords a hold on reality that allows man to surrender optimism and illusion without losing hope and purpose. It builds less exclusively on reason than does pragmatism; yet it demands of unreasonable man that he reason. It even insists that he be responsible for his every choice. It recognizes the enormous potential for evil in the human; then it places the root, source, and responsibility for evil in the choices that the human makes. In no sense is the existential incompatible with the pragmatic and therefore may be extended to the philosophical assumptions of a pragmatic existentialism.

Curriculum needs a philosophical undergirding that stresses these elements:

1. A development of both the intellectual and affective potential of man

2. An attempt to strengthen the conscious control of choice, through the *willed* intelligence

3. The close interrelationship of means and ends (as with method and content)

4. A recognition of social and cultural forces as well as assertive, responsible individualism

5. The necessity for education to furnish "binders" and "linkages" (respect, communication, love), to establish community, to rescue man from his loneliness, and to prevent social breakdown

6. The need to bring man's values and value sources to the school

The foregoing includes standard elements in the vocabulary of the American educator. Item one is at least half familiar; item two is standard, except for the "willed"; item three is directly pragmatic or instrumentalist; item four is acceptable to the pragmatist in some implications; item five is supported by much in pragmatism though the vocabulary may be unfamiliar; the pragmatist will hold item six suspect until he is surer of its intent.

Though familiar to the pragmatist, this is not the standard vocabulary of pragmatism. It is not contrary to pragmatism, but it contains an added dimension: a sobered view of the human condition, an awareness that the condition in part is a predicament as well as a nurturing and sustaining environment. The vocabulary is familiar to the modern mind and is in that broad, permissive and essentially nondidactic mode labeled "existential."

Though our philosophical grounding in this book is eclectic, we naturally have not included everything from all sources. We have rejected a great deal of perennialism, essentialism, reconstructionism, and even some parts of pragmatism. Varied philosophical approaches have certain incompatible elements, and it is unfortunate that men of good will regard one another as educational enemies when they are often merely separated by the devices of their rhetoric. Man is finally more important than the ideas he holds; when each recognizes the common denominator of humanness, increased attention may then be given to the common denominators in thought.

It is often assumed that John Dewey, Theodore Brameld, Arthur Bestor, George Counts, Robert Maynard Hutchins, John Childs, and Mortimer Adler represent a potpourri of incompatible and hostile viewpoints, especially in light of the acerbity of much exchange among them. Without diminishing the disparities or the incompatibilities, however, it is wrong to call them enemies. On the contrary, essentially they have been on the same side, working for human enlightenment in a fundamental enterprise. No easy resolution of differences need be sought. A communicating society highly regards differences an essential element of social cohesion.

If values are centrally to be brought to the school, a broad philosophical umbrella must be sought. The existential mode seems to afford just that. Such varied figures as Shakespeare, Goethe,

Kierkegaard, Jaspers, Heidegger, Locke, and Rousseau have been identified within the camp. Jacques Maritain is a Roman Catholic existentialist; Paul Tillich was a Protestant. Martin Buber, a Jewish philosopher, Nikolai Berdyaev, of the Eastern Orthodox church, and Jean Paul Sartre, an atheist, have all shared the umbrella.

Among the existential camp (often wrongly termed a "school"), there is either tacit or articulated willingness to emphasize some measure of agreement. As members of a community without union, they do not minimize their disparities, nor do they inhibit themselves from going in their own maverick directions. But, insofar as the disparities are either irrelevant or marginal to items of common concern or common commitment, they will not prejudice the existential common denominators with unnecessary conditions or provisions.

For example, Reinhold Niebuhr, Christian theologian, and Jean Paul Sartre, atheist, obviously have many divergences of thought. Yet, note a similar mood of emphasis between them:

> Existentialism isn't so atheistic that it wears itself out showing that God doesn't exist. Rather it deduces that even if God did exist, that would change nothing. . . . Not that we believe that God exists, but we think that the problem of His existence is not the issue.[6]

> I would say the ultimate religious problem is not whether we can justify belief in God, however defined rationally, but whether we can bear witness to a faith that in some sense has an idea of responsibility for its civilization . . . —and in some sense transcends it in the way that Lincoln transcended the Civil War struggle.[7]

What is the common bond? It is the agreement, whether altogether alone or not, that man is largely on his own in the universe, sharing a common condition. Both Sartre and Niebuhr seek to build man's morale to accept the austere and burdensome assignment of human responsibility.

The existential burden of responsibility is not merely in terms

[6] Jean Paul Sartre, *Existentialism and Human Emotions* (New York: Wisdom Library, 1957), p. 51.

[7] Reinhold Niebuhr, interviewed by Henry Brandon, "A Christian View of the Future," *Harpers* (December 1960), p. 76.

of what one *does* but of what one *becomes*. The cliché "existence precedes essence" means that the person substantially determines who he is or what he becomes in the process of living. "It means," says Sartre, "that, first of all, man exists, turns up, appears on the scene, and only afterwards, defines himself. If man, as the existentialist conceives him, is undefinable, it is because at first he is nothing."[8] Of course, in the extreme statement there is a flaw; there is a human essence, even biological, in the shaping. However, existentialism, to a greater or lesser degree, insists on each person's responsibility for the definition of his essence in the course of his existence.

For American educators to comprehend the press of the modern mind on curriculum they must fully comprehend where man has been and where he has come. In this century the American experience has lacked some dimensions of war and poverty. We will take Dewey as a representative of many central tendencies in American education, to establish the relationships and distinctions between these tendencies and existentialism.

Existentialism is respectful toward science, but more conscious perhaps of its limitations than is Dewey. Existentialism is humanistic, though more specifically so than is Dewey. Existentialism and pragmatism are similar, if not identical, in their emphasis on choice and in their rejection of the a priori. Pragmatism insists much more on the conditions in which freedom is to be nurtured; existentialism is more concerned with the intent of the man who determines to be free. Existentialism does not universally share Dewey's naturalism, and existentialism is more concerned with explicit questions of value sources. Existentialism bolsters Dewey with respect to Freud, though not directly. On occasion it neglects the political and social science of democratic behavior; pragmatism does not. Pragmatism tends toward neglect of the irrational; existentialism acknowledges its potential fully but demands its conscious control rather than releasing man from accountability for subconscious drives and motivations.

8 Sartre, *op. cit.,* p. 15.

Functional Eclecticism

Withal, philosophy is philosophy, and curriculum is curriculum. They do meet and merge, but social realities condition the very philosophy of American education. The curriculum for American public education is not built, and is not likely to be, upon a single systematic and categorical philosophical system. It thereby serves American society and humanity the better. The prevailing educational philosophy may well be termed "functional eclecticism."

No one is likely to be completely content with such a philosophical condition. This is its great virtue. Complete satisfaction for some with the philosophical foundations of the American school curriculum would be purchased by acute discontent for many others. The curriculum is working well when it is regarded with reasonable content by all, with mild dissatisfaction by many, and with particular dissent by each.

This assumption is a familiar one and should meet with about the same degree of acceptance as will the curriculum. It is merely an application of the basic American democratic consensus, for which the verbal shorthand has become "cultural pluralism," the slogan, "unity amid diversity." It makes a virtue of the necessity for human community; it exists with the inconsistencies that permit people to live together.

The eclecticism necessary for a curriculum theory based on reality is not the pragmatic philosophy. It is a rare pragmatist who does not wish the rest of humanity to become pragmatic. The intent of functional eclecticism is not antithetical to pragmatism any more than it is to perennialism, reconstructionism, essentialism, or existentialism. It is, however, antithetical to the authoritarian.

Neither the American curriculum nor the American nation is built upon a philosopher's philosophy. There is no ideological strait jacket on either, and none appears likely. Thomas Jefferson has had as much influence on American political philosophy as anyone; yet in some respects he is almost universally ignored. Both

50

major parties claim and reject him in almost equal measure. John Dewey occupies a similar role in educational philosophy. The outcome of what some call our philosophical confusion is a happy one; because we have never raised a Karl Marx to the status of prophet, we have never suffered a Josef Stalin.

The confusion of the American mind is not necessarily as great as the discontent of any given philosophy. The American mind has considerable complexity and is deeply historical. It compels no confusion. It says in effect: *you* may be as certain as you like, but *we* can never be too sure. And then it adds: but we really must learn to live together. Insofar as it says these things with deep conceptual awareness, the American mind is healthy. It is rooted in life and rejoices that a great declaration of its national commitment is to "life, liberty, and the pursuit of happiness." The commitment is to life, and a joyful view of it at that. It is a good human view and one that man ordinarily understands.

With a View of Man

American education is matter-of-fact and nonexclusive. Its ordinariness had led to vast misunderstanding of its philosophy. At worst, it is alluded to as mass education. Public education is *not* mass education. A mass is a homogeneous aggregate, and when humanity is regarded as a mass, it is taught in order to be manipulated.

The mass educator has a fundamental disrespect for man. He seeks responses from the mass in ways which he conceives to be in *his* interest. If it serves his purposes, he will seek to persuade the mass that it acts in its own interest. This is the way of the propagandist, the totalitarian, and the huckster, and he does have leverage. There are human realities on his side. Mankind has certain identifiable drives and appetites; in given situations man has accultured tensions and aggressions that can somewhat be predicted and played upon.

But to say that humanity in the aggregate can be sold a bill of goods, deluded, manipulated, and psychologically coerced does not

51

tell the whole story of its unauthoritatively defined nature. The fact that man is falsely sold, is deluded, and is betrayed also says something in respect to the quality of social arrangements, motivations, and value systems. And this includes a commentary on the quality of education involved.

To be sure, there is a near common denominator in mankind that makes it possible on occasion to manipulate, coerce, and even enslave him. Certain types of political, social, and economic institutions make the process easier; certain motivations produce characters who thrive on the exercise of human betrayal.

But this is not the whole story. Man's vulnerability is less significant than his dignity. Men have created varied institutional arrangements and have behaved variously toward one another. They have had time (which constitutes history) to observe the effects of these institutional arrangements and behavior patterns and to render judgment on them. For a long time man has been ready, willing, and able to state the conditions for human association that he enjoys best. His judgment and his record have been fallible, but Meletus, Judas, and Booth have a poorer reputation than Socrates, Jesus, and Lincoln.

Public education (not mass education) is rooted in attention to the dignity of each man. It sees the array of humanity not as a mass but as a vast collection of individuals. It seeks to discover, to identify, and to recognize each as fully as possible. It does not seek to use; it seeks to establish purpose. Public education wants the individual to learn to choose what is truly best for himself. It too counts on a common human denominator but not the lowest.

History, philosophy, literature, religion, and ethics give some confidence that to discover himself man must discover humanity. These fields support the view that man behaves better in relation to other men when he is a self-directing part of a self-respecting human community than when he is a directed and conditioned respondent in an irresponsible but regimented aggregate or mass.

It would be a mistake to accept the foregoing simply because it sounds good or because it is a relatively conventional American viewpoint. If the view be weak or sentimental—and it has been accused of being both—it is a poor foundation for American education for this time of continuing crisis. Great marching societies have challenged it; some of them still march. Some philosophies deny it; some social scientists regard it as naïve. The tough-minded may, however, find their own evidence of the persistence of human dignity.

Of those who doubt its persistence, no one expressed the case better than George Orwell. His *1984* is a grim prediction of the triumph of thought control, manipulation, and coercion. The instruments of modern psychology and of age-old tyranny combine to crush the stubborn claims to personal choice and decision-making. Each man is ultimately only self-seeking; each man is ultimately vulnerable. He has his price, if not in rewards of position or status then in an eventual unyielding terror of something or other. Eventually, the dehumanized man comes to regard mankind and the universe in the same way as his coercers. That is what it means to be brainwashed.

Although skepticism concerning man's dignity is not new, it could scarcely be more persuasive than in the twentieth century. This is the century of motivational research, subliminal advertising, psychological warfare, to say nothing of the Gestapo and NKVD. What decency, dignity, and ethics availed in Dachau, Auschwitz, Buchenwald, or the Polish Ghetto?

Anyone schooled in traditional Western education would deny that every man has his price, that he will betray any person or any principle to save his skin, that every man can be taught to deny himself or to call error truth and truth error. One element that traditionalists may proudly claim is that tradition keeps human experience alive, that man may live sustained by what mankind has already learned.

The great crime of Socrates, for which he calmly died, was that he denied these cynical errors. The Romans believed these things until the unvanquished conviction of the martyrs in the ruddied sands of the arena instructed them to better belief. In *Murder in the Cathedral* T. S. Eliot demonstrates that through conviction, man may keep his courage instead of cowardice and may have his fears and weakness forged into an unassailable strength and witness.

Man expects brave words from other men, but he is suspect

53

when they come easily. Yet, a work of fiction gave the proof; in our troubled time came an affirmation of the human spirit and the demand for freedom. It came not from the West, from America where conditions almost compel the assertion but from the East. Boris Pasternak wrote in a land where the institutions of *1984* were far developed. His *Dr. Zhivago* was a proof that the *willed intelligence* may always see things straight and assert itself. Zhivago saw black as black and white as white, but this was not his major accomplishment. A fanatic may recognize polarized extremes. Zhivago also recognized shades of gray; he maintained the discriminating quality of critical judgment and the subtle ability of artistic, even poetic, expression in adversity and suffering.

Public education too must build its program on a discriminating confidence in man. The human record gives no assurance that human dignity prevails easily or that freedom is lightly won or retained. It does assert that man has regarded himself well and has sometimes considered his freedom worth any effort, even any sacrifice.

The curriculum of public education is not based on a precise, ultimate, or categorical view of man, although such views of man do exist. Many are linked to religions; such doctrines as "original sin" and "total depravity" are elements of large and complete theological and metaphysical systems. These views do not come directly to the school. The necessity for maintaining the secular nature of the schools derives from sorry experience with categorical dogmas. However, religious views and theological constructs that are part of the common culture do affect the curriculum.

The children in a given public school classroom are regarded philosophically with much variation by parents. Some are held to be good by nature; others, corrupt. (The view does not reflect on the quality of parental love, which is not required to be philosophical.) One child is nurtured in the fatherhood of God; another, as a child of nature.

Educational philosophers hold systematic, logical, and precise views of man; the most common element is their disagreement, which does not distinguish philosophy from the common culture. Teachers, administrators, and students bring philosophical assump-

tions to school that enter the mainstream of intellectual consideration. These affect program, courses, disciplinary attitudes, and all
other aspects of the school.

For better or for worse, the child in the public school is exposed
to the full range of man's philosophical assumptions. This could
only be avoided if history and literature were eliminated from the
school or if the strait jacket of parochial censorship were employed.

Even in its limited consensus, the school reflects a significant
commentary on the nature of man. This commentary, as an "ordinary" agreement, differs from philosophically precise views in one
salient respect. Although much blood has been shed over philosophically conflicting theories of man's nature, the school consensus
represents ideas that have not brought bloodshed. This is the view
of man on which the public can agree when it sends its children to
school:

1. The chances seem to be that the child can learn.

2. Whether his nature be good or bad, divine or mundane, the child
may be improved in some respects by the school.

3. The child is fit to associate with others, and others are fit to
associate with him.

4. The school may be entrusted with the child and the child with
the school.

5. The child is worthy of attention.

This leaves a good deal that is not agreed upon, particularly in the
realm of the abstract. But before the foregoing area of agreement is
dismissed as inconsiderable, let it be restated in terms more customarily academic so that it may be weighed.

In the first instance, the public seems to affirm its agreed belief
that man is an intelligent creature. It commits itself rather specially
to this belief by supporting the school and by leading the child to
the school on this assumption. Man learns and is made to learn: this
is no small element in defining the nature of the creature.

Second, whatever the judgment on his ultimate human nature,
the public agrees that the child's behavior may be altered and improved. Thus, by sending the child to school the public adheres in

partial definition to the agreed element that innate attributes are not fully deterministic and that society and culture may shape human growth and development.

Third, the public affirms the notion that man is social by nature. He is disposed toward the group. Whether he is or is not instinctively gregarious, the public seems to affirm that there is something in man which wants society.

Fourth, the public, despite its cynical protestations, risks its children by entrusting them to the very humanity it sometimes professes to distrust.

And fifth, the public confirms publicly its good opinion and preoccupation with the child. In effect, the school is by intent another act of love on behalf of the child.

The Basic Questions

Following now is a progression of questions answered in terms of appropriate evidence from the modern mind. The evidence is cumulative; therefore, the questions may be viewed as steps in this arrangement:

8. What is the meaning? (the reality of life)

7. What is the school? (institutional realities)

6. How does the person find himself? (identity)

5. How may his development be thwarted? (patterns of deprivation)

4. To what is this person heir? (the legacy of civilization)

3. On what does this person thrive? (freedom, choice, responsibility)

2. To what is this person bound? (the human condition)

1. Who is this person? (the human potential)

We shall construct a synthesis of philosophy and psychology to demonstrate the assumptions from which a view of conceptual learning, of curriculum, and of the school's role in the life of young humans may be derived—in other words, we shall develop a view of modern man in the human condition.

Who Is This Person?

An obstetrician holds in his practiced hand the up-ended body of an infant whose squall announces its first vocal response to life. Who is this creature? What is its nature? What are its capacities? What is its potential?

Many institutional sources supply formally structured answers. The basic nature, according to Calvin, was man's total depravity. By other fiat, the person is born into a condition of original sin. To the Marxist, he is a material object in a material universe, a hungering animal in search of food. On the other hand, in the eyes of Rousseau and subsequent romanticists, he is an innately good creature; if he can be nurtured away from the corruptions of society, the fruits and consequences of his existence will likewise be good.

In the latter nineteenth and early twentieth century the debate over his potential raged in psychological rather than essentially theological or philosophical terms. The nature-nurture controversy[9] wore to an indeterminate truce with environment, on the basis of scientific evidence, winning a considerably larger acceptance over heredity as a determiner of human potential.

The human record seemed to indicate that whether a creature of environment or heredity, animal or soul-possessed, the potential of the human creature was indeed broad. In the most secular terms, human behavior across the centuries has written very adequate and often ultimate definitions, on the one hand, of deviltry and cruelty, of sadism and bestiality, and, indeed, of evil; on the other hand, it

---

[9] Nicholas Pastore, *The Nature–Nurture Controversy* (New York: Kings Crown, 1949).

has written adequate and almost immortal definitions of courage and gallantry, of selflessness and love, and, indeed, of saintliness. Somehow or other, the potential of this infant may be to become an Adolf Hitler or a Winston Churchill, a Caligula or a Marcus Aurelius, a predator or a savior.

To enhance the effect of culture (of the environmental thrust) is to increase the significance of education. However, the purist on the side of heredity often had deep concerns for education; the determination of inherited characteristics, the measurement of innate capacities, the training and development of natural attributes were all important. The view of man's potential tends not so much to affect the degree of concern for education as to alter educational preoccupations and notions of curriculum, purpose, and method. The cultural determinists at the extreme tend to believe that society accounts for everything in the human potential. Educational consequences tend toward concern with group and social relationships, the effect of social forces on education, and the school in its interactions with other social institutions.

Withal, no view of man, however dogmatic or antique, seems to preclude acknowledgment that the infant *can* and *will* learn. Knowing this, men with varying views of the human potential and varying intents toward the young vie and contend for the control of education. Gardner Murphy summarizes the human potential for learning in this way:

This ability to learn entails at least five processes:

First, the ability to form simple associations—*e.g.*, to withdraw from danger signs and pursue signs that may mean success.

Second, the development of gesture and vocal sound to stand for present or distant or future objects, communicating with oneself and with others, standardizing a language of symbol.

Third, the utilization of such symbols to develop the higher capacity to think abstractly, to grasp that what is true of four apples and three apples is also true of four pears and three pears.

Fourth, the capacity to invest feeling in specific objects . . . , the capacity to form stable objects of deep personal significance.

Fifth, the capacity to systematize both these investments and these forms of symbols so that they become socially shared, and indeed are shared with the young, establishing a continuity of group attachment and ultimately a culture.[10]

Beyond innate characteristics and the environmental press, what of the human potential? Social science, which is entranced by anthropological preoccupations with enculturation, sociological concerns with social forces, and psychological concerns with learning theories derived from animal training and behaviorist models, tends to answer little of significance. But human behavior is too complex for narrow inquiry to encompass. The human view of man includes awareness of the reality that man is, and can be, a self-determiner.

What we call the "willed intelligence" is of utmost interest to education. This does not mean that education is not important without it or that the other determinants are inoperative and of no consequence to education. Through the willed intelligence, education acquires dignity from the dignity of man himself. It reckons with and counts on man's ability to discover and to use self, to redefine and redevelop self, to transcend biological limitations and culturally imposed errors and misperceptions in significant measure. This view of the willed intelligence links the classical respect for man with the stubborn insistence that man remains of consequence despite the redefinition of the universe.

Biological, economic, theological, or cultural determinism always invites the informed manipulation of the many by the few, in the name of advantage for the masses. Such brave new worlds as Stalin's Soviet Union, *1984*, the Geneva and Massachusetts Bay theocracies, and *Walden II* show the patterns of consequence. Even if man had no evidence of his capacity for self-determination, the gloomy alternatives of deterministic myths, which are always authoritarian models of one ilk or other, would force him to a more attractive myth. But the willed intelligence is no myth, and the solid accomplishments of democratic education in a democratic society hinge upon no chimerical delusions.

In terms uniquely his own but consonant with the view of this text, Gardner Murphy eloquently phrases this essential, this "third human nature":

[10] Gardner Murphy, *Human Potentialities* (New York: Basic Books, 1958), p. 49.

. . . there is a still small voice, a tiny, dissident voice, which may at times erode and even ultimately destroy vast rigid blocks of cultural tradition. There are deep forces within us that strive fundamentally for gratification of the need to *understand;* forces resistant to standardization and the molding process; forces that nervously and restlessly cut through the chrysalis of culture. It is just as human to fight against cultural standardization as it is to submit to it; and, under conditions of modern living, the creative forces of curiosity and of artistic and scientific reorganization of the materials and ways of life may overpower many of the massive conservative forces of culture. This creative thrust of understanding is a third *human nature.* . . .

This urge toward discovery, this living curiosity, beginning with a sort of "freeing of intelligence" from cultural clamps and moving forward in a positive way activated by thirst for contact with the world and for understanding and making sense of it, will begin to develop a society in which the will to understand is the dominant new component. Both science and the philosophy and ethics of a mass democratic movement provide reasons for believing that the whole thesis of a hopelessly uncontrollable culture can be annihilated, and that the conception of building a society largely motivated by the will to understand—including the understanding both of its place in the cosmos and of its own inner nature—may be fulfilled.[11]

To What Is This Person Bound?

Man is born into the human condition and does not escape it in his lifetime, though he may more or less modify it. Today a man may orbit the earth at the rate of 17,500 miles per hour; tomorrow this accomplishment may assume small proportions beside other, more spectacular feats. Does this diminish or enhance man's stature? Surely it is unendurable for modern man so to shrink the barriers of distance and see for himself that he dwells in one world, while at the same time to retain his anachronistic tribalism or reject the obvious dictates of a common fate. As with any occurrence, man must ponder the meaning of his space adventures to render them into experience, to conceptualize the happening. Without reflec-

11 *Ibid.,* pp. 18–19.

tion, the quest for meaning in the space flight may be just as spectacular (and essentially as witless) as the firing of a gigantic sky rocket. Our adventures, if thoughtless, may furnish mere distraction from the pressing business of our earth home. As Hannah Arendt has said: "The earth is the very quintessence of the human condition, and earthly nature, for all we know, may be unique in the universe in providing human beings with a habitat in which they can move and breathe without effort and without artifice."[12]

Man, whether one likes it or not, is born into a set of defining and limiting conditions. He is born to the earth home and is basically confined to the earth. Even at the apogee of space flight, man has only briefly extended the radius of the earth by less than a hundredth. Man is a large family, living in a finite and limited environment. If his numbers were less and his resources infinite, his problems would be different. But there are so many of us and only so much stuff. Thus, the content of the population problem, the distribution of goods, the conservation of resources, the relationship of the affluent with the needy (the advanced and the underdeveloped), become curriculum dictates, for there is no escape from these realities.

Man is born to mortality, another part of the definition of the human condition. Though man is culturally disposed to varying views of his postmundane fate, he is here awhile, inclined to prolong his stay, and to make the best of it. Philosophers ponder the meaning of life and biologists seek its secret. What is life? That is a question, in one sense, past our ken; yet men have a working understanding adequate for most purposes. (The biological limitations, though not fully defined, are perhaps more clear-cut than the intellectual and emotional dimensions.) In view of the numbers who have broken the once mythical four-minute mile, we would pose no absolute limits to man's physical achievements; yet we would be surprised at the first human runner who won the Kentucky Derby. However, the student of the human record is past surprise at any intellectual or creative achievement of the species.

Man is born into time. Our immediate concerns are with edu-

[12] Hannah Arendt, *The Human Condition* (New York: Doubleday Anchor Books, 1959), p. 2.

cation of youth in the twentieth and the twenty-first centuries. Of time, we know little enough, though we know the measure of days, moons, and years. We know something of the meaning of past, present, and future, but time is a dimension peculiarly relativistic. It speeds with activity; it lags with ennui. Our sense of its passage varies with age and the state of our health. As a commodity, it is constantly perishable. We say it is priceless, yet we permit the common culture to annihilate it with witless time-killing devices. The curriculum problem is tied to the dimension of time. We do not refer to such vulgar demands as scheduling, but rather the necessity to recognize that the job is tremendous and time is scarce and fleeting. The necessity for value judgments, priorities, and selectivity thus becomes apparent.

Man is born into culture. There is a mass of accumulated views and institutional patterns on everything that affects man. Sexual practices, marriage forms, religions, and languages abound in variety. However, culture cannot do everything for man; it affects most of his perceptions, but, rarely, except punitively, it does not deprive him of his five senses. Man's condition includes common denominators: he is born, he eats, he breathes, he excretes, he procreates, he feels, he dies—regardless of the culture. However, the effect of culture must not be underrated. Its influence on perception is clear: observe the varied ways of interpreting events by plutocrats and proletarians, by communists, fascists, and democrats, by liberals and conservatives, or in the classic anthropological case by Zuni and Kwakiutl.

Man can escape from being a prisoner of cultural determinism only through the discipline of his own senses and confidence in them and through the assertive use of willed intelligence.

Man is born into society—a vast complex of social groups, institutions, and myths. Throughout his life he will be subjected to a barrage of such societal predispositions as: everyone is out to get you, equality of opportunity, material success is the reward of superior virtue, poverty induces virtue or crime; these people have no sense of humor; those are stingy, devious, or upright; they are clannish; one race is superior to another; free enterprise is a competitive economy; Karl Marx, or Adam Smith, or John Maynard Keynes was the only sound economist; and so on.

Myths about the human condition are part of the human condition. They are not immutable. An education that goes beyond mere transmission of the culture examines them and seeks the reality. A myth believed, a legend acted upon, a chimera fondly pursued may have as significant an effect on human behavior or on history as reality. But the leprechaun's treasure is yet to be found, and humanity has learned much of anguish from its pursuit of illusion.

The vast differences for education are found in distinctions or degrees of difference between rigid and flexible cultures, closed and open societies. If a society prizes the individual and seeks his maximum development, its education will (1) seek to know the full reality of the human condition and (2) make maximum use of that condition for human welfare and development.

On What Does He Thrive?

The human record indicates that the human thrives best if nurtured on freedom, choice, and responsibility.

Freedom is the ability to make uncoerced choice. Obviously, freedom is not an absolute. To say that nowhere has man achieved enough of it is not to argue that theoretically he might not have too much of it; it only suggests that it is safe for him to seek more of it. Freedom is limited by concessions to security, though security and freedom are more interdependent than antithetical. Love also puts bonds on freedom. Man's desire for social approval or acceptance also hedges him. Freedom is limited by arbitrary impositions of power, though never completely, even by the most absolute authority. And freedom is limited, perhaps most of all, by timidity and ignorance.

Educational choice begins with the infant. Freedom and responsibility are inextricably linked: man is free to take the consequences of his choices. The school sometimes slips here, as freedom is not an easy road. It is wrong to deprive children either of choice or of consequence. The girl who picks her winter coat unwisely can learn only by wearing it; the school committee that lets a class down

63

does not necessarily learn if the teacher is able to rectify the situation.

The source of freedom lies in the ability of the human intelligence to perceive reality. Is *1984* possible? Is it possible for arbitrary power to engineer and coerce humanity out of all resolves of decency and respect? Not so, say the facts of life and of love. Men have often suffered rather than betray love, loyalty, or devotion.

A free society is desirable, but men may be free in another society as well. Sartre and Camus both recount that they were never as free as during the German occupation, when they saw reality clearly, knew the necessity and the obligation, and acted accordingly. This is the stuff of freedom: reality, responsibility, action! And *Dr. Zhivago* was written in the Soviet Union of Stalin. The institutions of freedom were won by men who had learned from experience the unendurability of "unfreedom" to human kind.

To What Is This Person Heir?

The infant is born heir to civilization, to a vast inheritance of human experience. Civilization is an aggregate of institutions and achievements rendered meaningful through history, philosophy, and the arts. The legacy includes treasures and millstones—much that elevates and liberates, much that confines and even stultifies the human spirit's development. The "priceless heritage" of the past and of tradition is a major preoccupation of the conservative, the educational essentialist, and the educational perennialist.

There is much that is priceless in the attic of civilization, but there is also rubbish there. An attic is valuable as a storehouse and provides a place for items of use and value, for lessons of experience, for restoration of meaningful sentiments, and for remembrance of times past. Attics, though, want cleaning and culling too. To dwell too long in the attics of the past may be an escape from present reality and an inducement to morbidity. Civilization imposes not merely the "lessons" of experience but also its limitations—the yoke of the past, outworn traditions, wrong notions, and irrational institutionalisms.

Man is not born precisely into civilization. He must be made heir of it; he must be inducted into it. Civilization is neither complete nor perfect. Therefore, sound curriculum must derive from social philosophy and a continuing application of *social criticism*.

Man is not obligated to his past but to his future; he is entitled to shape institutions toward the ends he would like to achieve. The past is used in this sense to analyze human experience; humanity has performed many social scientific experiments on itself. What does the record say of the times when humanity has proceeded on assumptions such as doctrines of the elite; ideas of human inequality, caste, and status; notions of special supremacy; the existence of man for the sake of the state; the justification of the means by the end? The record clearly suggests that some alternative assumptions might supply better results for humanity.

Civilization also inspires. Once the dross is culled, it provides for exposure to the best. It allows man to diminish the limits of time; through the vicarious but real experience of history and literature, the man who reads can have the advantage and the enjoyment—and some of the burden—of many lifetimes.

Civilization can be for or against man. History is a sorry account of antique grudges, sins and slanders, revanche and irredentism. Some of its musty tomes might well be left under the cobwebs. What must one nation forgive in other nations so that the world can achieve a community of trust and institutions of world order can aspire to human survival? Germany and the Soviet Union come to mind, as well as England, France, Belgium, and Holland, and the United States as well. The Middle East reveals how man misuses history when he permits it to be a storehouse of grievance.

How May His Development Be Thwarted?

If one would really seek to stunt human development, the formula is relatively simple: deprive man of love, choice, and learning. This formula is not intended for the use of those who wish humanity ill but rather as a corrective to those who combine good will with ignorance or ineptitude.

More precisely, human development is not simply stunted, but is also perverted. Humanity will out; individuality is stubborn and

65

slippery. Deprive the person of love, choice, and learning in a setting of freedom and responsibility, and watch him seek them out. He will love and choose and learn, but they may be strange objects and strange ways.

An education designed to thwart human development will be built on imposition of dogmas and inhibitions of inquiry. This sums up the platform: Give man false gods, and forget that "ye cannot serve God and Mammon." Smother him in goods and materialistic motivations. Keep him on the run with the activities, the routines, and the strivings of the common culture. Give him games, beer and hot dogs, and TV (his own bread and circus in his own living room). Particularize his education; render it training by "learning theory" based on observations of rats, pigeons, and other creatures. Subordinate all other goals to the achievement of security. Divert his attention from the human condition; focus it on what he has and what he wants, on space dreams, or exclusively on postmundane aspirations.

These prescriptions are difficult to effect because they run against the grain of humanity. The way of the authoritarian is well mapped but it is as hard to achieve as that of any transgressor. The devices are those of thought control, rigid elites, elaborate patterns of rewards and punishments, party lines, proscriptions, censorship, definitions of heresy, witch hunts, conformity drives, manipulation, and propaganda. The pattern of affinities may be used for observation in reverse. If you find these devices, expect educational a priori conclusions and the obscuring of reality; if you find such education, expect to find humanity thwarted and in pain.

It *is* humanly possible to exterminate humanity; but, short of extermination, human freedom cannot be completely or forever suppressed.

How Does the Person Find Himself?

To "know thyself" is not easy. The human infant will in time ask himself: "Who am I?" He will continue to raise the question with himself throughout his lifetime. He never knows for sure, and for assurance of his identity and meaning and significance, he builds certain bridges of security. He seeks the assurances of love. He seeks food and shelter (a minimal social security, so to speak), for unless he is physically well nurtured, his *amour propre* tends to disintegrate. The Marxist counts on the affective response to hunger as anger and social bitterness, a natural materialistic error. The more sophisticated understand that the more serious consequence of physical deprivation is psychic damage to the ego. This is the basic reality of cultural deprivation.

The person seeks a substantive role to aid in self-definition. He assumes responsibilities partly so that he may feel needed, which gives him an assurance of being. A useful occupation (the assurance of employment, in which he is bossed or obeyed or paid) again gives him evidence that he is really present. Man also seeks assurance through attempts to establish continuity. Meaningful developments, cause-and-effect relationships, sanity and order in social arrangements, the sense of building something that may last give the person an assurance of existence and a foothold in security helpful in defining self. The Hindu axiom has it that there are three ways to achieve immortality: plant a tree, have a child, write a book.

It is well that curriculum discourages the seeking of self through blind alleys. Power and access of material goods help only as narcotics do, in dulling the question. In *After Many a Summer Dies the Swan*, Aldous Huxley portrayed the disintegration of self into the abysmal fear of death through a parody on the life of a famous man of wealth and power. Napoleon in exile, Hitler in the flaming bunker, Mussolini dead and reviled in the public square show the futility of dreams of personal glory.

Modern man soon learns that he is loose in a terribly complex environment. Complex social expectations, rapid role changes, conflicting patterns of loyalties, social mobility and transience, value conflicts, success versus ethics, religion versus religiosities—all these tend to confuse, to lose the individual in "the lonely crowd."

Where does this lead? It leads to consequences that we can observe in all our classes if we are psychologically aware: to compartmentalization of the mind, in areas of reason, areas of dogma, areas of irrationality, and to a fragmented image of self. (One must distinguish between fragmentation and versatility, of course.)

The curriculum must help the person to find himself. It appears that he can find himself only in meaningful relationships with others and in recognized roles of responsibility achieved in communication and in loving and being loved. As a participant in society, a person begins to find his central tendencies, his dominant role, his clearest self-image. In ascertaining his dominant role, it is important that he don a fully human and unconstricting suit of clothing, fit for breathing and movement. If he is fitted into something less than human, into a uniform or strait jacket of oversimplification of self—*only* a soldier, *only* a scientist, *only* a businessman, *only* a teacher—it will not do! The only self fit for man is the human being. The uniform may fit nicely and give a spurious assurance of self, but if the seams split, the self disintegrates.

What Is the School?

The school is a human institution, mortally conceived, mortally operated, mortally concerned with mortality. It is at least this, and it may be more. The school obviously reflects the society and its culture, its purposes and its confusions; and it may do more.

Although the school is supposed to be an educational institution, it may be, but "it ain't necessarily so." At best, it may be a place where the person is truly at home, where his most constructive potential is led out and developed, where he gains in knowledge of life, man, and self. On the other hand, the school is more often than not an institution for academic learning (learning whose principal consequences are limited to the school itself), a place where the person is set against his fellows, where he learns to accept the purposes of others as his own, and where he is "housebroken" to apathy and conformity. The school is not necessarily an educational institution. Too often it is not, but we would have it be just that.

Considerable evidence indicates that the school is an unnatural intrusion on human development. The encultured individual is well housebroken to his institutions. The alien aspect of the school to the young human may not be too visible. In that event, an extreme corrective would be helpful. To read Rousseau's *Emile* or A. S. Neill's *Summerhill* may not afford a model on which to build, but it will surely induce toward a more pristine perspective, or anthropological distance, to the going institution. The child on his own is undisciplined, responsive, playful, animalistic, restless, joyful, roving, inquisitive, learning, affective. The key question we need to know of a school is: Does it reflect conditions to aid or to thwart human development? What would the good school be? It would be these things, among others: a critical analyzer of human experience; a developer of essential social values; a builder of useful skills; a place well adapted to stages of human development; a joyful place to spend a large chunk of life; an environment conducive to growth and fulfillment and low in frustration factors; an institution dedicated to the worth of all, the potential in each, and the love of man.

What Is the Meaning?

A suggested answer to the above question is that the meaning lies in the reality of life. The alternatives would seem to be that life is unreal, illusory, and mythical. Humanity's best hold to sanity appears to be its grasp on reality. We perceive life to be real and meaningful; it is an assertion, an article of faith.

Reality lies in what is known and what is knowable, in probing the unknown, *and* in accepting the unknowable. Reality is concerned with probabilities, degrees of certainty. It is sometimes necessary to act on scanty evidence, but it hardly seems realistic to act most confidently when there is little or no evidence. A single question may provide a clue here: Do the children look more *alive* as they enter the school or as they leave?

The school as an educator does not always serve good social value. We tend to accept the school in its stereotype as enlightener, as liberator, and as human. Yet there are some schools where the better the lessons are learned, the worse it is for man, for example, the schools of the Nazis and Communist indoctrination. Schools exist that primarily teach lessons of caste and status, the "better-people" biases; there are schools of unculled tradition, where the whole attic of civilization (treasure and rubbish alike) constitutes the curriculum; there are schools of the most antihumanistic trades (the war colleges of all nations); there are schools of closed-mindedness and closed traditions. *School* is a relatively meaningless term until we know something of the curriculum.

The American school should be of the modern mind, of freedom, of scientific spirit, of human inclusiveness, of dignity and respect. In this respect, the school is largely independent of structure and arrangement. To be sure, in our society, the quality of the facility is likely to be a symbolic index of the community's concern for education. But it would be well for education if that index were sought in the excellence of program rather than in chrome and brick and glass.

The school is half-bound by the common culture, half-free. It has been weakened by pet errors and institutional dogmas, economic, political, and cultural, and by the acceptance of games, vulgarity, and trivia. It need not be so. Modern man has come upon some special realities of his own. They are not all new, but they are specially relevant to modern meaning. However, if price be any criterion, these realities have come high.

Commentary: Toward the Historical Moment

Education should seek its meaning in a serious view of life. This meaning will be contemporary but rooted in history. Illustrative of the point are certain great learnings.

The educated man is a rebel. "Whoso," wrote Emerson, "would be a man must be a nonconformist." This well-worn quotation does not mean the educated man is dangerous to the commonweal. However, the accusers of Jesus and Socrates disagreed, and both were executed, though their crimes have never been historically apparent. In fact, their teachings are among the roots of law and order in Western civilization.

Albert Camus states in *The Rebel* that:

Man's solidarity is founded upon rebellion. . . . In our daily trials rebellion plays the same role as does the *cogito* in the realm of thought: it is the first piece of evidence. But this evidence lures the individual from his solitude. I rebel—therefore we exist.[13]

This rebellion may make a man discontent with conventional errors, may render him unfit for an organizational or bureaucratic strait jacket, or may give him fury at the thought of atomic incineration. But it "lures the individual from his solitude." It causes him to respond to his environment, and it moves him to thoughtful action. Perhaps only in rebellion can the modern American find a solution to "the lonely crowd" where David Riesman said man has lost himself.

The individual is fit to think for himself. It seems axiomatic and obvious that a person is capable of thinking for himself. But the progress of human engineering and motivational research has made us apprehensive. Today the methods of brainwashing and the selling of detergents are not dissimilar. Politicians and pat phrases are packaged and sold like cereals. In *Escape from Freedom,* Erich Fromm states that:

> . . . modern man lives under the illusion that he knows what he wants, while he actually wants what he is *supposed* to want. In order to accept this it is necessary to realize that to know what one wants is not comparatively easy, as most people think, but one of the most difficult problems any human being has to solve. It is a task we frantically try to avoid by accepting ready-made goals as though they were our own. Modern man is ready to take great risks when he tries to achieve the aims which are supposed to be "his"; but he is deeply afraid of taking the risk and responsibility of giving himself his own aims. Intense activity is often mistaken for evidence of self-determined action, although we know that it may well be no more spontaneous than the behavior of an actor or a person hypnotized.[14]

Not only must the student and the teacher learn that each person is fit to think for himself; he needs to know that he *must.* Only if the individual retains his integrity of judgment whole will the fabric of this civilization endure.

[13] Albert Camus, *The Rebel* (New York: Vintage Books, 1958) , p. 22.
[14] Erich Fromm, *Escape from Freedom* (New York: Rinehart, 1941), pp. 252–253.

In one paragraph of *Dr. Zhivago* Boris Pasternak isolated the root and cause of all the totalitarian horror that came to Russia.

> The main misfortune, the root of all the evil to come, was the loss of confidence in the value of one's own opinion. People imagined it was out of date to follow their own moral sense, that they must all sing in chorus, and live by other people's notions, notions that were being crammed down everybody's throat. And then there arose the power of the glittering phrase, first the Tsarist, then the revolutionary.[15]

Zhivago warns America too—the main misfortune is the loss of confidence in the value of one's *own* opinion. This vital nonconformity, this socially valuable attribute of individual judgment, is a signal objective of education.

The times are sad. Education is hopeful; indeed it is *the* hope. Learning is work, but it is joyful. Yet somewhere the boy must become the man; he must learn that tragedy is a part of life, and that tragedy is not only rare and personal, but it is universal and human.

We live in no easy century. It has been racked by wars of new dimensions. The twentieth century has recorded the greatest crimes against humanity in all of history. Each American should also examine his own conscience for responsibility in the sorrow of our time. We should ask what our share is as we read the schoolboy theme of ten-year-old Toshio Nakamura:

> The day before the bomb, I went for a swim. In the morning, I was eating peanuts. I saw a light. I was knocked to little sister's sleeping place. When we were saved, I could see only as far as the tram. My mother and I started to pack our things. The neighbors were walking around burned and bleeding. Hataya-san told me to run away with her. I said I wanted to wait for my mother. We went to the park. A whirlwind came. At night a gas tank burned and I saw the reflection in the river. We stayed in the park one night. Next day I went to Taiko Bridge and met my girl friends, Kikuki and

15 Boris Pasternak, *Dr. Zhivago* (New York: Pantheon, 1958), p. 404.

Murakami; they were looking for their mothers. But Kikuki's mother was wounded and Murakami's mother, alas, was dead.[16]

Such knowledge is important; it shakes one's affability, and one does not confront everything smiling and happy. Surely it is worth knowing. Are children, all of them innocent, safe anywhere, unless the mind of man remembers the sorrow and horror of our age and thoughtfully resolves to find peaceful solutions?

True meaning is complex and extended. A great error is to try making complex things simple. Who but the arrogant or uninformed will give *the* cause for the fall of Rome, the Civil War, the Great Depression, the political confusion of France, or the rise of Hitler. Scholars and philosophers endlessly search for answers. They suggest patterns, they raise questions, sometimes they speak in confidence—but they do not propose a final cause.

The search for extended meaning liberates the person from the semantic confines of the ordinary. It permeates the whole of life with the richness of all learning. In *The Philosophy of Literary Form* Kenneth Burke illustrates the release from apparent exactness into more precise meaning. To say, as he does, that "New York City is in Iowa" appears to be a simple misstatement of fact. But note what Burke has to say about it:

> Has one ever stood, for instance, in some little outlying town, on the edge of the wilderness, and watched a train go by? Has one perhaps suddenly felt that the train, and its tracks, were a kind of arm of the city, reaching out across the continent, quite as though it were simply Broadway itself extended? . . .
>
> "New York City is in Iowa" is "poetically" true. . . . To have ruled it out, by strict semantic authority, would have been vandalism.[17]

The unliberated are victims of a woeful literal-mindedness, which, at best, makes no more of the moon than green cheese. Thus,

[16] John Hersey, *Hiroshima* (New York: Bantam, 1946), pp. 115–116.

[17] Kenneth Burke, *The Philosophy of Literary Form* (New York: Vintage Books, 1957), p. 126.

when two liberated minds meet, each can never say all that he means, but the other will always hear much more than is said.

What are we trying to do? We most certainly are not delineating or defining the scope of a curriculum. Here we mean to emphasize that education involves the whole of man. Education is serious. It places demands on the intellect; it demands the individual and seeks him out alone. It re-creates the self even as it makes more meaningful all humanity and the very universe. In this process, mature adult concepts of intellectual integrity, of civic responsibility, of the good life, and of ethical and spiritual values should develop. The next task for the student of the school is to address himself to the historical and social foundations of these matters.

Chapter III

Historical and Social Foundations

What then is this American, this new man? He is either an European, or the descendent of an European, hence that strange mixture of blood, which you will find in no other country. I could point out to you a family whose grandfather was an Englishman, whose wife was Dutch, whose son married a French woman, and whose present four sons have now four wives of different nations. *He* is an American, who leaving behind him all his ancient prejudices and manners, receives new ones from the new mode of life he has embraced, the new government he obeys, and the new rank he holds. He becomes an American by being received in the broad lap of our great *Alma Mater.* Here individuals of all nations are melted into a new race of men, whose labours and posterity will one day cause great changes in the world.[1]

—*Michael Guillaume St. Jean de Crévecoeur*

American schools have always been rooted in a value structure. Colonial schools were literally an arm of Protestant religious enterprise. They sought to cultivate literacy to gain access to spiritual

[1] Michael Guillaume St. Jean de Crévecoeur, *Letters from an American Farmer* (1782; London: J. M. Dent, 1912) , p. 43.

75

authority, namely the Holy Scriptures. In the words of the Massachusetts school law of 1647, they were part of an effort to foil "that old deluder Satan."

The school in colonial America stood far from the modern school as a fundamental American institution. Most schools were on the elementary level. They were neither universal nor compulsory. Most children did not attend, but those who did went only for a matter of weeks, for a few months, over a few years. Colleges were founded in colonial America; yet at the time of the Revolution only one in a thousand Americans held a baccalaureate degree from one of the colonial colleges.

In the twentieth century the progressive education movement stressed learning as living. In colonial times the larger curriculum for the child was life. To a marked degree, the family was a cohesive and an inclusive social institution. It was principally in the family that the child learned, and the curriculum was largely *work*.

Necessity, Work, Utilitarianism

Serious-mindedness was intrinsic within the heritage of American education. Work was a necessity of circumstance; it was imposed not by theory but by reality. In the twentieth century, with its technology and automation, a recognized school function became the delay of youth from entering the labor market until later adolescence. In the older tradition work held precedence over school, especially at times of planting or harvesting. The priority even holds occasionally in rural America today; in fact, in 1961 it drew a critic's protest when Idaho schools excused their students to gather the potato crop.

Colonial America was predominantly rural. Fields had to be cleared, fences built, crops tended, animals cared for; households had to be kept, yarn spun, cloth woven, bread baked—and all these were jobs done without machine power. Horses and oxen were harnessed to man, of course, but the basic energy was applied through the muscle of man, of woman, and of little boys and girls.

So it was in the hard climates of New England and the Middle States and in the South as well.

Work was sanctioned not only by necessity but by the value structure as well. Max Weber in *The Protestant Ethic and the Spirit of Capitalism* and R. H. Tawney in *Religion and the Rise of Capitalism* recorded a relationship between the Protestant ethic and success materialism. That "Satan will find mischief for idle hands to do" was part of the common culture of early America. This expressed merely the negative aspect. Worldly success came to be identified with spiritual fitness, depending on the theology, either as a reward of faith or as a token of redemption. The attributes of thrift, prudence, sobriety, and industriousness were somewhat demonstrably related to economic or business success; they were also at least coincidental with virtues sought in the Puritanical codes. Therefore, it is not surprising that work became established in American values not merely as a means, a dictate of necessity, but as an end, a virtue in itself.

Long consequences follow from this fact. The McGuffey readers, for example, illustrate the established emphasis on the virtue of toil in nineteenth-century education. Busy work, ritualistic homework, and punitive assignments all bear a relationship here. In the latter nineteenth century, Puritanical support was buttressed further by pseudoscientific doctrines. Darwin's theory of evolution led to the popularization of the phrase "survival of the fittest." Intended as a biological tenet, the concept was given spurious sociological applicability. Herbert Spencer and William Graham Sumner developed social Darwinism. According to their theorizing, the poor were not so much the victims of circumstance, ill-fortune, environment, or social injustice as they were the victims of their vices and innate limitations of indolence, laziness, insobriety, viciousness, and general incapacity. Thus, material success became proof of both spiritual and social fitness. Humanitarianism in this perspective therefore became not effective philanthropy but erroneous antisocial sentimentality, weakening society by preserving the unfit.

The linkage of religion and education in colonial times is indisputable. Some scholars assumed that this laid a dead weight on educational progress. Some reckoned that religion served as a social static. Such was not the case. Religion in the seventeenth and eighteenth centuries was itself an arena of ferment, contention, dissent, and movement. The movement was both organizational and theological.

The Massachusetts theocracy constituted a Geneva-like effort to merge ecclesiastical and temporal authority. But if authoritarianism was the major theme of the seventeenth century, dissent was its *leitmotif.* Schism and fragmentation were characteristic of the age; Anne Hutchinson and Roger Williams are as much its symbols as John Winthrop and John Cotton. John Wise, in his essay "On the Government of the New England Churches," was writing for ecclesiastical purposes, but this essay was an early exposition of thought that is prodemocratic and, further, is explicit in anticipation of democratic political science:

> This [democracy] is a form of government, which the light of nature does highly value, and often directs to as most agreable [*sic*] to the just and natural prerogatives of human beings. . . .
> That a democracy in church or state, is a very honorable and regular government according to the dictates of right reason.[2]

Jonathan Mayhew, in the same line of religious dissent, uttered sermons with clear-cut secular, revolutionary implication. In attacking "absolute submission" as early as 1750, he voiced the logic of political severance, should persistent abuses warrant it:

> A people, really oppressed to a great degree by their sovereign, cannot well be insensible when they are so oppressed. . . . For a nation thus abused to rise unanimously, and to resist their prince, even to the dethroning him, is not criminal; but a reasonable way of vindicating their liberties and just rights; in its making use of the means, and the only means, which God has put into their power, for mutual and self-defence. And it would be highly criminal in them, not to make use of this means.[3]

2 John Wise, "A Vindication of the Government of New England Churches" (1717), reprinted in H. Shelton Smith, Robert T. Handy, and Lefferts A. Loetscher, *American Christianity* (New York: Scribner, 1960), pp. 390–391.

3 Jonathan Mayhew, "A Discourse Concerning Unlimited Submission and Nonresistance to the Higher Powers" (1750), reprinted in Smith, Handy, and Loetscher, *ibid.,* p. 414.

Theology too was in movement. Fragmentation led to attempted coercion; and the ugliness of coercive doctrine and behavior made tolerance shine out first as essential expedient and then as tested principle, even virtue. The austerities of Calvinism were softened by debate or lessened in impact by competition. Unitarianism entered with its rational course amidst theological diversity. Indeed, if education were linked to religion, its problem was not simply to escape from constraint but to adjust to the winds of change.

Most significant for education, however, were the beginning applications of the dictates of conscience to humane behavior. In 1700 Samuel Sewall, a judge repentant over his role in the Salem witchcraft hysteria, revealed a precocious social conscience. In a tract entitled "The Selling of Joseph" he anticipated abolitionist sentiments on scriptural grounds. The Quakers linked humanitarianism most basically to faith; John Woolman and Anthony Benezet, like Sewall, the Puritan, perceived human slavery to be both inhumane and un-Christian.

Colonial America, though simple in retrospective terms, developed real complexity. It was, after all, almost as long a time from 1607 to 1776 as from 1789 to the 1960s. It was a predominantly rural society with varied patterns of landholding. There were proprietors, planters, and patroons; there were freeholders and yeomen farmers; there were indentured servants, hired hands, and slaves. Some early settlements grew into cities; some by the time of the Revolution were already well into their second century—Boston, New York, Philadelphia, Charleston. Social class lines were drawn. There were aristocrats, merchants, planters and farmers, freemen and slaves, employers and workers, creditors and debtors.

Any picture of colonial society as simple, classless, and homogeneous in background and economic or social interests is romantic and illusory. America was culturally diverse. It did not yet consider itself a melting pot, nor were the dynamics of cultural pluralism yet understood, but the population was significantly heterogeneous: English, Scotch-Irish, German, Dutch, Swedish, Jewish, French, Irish, Negro, among others.

With complexity, complication developed in the school curriculum. The colonial elementary school was first directed toward literacy with a religious purpose in view; the grammar school was directed toward college entrance; and the college was primarily intended for training to the ministry. As the work-a-day world became more complex and its urban dimension increased, family domination of the work curriculum diminished. Businesses, mercantile houses, institutions of commerce, and such offered new opportunities and demanded new skills. The crafts and practical arts (smiths, carpenters, wheelwrights, coopers) possessed formal or informal apprenticeship systems, but in a complex society education on the job became inefficient, unsystematic, and expensive.

Demands for anticipatory instruction in formal schools were sure to follow the discovery by practical men of affairs that they needed trained men to work for them. Commerce discovered the practicality of geography and navigation; inventive inquiry enhanced interest in the natural sciences; trade and travel saw values in the study of French, German, Spanish, and Portuguese that were not apparent in Latin, Greek, and Hebrew; handwriting and accounting commended themselves to the keepers of books and ledgers. Benjamin Franklin, practical man that he was as well as civic guardian and statesman, was a leader in the demand that the school program face toward an extended practical necessity.

Thus, the emergence of the features of modern America enhanced the *utilitarian* emphasis in American education. Work as a discipline was not enough. Practical America sought usefulness in terms beyond the moral. It was busy with enterprises demanding developed skills, and it required an immediate utility of education.

One constant in American history enhanced this dynamic. For a century after 1789 the nation was busy encompassing and settling what became a 3.5 million-square-mile share of North America. The frontier, in the official census view, vanished in 1890, but new enterprise continued to preoccupy the nation. Frontiers were not merely lateral and usually westward movements of settlements, they also consisted of internal shifts of basic economic and social preoccupations. The twentieth century has seen, for example, the industrialization of the agricultural regions of the nation. In Iowa, which is considered a farm state, and an important one, the value of industrial output has exceeded that of farming for over three decades. When settlement slowed, industrialization increased. Furthermore, new enterprises followed the nation's adventures in imperialism and world trade. Today, deep commitments and involvements in world affairs, as well as the sanction of scientific and technological discovery, give renewed support to utilitarian and practical concepts in education.

The utilitarian view became part of the value structure as did the work ethic. It too became an end as well as a means. When Emerson wrote of "Self-Reliance," he expressed the idea of utility. Busy enterprise led to the common recognition that the worthwhile man could do something. This view was not necessarily anti-intellectual, but it could lead to a particularistic appraisal of the outcomes of curriculum. It tended to create appraisals of both men and curricula in terms of adequacy for the jobs at hand. It was democratic in that rank, prior prestige, social status, and family had little bearing on the appraisal. The largest pitfall lay in mistaking the nature of the job at hand or in assessing either its scope or direction too narrowly.

Lester Frank Ward, whose biographer dubbed him the "American Aristotle," wrote the first comprehensive sociological appraisal of democratic education. In *Dynamic Sociology* he stressed the significance of "useful knowledge." His work had acknowledged influence on the subsequent ideas of John Dewey.

The utilitarian emphasis in education was not exclusively directed toward external accomplishment. The aims of self-improvement and social melioration were closely associated. Deep-rooted in the historical development of the American curriculum is the humanitarian precept.

Humanitarianism and Education

In colonial times an individualistic revolt against authoritarian dogmas and theocratic rule began to produce the assertion of the dignity and worth of the individual. Roger Williams, John Wise, and Jonathan Mayhew again were among those who insisted that conscience had consequences in political and social theory. And love of man as a consequence of the love of God influenced such Puritans as Samuel Sewall and such Quakers as John Woolman and Anthony Benezet.

The commitments of the new nation, however, turned humanitarianism from a matter of private conscience into a social dictate. If the Declaration of Independence with its egalitarian premise and the Constitution with its Preamble and its Bill of Rights were to be taken seriously, the gross disparities in opportunity, the cruel denials of essential human rights, and the social evils that obstructed the general welfare literally stood in the way of fulfillment of the avowed national purpose.

By no accident do the two great statesmen of the American public school movement, Horace Mann and Henry Barnard, stand central in the humanitarian movement. Educators they were in career emphasis, but humanitarians they were in the full meaning of the term. Both were concerned to establish schools, to educate teachers, and to develop professionalism, but only Mann committed himself to the abolitionist crusade. Both, however, were involved in matters of peace, temperance, the condition of workers, prison reform, the library movement, and care of the ill and insane—quite the gamut of humanitarian causes characterizing the years labeled "freedom's ferment" by Alice Felt Tyler.[4] A basic purpose of the American curriculum was firmly established in humanitarian goals; "do-gooders" and doing good are historically fundamental to the aims of American education.

For curriculum development humanitarianism as a basic and reputable element in American thought is fundamental. The American Revolution established a republic and a constitution that made possible the development of a democratic political science. But democracy is not merely a political method—a "government of the people, by the people, for the people." It is a way of life based on tenets of human worth, equality, and brotherhood. The ideas of

---

[4] Alice Felt Tyler, *Freedom's Ferment* (Minneapolis: University of Minnesota Press, 1944).

social and humane concern thrive in this environment. Men decide to do things in concert for themselves and for others. Thus, after the Revolution, political democracy would have been meaningless or unfulfilled as it developed, had not the deeds of social conscience enriched it. In the logic of the context, humanitarianism burgeoned in American life. Without the humanitarian movement American history would lack meaning.

Public education was one of the greatest streams within the humanitarian movement, reinforced by the logic of political democracy. The eventual acceptance of the obligation to educate all the children of all the people was a direct outcome of initial egalitarian impulses. Its greatest institutional product, the American secondary school, was unique among educational systems; it made the high school common to all, free, tax-supported, considerably compulsory, and practically universal.

Equality of opportunity as a derived concept became the great discipline for the American educational effort. It spurred curriculum advance and experimentation to find learning experiences suitable, relevant, meaningful, and useful to all. On the one hand, it led to the comprehensive high school with open admission and a large common program for all; on the other hand, it led to a broad range of special and vocational programs on the assumption that equality demanded equal chance for personal growth but not identical learning patterns. The dictate of equal opportunity lies behind programs of state aid and equalization plans; it is a basic motivation for programs of federal support. As a premise, it has been a great source of constructive discontent—discontent with inadequate support of schools, with conditions of child employment that stand in the way of schooling, with parental neglect, with social irresponsibility toward such large aggregates of children as the children of migrant workers and the children of urban ghettoes of color and poverty. Equal opportunity was the root of the drive for the desegregation of American schools.

Humanitarianism and the materialistic ethic came into conflict in the latter nineteenth century. A spurious social science (as discussed earlier) had bolstered the notion that unrestrained competition somehow constituted the essential basis for a sound society. To social Darwinism, "survival of the fittest" made humanitarianism an enfeebling sentimentality. But the increase of democratic commitment was bolstered by an outpouring of social criticism and a new social science. The social scientist at the turn of the century was concerned with establishing a science of society. His concern was purposive: to use knowledge as an instrument to build a better social order. These social scientists were active social critics. Thorstein Veblen, Simon Paten, Charles Cooley, and Richard Ely were the social humanists.

America has moved toward definition and was never as simple as presumed in retrospect. To know America is to become aware of its complexity. Indeed, the curriculum for the American must be designed to render him capable of understanding and moving amid a complexity of institutions and cultural forces.

Cultural Pluralism

The cultural pluralism of the American nation is noteworthy in degree. The factor of pluralism itself does not render it unique. Other nations of the Western hemisphere have considerable diversity, but no nation of such considerable size even approximates the complexity of the American population. Its diversity is extensive by any categorization—national origins, ethnic roots, religious affiliations.

Pluralism characterized the American settlement from its origins. Of course, the waves upon waves of immigration in the nineteenth century enhanced this dimension beyond any historical experience. The immigration was variously motivated. Sometimes America represented a vision realized—as Mary Antin called it, a "promised land." Mainly, the motivation was the search for something better; opportunity meant all things to all people and was the key. And the key to the reality of the American opportunity was the remarkable degree of openness in its society, amazing by comparison with the places from which the immigrants came. Rich lands, abundant natural resources, security from foreign foes, relatively invisible class lines, burgeoning educational facilities, democratic political institutions, and exploding economy spelled openness, elbow room, and opportunity.

The immigrants usually left because of dissatisfaction. This ranged from the slowly realized complex of chronic discontent to the acute distress of injustice or famine. In a word, they came to escape Europe. It took strong reasons to impel millions upon millions to migrate so far, but they came with hope; they came to a land of hope.

America's historic function meant something new, something special and remarkable. Unlike the older nations of the world, America was built for human fulfillment and the liberation of the human potential. Its failures were never those of national commitment, a commitment that lifted men's hopes and offered many a choice available to them for the first time.

The new American came here seeking better things and escaping earlier grievances. He brought along some baggage: clothes, hard-earned cash (often little indeed), a mother tongue, a faith, a nationality, a culture, a bag of songs and stories. He brought skills, brains, muscle, aspirations, and feelings. Having been born and nurtured in a tight and confining European culture, he often brought some rubbish—not material, but of the mind and emotions. Ethnocentrisms, particularisms, and old hates, biases, and suspicions deeply implanted by myth, history, family, parish, and nation were brought along, as was the demon fear.

The new Americans represented a wide range of choice. Some came freely and uncoerced, seeking new opportunities and broader horizons, because their life choices were limited in Europe. The trip was motivated at least as much by the circumstances they fled as by what they sought. On one side of the coin there was famine, persecution, economic scarcity, and political oppression; on the other, food, tolerance, opportunity, and freedom.

Others came through no choice of their own. They came as captives and entered the new continent as slaves. This was the singular characteristic of African immigration. For centuries the facts of this immigration have stood paradoxical and contradictory to the main currents of American development. In fact, the African immigration represents a case so special and conditions so opposite to ordinary American historical premises that most often it simply is let go by default and a "white man's history" is written, either because of embarrassment or neglect. The most pressing issues in contemporary education center upon the children of this very group of Americans, and the paradox of their special conditions of immigration has direct bearing on the most crucial dilemmas of our time.

The European immigrant had various patterns of opportunity and acceptance; he could move; he could bargain. But the African was fed and lodged as property at the discretion of his master. He had no say whatsoever about his "being."

In the era of the slave controversy apologists for "the peculiar institution" used to point to the exploitation of workers in northern mills as a comparable situation. In the historic moment the lot of the factory worker may not have been materially better than that of the slave. But the apologist rationale neglected significant realities.

Institutional patterns were developing through which the factory worker could significantly improve his condition by his own efforts. The institutions that he would seize upon as his most effective instruments were the labor union and public education. These were denied to the slave; even for many decades after emancipation they were largely denied to the Negro by many devices of "social control."

The avenues of geographic and social mobility were open to the free worker, not wide open, but open. The slave moved as property; he himself could move only in the hazardous role of fugitive. True, the Civil War "freed" the Negroes, but their social and economic ceilings of upward mobility were so general that the few who really achieved considerable upward gains were rare exceptions. Horatio Alger's great leaps of upward mobility were denied the Negro, and far from aspiring to marry the boss's daughter, he was wary under pain of death not even to cast a glance upon her.

The European immigrants suffered varied degrees of cultural

coercions, even social cruelties, in the rough-and-ready community of the melting pot. They knew sticks and stones, on occasion, as well as rude names. But often within a generation or two, they were governing the towns and states that ridiculed and abused them. Their children were educated with the children of those who had patronized or reviled them; their family structures were preserved; and their grandchildren intermarried.

The African as slave experienced the entire structure of his family and communal life at the sufferance of his owner. His bondage largely obliterated his connection with previous family, clan, and culture. In the whole period of enslavement his efforts to reconstruct meaningful familial and communal relationships were built on shifting sands.

No other immigrant group came so unwillingly and unwittingly to these shores. No other group was so long subjected to such general exemption from the rights and privileges of the total community. No other group was subjected to such enduring patterns of specially assigned indispositions and indignities, and the historic consequences of this "special" treatment have only lately begun fully to assert themselves.

Within the human condition, the case for equality is clear. The difference in historical condition defines no inadequacy in human potential or worth, nor the potential to make continuing contributions to the cultural scene. The Negro too has a great capacity for work and life.

The heavy weight of cultural pluralism must be acknowledged. The implication of burden need not imply a fugitive or negative attitude. Burden is a reality and means there is work to be done. Man often finds it hard to accept the difference, but to pretend that the differences do not exist is social hypocrisy. Public acceptance and private rejection are a half-way house mainly inhabited by prejudice.

A great deal of hatred infects the American scene. A vast complex of ethnocentricities, biases, and suspicions weaves its way the length and breadth of the land. "Unity amidst diversity" is a fair concept, well phrased, but the schools cannot bear their share of work in achieving social cohesion if they merely echo clichés and sentimentalities.

Henry Steele Commager has said that our schools have kept us free. As an historian he was speaking on the achievement of the public school with respect to our pluralism. In a seeming Babel, the school established a common tongue and a rudimentary sense of common institutions. It has gone on toward enlightenment. Prejudice and ethnocentrism are identified in terms of liability. Students are alert to prejudices and ethnocentrisms, at least among others. The burden of work to be done is the teaching of the ultimate reality that nobody's ethnocentrism is any good.

To achieve social cohesion without cultural coercion requires strict discipline. The old concept of the melting pot was badly used in two respects. First, coercion was implicit: the melting pot was to liquefy human matter and to recast man in the image of Jack Armstrong. But social process simply does not work that way, as anyone who ever read the Book of Daniel could tell. To the degree that it was merely naïve, the melting-pot thesis was innocent. The taint of nativism was in the crucible, however.

What does the American need to know? He needs to know his neighbors, in a simple culture, beyond the reach of transport and media. To know one's neighbors is to know one's family multiplied to clan and village size, with minor variants of personal idiosyncrasies. Human encounters among those who live similar lives tax neither vocabulary nor the psyche.

The American's neighbors all around him challenge him to be educated, to grow, to set himself free. He is challenged if he is alive, healthy, resilient, and freedom-loving. But what if he is frightened? Then his neighbors threaten him; he sees them as his natural enemies, or they are grandchildren of enslavers or enslaved. They pray strangely; they cook with different herbs; their children are noisy. And those neighbors are everywhere, next door and in the schools.

One of the ways the curriculum can best serve the public in the context of cultural tensions is to recognize the great and inspiring American commitment and the considerable achievement of the

American dream. Reality closely regarded will reduce the insecurity that causes us to minimize our problems and will ease the apprehension that great efforts have been unavailing.

Social Class

Since 1950 several important sociological studies remarking and defining the scope of social-class and status alignments within the American community have been published. A. B. Hollingshead's *Elmtown's Youth*[5] was the most interesting to educators in its explicit delineation of class configuration among adolescent school children.

Awareness of the reality of such attitudes and distinctions is of importance to the educator who would know his school and community in their true pattern of social and human relations. Such knowledge is pertinent to understanding elements of class-directed patterns of culture, taste, and behavior, social cliques, school politics, disciplinary difficulties, and patterns of teacher-student success and failure. Social-class analysis is a useful tool in understanding the society of the school.

The functional attitude toward the relevance of social-class findings to education is a veritable index to the quality of the educator's statesmanship. Social scientific inquiry must be objective and value-free. The service of the social sciences to education is in the special techniques of inquiry. The mission of the sociologist is to define and describe certain dimensions of reality in reasonably specific and accurate terms.

Education as a discipline and as a profession is not value-free. Education is a value system put to work. It does not scorn the evidence: the evidence of man's intelligence is real; the evidence of his will to learn is impressive. Education rests on evidence that children can and will learn. As a commitment and as a nonnego-

[5] August B. Hollingshead, *Elmtown's Youth* (New York: Wiley, 1949).

89

tiable value, it asserts that *all* children ought to be taught and that it intends to do the job.

Facts demand either recognition of reality or a turning away from it. Values compel choice, or what to do about something. To say that social class is real is not to say that reality dictates a class-centered curriculum. Class is real only as illusions have the force of reality. All men walk on the same earth. Yertle, the Turtle[6] found out how transient are the illusions of ascendancy.

Sociologists are not historians; they give evidence but not perspective. Status symbols are nothing new. Steam yachts and private railroad cars were considerably more impressive in their day than foreign-built sports cars are in ours. The tycoons and robber barons of the latter nineteenth century enjoyed a more feudal privilege than the most bloated of contemporary plutocrats. Little over a century ago, one group of our people was in literal slavery. Another dozen nationalities within this century experienced the slanders and intolerance that we now regretfully dub "second-class citizenship."

Class structures and conditions change, but one definitive characteristic of the so-called lower class has always been *poverty*. Middle class is indeterminate; many of its dimensions are psychic. Upper class is well defined, but so narrowly as to be inconsequential to most social decisions. But poverty provides visible signs. It cuts the person off; it leaves him out.

Social-class barriers diminish communication. Cultural deprivation is a class-wide result of diminished communication. Where communication is drastically diminished the outcome is *alienation;* this is true of today's many children of the poor and is the root and nature of the school dropout problem.

A war on cultural deprivation can be a mere doctoring of symptoms, but the malady is social class itself. Democratization is the process that must be studied and put to work if cultural deprivation is to be ended, if all children are to be educated into American life, and if poverty is to be eradicated. If the school is to serve "the great society," it must successfully educate amid and against

6 Dr. Seuss, *Yertle the Turtle and Other Stories* (New York: Random House, 1958).

90

poverty. To do this, it must encounter the children of the poor in terms that they will comprehend, and in this encounter the school must remove its blinders.

Educators now recognize an obligation to these children although some seem to use this recognition as an opportunity to gain grants and headlines. "Cultural deprivation" has been added to the jargon, but the term is helpful only as a description of a symptom; it is not an analytical term. To say that the poor are culturally deprived is as profound as to say that they lack money.

Poverty means rejection and stigma. There is a clear-cut repudiation in the common culture of the quondam connection between poverty and virtue. The belief that a positive relationship exists between goodness and poverty is rarely invoked even hypocritically in the American community. American civilization has instructed profoundly in stigmatizing the poor, and if a relearning is to take place, it will have to be equally profound.

America is something more than materialistic. The very effort of education is rooted in value structures far removed from concern for "things" alone. However, it is no slander diagnostically to assert our considerable materialism. Americans like things, they seek them, they admire their presence, they define success appreciably as the ability to gain them. Americans trust things, they are at a loss without them, they distrust their absence. Thus, Americans have a real problem in association with the poor, for the poor lack things.

Historically, the Puritan thrust in American history gave deep credence to the belief that material success and spiritual fitness were signally related. Darwin and McGuffey added sanctions to the belief, and the poor continue to suffer under a weighty bill of attainder in American civilization. This poses its problems for education; it poses special problems for the teacher and administrator who feel that poverty is somehow the result of a lack of virtue or of congenital inadequacies. Such attitudes must be clarified. Poverty is a human condition from which Americans are generally exempt.

Poverty is subject matter for the school. Education will not affect the poor until it studies its present curriculum and changes it. A superficial attitude toward the poverty problem would read as follows:

1. This is a rich country, but some people are poor. Such contradiction does not look good. Perhaps something should be done about it.

2. Who should do something about it? Maybe the government or maybe some idealistic young people will know what to do.

3. The poor deserve something. Perhaps they deserve a chance to do something for themselves.

4. Lower-class values are not the same as middle-class values.

5. America is a land of opportunity, but some people don't take advantage of it.

6. Possibly there is something fundamentally wrong with those people who don't escape poverty.

7. Fortunately, most of us don't have to see much of poverty.

This easy bill of particulars is precisely the foggy and superficial analysis upon which much of the current approach to education rests. Its inadequacy was brought home during and after the summer of 1967 not by academic criticism, but by a succession of devastating events throughout the land.

The key to the relationship between social class and curriculum lies in communication. Consciousness of class and awareness of class distinctions set up barriers to communication. Candor and honesty suffer in the process of crossing class lines. The Negro in a community of discrimination calls one who crosses the line "Uncle Tom." Enlisted men think nothing of holding back some of the facts or in conveying something other than the facts, when communicating with their officers. Similarly, students have one standard of honesty among themselves and another for dealing with school officials.

Open, honest, free communication exists only among equals. The more pronounced the barriers of class, the more they resemble the frontiers of cold war. Words and symbols become tools of psychological warfare. "Uppers" communicate defectively to "lowers" because they feel no obligation to explain themselves and because they have certain privileges which might be lost if revealed. "Lowers" communicate defectively "upward" because they have a sense of vulnerability to coercion and exploitation, because they have learned that in crisis blame is always affixed downward, and because candor is something satisfying to withhold from those who are in a position to demand so much more.

Honesty and ethics are effective disciplinary codes among groups who perceive themselves in a peer or kin relationship. Students judge the trustworthiness of one another by dealings among their peers, not by how students relate to the school or adult authority. The positive corollary to this is: *The more democratic the pattern of human relationships in an institution, the more uniform its conditions for communication and the larger its quotient of common trust.*

In the school it follows that the greater the sense of common purpose among students, teachers, and administration—and the less the sense of exercise of arbitrary power by "greaters" over "lessers" —the fuller will communication be in every sense. Learning is built on communication; whatever impedes communication damages learning. Social-class illusions affecting the schools as reality cannot be viewed with complacency or detached academic interest. Social-class perceptions divide people and hurt learning.

From Optimism to Anxiety

The atmosphere of the years after the victory of World War II was initially charged with exuberance and rededication. Veterans flocked to the campus and infused it with adult vigor and critical participation. Many turned to education in a mood of seasoned idealism. As one veteran summed it up: "I had a good job ready and waiting in my father-in-law's office. But I had to put my life on the line for democracy, and I did a lot of serious thinking about what that meant. I was lucky. *I* made it! I guess that going into education seemed to me like the best way to help make sure that what we went through meant something."

This was optimism, somewhat guarded. Yet only a few years later, the general mood was characterized as an "age of anxiety." The cold war, the awful knowledge of the hydrogen bomb, the Korean War, the Sputnik shock, the intensified domestic problems

93

all produced anxieties and tensions that caused this victorious and powerful nation at times to assume the postures of a weakling. The McCarthy phase in the early 1950s is the historic measure of the psychic malaise of the time. The progress of American education was not summarily halted overnight. Yet the developmental pattern of American education was suddenly set upon, torn, altered.

Education had much to build upon. Before World War II it had already made the secondary school practically universal. In methodology and in curriculum the schools had taken long strides toward developing an education based on the realities of life and learning rather than on academic pretensions. The mood had been confident and progressive; the schools had never become generally progressive, but progressive education had begun to show the way to a multidimensioned and humane school.

In the course of building the American educational system, a profession had appeared: a group of professional educators. Not without flaws or mortal limitations (any more than doctors, lawyers, or engineers), these educators had sought to qualify themselves as professionals by the only possible method—by learning to know what they were doing. This they had arduously begun to do at high levels of performance. The qualification of the professional educator meant long years of preparation, long years of practice, almost constant thought on the problems of education, and a tireless inquiry into causes and solutions. The profession had enlisted the energies of some remarkable men. Their motivations were something other than ordinary, for monetary rewards in this profession were less than in others.

But the building of the schools by the people who had been ready to devote their lives to finding what education was really about had made enemies. The charges upon the public for support offended those with a myopic view of tax benefits. Democratic commitment stirred antipathy among the reactionary or elite-minded. The independent course of curriculum development stirred resentment among the collegiate custodians of the academic mysteries. The very suggestion of profession provoked an invidious anti-intellectualism, not among the great public that wanted its children educated but among the gifted, well-educated, amateur know-it-alls who stood ready (in rhetoric at least), to reconstruct the school around notions that would have made it more subservient to the unusually gifted schoolboy they believed they had been.

In the deep national insecurity of the 1950s, a strange coalition of critics and amateur crusaders stood ready to redeem the schools. To effect their reforms it was essential either to discredit or to suborn the leaders of the schools, the professional educators, either to remove them from decision-making, to induce them to betray their knowledge, or to lose confidence.

Great changes were urged and some were thrust upon the body of American education. New treasuries were unlocked to endow the school with a far from unconditional largesse. Education, which had seldom made headlines, became a daily source of news and the bread and butter of a new breed of pundits. Did money and attention presage Utopian vistas soon to be achieved? It would be pleasurable to be able to speak thus, but responsibility compels a less happy assertion.

A Regressive Era in American Education?

The necessary assertion is that the period since 1950 qualifies as a regressive era in American education. The assertion does not derive from such sad realities as the lag in teachers' salaries, the shortage of teachers and classrooms, or the time wasted in refuting the charges of irresponsible critics. Furthermore, the generalization is made in the face of many hopeful auguries, among them these:

1. The establishment of communication for curriculum building among such established authorities on subject matter as teacher educators, curriculum specialists, methodologists, and classroom teachers.

2. The development of truly conceptualized approaches to content (intrinsic method) in mathematics, physics, chemistry, biology, and the social studies.

3. The unanimous ruling of the Supreme Court in 1954 with respect to the desegregation of the schools. Despite tensions and obstructionism, considerable action and facing up to the decision, a firming of purpose including the 1961 "strong resolution" by the National Education Association.

4. A rise in public awareness of the basic national significance of education—with the following corollary:

5. The enhancement of the newsworthiness of education, with its attendant vitalization as subject matter in the forum of American opinion.

6. The discovery on a significant public scale of the socially damaging consequences of high dropout rates, of the relationship between automation and increased necessity for education, and of the reality of cultural deprivation in creating slow learners and poorly motivated students.

7. The continued labors of schoolmen, teacher educators, and classroom teachers in working with students toward deeply thoughtful purposes and with some of the best instruments of a century of educational experimentation and research.

American education has turned into a succession of blind alleys and has listened too closely to a number of false prophets. The chief characteristics of regression have not been nonproductive efforts, which are inherent as a hazard in experimentation, but such phenomena as these: (1) protagonism and demonstration ahead of evidence; (2) the bandwagon overadoption of educational panaceas, on some of which the research evidence is alarmingly negative; (3) minimal attention to the substantive (the what to teach and why) and the exaggeration of interest in administrative arrangements, instruments, and gadgetry as solutions to curriculum problems; and (4) the accession of a good deal of educational power in the hands of amateurs, whose least fault has been enthusiasm for the ephemeral and whose worst offense has been a philosophical disdain for fundamental assumptions of democracy and lack of respect for the accomplishment of American education and its professional leadership. Ironically, these basically nonintellectual matters have found their most ardent proponents among those who have long delighted to regard "educationists" as anti-intellectuals.

A single or simple factor analysis cannot account for large complex events. Many elements affecting the regression derived from institutional characteristics unrelated to one another. The National Education Association, the federal government, the foundations, the press, the irresponsible critics all (but not in common purpose) have had something to do with determining the result, the direction, and the velocity of the trend.

The first factor was the vulnerability of education itself. Raymond E. Callahan sums up the net effects of the school administrators' preoccupations between 1910 and 1929 as "an American tragedy in education."

> It was not that some of the ideas from the business world might not have been used to advantage in educational administration, but that the wholesale adoption of the basic values, as well as the techniques of the business–industrial world, was a serious mistake in an institution whose primary purpose was the education of children.[7]

Educational leadership may also have been vulnerable, if not in anti-intellectualism, at least in inadequate intellectualism. More likely, some educationists tended toward an error equal and opposite to that of the extreme academicians. Where the latter tended to sanctify subject matter and to deem method either irrelevant or inferior, the former came to a preoccupation with method and process that seemed to imply that the content and the process were identical. For a decade after World War II the Association for Supervision and Curriculum Development traveled in this direction. Its national meetings were refreshingly devoid of prestigious harangues and were models of process involving thousands of delegates in active conference participation. Increasingly, however, its members felt a repetitive sameness in the devices and subject matter of discussion groups, and it has moved toward more substance and greater conceptual depth as a result of its own continuing self-appraisal.

The National Education Association (NEA) may have contributed to a certain vulnerability. Some critics within its membership noted a certain school-teacherish fussiness about some of its interests. As it attained size, its concerns and its cautions appeared to have some attributes of the bureaucratic organization. To some extent, legitimate concerns with membership, lobbying, and legisla-

---

[7] Raymond E. Callahan, *Education and the Cult of Efficiency* (Chicago: University of Chicago Press, 1962) , p. 244.

tion overshadowed its interest in the substance of education. The NEA, however, is not altogether a bureaucratic monolith; some of the most constructive pioneering work in curriculum and content has been done under the aegis of such component groups as the National Council for the Social Studies, the National Council of Teachers of Mathematics, the National Science Teachers Association, and the Association for Supervision and Curriculum Development, among others.

A larger vulnerability of education itself that is seldom if ever identified by the critics may have been its essential conservatism. Whatever the faults of the educational establishment have been, they not included erring in the progressive direction, humanizing the school too rapidly, adopting such practices as "lighthouse schools" too soon, or being too responsive to the implications of educational research.

A second factor conducing toward regression was the mood of the American public. Earl Kelley stated that we reacted to the launching of Sputnik in October 1957, in "fear and hurt pride." Deeper rooted was a threatening anti-intellectualism in the American public, with McCarthyism as its most alarming indication. American education has done a good deal to enlighten our society, but only recently has most of the public been to school for a considerable education. We have yet to see a voting generation with a majority who have finished the secondary school.

Eager critics of varied motivations responded to and capitalized on this mood. Against the evidence, or in ignorance of it, they compiled a bill of fallacious particulars—that the NEA was some kind of conspiracy, that subversion ran rampant in the schools (especially in social studies), that the teaching of controversial issues, modern literature, or art was somehow treasonable, that European models of education were more successful than our own, that Johnny (presumably the typical American schoolboy) could not read, that the basic skills (reading, spelling, writing, computation) had been better learned by earlier generations, that the modern classroom was a "rat race" with no discipline, that vigilantism was necessary to protect children against radicalism and indecency in textbooks. The net result was to obscure the legitimate efforts of responsible critics and to make the job of hard-working educators more difficult.

A third factor was the growth of the notion that education is basically an instrument of national policy. An increased national concern for the quality and support of education was constructive. To conceive of education as a fundamental and essential institution whose unique and autonomous function is to educate and develop free men to self-determination in the fullness of their capacities is sound. Free men, fully educated, will take care of their nation's future.

However, education can render less than full service to the nation if it is an instrument to be mobilized rather than a basic institution to be encouraged and supported. Among the intrusive evidences of this notion are propagandistic and coercive approaches to career choices, especially of the gifted, the privileged position of mathematics and science, and the rumors of national curricula, national certification, and national testing programs. Tangible in its effect was the National Defense Education Act of 1957. Under this act science, mathematics, and language instruction received direct preferential treatment. Guidance, audio-visual devices, and vocational education shared in the preferment, even though the act distorted the balance of education in terms of facilities, curriculum, appeal to students, and recruitment of teachers. In effect, the act represents substantial federal control (direct influence) through subsidy.

A fourth factor potentially effecting regression has been the Fund for the Advancement of Education of the Ford Foundation. The Ford Fund has exerted considerable influence on the American educational scene. Criticism of its policies, goals, and projects has been abundant. Unlike most educational foundations it has determined its educational purposes and has awarded its money to furthering these objectives. Its goals have sometimes been perceived as the redemption of American education from the hands of the educationists and progressive education, toward a more substantive and intellectual academic program. To date, it has done more to control and influence education than to produce positive effects upon the content of learning. Its project enthusiasms have been for the mechanical and administrative: teacher aids, instructional television, team teaching, teaching machines and programed instruction, special arrangements for the gifted, educational speed-up, schoolhouse design. While none of these projects has been unworthy of experimentation, there are others that are more worthy.

Historically, the Fund for the Advancement of Education represents an educationally bankrupt philosophy come into great wealth. Prior to World War II Robert Maynard Hutchins, Mortimer Adler, Clarence Faust, and Alvin Eurich represented an extremely responsible and articulate body of critics on the course of American education. The classics, the absolutist philosophical premises, and the Great Books were their platform; anathema to them were pragmatism, progressive education, John Dewey, Columbia Teachers College, vocationalism, and teacher education.

These critics were learned and civilized. They argued, even "slugged" hard with logic, rhetoric, and philosophy; they inveighed against but did not slander; they entered the lists of debate—and lost. They wanted better education, but their ideas were anachronistic. Their view of American civilization was distorted and their knowledge of the schools inadequate.

Robert Hutchins, the idea-maker of the coterie, twice took his falls. In *The Higher Learning in America*[8] he exposited his classical, aristocratic, elite view of the university. Harry Gideonse, then a professor under Hutchins at the University of Chicago, later president of Brooklyn College, took issue with Hutchins in *The Higher Learning in a Democracy*.[9] In a *Fortune* article of August 1944, "Challenge to Liberal Thought," John Dewey exposed fallacies in the traditionalist view, exploded the canards about progressive education and pragmatism, and made it clear that anti-intellectualism and unintelligibility were charges to be brought against Dewey only by those who had never read him.

In the postwar world the luck of inheritance fell to Hutchins and his coterie. No vast fortune came to the hands of those who had

---

[8] Robert Maynard Hutchins, *The Higher Learning in America* (New Haven: Yale University Press, 1936).

[9] Harry David Gideonse, *The Higher Learning in a Democracy* (New York: Farrar and Rinehart, 1937).

worked for democratic education. The Ford Foundation, indeed, worked considerably against such outlines for progress. It exerted this influence in two ways: (1) by direct subsidy; and (2) by discouraging criticism because of its very nature, through the indirect influence of its purse strings. The biases of the Fund are known, and many magnificent gifts have come to universities through skillful use of this knowledge. Awareness that criticism of the Ford Fund might tend to prejudice it against an institution or against colleagues in need of funds may silence a professor who would willingly bear the personal hazards of such prejudice.

A critical bias is implicit in our analysis of the effect this powerful foundation has exerted on curriculum development:

1. It has enhanced the influence of the academic; the collegiate domination over the course and direction of the lower schools has been reinforced.

2. It has consistently pressured toward the minimizing of the professionally educational, as against the academic, in the preparation of teachers.

3. It has moved strategically through major grants to put leaders of its own persuasions in key positions.

4. It has continued to press for its pet projects through publicity and support, even when professional opinion and research have examined them and found them wanting.

5. It has pushed such interests as instructional television and programed learning with only a partial reporting of the research and professional judgment on these instruments.

6. Withal, it has endowed constructive adventures in teacher fellowships, school-building design, scholarly approaches to the history of education, teaching internships, and experimental approaches to urban education.

7. But it has distracted much potential energy from examining more basic needs in American education because of its preoccupation with its own bill of particulars; it has erred perhaps innocently in underestimating the substantial influence of the wealth it administers.

In spite of the evidence of regression in American education, substantial grounds for optimism do exist. Education is important to the American people. It is more central to public dialogue than ever before. The people, despite their apprehensions and occasional tax weariness, give no sign of retreating from basic commitment to the schools. Enrollments in public elementary and secondary schools in 1966–1967 totaled more than 44 million, and roughly represented an investment of $25.9 billion. In the spring of 1967 about 2.7 million young Americans graduated from American public high schools.[10] This is not quantitative achievement alone, but professional leadership must rest smug neither on scores of quantity or assumptions of quality.

The 1960 Report of the President's Commission on National Goals reaffirmed and bulwarked the American commitment to education with these words:

> The development of the individual and the nation demand that education at every level and in every discipline be strengthened and its effectiveness enhanced. New teaching techniques must continue to be developed. The increase in population and the growing complexity of the world add urgency. Greater resources—private, corporate, municipal, state, and federal—must be mobilized. A higher proportion of the gross national product must be devoted to educational purposes. This is at once an investment in the individual, in the democratic process, in the growth of the economy, and in the stature of the United States.

Historically speaking, these words served notice that the American concern for education was far from diminished and that it was indeed affirmed more positively than ever before.

The New Historical Moment

The American of today must be concerned with considerable accomplishments and weighty responsibilities. He abides in a great and complex nation, diverse in class, nationality, culture, and geography. Education must help this American to appraise his his-

10 *Education U. S.*, National School Public Relations Association, May 27, 1968.

torical and social position and meaning. It must help him find out who he is, where he is, and how he is perceived. Most important, education must help him find the why of all of it—the most neglected and most powerful lever in learning.

Not one in a hundred American teachers has ever seen or experienced the phenomenon of real physical hunger among men; ninety in a hundred elsewhere in the world have experienced it. The American standard of living is the envy of much of the world. This fact is much misunderstood. We are not basically envied our bathrooms, our television sets, our automobiles, our chrome and plate glass. Some foreign observers are intrigued with our material goods. However, our large preoccupation with things is less envied than regarded as a fundamental sign of our materialism and cultural immaturity. The major factor in our standard of living that is truly envied is simply that we have enough to eat. Most Americans do not know what it is to be hungry except between meals. We share this distinction with a rare few of the earth's peoples such as the Swiss, the Scandinavians, the Canadians, and the Australians.

There is an ideological division in the world. Its expression is known as "cold war." Another equally meaningful division is that between those people whose chief preoccupations are the basic needs for human survival and those who have been somewhat liberated from this preoccupation. Such films as the French allegory *He Who Must Die,* the Italian classics *Paisan* and *Bicycle Thief,* the Indian masterpiece *Pather Panchali* point up the great differences of experience and everyday concern between us and those who live ever in doubt of tomorrow's bread.

Our culture takes its basic affluence for granted. (To be sure, this glosses over the real needs of the one family out of five who must live on an income of less than $3,000 per year.) Generally speaking, the vast majority of Americans can and do afford eating, drinking, and smoking more than is good for us. We are able to protect ourselves against the winter's cold and increasingly against the summer's heat. We seek most of our goods for display, for pleasure, for decoration, for emulation, for social approval. The common culture, with few real needs and fewer developed values, is a constant target for those who wish to create an economic demand for goods that hardly anyone needs but that many may be taught to want.

Such writers as Vance Packard in *The Hidden Persuaders* and *The Status Seekers* (among others), and John Keats in *The Insolent Chariots* assert that we victimize and make ourselves ridiculous by our irrational wants. David Reisman in *The Lonely Crowd* sees contemporary man rendered loud but lonely by his lack of inner convictions, by his aimless outer-directed wanderings and strivings.

Of striving there is plenty, and a good deal of arriving too. Our resorts are crowded with those who pay more than $50 a day (American plan) in season and one area alone is ornamented by the residences of a reputed 1,700 millionaires. There are more permanent patients in our mental hospitals than there are seasonal guests at our resort hotels.

Two ways of life are coming to the fore in our time: the Successniks who accept the goals of the common culture and achieve them, and the Hippies who reject these goals and retreat to a nihilistic existence on verse, vine, and virility. Another choice, the one which education would seek to foster, is the goal of the examined life. In modern terms this examination is not only philosophical and moral but also sociological and psychological.

Our society makes the necessities generally available. Then it skillfully adorns the useless with the togs of need. It provides activity as the counterfeit of action, noise in place of reflection, persuasion in lieu of examination. It is obviously a pretty good society in its material accomplishments, in its opportunities, in its political freedoms, in its generosities, and in its free institutions. It may be that its educational frontier lies in developing tastes and values for the common culture, in teaching the common man to enjoy freedom constructively, and allowing him to live at peace, first with himself.

Commentary: Toward Methodological Necessity

The educational direction of the future may lie mainly in this quest. The search for talent in the selective sense is an exaggerated contemporary preoccupation. America may need to search out and develop the fundamental talent of humanity—the talent for life itself. Lester Frank Ward said that there is no need to search for talent; it exists already and everywhere. The thing that is rare is opportunity, not ability.

Ward wrote in the late nineteenth century. Universal public education has gone far toward vindicating his position. Critics have declared that public education is a mill of mass production, conducing toward a dead level of mediocrity. There are such conducing forces in our society, but they are the common culture and its raucous voices, known familiarly as the mass media. The schools, even with their faults and obstacles, have done quite another thing: *They have made excellence commonplace.* In fact, one of our great problems is that we do not know what to do with the excellence we produce. Most Americans have jobs, but all too often the individual works far below his potential.

If we seek a democratic society in this land and foster its growth through education, how can we justify our misuse of the individual and his potential? Legally we are committed to a constitutional system and a pattern of justice under law. In the documents of the American spirit—the Declaration of Independence, the Gettysburg Address, the writings of Jefferson, Emerson, Whitman—our commitments to individual worth, the dignity of man, social justice, and human brotherhood are stated explicitly.

In present-day America, democratic frontiers continue to face problems. True, real wages, labor conditions, health, and social conditions have improved within our time. But the open-eyed observer sees much that disturbs his sense of social conscience, human potential, and democratic idealism. He can see wretched exhibits of rural poverty, large areas of miserable urban slums, whole cities of almost unrelieved squalor, decayed and depressed mill towns and mining towns. All this persists in America.

Democracy does not exist merely to assure good housing and adequate diets. A system concerned with breeding a race of healthy animals would do as much. But for man, our concern is with "democracy for what?" The human spirit may wither too. Democ-

105

racy should increase the community of man, while it decreases man's loneliness and alienation.

Technology (automation) can increase the individual's spare time; democracy can provide the arena for his use of it. But the individual must determine the use he will put it to. Is he to drowse, drink beer, watch television? Is American society to reach its high-water mark if its people become the greatest players of games in human history?

Democracy is already lost to a people who regard its opportunities no more seriously than this. The American is progressively acquiring more free time. The individual and his society will be fulfilled only if priority is given to: an increase of true communication among *all* men, a concern for and participation in the creative arts, a deep and active concern for public problems, a search for social faults and injustices and determination to set them right, an increase of common efforts in community building and good works, a vast increase in love of learning for its own sake, a more serious and therefore more joyful view of life, a concern with all of humanity, and a search for the roots and truths of moral, ethical, and spiritual values.

The attainment of these priorities cannot be achieved by phrasemaking. The highest priorities for the schools demand the most rigorous attention to method. Surely the needs are worthy of effective responses.

The instructional model that serves these high priorities will then by definition build in these features. It will provide an effective system of communication, an environment conducive to creative behavior, a free forum for the examination of issues, bridges from learning to action, intrinsic motivations, and a classroom methodology that itself employs the values which it articulates and seeks to perpetuate. It is to these matters, among others, that the next chapter is centrally directed.

Chapter IV

The Methodological Foundation of Curriculum

The basic teaching technique is still the lecture-read-recite system, in which the teacher does most of the talking, and the student counters by doing as little listening as possible. Teachers insist on talking because they find it helps to pass the time.[1]

—John H. Sandberg

Content exists in a curricular sense only when subject matter is related intrinsically to a method by which it can be learned. When a thing is learned conceptually, it meets these conditions: (1) it is clearly perceived; (2) it is retained; (3) it builds over time; (4) it can be put to work; (5) it enhances being; (6) it affects behavior. Subject matter that does not fulfill these requirements must be held suspect in terms of its content.

As the progressives have long insisted, learning is an active, participative process. Action is neither learning of itself, nor is participation. Nor is what goes on around a person his experience.

[1] John H. Sandberg, *Carnegie Review*, No. 2 (1964–1965).

What one actively participates in or undergoes does not necessarily constitute experience either, or it may be experience at a relatively low level. Experience is not happenstance (or a "happening" for that matter).

Experience is the rendering of occurrence meaningful. Experience is the result of deliberate awareness, of willed attention to cause, effect, and consequence, of cognitively weighing evidences and values, and of affective explorations and judgments. It is the encounter of a whole being with the whole dimension of a person, an act, a situation, or a process.

The relationship between experience and learning is complex. In this chapter, we shall discuss this relationship, which is at least fourfold: (1) learning *mobilizes* experiences; (2) learning *creates* experience; (3) learning *re-creates* experience; (4) learning *exploits* experience. Thus, curriculum must be (1) systematic and organizational, (2) creative, (3) historical, and (4) opportunistic. It must be all these not altogether incompatible things without being largely contradictory. It must seek balance and try not to achieve one good at the expense of another. Method itself must be conceptualized, and this conceptualization must begin with a sound appraisal of the resources that the learner himself possesses.

Man—The Natural Learner

Glimpses of the truth often reveal profound errors. For instance, a teacher may say: "I am teaching my students to think." Reciprocally, appreciative students who perceive a teacher's work to be beyond the ordinary may say: "He has taught us to think." In both cases the intent is good, but the perception is faulty.

The fault lies in the fact that the person does not need to be taught to think. *Man thinks.* This is an axiom, a given attribute of his human peculiarity, upon which all sensible learning theory and educational methodology ought to be based. Nothing is extraordinary in this fact. Fish swim, birds fly; man thinks.

What is extraordinary about schools is that so little is made of this peculiar human attribute. Respect for thought in the classroom, where it should be commonplace, is apparently so rare as to be remarkable. The teacher who respects thought is too often seen as performing a feat beyond the call of duty, when, in fact, he is only doing what is ordinarily sensible and what all teachers should do.

The best teaching is that which liberates and encourages thinking. However, the evidence in schools everywhere does not support this goal. *In the main the schools do not liberate and encourage thinking; instead they put fetters on the processes of thought and discourage the true activity of the mind.*

The schools work their damage in the name of high principles: systematization and methodology. Is it then presumed that we speak amiss of these sacred cows of pedagogy? Yes, in fact, and more—we propose to slaughter and dissect them.

Only one methodology bears sensibly upon the matter of education: this is the method of intelligence. In brief, education must utilize, must cease to ignore, and even to contradict, the way people learn. How do they learn? By doing what they are born to do—by thinking.

Never doubt it, thought goes on. In the dullest classroom, in the deadliest academic denial of learning, even lively thought goes on. The teacher may drone on or quiz with sterile, witless, bookish questions while the students slump in apparent apathy. Not thinking? Oh, but they are—and very positively, too. The very apathy constitutes a thoughtful decision to participate as narrowly and marginally as is possible and socially permissible in a situation that they have judged meaningless and useless. Students discriminate and judge acts of thought, not because they ought to (though it is good that they do), nor because they are always encouraged to do so (though they should be), but because it is the nature of the human organism to do these things, to respond in this way. They do these things (this thinking) because being human they cannot help it. However, when social penalties are placed upon such evidences of mind, they are mindful enough of their skins to hide these evidences.

We do not intend to dissociate thinking from learning. This

would be a patent absurdity, but it is exactly this absurdity that teachers often commit. The poetry of the military says:

> Theirs not to make reply,
> Theirs not to reason why,
> Theirs but to do and die.

How much so-called learning in the classroom is undertaken in the same spirit?

Thinking and learning should truly be inseparable. It is a crime against education that the school often tries to promote learning while discouraging thinking. Is this a false premise? Does not the school too often do the following?

1. Encourages the study of conventional artists and writers, but discourages the students' critical appraisal of their works.

2. Organizes the subject matter of its sciences as bodies of knowledge, but discourages those methods of inquiry that, from Archimedes through Galileo and Newton to Einstein, have extended and revolutionized so-called bodies of knowledge.

3. Organizes subject matter concerning government and society, but discourages the active and critical discussion of political and social problems and issues.

4. Presents the student with works of creative writers who have changed and extended the forms and styles of human expression, but represses experimental and unstructured methods of communication.

Are these not typical illustrations of the ways in which the school attempts to develop "learning" while at the same time it discourages the student's own thinking? Academicians who deny these charges couch their defenses in familiar phrasings: "This may be true, but a child must walk before he can run." "One must learn respect for the structure of learning before one experiments with new forms." "One must acquire discipline before one can indulge in self-expression." "Instruction comes before education." "The job of the school is to transmit the culture, not to serve as an agent of change and uncertainty."

Surely there are many who think these things, and they may be right. The damning fact is that many teachers take refuge in these defenses, and the observable result in the schools is that thinking is all too scarce. Those students who think most actively too frequently either are forced to hide the fact or are in trouble with their teachers. Teachers cannot afford to be smug and complacent about their work. Teaching is not of itself virtuous; only good teaching can claim virtue. What of the teachers of Winston Churchill who judged him to be a mediocre student of the humanities and those of Albert Einstein who failed him in mathematics? And when grades and marks are allotted, which is rewarded more highly, the regurgitation of facts and figures and respect for formal categories of knowledge or the raising of critical judgments and opinions and the creative restructuring of problems and materials? Do most teachers cast their academic vote for the *absorptive* or the *inquiring* mind?

Teaching is a noble vocation. Nonetheless, teachers are occupationally inclined to be "schoolteacherish." How does it happen that the schoolroom, which should be a place that is vital and alive with thought and learning, is so often the abode of mere thoughtless recitation? A searching analysis of the problem is needed.

Thoughtful learning is always more concerned with unknowns than with knowns. Nor is perception of reality an easy matter; facts are not as easy to come by as overconfident instructors seem to believe. Reality and facts are not nearly as important as what students think is real or what they think about the reality that they perceive. The import of this existential assertion is that the significant reality is what is in the students' minds. It is not what is in books, nor a teacher's structures of learning, nor in notes or outlines, not even what is in the "real world." Remember that in the Hindu parable of the blind man and the elephant, the man who seized the elephant by the tail perceived this quadruped to be "very like a rope."

Too many teachers and learners are inclined to like formal learning. They adore formulas for universal application; they admire categories and classifications; they think in terms of neat, step-by-step arrangements. They spend so much of their classroom time living by these abstractions that they begin to see life in this way. Thus, the academic elephant becomes "very like a rope." Yet, real

111

experience intrudes to shout the fact that the academic concept of life does not resemble life as it is really lived. Categorization and neatness are not what is encountered when the driver follows the kaleidoscopic patterns of highway traffic, or when the citizen tries to make sense of the election returns, or when one lives amid the complexities of family and community life.

Let the responsibility for unreal approaches to learning now be assessed in social and cultural terms. Schools are under both conscious and unconscious pressure to diminish inquiry, awareness, and discovery. Emerson said: "Society is in conspiracy against the manhood of every one of its members." That is a thesis to be respected and a circumstance to be abhorred. What makes this so?

Consider the parent who considers himself responsible in dealing with his child. Often he feels that his prerogative is to mold the child to fit his image. The parent may have the wit to see that this is a ludicrous presumption on the part of his neighbor, but seldom does he see the comedy of his own efforts. Paternal pride waxes upon conformity and imitation. "The little boy is getting to be more like his father every day." Even the drunkard or the thief would take this as complimentary both to himself and his child. But how often are the signs of human dignity and incipient manhood applauded and encouraged? The father is not proud of his son when the child shouts, "I hate you." The father does not nod and listen when his teen-age son asserts, "You are wrong, and I know it." What father cherishes the character of the youth who catches him in a lie and confronts him with the fact? What father refuses to reach for an instrument of authority when the youth says, "I won't do it unless you give me a good reason for it?" What fathers? Only the wise ones. And not many teachers or students have yet been nurtured in such responsible human relations to make the role of respect easily understood for the school.

Let us consider again the two important facts that the school often forgets: (1) man is a natural learner; (2) he always learns, but not always what is intended for him. What can be set forth as the basic principles of *natural* or *informal* learning? If systematic observation is made of these principles, then perhaps they may be applied in deliberately planned learning. In other words, perhaps learning in the schools may be improved by making it more natural. Certain principles are suggested:

The natural learner constantly conceptualizes, explores, and reconceptualizes. Like the blind man, his first perception of any field of reality is partial. It is faulty; it leaves out something. But when an elephant is perceived to be "very like a tree," the learner has hold of something—in this case, the leg of a pachyderm. But that is not all. He perceives strength, solidity, mass, and body; and these are "very like an elephant." No reality can be explored intact. But the learner must conceptualize. Then he must go farther, find out more, and formulate a larger and more complete perception. Undoubtedly most people think that they have a fairly complete conception of an elephant. On the other hand, though it is doubtlessly better than a blind man's view, have they ever seen elephants dance, make love, fight one another to the death, work for man, or die? Lacking such observations, who can claim complete perception of the elephant?

Too often the school formalizes a concept. It neatly parcels out limited truths to purvey them as complete truths or reality. This impedes exploration. It captures inadequate images so that the student lives perennially with incompleted concepts. Should the school thus put obstacles in the way of natural learning?

The natural learner responds eagerly to his own "felt needs." John Dewey talked much of this. How is it possible to dismiss this reality? How will a person learn naturally unless he feels a need to know? With rewards of candy and other incentives, a child can be induced to say that 4 and 3 are 9, and in time he will even believe it. But his need, in this case, is to know the meaning of 7. And the time will come when he will explore and discover the real need, which will give him the real answer to his problem. Let us then ponder this, and in our learning situations let the curriculum pursue the child's needs with more frequency and more depth.

The natural learner is tireless. In schools there is much concern with attention spans and motivation. But these are problems when

113

trying to force people to learn things they do not feel are worth learning. When a boy gets a horse or a car, how difficult is it to persuade him to learn to ride or to drive? How many hours will small children spend in planning a game or a show? When a man decides to climb a mountain, what will he not do? He plans, he organizes, he practices skills, he tests his tools, he tries, he fails, he tries again. He enlists all his forces, his strengths, his agility, his élan, his very life.

Too often the school slanders its pupils. It judges them lazy, weary, or inattentive; it acts as though these were natural characteristics of learners. On the contrary, these are protective poses of people who are unwilling to invest themselves in adventures not their own. When the school helps students to discover the mountains they want to climb it also discovers their energies and capacities.

The natural learner derives systems from what he learns; he does not impose systems upon the unknown. A boy who forages in the woods puts nuts in his pockets and berries in his cap. He puts his knife in one pocket and his candies in another. In other words, he sorts and categorizes as it makes sense to him. In the words of modern mathematics, he establishes his own sets.

The formal lesson often provides categories before explorations, before discovery. Thus the school sends children for water with wicker baskets, for rocks with paper sacks, and for bread with an empty bottle.

If the principles of natural learning are regarded seriously, the school has a clear mandate: it must encourage the student to state his view of things, to look further, and then to state a revised view over and over, again and again. It must refer constantly to the interests and needs of the learners. It must count on a natural willingness and energy for learning. When the school finds these lacking, it should hold its own prescriptions suspect. And it must hold back on imposing outlines or systems, in confidence that the best foundations of order will be in the nature of discoveries made, in the shape of the things that are learned.

The Profession of Teaching

To speak of "the teaching profession" is not uncommon. To be professional is a laudable aim for the teaching force. After all, it is paid, however inadequately, for its services. In certain games being paid constitutes a criterion for the professional; the baseball player who plays no better than the novice on his first day out cannot exist as a professional.

The performance on the job at a high level of knowledge and proficiency also defines the professional. And here, insofar as teaching is concerned, is the rub. It is true that performance on the job can be professional in the most demanding sense of the term. A factor analysis of the knowledges and skills demanded of true teaching reveals its complexity. To claim professionalism, to practice among those who really know what they are doing, a teacher should have a confident mastery of three basic factors:

1. *A substantial understanding of a field of knowledge.* This knowledge must be more than mere competence. The teacher must know more than an examination might have tested. The teacher must also know his field in relation to the other subjects that the student has studied and is studying concurrently. The field must be related to those with which he will organize learning experiences. In short, the teacher must have not merely knowledge of subject matter but also curricular competence.

2. *A practiced skill in organization of a learning situation.* This implies a good deal more than rapping for order and beginning to talk. The professional teacher is an accomplished administrator, one who balances and deploys economically toward the achievement of diverse ends. He is responsible for the establishment of large and small group activities, functional task forces, and individual responsibilities in an ever-shifting flux of social process. The teacher must be accomplished in group dynamics, human relations, and fundamentals of administration not as credit dividends toward certificate or degree, but to function professionally.

115

3. *Knowledge of the learner and the matters relevant to his learning.*
The keepers of filling stations, barbers, butchers, all have established
notions about child rearing, teen-agers, discipline, and the school.
Teachers' views often mirror the notions held by ordinary citizens.
Because the ordinary citizen is usually not well informed, this often
simply means that the teacher lacks the necessary degree of professionalism. The real teacher moves amid a complex. The consequences of social class, emotional crosscurrents, ethnic origins, and
regional backgrounds all have a bearing on learning, which the
professional recognizes and responds to gracefully and takes in his
stride.

It is not to be anticipated that the new teacher enters the
classroom in full-blown possession of an impressive arsenal of professional attributes. But great golfers do not develop by practicing
the errors of the duffer for a lifetime. Too much teaching, however,
is practiced in proud or conventional disdain for the very attributes
that constitute the professional. It would be interesting to go to
restaurants, drug stores, and barber shops, for example, and select
from among the waiters, clerks, and barbers a cross section of
reasonably personable alert persons between 21 and 65 (the common teaching ages). After ascertaining that they are high-school
graduates, these people could be given licenses to teach and a day's
briefing on the job. Our hypothesis is that they would not be distinguishable from *most* of the teaching force. The lack of a college
degree or of high professional attributes would not be noticeable.
They would teach much the way too many elementary and secondary school teachers and most college professors do.

The fact is that everybody knows how a teacher teaches. You
walk into the schoolroom; you smile, you frown; you ask for attention; you assign lessons and tasks; you scold the noisy, the idle, the
mischievous; you severely punish the chronic offender; you indulge
private idiosyncrasies; you motivate with the "sugar candy" of your
smiles and compliments and with the threat of tests, grades, and
college entrance; and you join forces with those who make the going
easy against those who obstruct the smooth passage of well-rou-
tinized hours from 8:30 A.M. to 3:15 P.M. and from payday to pay-

day. Because this is the school to which most have gone, its rules are not hard to learn.

Society conventionally exacts a college diploma to exercise these functions. In essence, however, it does not take a college degree to perform such tasks. In effect, one could say that the degree represents a unionlike requirement to keep numbers down and wages up. Because the college has long expressed an articulate disdain for professionalized teaching, it has no quarrel with the *amateur* or, more appropriately speaking, *duffer's* model of instruction. Therefore, except for the education courses that have at least a professional potential, college does the future teacher no harm (that is, it awakens no insecurity over his lack of competence) and does at least increase the likelihood that the teacher will be a year or two older than those whom he will first teach.

The duffer's model may be redesignated as the antieducational model of instruction. Unfortunately, this is the model that is fairly commonly accepted; that is, to become professional is not so much to reject this whole bumbling procedure as to learn to do these things better. The teacher learns skillfully to reinforce (smile, scold, give candy, or spank) and to enhance the "pernickety"—get down to the very basics of everything. If the teacher (or re-employed waiter or sorority girl) is not school-teacherish enough (that is, deadly dull), a machine may be programed ad nauseam. If the teacher is insufficiently talkative, the school may bring in a televised talker.

Teaching must be gauged against a new model—a professional model—or educational research will continue to direct its efforts toward the unprofessional.

A New Model for Instruction

Since method is implicit in content, a laissez-faire attitude toward the concept of the learning situation must be rejected. Certainly the full dimensions of any school program will not be realized if method or the lack of it: (1) discourages inquiry and creativity, (2)

117

ritualizes procedures, (3) fails to accept individual differences (or perceives or relates to them in superficial terms), (4) ignores scientific or scholarly techniques or attack, (5) maximizes memory and minimizes discovery, (6) neglects the potential for achievement through either the individual or the group, (7) employs teacher resources in a single rather than in a multidimensional role.

A certain schema for instruction best fits this curriculum theory. Its essential characteristics are freedom of movement, flexibility and adaptability, and full employment of all available resources.

Students of methodology will not find the new model so new after all. Its genealogical roots are deep in Quintilian, St. Augustine, Vittorino de Feltre, in Rabelais, Bacon, Locke, Rousseau, Comenius, Pestalozzi, and Dewey. But it acknowledges no debt to Calvin, Marx, Gentile, or Skinner, and little enough to observation of good practice in the schools.

However, Morrison's unit method is significantly used and altered. We do not intend to minimize or patronize his approach by claiming a distinctiveness beyond it. The unit method had both beneficial and revolutionary impact on instructional practice. Most of the instructional situations in the country would be improved significantly if the teacher conceptualized and used the Morrison model of practice.[2] The method did not fail, but it was not widely used because it demanded too much professionalization of teaching.

Our model here is new in scope and purposes. It is a reconceptualization of the basic instructional function of the school and is related to the uses and conception of intelligence. We will use the phrase "built through" to describe the learning situation in this model. The phrase is deliberate and significant; it implies *construction,* cumulative experience, purposiveness, design, direction, continuity, and eventual completeness.

The five phases include:

1. Exploration and planning

2. Inquiry, activity, and research

2 Henry C. Morrison, *The Practices of Teaching in the Secondary School* (rev. ed., Chicago: University of Chicago Press, 1931).

3. Presentation, organization, and conceptualization

4. Appraisal and evaluation

5. Utilization, reflection, reconceptualization

Exploration and planning. The opening phase involves the search for the possibilities of learning experiences within a unit. While the teacher's scholarship is naturally included, it does not preclude the necessity to involve all learners in exploration and planning. (It is assumed that the teacher too will be an active, participating learner. This phase includes assessment of such study resources as textual accounts, library research, guests, field study, and projects. It involves review and discussion of what the class, or individuals within the class, already know or have experienced relating to the unit being planned. The overview is established; the scope of study is limited and defined. The hypotheses are set forth as generalizations that will be examined to discover whether the results of inquiry (facts or evidence) support them, to what extent, and with what qualifications. Planning will include preparation of study-guide materials and the division of labor.

Planning should axiomatically be cooperative. Though most teachers seem unaware of the skill of cooperation and most schools devoid of it, it would be anachronistic and patronizing to set forth a theoretical justification of cooperative planning and cooperative classroom procedures. Such devices are related positively to self-realization, initiative, creativity, democratic attitudes, and motivation. The point here is simply that exploration and planning are a phase of learning; therefore, to exclude intended learners from this enterprise is to exclude them from a part of the intended learning.

Inquiry, activity, and research. Phase 2 implies the study of evidence and subject matter and the systematic collection of data: readings, references, projects, field studies. It also includes the discussion and interchange of knowledge and ideas.

It may be noted that a strand of scientific method runs through this model, for example, the formulation of hypotheses in Phase 1 and the systematic collection of data in Phase 2. However, it is not

119

the sole support of the method, as this model conceptualizes a complex learning situation, involves groups of young learners in a context of many social and psychological factors, and includes content goals that encompass more than pure discovery.

Nor are the phases sharply cut off from one another. In brief, they are not "formal steps." For example, somewhere in the middle of Phase 2 it may be necessary to admit blunders in direction that require stopping to reassess, turn back, reexplore, or replan. The central characteristics of each phase are clearly discernible, but the learning enterprise should be one that exhibits flow and continuity rather than jerkiness, and spontaneity rather than scheduling.

The signal element relevant to the instructional model that awaits subsequent development is the delineation of content resources on which the learning situation will be based. A conceptualization of the substances of experience has been developed for its intrinsic consonance with this model of instruction. The procedural aspect of exploitation of the full dimensions of experience are set forth in Chapter V and substantively developed in Part Three.

In Phase 2 the competence of the teacher as an organizer of learning is at a premium. The teacher's scholarship is now put to work by making appropriate resources known and occasionally steering inquiry away from blind alleys and disappointing by-paths. The teacher may give brief, well-planned presentations of material while helping students to develop skills, techniques, and effective use of their time and efforts.

The teacher's most important role is attending to individual differences with constant press toward maximum growth and development. The teacher must be certain that each student finds tasks most appropriate to his abilities, interests, and motivations. This must be defined intersubjectively among individual students, the group, and the teacher, in open communication that reflects phenomenological views of self, situation, and one another.

Presentation, organization, and conceptualization. Phase 3 is concerned with bringing together the findings of study, experience, and research in meaningful patterns. It is here that initial hypotheses and assumptions are checked out in light of what has been discovered.

The goals of "generalization" responsibly are confined to the evidence and carefully qualified as to limits and exceptions. If the inquiry has been basically scientific, the generalization may be made quite firm if its limits are strictly defined. In a social scientific setting certain generalizations may be phrased in terms of probabilities or limits of confidence, or something akin to these. But generalizations on moot issues, on humanistic matters, on questions of taste and judgment, or on values must be phrased carefully. When they are not, they may become instruments of semantic or psychological coercion. Dissent as well as consensus is a valid source of generalization.

Conceptualization takes shape here as the articulation and personalization of meaning in a form that is susceptible to use, to growth, and to continuing reappraisal. The students may come to speak of this process in just such terms, but the process is more important than the words. In the actual classroom the process of conceptualization may take place as the learning addresses itself to questions like these:

What conclusions shall we draw from our findings?

What early questions have we satisfactorily answered?

How would we restate our initial questions and hypotheses if we had known at the beginning what we know now?

On what matters have we found less evidence than we were seeking and what should we do about it?

What implications, if any, do our findings have for action?

What avenues or interests have we opened for further study?

Appraisal and evaluation. Phase 4 directs attention to two questions: (1) How have *we* done? (2) What have *I* learned? The first question implies a procedural review, a critique on the learning method. Such a critique is a basic element in developing skills, scientific attitudes, and critical thinking. It is also a means by which classes grow in learning competence (a rarity in the educational

121

process). The second question implies not merely the vulgar necessity for tests and grades (which ought to be outside the patterns of motivation); it implies that the learner is intrinsically concerned with evaluation of self. It assumes that a participant in a learning situation developed with this model wants to learn certain realities about self and achievement from the process of evaluation and its outcomes.

The ordinary tests employed either in old academic or recent technological models of instruction primarily measure activities in Phase 2, and these usually in a vacuum. Tests are legitimate but severely limited instruments within a learning situation. Testing presupposes a connection between the ability to give back subject matter on cue in an arbitrarily sought pattern and real-life consequence, which should be the outcome of learning.

Typical testing serves to diminish the person. It is a poor basis for self-judgment and often gives him conscious feelings of inadequacy. To know what we do not know is profound learning. For example, to conclude that we cannot learn to ride a bicycle because we cannot name the identifying characteristics of seven manufacturers' types is the kind of false self-conviction toward which the typical academic approach is directed. The test forever doubles back on itself; it says to go back and memorize the items missed. Evaluation reaches forward; it invites the learner to dare, to assess his strength, to try, and to discover what can be done. A child would never learn to walk if he had to pass a test of competence beforehand.

Evaluation in our model eliminates mystic assumptions. This model inquires directly into consequence. It seeks to assist the student in finding out what he has learned by directing his attention toward self-inquiry: Can I do anything now I could not do before? Have I new or improved skills? How can I find out or demonstrate these consequences? Real evaluation is expansive; it moves out, it demands more.

Utilization, reflection, and reconceptualization. If the first four phases mainly represent a restructure and extension of earlier reform models of instructional practice, Phase 5 constitutes a radical theoretical departure and innovation. Elements commonly ignored, or at best merely acknowledged in good words and pious hopes, are herein incorporated with the basic intent of instruction.

This is the phase *beyond* formal learning in the school, but its importance and reality should not be overlooked. Full learning does not take place without this phase. This is so apparent that anyone may acknowledge and dismiss it. But this model for instruction demands that the school not hold optimistic, careless, or laissez-faire attitudes about desirable outcomes. *Instruction must deliberately and intelligently improve the likelihood that culminating learning will eventuate.*

At this point the model demands consummate teaching (the utilization of professional know-how at its highest levels) to effect consummated learning (the wedding of behavior and experience). Such teaching perceives that learning is not a capsule to be swallowed, not a set of hurdles to be run, not a bundle of neat generalizations to be wrapped and stored away, not a series of academic exploits to be catalogued, scored, recorded, and forgotten.

The teacher can directly invite realization of Phase 5, as the class progresses from one unit to another, by such leads as these:

1. The next time such a situation occurs, think of what we found out with respect to hypothesis X.

2. Here are some good books on the subject that we have not used, and which you might like to read on your own.

3. Remember the generalization. Since we disagreed, keep looking for evidence and thinking about it.

4. I think we have some clear ideas about this subject now, but remember, things change. Keep your minds open. Some new evidence may develop, which means that we'll have to reconsider and reshape these concepts some day.

Phase 5 must be thought of in harder terms than invitation. The key words, *utility* and *necessity*, do not mean the same. Even the most traditional academician warns: "Learn this, it will come in handy" or "You will need to know it in college."

Utility must be a demonstrable as well as a claimed characteristic of learning. Nothing argues harder for articulation of curricula than this. The school must know at every level what it has enabled its students to learn so that it may deliberately give occasion for its use. Does the school too frequently destroy what it has created by denying opportunity for its use? Does it do the following too often?

1. Teach children songs and deny them the chance to sing.

2. Teach them skills of critical thinking and penalize them when they criticize.

3. Nurture them in choice-making and veto their choices.

4. Attend to their physical health and then restrict them to the most sedentary of routines; reward vigor with captivity, as it were.

5. Keep them in school in their biological prime and refuse to deal respectfully or candidly with their expression of sex.

6. Teach them to love to read and give them no time for it. Teach them to paint and take away their brushes and palettes. Teach them to talk and penalize them for speaking their minds.

7. Sometimes teach the real, but usually test the absurd.

8. Speak of individuality and reward conformity.

How shall the child determine what is useful when the use of what he undertook to learn in good faith is so often denied by the very institution that undertook to get him to learn it?

Beyond utility lies necessity; the necessity in learning is its exercise. In our time, three dozen people watched as a woman was murdered, and nobody acted on her behalf. We can assume that many had studied civics in school and had passed the course. Some had probably written good tests, but they failed the *ultimate* examination. The school had not stressed fifth-phase learning, necessity. In sum, it is that aspect of the new model of instruction which insists that learning in the school must have a life consequence. The fifth phase is no less than the assumption of *human responsibility*.

The returns for the student who participates in the new model of instructional practice are great. Three specific advantages may be noted:

The skills of learning are made intrinsic. No choice exists between the development of skill and its use. The traditional classroom may make "the skills" its subject matter; that is, it may assign their study and use. The new model exemplifies the skills in action. The automated classroom simply extends the conventional teaching approach; it renders the skills extrinsic and delegates their exercise to the machine.

Students in the new model become searchers and researchers. They locate, record, and appraise resources for learning. They learn to budget time and energy. They acquaint themselves with the devices of cataloguing, indexing, locating information and ideas. They live in the mode of the modern organization, in which they must survive as individuals while operating in a constantly changing panorama of functional subgroupings. The skills of cooperation that the students employ are not utopian; they have social and ethical value, but they are skills in the context of the complex institutional structures in which most people live.

The student finds his learning situation consistent with his evolving discovery of the modern mind. He learns that man is in a predicament, not wholly of his own making, where intelligence and enterprise are his chief resources. He finds similarities in his situation as well. In the conventional classroom his signs of growth are often held against him. In the new model, growth is both sought after and counted on.

Obviously, no learning situation can succeed without the student. But many instructional models leave this at the axiomatic level. Student involvement in the new model is real; in fact, student involvement in responsible rather than perfunctory roles is necessary to its success.

The new model brings the student into the pattern of inquiry that is most typical of sophisticated study. Older models are naïve and sterile: assign, recite, test, or lecture, discuss, test, or program, study, reinforce, test. These are patterns of learning familiar only within the school. They are not common to man in his natural habitat, life.

The phases of the new model parallel and incorporate the very structure of modern research. Phase 1—exploration and planning—parallels the design of the project and the statement of hypotheses. Phase 2—inquiry, activity, and research—is the accumulation-of-data stage; its classroom instruments may be those of any research discipline (documentary, survey, statistical, or field). Phase 3—presentation, organization, and conceptualization—is like the data-processing and reporting stages of a research project. Phase 4—appraisal and evaluation—represents the critical intelligence applied to findings of inquiry, an application both by the researcher and by his peers, on behalf of both. Phase 5—utilization, reflection, and reconceptualization—reflects the outcome of research, which includes every step from rejection to replication to utilization.

What is important is not that the new model teaches the ways of science, but that it involves the student in the method of scientific inquiry. Scientific method is intrinsic rather than extrinsic to the new model. Learning will be experienced as problem solving, whether the problem be the determination of the amount of energy brought to bear by a machine, the creation of a poem, or understanding the roots of prejudice in a community. The results of the method will be new knowledge, deeper perceptions, and experience itself.

Perhaps the most significant feature of the new model is in its regard to individual differences. Token acknowledgments have included some allowance for adjustments to individual differences, but such tokens are often patronizing or exploitative, or both. Johnnies-come-lately to the educational scene have waxed excited over a one-dimensional view of individual difference: the fact that some students learn faster than others. But a footrace does not constitute a full-dimensioned physical education program; for that matter, though speed is involved in both, a runner does not train for the Marathon as he does for the 100-yard dash.

The new model does not do anything *to* individual differences. It accepts them, respects them, and liberates them. It puts all of the complexities of individual differences to good use, including: biological differences, variations in cultural background, assorted depths of experience, emotional differences, wide variations in maturity and motivation, varied skills, broad ranges of developed and potential strengths, disparate capacities for communication and response, diverse moral and spiritual sensitivities, and the fact that some work faster than others. Variety is not a problem; it is the foundation of the method and includes the complex, diverse patterns of mankind and expression of the full human potential. When it is reduced to oversimple dimensions, it results in confinement to tight little boxes, circumscribing and distorting the human potential, and the curtailment of learning. Real education recognizes, appreciates, and uses differences.

Discipline as Curriculum

Discipline is not a "bad" word; it is an educational necessity. The necessity in educational discipline is the maintenance of a learning situation. But it is necessary to beware of appearances. The appearance of perfect order need not mean that learning is taking place; neither need disorder mean that dynamic learning is in the making. Schoolteacherishness and hooliganism are both equally productive as springs of bad discipline.

"Schoolteacherishness" is our term for most of what is wrong—of what is unprofessional—about instruction in the schools. Two factors in schoolteacherish discipline are tradition and insecurity. Most adults, if told to perform the role of a teacher, would exhibit schoolteacherish discipline. Children also know the role well, and when playing school, they parody the classroom from time immemorial: "That was the bell. Quiet now. Johnny, are you chewing gum? Spit it out. You know very well we don't chew gum in school. Now, class, let's all turn our books to page 111. We don't speak without raising our hands. Did you have permission to speak? Nice little girls don't whisper; do they, Mildred?"

A realistic analysis of the disciplinary problem also includes "hooliganism." We shall use the term as a descriptive label for customarily destructive or disruptive models of behavior. A student may exhibit hooliganism but is not necessarily a hooligan. The mode of behavior should not be used to stereotype the individual or generalize overconfidently on his essence.

The romantic would tell us that "there are no bad boys," but even he must admit that there are boys who behave badly. Challenge rather than theory confronts two million teachers daily. Often this challenge is in the form of a personal or organized attempt to resist the establishment of a learning situation. The challenge must not be minimized; it is a challenge to the institution of the school itself. The school does not solve its problem by labeling its students "bad," but it should begin by acknowledging and defining bad conduct.

Bad conduct is part of the culture of the school, and not all of it is grim. The school as an academic institution has often taken itself too seriously, and this has invited comic perceptions quite often. Students tramp in unison while visitors walk the aisles of study halls; sneezing fits run epidemic through assemblies when dull speakers hold forth; a dozen students exhaling through old pipestems turn a library into the atmospheric counterpart of a corner pool hall; snakes, toads, and mice still appear in surprising places; whole classes resist efforts to be brought to order; erasers, books, doughballs take wing; paper gliders float lazily in somnolent classrooms in late September afternoons; and we can recall a day after Halloween when a live horse was found in a third floor room, a legend that will endure as long as the author's alma mater stands. Such deeds scarcely facilitate learning, but they wrench the school from grimness; they remind the schoolteachers that people are around; they assert that the drama of the school, like that of life, is incomplete without comedy. The school very often can control overextensions of such correctives by joining in the laughter. Let one teacher join the burlesque of sneezing fits and the epidemic ceases in appreciative laughter.

Not all bad conduct derives from philosophy. Students may

steal, lie, betray, attempt rape or mayhem, commit arson, and burglarize. They may blackmail, bully, and extort; they may serve as agents in the peddling of dope and pornography among their fellows. Students have even murdered within the school. These deeds are too serious to be funny, and they do not contribute to constructive learning. Fortunately, such deeds are not typical of the school, although they are brought to the school. Their incidence should rule out sentimental conclusions or retention of the thesis that discipline is a term somehow inappropriate to the modern or humane educational vocabulary.

Conduct that is bad in the societal sense is criminal behavior and is sometimes brought to the school. Even this behavior must be understood as well as policed, but it is beyond the school's capacity to cope with criminality. School discipline must be such that it competently copes with the challenge to maintain a learning situation. Students come to school "damaged," and sometimes the school contributes to this damage. The damaged personality presents a real danger to the school because of four basic misperceptions that such a person brings to the classroom:

1. A damaged view of human worth and dignity

2. An inadequate view of what learning means to the particular individual

3. A hostile or disparaging view of the school

4. A disregard for and a sense of disaffiliation from the institutions of society

The school does have an obligation to help the damaged individual, but it also has an obligation to prevent such students from denying others the right to learn. Thus, there is a real necessity for discipline.

To attain discipline, it is necessary to establish a solid theoretical base derived from the necessities of the learning situation. This done, the disciplinary function will be exercised educationally. Sound theory will divest the disciplinary function of the schoolteacherish, the personal, the crotchety, and the arbitrary. It will bulwark against extremes of neurotic or dogmatic self-indulgence on the part of students or teacher.

Respect is the key concept of discipline. It is fundamental to the learning situation in four aspects: (1) respect for the *person* (each person), (2) respect for *learning*, (3) respect for the *school* as an institution, and (4) respect for the *basic institutions* of society. This then is the foundation for solid disciplinary theory.

RESPECT   RESPECT
FOR THE ⟷ FOR
PERSON   LEARNING
↕   ↕
RESPECT   RESPECT
FOR THE ⟷ FOR BASIC
SCHOOL   INSTITUTIONS

THE CONSTRUCT OF RESPECT
IN THE CLASSROOM

Respect is not an authoritarian concept. Respect derives from internal directives, self-knowledge, appraisal, participation, and consent. It may be sought but not commanded. Allegiance may be bought, coerced, duped, or traded. Respect does not exist without freedom and understanding.

In our construct there is no statement on respect for authority, nor is there need for it. What is sought is a source of functional order to maintain a learning situation, but respect for authority is a tired appeal of tyrannies too febrile to make sense. Not infrequently statements of school "philosophies" include the development of respect for authority as a primary objective. Such an objective would be more appropriate to the schools of Hitler, Mussolini, or Stalin than for those of a free society.

130

False coin, too, is made of the appeal to respect the teacher. In a true community of respect the teacher as a person and as an agent of learning needs no special status. The other side of the schoolteacherish desire for special tokens of regard is the teacher's traditional willingness to treat students with arbitrary indignities and tokens of disrespect, in the name of respect for adult and authority alike.

The source of discipline is *not* personal. The notion that power resides in teacher prerogative is an antieducational tenet that lies at the root of many unnecessary classroom problems. The source of the teacher's disciplinary force is official and resides in his role. His obligation is to conduct learning situations. Professionalization of teaching simply means an ability to establish and to maintain learning situations. Functional discipline is essential to learning, and the teacher has no need to personalize this function. To insist upon irrelevancies of conduct or manners that neither obstruct nor advance learning is personalizing discipline and is unprofessional. To allow conduct to persist that interferes with the basic learning situation, whether from indolence, good nature, laissez-faire attitudes, or sentimental permissiveness, is again to personalize discipline and constitutes dereliction of duty. The dictate of discipline is not what teacher likes or dislikes, tolerates or detests, but simply what the learning situation necessitates.

This concept alters the very vocabulary of the classroom. "I don't like that sort of thing" or "not in my classroom," in terms of functional discipline becomes, "We are here to learn, not to fool around," or "Can't let you sleep, John; we'd be cheating you and the taxpayers."

Obviously, the function of discipline varies with the individual activity. It cannot be the same pattern for the multiplicity of arrangements and involvements that make up the normal day's work within the new model. In the classroom, even as in architecture, form follows function. Rows of empty houses are orderly enough, but they lack function. If a vital learning situation is complex, then the forms around or within which students structure their efforts will be as varied or complex as the purposes of their learning.

The Elements of Respect

Respect for the person. The classroom can only be well disciplined for learning if it is grounded on the principle of human dignity. Indignities visited upon persons by other persons deny respect; they destroy functional discipline. Intrusions on personal dignity have been common, even conventional, in the classroom. The classroom has too often included class-oriented patterns of teacher preference and favoritism, psychologically cruel and unusual punishments (such as exposing a student to ridicule in his most vulnerable attributes), corporal punishment, ridicule of error (by teacher or fellow students), suppression of dissent and free discussion, neglect of any, many, or a few on personal or preferential grounds. Respect for the person implies acceptance of each student's weaknesses as well as strengths, and these often masquerade in one another's togs.

A free climate of expression is the first requisite of respect, and all effective social intercourse should contain relevance of comment. However, teachers often err in cutting off comment before a student has established relevance while they are more generous anent their own discursiveness.

Treatment of error is the acid test of respect. Freedom is based on the assumption of mortal fallibility. It follows that error deserves correction rather than punishment or ridicule. Indeed, the good teacher seizes upon and emphasizes the one correct statement in ten from a poor contribution; the weak teacher gloats upon the missing 2 percent of a 98 percent sound statement. Error maltreated becomes stubborn, loyally defended. In a good learning situation student and teacher alike recognize that they have no stake in being wrong. Correction is a favor, not a rebuke. These are essential although not painless lessons for maturity, but growing up is never easy.

Respect for the teacher is adequately secured in the concept of

132

respect for the individual. A new, inexperienced, or insecure teacher should remember that respect must be reciprocal if learning is to take place. The teacher is accorded the same respect that is extended and maintained among and for the students, each of whom is responsible to the learning situation.

Respect for learning. Respect for learning begins with professionalized teaching. A classroom ought to be a place characterized by well-mannered, reciprocal human behavior because it is a place where people associate, because it is in a school, and because it is a part of the larger community. Such a classroom presupposes *functional discipline,* and it is a necessary component for learning to take place. In fact, the expectation and raison d'être of the school are learning, but it is not easy to assure that learning takes place. It is not evidenced by simply assigning, reciting, praising, scolding, quizzing, and grading.

It would be sentimental to assert that the opportunity to learn compels respect. It does for a few, but learning is not effected by throwing either a ball or a textbook to a group of students. For teachers to move from the pillar of strength that respect for learning is, they must know what learning is all about. A sterile pretense of learning compels disrespect! Indeed, student rebellion against sheer boredom should not be construed as a result of bad discipline. On the contrary, it may be a responsible expression of respect and even hunger for learning.

Respect for the school. The school is an institution created by man. Candor compels its officers to admit its errors and absurdities. Honest self-criticism is a sign of confidence, but the school may become debilitated by morbid introspection on its shortcomings. Even the poorest schools represent man's best hopes. To criticize the school is an act of loyalty, but to permit damage to its basic function is to sit passively and contribute nothing.

Respect for the school comes more readily when it is broadly based. A democracy stands on firmer grounds than an autocracy. A school may be forgiven its inadvertencies but gains respect from its achievements. There must be consonance among the four pillars of respect. Respect for the school cannot endure when the school abuses persons or neglects learning.

To deserve respect the school must study justice within the academic setting. This includes the study of equality, due process (fair procedures), participation in enactments by which one is governed, rights of petition and appeal, freedom from coerced testimony, absence of cruel or unusual punishments, presumption of innocence, no mass punishments to get at the guilt of a few. These hard-earned principles have served free men well. The school should examine its disciplinary system in relation to constitutional principles of justice.

Respect for the basic institutions of society. Respect within the school does not stand alone. The school that neglects the development of respect betrays not only itself but society as a whole. Those roads that lead to school, the homes from which its students come, the regulations which affect students and their parents are the products of a long, historic achievement. A school contributes to much more than the solution of its disciplinary problems when it gives its students some sense of value for a man's achievements. Let the school bolster itself by teaching children the worth of their heritage. And let the school also teach a corollary obligation: he who betrays one basic institution betrays all.

The school's insistence on respect for basic institutions does not mean pious verbalism or dereliction of civic responsibility. Schools cannot endure, or expect respect for long, in a community of corrupted basic institutions. The school must teach students to recognize community betrayal, whether it be by labor leaders who connive with hoodlums, industrialists who defraud the government, bankers who embezzle, or public officials who raid or carelessly guard the public treasury.

Without doubt, professional insecurity has been a source of much *bad* discipline. Bad discipline does not describe any particular pattern of order or disorder; it implies social incoherence that obstructs or detracts from the realization of a learning situation.

Parents also contribute to bad discipline. Parental relationship to bad curricular practice warrants exploration, but for our purposes, the three listed here include the basic problem:

1. Parents are often baffled by their children; they too need to be educated.

2. Parents are often the products of authoritarian subcultures: one or both dominant parents, closed-circle ethnic groups, dogmatic definitions of evil nature, antique notions of child-rearing and family life.

3. Parents are often in pursuit of their own youth and refuse to give up their games. They often refuse the responsibilities of maturity. When they are aware of their limitations, guilt debilitates their efforts to create responsible standards of behavior for themselves and their children.

With an understanding of its four pillars of respect, the school will stand beside responsible parents in developing the pervasive respect upon which the human community depends. When necessary, the school will not hesitate to move into the social vacuum occasioned by parental insecurity or abdication. Here, equal opportunity means that the school will make its civilizing impact available to all.

One further insecurity sometimes debilitates the teacher's will to assert the disciplinary obligation. This is the notion that good discipline is somehow undemocratic. Primitive progressivism suffered from this misconception. It abhorred classroom tyranny, and it was right. It maintained that authoritarianism in the schools of a democracy was an anachronism and a contradiction. But the fallacy that weakened this premise was the prevalent assumption that anything not authoritarian must be democratic. Too often the lid was off, and harassed teachers found themselves defending constant chaos in the classroom because it was not authoritarian.

Neither was it a democracy. Laissez-faire permissiveness is neither authoritarian nor democratic, but it does move toward tyranny. The classroom without functional discipline becomes chaotic, and chaos invites tyranny. The alternative to tyranny need not be anarchy. Teachers are obligated to maintain learning. Learning rests upon the pillars of respect, and these are the pillars of democracy as well. The teacher need not feel that by serving one well he is in great hazard of neglecting the other. Discipline that maintains the learning situation is the foundation of curriculum itself.

Method in Action—Two Case Studies

Case I

A real learning situation builds trust in intelligence and puts that trust to work. It also helps the person to recognize, authenticate, and mobilize his experience. The school is forever erring against these basic dictates: respect the mind and build on experience. Too often the teacher seems to have assumed children's minds are vacant, fragile, and that their experience is limited to the sum total of the syllabuses for previous academic years.

The school should never present such a picture. Respecting the mind and building on experience will effect marvels, yet it need not cost a penny or disturb a single vested interest in the school program. It will not even require the change of a textbook anywhere. This is not to assert that all school improvement can be cost- or trouble-free. But, in this case, education gains a rare dividend through an attitudinal modification.

The school can assume that the student's intelligence is ready for work—and have work ready for it. However good the student, no matter how much he has learned in school to date, the school can assume that his experience out of school (his learning out of school) far exceeds his learning within the academic halls. This is not assumed to sell the school's contribution short; rather, it roots the program design within reality in order to strengthen its curriculum by a daily mobilizing of the student's entire experience.

At this point the recapitulation of a methodological demonstration will clarify our discussion. The substantive is important; that is, some things are worth learning. If this premise is accepted, it is probably safe to assume a fair consensus that: (1) the Industrial

136

Revolution is substantially and topically a subject worth modern man's study, and (2) through such study man will better understand who and where he is (that he more fully comprehend his condition and his predicament).

When the school *teaches* the Industrial Revolution, what does it commonly do? Its students are of junior or senior high-school age—twelve to eighteen years old, perhaps. They have been living in a society that is largely the product of the Industrial Revolution, and they will be at home with much of its most fascinating technological products. They know what the Industrial Revolution is. However, they may not know that they do or be aware of how much they know. But since they do know what the Industrial Revolution is, the learning situation that proceeds as though they do not is subjecting them to a dual indignity: it teaches them distrust of their intelligence, and it acts as if their most real experience is not authentic.

The job of the school is to show the students what they know, to assist them in effectively organizing and conceptualizing this knowledge, and to help them grow by assisting them in recognizing and authenticating their experience.

Too frequently the teacher functions as though he were in a vacuum; he looks for resources exclusively in textbooks, encyclopedias, and other reference books. This is not to say that such references should not be consulted, but they are not the proper place to begin the search for knowledge. The resources to explore first are intelligence and experience. However, the too typical teacher "discovers" seven pages in a textbook "covering the Industrial Revolution," locates "further references" in other books, and perhaps shows a film or two. These are "covered" and a test is given. If the teacher thinks that gadgetry modernizes, the textbook may be "programed," and the student may come upon James Watt, or Richard Arkwright, or Robert Bakewell either at the end of a branch or of a line. There will be definitions, some inventions and inventors, and some minimal consequences. The consequences will be a separation of these little matters learned academically from what the student *already* knows. A corollary consequence will be a diminished sense of self as the result of one more academic occurrence which instills the notion that personal perceptions of reality have been worthless or invalid. And when tested, learners will perform according to a relatively normal curve.

Real learning seeks mastery and begins with the instructional responsibility to proceed from a masterful view of the subject at hand. Let us consider a classroom where this condition is met; the learners are tenth graders and in a world history course.

The teacher introduces the term Industrial Revolution and asks what it means. A student may or may not have enough confidence to offer a definition. Whether the students define the Industrial Revolution or not does not matter; the teacher knows that they *do* know what it is. If they say that they do not, the teacher says, "You will find that you are so wrong, and you will learn that you know something you didn't know you knew." Or, if they supply definitions, the teacher may say, "Of course, now let's talk about it."

The teacher may then supply some background information that students do not know. For example, the term the Industrial Revolution refers to the historical process and events that effected a drastic change in the method and condition of making products from raw materials. The initial, historically significant first phase and locale was between 1750 and 1825 in England. But what *do* the students know? Ask them where the things they buy or want to buy come from, and they will most likely answer "factories," probably automobile factories at that. "Were goods always made in factories? If not, then where?" Students discuss the fact that goods were made at home and sometimes still are. This anthropological view can help them understand many present world problems.

The class is now more aware that today means the factory; yesterday, the home. And they will also learn about the process of changeover. What do they know before they begin to study the topic? Will students in Bridgeport, Pittsburgh, Birmingham, or Detroit be told to open their books to read a definition of a "factory"? *They know what a factory is.* The aware teacher will not patronize the students by doubting this; he will put their knowledge to work. The problem is not first to seek new knowledge but to mobilize the method of intelligence, to authenticate experience, and to conceptualize it.

One way to begin is to write on the chalkboard:

| home manufacture | Industrial Revolution | factory |
| (the domestic system) | ———————→ | |

"What do we know about factories?" is the next question to ask. As the "factory" column fills, the students will be responding on the basis of knowledge they have taken for granted.

factory

machines	assembly lines
mass production	fewer skills
raw materials from elsewhere	wages
power supply	bosses
many workers	capital
division of labor	cities

How about the domestic system? Do the students have authentic knowledge here? They have probably read *Silas Marner*. They have experienced colonial times and frontier days hundreds of times at school, at the movies, and before the television screen. They do know; they merely need to recognize the fact. In other words they merely need to make their experience respectable in the school's eyes—and their own. Perhaps there is a domestic manufacturer at home or even one among themselves. They will fill the "home" column too.

home manufacture

(the domestic system)	skill and pride in labor
small output	simple barter
raw materials at hand	family unit
simple tools	subsistence agriculture
worker completes the task	village life

The development of such a list provides evidence to the students themselves that they already knew much of the lesson in history *before it had been taught them.* The first law in developing intelligence is to show the learner that he possesses and can depend upon his own knowledge and intelligence.

What is left to find out? Does the student perhaps have the ability within his experience and understanding to construct the meaning and essence of the Industrial Revolution itself? He has the *before;* he has the *after.* The bridge across the process alone remains to be built.

The domestic system is here. ⟶ The factory system is here.

What must have taken place in this period of historical transition that is called the Industrial Revolution? Should the students now turn to their books, they will find storehouses of meaningful evidences. It would be appropriate to the method if the books were opened at this point. The method of intelligence does not war upon books; it does resist the substitution of the symbol for the real, of making ends of implements. To test the method thoroughly, we shall leave the books closed awhile.

From awakened confident intelligence, students are now ready to set forth the historical necessities.

Industrial Revolution

inventions
new raw materials
increased commerce
expanded markets
new sources of capital

credit and banking growth
new food supplies
agricultural revolution
movement to the cities

Now, indeed, books, films, and field trips may be employed profitably. Mobilized intelligence has established a sensible situation for them. It is now possible to make such generalizations for subsequent use as these:

1. The method of discovery is not restricted to fields of exploration or science.

2. Creativity is possible in a discipline where "the facts" are already established.

3. The liberation of intelligence may be planned and counted upon, but never programed.

4. The uses of intelligence and dimensions of experience must first be exploited in learning, lest gains in substance be at the expense of self-knowledge and self-trust.

5. Curriculum planning must concentrate on the resources of the learner himself. Delinquency in this respect leads to the most absurd consequence of all academic errors. It sets the classroom program against all of the participants. Such programs destroy the very potential of the school.

Case II

Another illustration may serve to point out the reality of a complex, sophisticated, professionalized learning situation.

Long ago we visited the Fairmont Heights High School near Washington, D.C. This school gave every evidence of knowing its job and purpose. The students, teachers, administrators, and staff all talked knowingly, clearly, and consistently on the school's goals. The exhibits and bulletin boards supported their views.

One of the classes that we observed was a Spanish classroom, and though we were not too familiar with Spanish, we were soon at ease in the classroom. At one table about eight students were scanning some pamphlets from tthe National Council for Social Studies on critical thinking and some from the now defunct Institute for Propaganda Analysis. The door was marked "Spanish," but we were not sure at this point.

However, at conventional chairs in the middle of the room, a dozen students were doing exercises in workbooks from what appeared to be standard texts, and the texts were in Spanish. It did seem to be a Spanish class at that. In the back of the large room (with several posters of Madrid and Barcelona and maps of Iberia), three girls were dancing the samba to a phonograph record. And four boys were watching (or *studying*) them. The room was "progressive" enough, and there were signs of learning and vitality in the classroom.

To find out what was going on, we asked a girl at the table if she was catching up on a social studies assignment. She explained that it was a Spanish assignment and that the students wanted to study the country, the people, and the institutions as well as the language. They knew that Spain was a dictatorship under General Franco, and this made it difficult to obtain "real" information. They got two kinds of stories: government pamphlets that made everything rosy and reports from enemies of the dictatorship who saw nothing good in the country. Because none of the students had been to Spain, they needed to learn how to get at the facts behind the biased materials, thus the study of the materials we noted when we first entered the room. As she spoke, the other students nodded their agreement.

But what about those girls dancing and the boys watching? We wandered back to the group. "Got all your work done and killing time?" we asked one of the boys. He smiled and shook his head but was shy. Another boy slid over to talk. "Wonder what this is about?" he asked. "Well," he said, "we're having a school party in a couple of weeks. Big Latin American dance. A lot of us don't know how to dance these dances. So, our teacher says it's logical to learn them here because Latin America and its dances are all kind of Spanish. I guess that makes sense." And it does!

As a perennial classroom observer, we wish that we could report more that made equal sense.

Commentary: Toward Intelligent Procedures

The main job of education is to enhance intelligence. But it should be apparent that this comment is not intended as a concession to reactionary views on the function of the school.

Education must operate from a modernized view of intelligence. The archaic view that mind is a muscle to be trained, exercised, and developed needs no further discussion here. Yet, the vocabulary of faculty psychology does persist, and sometimes one suspects that the concepts linger in some academic circles. However, it is unfortunate that members of these groups often hold the reins of educational policy-making.

The quasi-scientific view of intelligence that rose with the mental-testing movement is more recent, more sanctified by the apparatus of statistics, and dies even harder. The almost unchallenged view in the 1920s asserted that the individual possessed a native intelligence which was measurable, immutable, and was a primary and reliable predictor of academic success in terms of its measured outcome, the I.Q. It did sometimes identify academic talent, but it also led to invidious judgments, overconfident categorization of students, an abortive rash of ability-grouping experiments, and a tendency to sidetrack methodological inquiries away from motivation and conceptualization.

The modern view of intelligence is complex and eclectic. Intelligence is personal, social, cultural, methodological, and functional. The following generalizations comprise the context of a viable view of intelligence in the educational sense:

1. The hereditary aspect of intelligence, barring clearly established congenital defects, is quite ambiguous except in the generic sense (see the second generalization). The degree of native intelligence measured by so-called intelligence tests is an unknown and may range from negligible to considerable.

2. The human child inherits human intelligence. Even when his personal score on measurements in vogue at the time is at lower limits, his human intelligence is unique. A dull person thinks far better than the most intelligent representative of any other species. Therefore, humanity does have native intelligence. In its most significant sense this means it inherits the mind of the species.

3. The personal intelligence, in the measurable sense, is mutable. It may increase or decrease with changes in method of instruction, motivation, environment, or cultural opportunity.

4. The qualities measured are culturally affected as well as the measuring instruments. Cultural deprivation appears to limit intellectual capacity or the ability to use the mind.

5. Intelligence is situational. A person who functions intelligently in an area where his experience is clearly related to the problem may appear to be or may actually be unintelligent in a situation where he is insecure.

6. Intelligence is social. It is, of course, personal, but it is not solely that. Intelligence varies with its associations. Man's heritage affects his intelligence.

7. Intelligence is procedural. Regardless of its potential, the raw intellect is relatively helpless in many enterprises until methods are learned. With method, the instructed, ordinary mind can create marvels, build bridges, and indeed move mountains. Out of methodological frustration, native genius without technique may give humanity nothing more than an advertising campaign for a product nobody needs.

Learning is a basic human procedure that the human is prepared to undertake. If learning is to proceed intelligently, it must respect the method of intelligence, and it must utilize a broadly conceptualized view of intelligence. The procedures of curriculum change must be similarly grounded.

Curriculum change is a process of professionalized learning. It is to procedure in this context that we now direct our discussion.

Chapter V

Procedural Bases for Curriculum Improvement

> Sir, while you are arguing which of two things to teach a boy first, another lad has learned them both.
>
> —*Samuel Johnson*

Curriculum development is a form of social process. Like any other social change, it has its own political science. Yet curriculum change has a unique quality; its decisions are not simply the result of tugging and hauling among vested groups. Curriculum is the program of the school and the school is an agency of inquiry and enlightenment—its natural abode and its roots are in the world of scholarship and research. Thus, to an unusual degree, curriculum change is rooted in objectivity; it can be although is not always beyond various conflicts of power forces and personal ambitions.

To posit curriculum improvement assumes criticism; the approach to sound procedure is also by way of criticism. To distinguish between two species of educational criticism is essential. A rhetorical distinction has been drawn by defensive and beleaguered educationists between so-called responsible and irresponsible critics.

145

The distinction is sometimes drawn on the basis of qualifications: thus, admirals and journalists who offend are termed irresponsible, while college presidents and journalists who please are responsible. "Qualification" itself becomes a somewhat flexible term. Similarly, credentials have shifting market value. Thus, when Dr. James Conant (whose academic pedigree is impressive) speaks well of the comprehensive school, he is praised as "qualified" in some quarters; when he demonstrates his capacity for mortal error in his views of teacher education, his credentials somehow depreciate.

The distinction relates to substantive analysis, not to motivational research or a check of references. Thus, a man is responsible if he takes his stance and signs his name; he is qualified if he manages to make sense.

Responsible critics, including Admiral Hyman Rickover and James Koerner, have assailed the schools on the grounds of academic softness and intellectual incompetence. They have forthrightly challenged certain basic premises of American public education in favor of selective, intellectually aristocratic European models. They have not been sophisticated, but they have been responsible; they have signed their names to their assertions. They have not bothered to inform themselves particularly well, but they are in a way qualified: They argue with some skill. These critics attack the schools in behalf of intellectual excellence, academic standards, and national policy. For them the culprit is the "Establishment," which means roughly anyone ever on the payroll of public education. Though responsible, these men are often imprecise.

Other critics, also responsible, find fault with the school in many of the same areas that are most satisfactory to others. This group is represented by Raymond Callahan, Paul Goodman, and Edgar Friedenburg. As to credentials, they are both in and out of the field of education. They all deplore formalism, bureaucracy, depersonalization, conformity, narrowly defined efficiency, and sterility in the school. They believe in education but not in institutional rigamarole. They criticize the school on behalf of the child, the human person. They support his universal claim to dignity, his acceptance, and his development. They want to personalize the school, infuse it with creativity, refresh its atmosphere, expose its absurdities, and vivify its program. Their criticism is most functional to the development of curriculum theory.

Strange Modes of Change

The operational definition of a given school, the attitudes and policies of its board, and the theories and practices of its administration greatly influence the course of curriculum change. There are many modes of school operation—democracy, oligarchy, political ingroup, nineteenth-century "schoolmaster," administrative tyranny (including the benign manipulator), and dictatorship. There are also several modes within the definably democratic, the most sophisticated of which may be called the "democratic-scholarly."

The criteria used here for patterns of curriculum change are essentially pragmatic. High-blown premises in the context of inadequate or devious mechanisms are held suspect. The goals for better learning programs constitute no justification for corrupted means. Unless means and ends are truly independent, improvement in the school's operation can scarcely result from such strange patterns of curriculum change as those discussed below.

Sugar-coated conspiracy. A well-intended elite group in a school system may wish to reform the curriculum. The group might hold any educational bias, from a hard core of basic education to a Teachers College–Harvard evangelistic creed. Such a group might be convinced of its superior virtue, distrust what they determine are the unprofessional attitudes of *most* of their colleagues, and espouse verbal concessions to democracy but distrust majority rule or open process. Such a group might enjoy close connections with top administration or might even be its active agent. If not, their first step will necessarily be to conspire against the administration, then discredit it, and finally try to replace it with their own man.

These are essentially the steps in a revolutionary process. As in history, they are often a product of past abuses, high-minded (if

147

smug) good intentions, and personal ambitions. The process is full of hazards, inviting opportunists and idealists alike. On the record, it leaves great damage in its wake, is vindictive on accession to power, and is often disappointing in the degree of reform achieved. Not always, but more than once in history, the consequence of revolution has been retrogression. The steps of the process (though not so orderly as on paper) usually follow a pattern:

Frustration factors exist. These may derive from administrative abuses, "status quoism," restrictive working conditions, discontent with majority rule, delayed ambitions, or balked evangelism.

Dissidence develops. Dissident individuals begin to associate: first, to share grievances; eventually, to make plans.

Dissidence makes a platform. The avowed goals will be high-minded and will be entrusted to the idealistic. Meanwhile the power seekers will be charting tables of organization, making promises, and establishing alliances.

Strength is shown. Conspiracy prefers that this phase be as brief and as dramatic as possible (and, incidentally, nonprovocative). It likes the lightning stroke, the coup d'état. It does not like the long siege of struggle or open political debate. Any struggle or debate changes the nature of the conspiracy, subjects it to scrutiny, analyzes its motives, and forces it to justify itself. Conspiracy prefers to deal with its adversaries either before they are armed or after they have been disarmed. The administrative-faculty minority seeking to effect change in this manner may stun the majority with an elaborate plan, bulwarked with charts and visual aids and flashily rationalized with catch phrases and quotations from authority. Before critical studies can be made, before an opposition can unite, a school may be confronted with a *fait accompli.*

Power is consolidated. Sometimes, though fortunately only figuratively in school conspiracies, "heads roll." Adequate colleagues who are nonpartisan in behavior are reassured. Former leaders are shorn of functions, psychologically manipulated, and edged out. Idealists and opportunists vie briefly over the next steps; soon the idealists are writing lesson plans or are resigning in disillusionment.

After all this, life goes on. The results of this "upheaval" are a few new faces in the offices, new slogans on bulletin boards, maybe a new building to celebrate progress, but in classic terms, the peasants still find life hard—in our case, the students still find school uninspiring.

The public relations approach. Modern society has developed a smooth alternative to the choice between reasoned action or the exercise of power. It is not so much new as perfected in our time and is bulwarked both by psychological wizardry and new media. It is the so-called Madison Avenue approach; its ways are well known to con men everywhere and are those in which Machiavelli instructed his Prince.

Like political reform, curriculum change is often the instrument of the big-time operator in office. Such an operator knows the value of associating with present emotions, self-evident propositions, popular current catch phrases, powerful friends with open purses, and newsworthy enterprises. An operator of this ilk in education would not have any difficulty in associating himself with these propositions:

> *Present emotions.* Express awareness of the communist challenge, express confidence in America, play on insecurities and fears, raise hopes, promise expanded services and new economies.
>
> *Self-evident propositions.* Stress the fact that education can be improved. It must change or fall behind. Education is everybody's business.
>
> *Popular current catch phrases.* We need bold new programs, quality education, early identification for one group or another, research, team teaching, excellent, education for the gifted.
>
> *Powerful friend with open purse.* One grant is worth a thousand concepts (too often the new American educational proverb).
>
> *Newsworthy enterprises.* The question here is: What kind of accomplishments are making the headlines in a school district?

What is wrong with this approach? Is this not the way that things get done in our age? The point is that this is how the big-time operator uses institutions to further his own career and to keep

149

the public from closely scrutinizing the actual state of the institution to which he supposedly owes commitment. This is how the appearance of getting things done is created, not how things actually get done. Much deterioration is taking place in American schools today because of this approach, and slick operational devices are much more common than substantive changes in curriculum and method. Many school systems are more concerned with press releases and brochures that detail triumphs than with education in the classroom.

Exterior imposition. The sources of exterior imposition on curriculum are numerous. Included are legislative fiats, college admission requirements, pressure groups, and special interests. Legislative requirements especially affect the area of social studies and often include mandatory teaching of American government and history as well as state and local history. Pennsylvania, for instance, requires Pennsylvania history, American history, and world cultures, and thirty-six clock hours of economics. The usual effect of such mandates is to assure a jerry-built program.

Some actual or attempted exterior imposition is sophisticated and even enjoys quasi-legitimacy. One example of an organization with a "message" for education is the Joint Council on Economic Education. It directs its efforts to improve economic literacy through the schools. It works scrupulously to maintain respect for professional channels of communication. It enlists both scholars and methodologists. Its instruments, workshops, resource units and consultant services are professionally reputable and well conceived. It avoids the doctrinaire by the discipline of scholarship and by having all organizational and interest-group viewpoints of any reasonably defined relevance represented on its councils and its programs. In a field where many attempted impositions *are* doctrinaire and propagandistic, the Joint Council's relative objectivity and responsibility are both refreshing and fortunate.

Free but sponsored materials represent a powerful attempt at imposition. Those teachers who do not know their hazards should not use them at all, and should never use them textually. Basic

150

instructional materials should go through the processes of scholarship, publication, and criticism. However, sponsored materials do have their uses: They may be useful in explaining technical processes in a given industry; they may be useful as examples of points of view; they may even be useful as raw material for critical thinking or propaganda analysis. They are not texts and should never be accepted as such.

The efforts of the well-intentioned, the zealots, and the superpatriots to advance their causes through the schools are perfectly legitimate on their part. But the school would be acting foolishly and irresponsibly to allow them a disproportionate share of time, to be intimidated, or to let them in the back door. When the processes of curriculum building are regularized and professional, all viewpoints may be given audience, and the student can learn to think critically.

If the foregoing modes of curriculum building seem strange in at least some respects, what constitutes sounder procedures? The first great resource for building a better curriculum should be the professionalization of the teaching occupation in a fundamental rather than a rhetorical sense.

Scholarship and Professionalism

With respect to working conditions, teaching is most highly professionalized at the college level. The classic though not universal model is that of the "scholar–teacher." The scholar–teacher is selected for competence in his field; it is then assumed (perhaps too blithely) that by virtue of his competence he is also endowed with great teaching ability. Within his teaching assignment, which is somewhat tailor-made to his interests and competence, he is master of many decisions. He develops his course outlines; chooses one or more texts, or no text; assigns readings, projects, and inquiries; devises tests; establishes criteria for evaluation. He is officed rather privately, though not necessarily handsomely. Beyond meeting his

151

classes, his comings and goings are not dictated by a school bell, but by his professional obligations, his committee assignments, and his sense of responsibility.

In the main, the college professor is treated as an adult and as a responsible professional. He moves about in a grown-up world and generally converses and relaxes with colleagues without apprehension of supervisory or administrative scrutiny. Should *he* be caught reading, it is regarded either as matter of course or as a point in his favor; reading is a legitimate aspect of his work. Should he be observed with feet up, staring into space, he is presumed (at least by professional courtesy) to be thinking. Unless he is working as an intern, in a probationary status, or has requested observation, he is likely to be unsupervised, and any supervision will be constrained to avoid presumption.

His freedom of inquiry and of teaching are protected by deeply established traditions and formidable conventions of academic freedom. These are buttressed by an effective organization of his own making, the American Association of University Professors. Exceptions occur but are not too frequent. Nor is the use of the term "professional" or reiterated claims to "professionalism" prevalent in his vocabulary.

A familiar story tells of an alumnus who returned to his campus twenty years after graduation and called upon a former professor. During his visit he picked up a copy of an examination, perused it, and remarked, "I see, Professor, that you are still giving the same old examination in your course."

"Quite so," returned his erstwhile mentor, "however, the answers are different nowadays."

Curriculum revision as a consequence of scholarship is consistent and continuous. The scholar–teacher is expected to "keep up with his field." He does this by reading the journals and quarterlies in his field, by attending meetings of learned societies to which he belongs, by conversations with his colleagues, and by his own research. A normal curve of dedication to the pattern naturally exists, but this again is the central tendency.

Consider, on the other hand, the normal pattern of the schoolteacher's life. He hears and talks a good deal about the "profession." His largest professional obligation, based on the volume of words and pressures as evidence, is to keep his dues paid to the National Education Association (NEA) and to its state and local affiliates. But what is the job behavior of the so-called professional teacher?

The schoolteacher is, generally, job-bound by the school bell, the schedule, and the expectations he places upon his students. His professionalism in reality is only the result of the public relations material fed the public by his organization and his administrative officers. When the model of the responsible scholar–teacher is pointed out to administrators as one to be emulated, the common response is: "I wish we could make these assumptions and provide similar circumstances, but we cannot. That's just not the way our teachers are. They are not adequately prepared. They are too irresponsible. We just couldn't run a school that way."

The teacher then lives on the job something like this: He reports for work a half-hour before the tardy bell; when late, he is checked on and reproved for tardiness in the same fashion as his students are. Punctuality is high among the "values" sought in public education, and teachers are not exempted from its discipline. The elementary schoolteacher is often a virtual prisoner of the self-contained classroom. Should the high-school teacher begin his day with a "free" period, and should it be his regular habit to read from 9 P.M. to 1 A.M. each evening, it would not be a legitimate excuse for arriving ten minutes late more than once. "Can't make exceptions—bad for professional morale, you know."

If the school day consists of seven periods, the high-school teacher will have five classes, a homeroom or supervisory responsibility, a free period, and twenty or thirty minutes for lunch. The teacher may smoke in designated places during his free period while gossiping or snoozing among colleagues. Browsing in the library is not common to the culture; grading papers and attending to class registers are. Carrying student exercises during intermissions and especially on errands to the office is almost as effective against being perceived as frivolous as is wearing a worried look, something which teachers often manage without unduly taxing their thespian talents.

In rare instances a couple of teachers might leave the school on "free time" to have coffee at a local diner with some neighborhood businessmen. This would be remarkable and would be remarked upon. The teacher is not yet allowed to live as an adult; he is disciplined, scheduled, given assignments, supervised, and generally treated as one "who goes to school."

To what extent is the teacher's teaching even his own? Assume that the teacher is qualified, certified, holds a strong undergraduate major in his teaching field, has a Master's degree in the same subject, and has several years of successful teaching in his field. Assume further that he has paid his National Education Association dues, belongs to a subject-area affiliate, and is well read. Predictably, his qualifications will considerably exceed his prerogatives. His textbooks will be selected for him, with or without his advice; when chosen for him, he will not often now neglect their use. His assignments will include close roll-taking, prescribed patterns of testing and appraisal, and enforced formulas to derive grades. He will often be expected to provide evidence of his diligence by submitting daily lesson plans for inspection.

The larger the school (and the trend is constantly growing), the greater is the likelihood that there will be a ready-made course of study. This is a complete prospectus for a course, and includes subject-matter outlines, suggested or prescribed "activities," and time allotments for topics—often broken down as far as daily assignments. Where does the course of study come from? It usually descends from a committee of which the teacher is most often not a member. He may or may not respect its competence. A majority of its members may have credentials of competence in the field equivalent to his own, but often this is not the case. Or it may be an exterior imposition, inherited from labors of colleagues once revered, now retired. In highly organized systems, it may represent a gesture of bureaucratic largesse or a feat of supererogation performed by the experts of the board of education's curriculum division.

What is the teacher's *real* condition? To come to the existential sense of the matter, the teacher is an employee, either politely treated or gently disdained, hemmed in by restrictions, straitjacketed as to initiative and creativity, deprived of motivation for scholarship and curriculum building, and badgered by supervision that makes a travesty of the common talk about professionalism.

On Supervision

Other professionals are not supervised in any manner, degree, or kind comparable to the supervision of teachers. It is not a matter of *good* or *bad* supervision, nor of supervision masquerading under such euphemisms as "friendly visitor," or "big brother," or "teacher's helper." The simple fact is that teachers are *supervised* throughout their careers. We do not mean to imply that student teaching, or internships, or preprofessional probationary teaching should not be supervised, however prolonged. Let teacher education and school administration make the period of preparation, under supervision, as long as they deem essential, but sooner or later it must be decided whether or not the prospective teacher *is* a professional. At that time he must be treated as such; this means the removal of supervision.

Note that we are criticizing supervision only as a professional function. We are not attacking supervision as an instrument of teacher education, whether in student teaching, internships, or probationary teaching situations, where the only needed strictures are assurances of its educational soundness. Supervision can only contribute to growth toward professionalism under controlled conditions. Laissez-faire arrangements in any school with any critic teacher only frustrate the idealistic young teacher. The net result is to weigh the new teacher down in the accumulated frustrations of the mediocre. Teachers in preparation must be deeply grounded in the historical and social realities of their enterprise; they must be inducted early into real professional consciousness. They must be supervised in the full human dimension. This means that rapport, warmth, and communicativeness must supersede the devices, techniques, and pretensions of the clinical. Above all, teacher preparation must operate under sound theoretical models and be exercised

155

in situations either rigorously selected or arranged to carry the models into practice.

Supervision, then, is justifiable as teaching. The teacher of teachers must be able both to teach and to do. In one high school a B-squad was coached by a man from the Ozarks whose standard comment was: "If yuh cain't do it, ah'll show yuh haow." He could and did. The B-squad challenged the varsity, beat them 42–14, and four of their members immediately joined the varsity team. That is the kind of competence teachers of teachers, supervisors, ought to have. When students say they cannot do something, the teacher must be able to say, "I'll show you how." And if they cannot, what are they doing in their jobs?

Supervision and professionalism are incompatible. The professional is educated for his task and practiced in it. He has been examined by his masters and licensed. He knows his tools and how to choose them. He has learned discipline and humility as elements of his training. Better than anyone, he is aware of his limitations; he knows when he needs assistance and where to find it. The professional does *not* scorn help or consultation; he simply wants such help to be helpful. He avoids presumptuous advice giving or officious, bureaucratic job justification. The professional, be he doctor, lawyer, dentist, or the truly professional teacher, knows where to go when the demands of his task exceed his skills or knowledge: to books, to seek out his old masters, or to call upon distinguished colleagues.

Our assumption is that teaching *can* be professionalized, that teachers *can* be professionals. They will not become so by paying regular dues to the best-intentioned of occupational lodges. *The professional proves himself by doing an expert job on his own responsibility, with his reputation ever at stake.* To do such a job is both a joy and a burden. But if the majority of administrators and supervisors will not accept this criterion, what can be made of teaching?

Much false rhetoric has been spent in the debate over the institutional image of the teacher. The case of the so-called professional (the NEA member) as against the trade unionist (American Federation of Teachers member) has been argued ad infinitum and to varied conclusions among teachers, as witnessed by the New York City and Denver bargaining-agent elections in the mid-1960s. But the present condition and the growing direction of teaching as an occupation is toward neither of them; it is toward the civil service pattern.

The Civil Service Image

A civil service status is a decent social achievement and would represent substantial gains in security and perhaps repute for the teaching occupation. And while civil service status is not professional status, it is civil service gains that are most often sought under the misused appellation of professional by most teacher organizations (regardless of their organizational bias). And it is civil service attributes that are sought, prized, and rewarded in teachers. Finally, it is as civil servants that teachers are supervised.

Because the term is so confused in common usage, we reiterate that *the real professional proves himself on the job on his own.* The medical doctor does not prove himself as a professional by joining the American Medical Association (or by refusing to join), or by public relations campaigns, or by the scale of his fees. He proves himself in the sickroom or operating room, in the personally responsible exercise of his training, skill, knowledge, and competence within the discipline of his ethical code. So, too, the teacher proves his professionalism in the classroom. *Merely being there is not the proof.*

Teachers' concerns with civil service preoccupations are legitimate. Improved conditions of employment, equitable tenure codes, retirement plans, hospitalization, and fringe benefits are some of an employee's job rights in any well-managed organization in an affluent society. This is the American way. Curriculum improvement, however, is a job for *professionals,* for people who know what they are doing.

Civil service is well adapted to perform public chores, but civil service is self-perpetuating, not self-re-creating. Curriculum change

157

must build from the latter quality. Curriculum change demands experimentation, creativity, initiative, self-confidence, daring, and responsibility. Unfortunately, these are not virtues usually associated with civil service. The virtue of civil service is to carry out the public's assignments punctually, methodically, and effectively. As in the organizational world, there are also certain inner dynamics of empire building, aggrandizement, form without function, as witness *Parkinson's law*. School administrators and supervisors often seem to hold that the school's task is the same.

If the teacher *is* professional, in all likelihood only a colleague in his field is in any position to be helpful, and even the best supervision from anyone else will probably not be helpful. Not all teachers perceive the case this way, but most do, despite the barrage of propaganda to which they often have been subjected. Supervisors can rate or reward, but not on professional grounds unless they have knowledge of the specialized field.

Civil service merit derives from observance of form and punctilio, loyalty, subservience to superiors, selflessness in terms of giving higher echelons credit for any accomplishments or innovations, good posture, neat desks, tasteful, unostentatious and conventional dress, unassuming, unassertive speech and bearing, outward appreciation for suggestions (however irrelevant), uncritical attitude toward any organizational policy, restrained views on all public matters, avoidance of raising issues or suggesting troublesome procedural changes, and faceless courtesy to all guests.

To these merits, the good civil servant adds virtues of his own: ridding frustration through gossip; always avoiding the appearance of idleness; always having an escape hatch from responsibility; always having a scapegoat if anything goes wrong; and always evincing a tender, legalistic concern for all of his benefits and job rights. Are not these elements of "merit" what administrators and supervisors really seek in teachers? And are not the faults of teachers, of which they complain, more or less the consequence of being cast in the role of civil servants rather than the autonomous and responsible role of professionals?

True teaching professionalization is at the core of the matter in the school's re-creation of the basic essence of curriculum development. Our concerns here are naturally for administrators and supervisors, but more importantly, for teachers.

Sources of Coherence and Order

Foreign visitors are often skeptical of constructive consequences from local and state control of education. They expect chaos and confusion as major outcomes from an absence of central authority and control. For our purposes, it is important to distinguish between coherence and uniformity in this context.

First, we must note the degree of centralized authority that does exist within the American educational system. For example, the New York City Board of Education, under a tight hierarchical authority, controls more students, more teachers, more schools, and a vastly larger educational budget than many national systems, which are considered highly centralized. Thus, at close hand, American education can observe the efficiencies and corrosions of centralism not merely in New York City but also in other major American cities.

The United States Office of Education is not a ministry of education. However, since 1950 it has left its simple fact-gathering function behind. It now administers significant, far-reaching programs. Its controls have remained minimal, but its influence on American education is far more consequential than it was before World War II.

As a matter of fact, there are many forces working toward coherence in the American school, though not toward uniformity. A school in Bangor, Maine, is more likely to resemble a school in Ventura, California, than to differ from it. The schools of New York, St. Louis, Denver, Des Moines, Tipton (Iowa), and Butler (Pennsylvania) all differ, but students who transfer from one to another recognize the basic similarity of one school to another. How may this be accounted for? Numerous forces bear on this consistency.

159

The federal government. In several important areas the federal government enters directly into the process of curriculum development—vocational education, "subsidies" for science education, foreign languages, guidance programs, and grants for educational research.

Long-established precedents for teamwork exist in the field of vocational education. The increase of industry and technology, the extension of secondary education for all children, the needs of urban youth, and dedicated leadership led to rapid growth of the vocational-education movement in the early twentieth century. During Woodrow Wilson's administration the first major federal aid to education since the original Morrill Act was enacted—the Smith-Hughes Act of 1917.

This law gave direct federal aid to programs of vocational education; it left local control intact in some particulars, but it did make stipulations in other areas and somewhat control them. Local school authorities could decide whether or not to have such programs. When they sought to establish Smith-Hughes programs in vocational agriculture and home economics, for example, they retained certain local prerogatives. While they could hire and fire teachers on customary local bases, teachers' qualifications were mandated. The local school board could not hire a history major with a farm background as an agricultural specialist under the act on the grounds that he could milk and pitch hay as well as the next man. Nor could they hire a woman to teach home economics on the grounds that she sewed well or baked pies that took blue ribbons at the county fair. Graduation from certified four-year college programs in these fields was required; in certain technical fields practical experience plus collegiate training was accredited. The local district received Smith-Hughes support (up to half the program costs) only through compliance with certain high standards of space and equipment. An ice box, a used sewing machine, and a gas plate would not suffice for a home economics facility. Thus significant programs of federal aid in which local and federal controls operate together have been successfully conducted in American schools since the act was passed.

The National Defense Education Act of 1957 directly influenced curriculum by subsidized favor toward certain areas of instruction. It exerted influence with a less defensible rationale and was partly a product of Sputnik. The word "defense" in the title was both a cynical device to gain Congressional support and a description of some of the program intent. Direct favoritism to science education, foreign languages, and guidance programs was a feature of the act. This is not to say that money in these areas is wasted. Training institutes and support of graduate study as direct subsidies to teachers were a part of the program, but for the most part, teachers of English, history, and the arts, among others, continued to pay their own summer school tuition. In the schools, English and social studies teachers sometimes expressed thoughts less than enthusiastic when their minor fund requests for books, maps, and globes were vetoed while a language lab costing thousands of dollars was being installed. Interest in the advancing technology of the audio-visual movement found concrete support under Title VII of the act. As a result of aroused opinion among neglected areas, other fields have been added to the subsidy list.

Research programs by their emphases have drawn curriculum in certain bandwagon directions, along with more constructive results. Federal programs have tended to direct educational attention from the substantive concern to the instruments of education. It is easier to design tests of the uses of tools and instruments than to blueprint more complex substantive studies. Instructional television, teaching machines, gadgets, and organizational gambits have been studied well past the point of diminishing returns. Research on sophisticated methodologies and complicated conceptualizations demands rather too much ingenuity in design or exceeds the educational competence of the current crop of educational researchers. Thus, research may serve to divert attention from primary educational problems.

The textbook publishing business. Textbook publishing is a free competitive enterprise that rather closely resembles the model of the free market in classical economics. Many producers participate in the publishing market, and new entries into the competitive field are common. Competition is keen both for material in the form of publishable manuscripts and for sales. Competition is full-dimensional and includes price, quality, and force of persuasion. No single publisher or small group of publishers dominates the market. In an economy deeply characterized by oligopoly (domination of the market by a few producers), the highly competitive textbook industry is deeply responsive to the demands of the consumer. It is, therefore, peculiarly motivated toward quality control and careful study of the needs of its customers, namely, the schools.

The textbook market is preeminently national and in rare instances, international. Of course, such textbooks as those on Pennsylvania geography or Texas history have a circumscribed sale, and regional publishers do exist, particularly for the southern market.

Textbook publication is important business in dollars and cents too, though not big business in the sense of steel or automobiles. But major adoptions of schoolbooks, especially state-wide adoptions (of which there are some instances) mean large money by any criteria. The publisher is in business to make money, and sometimes commerce does override other considerations. However, it is wrong to assume that commercial motivations necessarily corrupt or vulgarize the trade.

The alternative to profit-seeking for a publisher is nonprofit-seeking. This sounds high-minded and is—in some fields. But if books are to be produced without profit, who will assume the undertaking? Presumably an agency of the state, perhaps a ministry of education, will do the job. This is not unknown: textbook publication is not a competitive profit-seeking enterprise everywhere. In such a "market" what is lost? Nothing more or less than the free market in ideas is at stake. Not all officially sponsored texts are venal, but they tend to be dull. Why produce alternative or competitive texts when it is possible to develop an authoritative "best" volume? Besides, alternative texts are expensive, and nonprofit ventures must by definition seek economy. But if not universal, venality is not uncommon. Not only is the officially sponsored text found in totalitarian educational systems, but it *is the only text* found in such schools. Neither the diminished quality and attendant dullness nor the opportunity for official censorship seem worth inviting.

The American textbook industry is not beyond reproach or error. We will point out certain vulnerabilities in the context of the large consonance between its aims and the function of education in a free society. Finally, the process of developing textbooks is the deepest assurance of this common purpose.

Customers for the publishers' products are presumably highly educated to their own needs. They are presumably professional in judgment of texts on these two basic scores: scholarly content and teachability. Presumably, this sound knowledge and educated judgment renders them sales resistant to the irrelevant. In brief, basically, where competitive free enterprise produces books for profit, the ultimate control of content lies in the hands of the users—in this case, the buyers. This is precisely what cannot happen when texts are produced without profit by the state.

To launch a text is a risk-taking entrepreneurial venture. A publisher could engage a literary hack to cut, paste, and put together a cheap, quick book and offer it for sale. If it won a large portion of the market, presumably it had been a good job, for it is assumed that the customers are competent to judge. Such a risk seems not worth the taking, however, as there seem to be no apparent illustrations. The text is offered to a critical potential market; it is offered in the company of numerous competitive works. But furthermore, the institution of the marketplace is bolstered by the institution of criticism.

The textbook business resides not merely in the marketplace but also in the world of scholarship and in the forum of ideas. The basic institutions of free speech and free press are made viable through criticism. If the customer—a high-school teacher in Sheldon, Illinois, a school administrator in Richmond, Virginia, or a textbook committee in Denver—withholds purchase until a few months after entry of a new text, he may be able to base his judgment upon study of published criticism. In various journals he will find reviews that scrutinize the book as to its scholarship, or its value as a methodological aid, its teachability, its biases and omissions, or even its aesthetics. The criticism will not always be objective or even competent; but it will be open, and like the book itself, will be open to countercriticism.

When considering a manuscript for publication, the publisher is prudent, even cautious, not to say scared. He has immediate profit to consider and a long-term reputation to maintain. The risks to both of attempting to market an incompetent product to a competent and critical public are sobering.

The publisher will naturally study the market as all purveyors do, and the characteristics of what is selling will influence him. Some of these characteristics, fads of design and illustration, will be less than fundamental to academic quality. If extraneous elements seem to sell books, it must be remembered who is buying them. The publisher assumes that his potential audience is intelligent and professional, and he makes his heaviest bet on this fact. He seeks scholarly competence, not merely in terms of name and title window-dressing. In an elementary reading series, in a sociology book, in a high-school physics text, the publisher knows his most formidable sales persuasion will be to establish the fact that his offering stands closest in its report to the best and most recent research in the field and that it is geared to high utility for the level of intended students.

Most American textbooks are attractive as a by-product of our sophistication in packaging and of our affluence. It makes our books enviable and admired around the world. Grounded by thirty years of critical and sometimes exasperated use of texts as well as much acquaintance among publishers and their agents, the author has had a rich opportunity for comparative education in this field. In 1950 we served as a member of the United States delegation to a UNESCO seminar in Brussels whose subject was the improvement of textbooks. After this intercultural exploration, we have felt better about the way American schools get their books.

However, content is what responsible publishers seek. Textbook teams are chosen to provide diverse strengths in scholarship, methodology, and usability. The manuscripts are screened and reviewed ahead of publication. And always in mind is the fact of competition.

Do commerce and caution lead to error? Of course they do, but publishers print the books that the schools buy. If the schools resist the pressures of anti-intellectual vigilantism and vested-interest coercions, they will find good allies among publishers as well as the American Library Association. However, the school must assume responsibility for protection of its freedom at home and can count on the press to support basic freedom. It is not that all publishers or schoolmen are heroic but that the process is sound.

An example will clarify our point. In 1950 a major textbook publisher refused a manuscript on the problems of democracy because its writers gave direct and explicit attention to questions of human rights. But the publisher did not feel there was an adequate market in 1950. The miscalculation cost the publisher two good authors, and the subsequent lag of his texts behind the spirit of his times cost him not merely at the point of principle but of profit as well. Social taboos affect publication, to be sure, but these originate in neighborhoods and communities much more frequently than in the corridors of power or in publishers' offices. The worst these fallible mortals do is to guess wrong on occasion. Errors do pile up. When the pile of errors gets high enough, an author makes a book of it, a publisher takes a flier on it, and sometimes a fair best-seller results.

Professional organizations. In 1968 the National Education Association and the American Federation of Teachers, with about 1.08 million and 150,000 members respectively, help the education force maintain a loose semblance of professional affiliation.

Local and state control of curriculum could theoretically mean thousands of curricula taking utterly maverick and localistic directions. Professional organization provides one reason that they do not. Affiliates of teachers around professional functions are legion. Among them are the National Council for Social Studies, the Music Educators National Conference, the National Science Teachers Association, the National Council of Teachers of Mathematics, all of which are within the NEA family, and the National Council of Teachers of English, which is not.

165

The particular contributions of these and other associations are considerable. Procedurally, they are important in identifying, developing, and exercising leadership in their fields; they provide national communication and intercourse through meetings and publications; and they develop and publicize new departures in content and method. They also attempt to bring teachers at the school level together with college teachers and research scholars, with varying degrees of success. (The National Council of Teachers of English has been more than ordinarily successful in this liaison role.)

The scope of these teacher organizations has been enhanced in recent years. The National Council for the Social Studies has enjoyed its closest relationships with historians. Joint efforts with the American Historical Association have produced a series of historical resource units for teachers, though the common effort has not by any means silenced the attacks of historians on "the social studies movement." The National Council for the Social Studies has also linked efforts with the American Council of Learned Societies.

The life of any curriculum specialist is difficult. Intrinsically, the burden of assumption is heavy. The demands of a scholarship in breadth strain one's mortal capacity. An extrinsic hardship is the vantage point afforded on the internecine struggles and parochial warfares among members of the academic community. If the humanizing impact of education were real, one would expect this community to be disciplined largely by magnanimity and objectivity; instead, vindictiveness and subjectivity often shock the viewer or participant. To remain serene and effective, one must, of course, perceive the ferment as the result of diverse phenomenologies of decent but involved men. (The numerous novels of C. P. Snow are a large help in attaining and holding this perspective, especially *The Search, The Masters,* and *The Affair.*)

Direct efforts of scholarly or scientific groups to affect the curriculum from the perspective of advanced research and substance are also now becoming common. Such bodies as the University of Illinois Committee on School Mathematics, the School Mathematics Study Group, the Biological Sciences Curriculum Study, and the

Physical Science Study Committee have been created for this purpose.

Surveys and consultants. The school survey is a resource for bringing individual schools into harmony with general good practice. It is also an established method of appraisal and direction finding. Its primary assets are the involvement of expert judgment, the utilization of objective instruments, the detachment of the critical point of view, the advantage of outside perspective, and the immunity from community pressure.

These assets can be put to good use, if the following conditions are obtained: (1) the school survey team is competent and candid; (2) the invitation to conduct the survey is deeply rooted in a consensus of need among the community, the faculty, the administration, and the board of education; (3) the school's involvement in the survey is deep, well-planned, and long-running; and (4) long-term follow-up and reconstruction is intrinsic to the plan. "Hit-and-run" surveys are worse than useless.

There are hazards in the survey. Commerce can affect objectivity quite subtly and perhaps even subconsciously. Surveys are often introduced for limited purposes: to condemn an administration or to whitewash it, to prove one factional claim over another, to serve political ends. A greater hazard is simply that the survey is superficial, that the team is no more than a casual group of visitors, and that the report is either mined for public relations releases or buried with other embarrassing and sometimes expensive documents.

The best study is self-study, though its force and objectivity can surely be strengthened by "outside" help. The evaluation system practiced by the Middle States Association of Schools and Colleges is a nice balance between self-study and visiting appraisal. Furthermore, the corrupting potential of the dollar is completely removed, for the survey team works on a voluntary basis out of a sense of professional commitment and obligation.

Consultants can be useful, but their engagement must be well-planned and their utilization specific. If the purpose is simply a day of moral uplift and a chance to give a distinguished guest a blurb in the local press, this is one thing. If the consultant is sought for the use of his name, presumably the only relevant inquiry is to establish his price. But, if there is work to be done, the consultant must be a worker. The consultant should outline in detail what he proposes to do and to what effect. Workers come cheaper than orators, and the value of the consultant is not in direct proportion to the size of his fee. There is also a point at which diminishing returns set in. One practice might immeasurably enhance the effective use of consultants on the school scene: when the consultant is introduced, let the amount of his fee be announced. (We would like to be present the first time that this is done!)

What Procedure Draws Upon

The basic resource for curriculum building is human experience. Experience includes but is not exclusively comprised of organized bodies of knowledge that may be designated as subjects, sciences, disciplines, and the like. Human experience may be categorized, but only with hazard to reality may it be fragmented.

As the source of potential education, human experience includes the following:

1. The humanistic–ethical
2. The creative–aesthetic
3. The scientific–quantitative
4. The vocational–utilitarian

For those who find it difficult to subsume the "religious–spiritual" within this framework, we grant that another category will be needed. The same holds for the "physical–athletic," although the Greeks included this dimension in the humanistic–ethical and modern man can see its implications in the vocational–utilitarian. In other words, a category of six can be made, but for our purposes, we will use four.

These are *not* the divisions of curriculum; neither are they simply the corresponding redesignation of the humanities, the sciences, the arts, and the practical subjects. They are the four areas of human experience, and they are also the areas of *potential human development*. (What man has been, man can be—only more so.)

Since these are not designations of curricular divisions, it is inappropriate to categorize the transient organizations of knowledge called "school subjects" under them. Human experience constitutes the scope of a complete learning experience. *Any learning situation should reach the person across the spectrum of his whole potential.* Any learning situation should draw upon what is relevant out of the whole human experience.

We do not assume that the study of literature or philosophy is designated under the humanistic–ethical rubric. Physics and chemistry are not categorized as scientific–quantitative subjects. Drawing is not listed as creative–aesthetic. The electric shop in this context is not regarded as a place for narrow vocational–utilitarian experience.

When a person studies any particular subject matter—be it drama, chemistry, guitar playing, or animal husbandry—potential learning is diminished if what is relevant from all areas of human experience is not drawn into that study. Furthermore and of graver consequence is the fact that the *learner* is diminished by any fragmented, censored, or tortured arrangement of experience which fails to nourish his total and constant human potential.

Acceptance of this concept would revolutionize the curriculum. But a practical revolution is intended, one that can be brought about by wit and perception largely within the existing framework of the subjects. It avoids war on the subjects partly on pragmatic grounds and sees no prospect that such a war might be won. Moreover, it discovers no ground of principle for moving to such an attack. The subjects become relevant when they are well taught. A new and vital conceptualization of "well taught" is offered here and includes the phrase "fully taught," and that, to be sure, gladly.

The concept is not intended as another gimmick. As with anything from orange juice to conviction, it can be reduced by zeal to an absurdity. Of course, some subjects draw upon certain areas of

169

experience more than others do or upon more areas of experience than others, and some subjects may draw most heavily on only one or two areas. Some legitimate and relevant subjects of study or inquiry may enrich most largely one or two dimensions of the human potential.

A planned learning situation must be held under suspicion when it seems to draw upon less than all areas of experience in some degree or when it fails to nurture the full potential of human development to some degree. It should be held suspect on two scores: (1) the planning of the learning may have failed to explore the full dimension of the experience resource—in other words, scholarship may have been defective, myopic, or laggard; (2) it may be less significant than something else that might be undertaken for study. Any planned learning in any subject should seek to draw upon available resources in the four areas designated as categories of human experience.

In Part Three, each area will be developed in its particulars. The point in our procedural analysis here is to suggest that any learning situation should seek to establish relevance in all areas of human experience. Figures 5.1–5.3 show some of the possibilities. Clearly there are implications for teacher education, for classroom arrangements, for scheduling, and for articulation.

Mobilization of the learning resource suggests basic questions that will be considered later: How does this concept relate to older notions of fusion and integration of subject matter? Could it be used effectively within, and perhaps to revivify, the core curriculum—or common learnings? Would team teaching be helpful or detrimental to the concept?

Commentary: The Professional Job at Hand

Figures 5.1–5.4 suggest a much broader base to instructional planning than is usually practical. If one keeps in mind the discipline of the new model (Chapter IV), it will be clear that such devices should not be asserted and clamped down upon the learning situation through unilateral teacher action. Rather, such models should be used illustratively with students in helping them to see the full range of potential in developing a learning program. When teachers use such devices in a pattern of cooperative planning, they will learn (perhaps in some amazement) that the mobilized experience and motivated curiosity of an entire class naturally far exceeds the creative efforts of the teacher alone, however ingenious he or she may be.

The process of curriculum development must derive from a viable curriculum theory founded on these elements: (1) an appraisal of academic realities, (2) historical analysis, (3) an examination of social bases, (4) the establishment of philosophical roots, (5) the derivation and application of methodology, and (6) sound procedural choices. Upon such foundations the substantive resources of human experience and scholarship may be structured into meaningful learning. We have categorized these resources as:

1. The humanistic–ethical
2. The creative–aesthetic
3. The scientific–quantitative
4. The vocational–utilitarian

Curriculum development must proceed from a program of priorities considered as first- and second-order priorities.

First-order priorities

1. A critical analysis of the reality of the school. (This is discussed in Part Two.)

2. The activation of human concern, opening of communication, clearing of channels

3. Hard work on the content–method nexus in all subjects

4. Recognition of the interdependence of cognitive and affective development

5. Development of comprehensive learning situations designed to tap the range of relevant experience and to nurture the range of the human potential

Figure 5.1

Full-Dimensioned Learning:* Case A

Subject:	Physics
Unit:	Sound
Topic:	Hi-Fidelity Reproduction

I. Scientific–Quantitative†
Antecedent resources
Nature of sound
Characteristics of elec-
tricity
Direct-bearing resources
Electronics
Mechanics of hi-fi
Vacuum tubes, transistors
Condensers
Amplification

II. Creative–Aesthetic
Music or engineering
Sound for its own sake
Hi-fidelity junk
Demonstrations:
trick sound recording,
Emperor Concerto

The Learning Situation

III. Humanistic–Ethical
History of recorded
sound
Great achievements in
recording

IV. Vocational–Utilitarian
Assembly of hi-fi set
Trouble-shooting hi-fi
assembly
Career survey
Talk by hi-fi repairman

Implications include one or more of the following: (1) unusually broad-gauge teachers, (2) common-learnings programs, and/or (3) cooperative (team) teaching.

† Primary resource field.

Figure 5.2

Full-Dimensioned Learning: Case B

> Subject: History (United States or World)
> Unit: World Tensions
> Topic: Regulation of Atomic Energy

I. *Humanistic–Ethical**

Discuss
- Decision to use the A-bomb

History
- Struggle for civilian control—the AEC
- Impasse in the United Nations
- Era of unrestricted testing

Question of human survival

Rights of the innocent

II. *Scientific–Quantitative*

Destructive capacity of the A-bomb

Destructive capacity of the H-bomb

The 100-megaton case

Scientific evidence on results of testing

The Learning Situation

III. *Creative–Aesthetic*

Literature of the atomic age
- John Hersey, *Hiroshima*
- Norman Cousins, *Modern Man Is Obsolete*
- Nevil Shute, *On the Beach*

Films
- *Dr. Strangelove*
- *Fail-Safe*
- *Hiroshima, Mon Amour*
- *On the Beach*

IV. *Vocational–Utilitarian*

Careers in
- Science
- Foreign Service
- Peace Corps
- Peace Organizations
- Religion

* Primary resource field.

Figure 5.3

Full-Dimensioned Learning: Case C

	Subject:	Social Studies (Grade 2)
	Unit:	How People Live
	Topic:	The Farm

I. *Vocational–Utilitarian**

What a farm is
What good it is
What a farmer has to do
What a farmer has to know
What a farmer's workday is like (in various seasons)
What the farm wife does
What farmers like about their work

II. *Humanistic–Ethical*

How farmers help town people
How town people help farmers

The Learning Situation

IV. *Creative–Aesthetic*

Slides and pictures of rural scenes around the world
Reproductions of paintings by Grant Wood, Benton, Curry, Corot, Millet
Observation of fine stock and produce
Planting and growing projects
Admiring and playing with young animals

III. *Scientific–Quantitative*

How big a farm is (nearby)
How much *stuff* a farmer grows
What price he gets for what he sells (local market)
What kinds of machines farmers use

* Primary resource field.

Figure 5.4

Full Dimensioned Learning: Case D

Subject: Track
Topic: Distance Running

I. *Vocational–Utilitarian**
  *Object: To Run a Good
    Race*
  Careers
    Great coaches and their
    methods
    Professional athletics

II. *Humanistic–Ethical*
  Read the "Advice of
    Epictetus to a Young
    Man Who Would Be
    an Olympic Runner"
  Discuss self-discipline and
    athletic success
  Values in competition
  How to win
  How to lose
  Successful athletes who
    overcame handicaps
  Black athletes protest
    1968 Olympics
  The democracy of
    sport

The Learning Situation

III. *Creative–Aesthetic*
  Novel and Film
    Alan Sillitoe, *The
    Loneliness of the
    Long-Distance
    Runner*
  Comic contrast
    Owen Johnston, "The
    Great Pancake
    Record"
  The Greek view of
    athletics
  Innovations and changes
    in technique

IV. *Scientific–Quantitative*
  The anatomy of
    running
  Time charting the four-
    minute mile
  Diet, training, and
    endurance

* Primary resource field.

Second-order priorities

1. An analysis of available research bearing upon institutional choice

2. A critical appraisal of established subjects with respect to their significance, relevance, and potential. (This obviously cannot be done effectively until first-order matters have been accomplished. When this is the common starting point, much "wheel-spinning" and lost motion derives from this procedural error.)

3. Methodological revolution—the development of new models of instructional practice. (We are not necessarily referring to the new model discussed here. The curricular theory of this work is intended to liberate rather than to constrict professional energy for program improvement.)

4. A disciplinary revolution with its primary dictate being maintenance consistently throughout the school and learning situations ever prevailing. (This is to be achieved with respect, through responsibility and viable democratic relationships.)

5. Replanning the working arrangements within the school

At this point, we may well summarize certain hazards to effective accomplishment. Some of these have already been set forth; others will be more explicitly exposited in Chapter XII. These hazards may be spoken of as academic millstones. Among the sources of regressive choices presently available we merely suggest the absurdity of attempting to derive learning theories for man, the most complex of creatures, from observations gained by manipulating such creatures as rats or pigeons. This source of error does not stem from the animal-learning enthusiasts' infatuation with lesser species. Rather, it is derived from mechanistic or deterministic views of man which effectively prevent adequate perception of the human being's great potential. The mechanistic view of man and life nourishes overenthusiasm for gadgets, gambits, and devices. However useful these may be in prospect, educators must be wary of the "hard sell" and the stentorian toot of the bandwagon.

Today, as never before, educators must be aware of the power of Parkinson's Law to run amok. Absurdly proliferated administrative and supervisory structures and a plethora of functionless forms are the outcome. Realism dictates that the effort must be only to hold the line. To attempt to cut back is worse than futile: open the doors to "reorganization" for whatever good purpose, even for avowed aims of "simplification," and the outcome is sure to be measured in the creation of one or two new echelons or layers of highly decorative personnel. When administrators (or guinea pigs) get together, multiplication is a predictable consequence.

Schools used as instruments of status striving, schools perceived as *instruments* of national policy, and programs dictated by vested academic interests are the conditions that stultify good institution building. Procedure is not an end in itself; procedure exists to do a job. The qualification of sound procedure depends on the abilities of those who proceed. Thus, the primary emphasis must be upon professionalization of the school. It has been established that good words alone do not do the job.

Professionals are independent and resourceful, but not maverick. Professionals build meaningful associations; in education, as elsewhere, this does not mean starting from scratch. Many meaningful associations do exist and include subject-area teacher organizations, scholarly societies, and regional associations of schools and colleges.

Though we have placed primary stress on up-grading the role of the teacher, no invidious intrusion on the *meaningful* role of administration is intended. To deprive administration of the futile office called "supervision" is to release its heavily taxed energies for productive enterprises. Briefly, these are educational statesmanship and program coordination. The professional competence of administrators to organize and get things done is respected and trusted. It would be patronizing here to discuss such matters as how to form committees, how to get people to work together, how to organize self-study, or how to get resources for program development in the hands of those who need them. Such matters are the very stuff of administration, and administrators are very good at them when they are relieved of extraneous chores or of duties for which they have no great professional qualifications.

In brief (but *not* in conclusion, for the weight of this text is cumulative on this as on other matters) the process of sound curriculum development may thus be summarized: Professionalization

177

of teacher functions supports the exercise of the professional function of administration. Respectful but not supine consultation with the community will lead to the assessment and accomplishment of priority tasks. The self-study and searching at-home analysis along with the incorporation of scholarly and professional resources (local, regional, and national) can move toward the restructuring of program, intent, and organization on tentative experimental lines. Such appraisal and reconstruction becomes a continuing exercise, encompassing constant rearticulation and refinement in use of the process.

Our new model of instructional practice is illuminating at this point. Curriculum improvement is *learning* and the utilization of the *product* of learning. Presumably the school takes its best methodology into the classroom where it undertakes to develop learning among its students. Should not the school (its faculty and administration in this case) apply its best professional knowledge to its own problems? Again, this "best professional knowledge" is simply *to know how to establish a learning situation and intelligently to utilize the product of that learning.*

In Part One our effort has been to mobilize essential foundational concepts directed toward the job of developing a more humanized school. Our next effort is to examine in depth the schools as we find them. However, the matters already considered are not completed, ready to be packaged, and put aside. On the contrary, the concepts forged thus far constitute the tools by which subsequent institutional analysis will be constructed.

PART TWO

THE
INSTITUTION
AND THE
PERSON

Chapter VI

The Elementary-School Experience

We grant space and time to young plants and animals because
we know that, in accordance with the laws that live in them,
they will develop properly and grow well; young animals and
plants are given rest and arbitrary interference with their
growth is avoided, because it is known that the opposite practice would disturb their pure unfolding and sound development; but the young human being is looked upon as a piece of
wax, a lump of clay, which man can mold into what he pleases.[1]
—*Friedrich Froebel*

The Child in America

The American culture is acutely child-conscious and in many
respects has become impressively well informed. Perhaps the measure
of the common culture's gain in sophistication may be the contrast
between the comic-page treatment of children in the "Katzen-
jammer Kids" and in "Peanuts," or even in "Dennis the Menace."

[1] Freidrich Froebel, *The Education of Man*, trans., W. N. Hailmann (New
York: Appleton, 1898).

Thanks to Benjamin Spock, Arnold Gesell, Frances L. Ilg and Louise Bates Ames, to the mass media, to the pediatricians, and even to the PTA, a good deal of useful information about child care and child development abounds in our common culture.

But what do they know of children who only children know? Child development is significantly affected in America by two factors quite independent of the child's nature itself. First, *parents are primarily responsible for the nurture of children;* second, *the American parent idealizes the image of youth.* These factors have curricular consequences.

No one in American society would recommend that children be taken by the state and reared in scientific objectivity by a social agency. But certain peculiarities of American parenthood should be noted and examined for their educational implications and consequences. We are discussing parents here, not family. The American household typically is a two-generation institution. In psychic terms it tends to be less than that, for often the household press is for children to conform to adult models while parents seek to prove their own youth. The immediate absence of grandparents, aunts, and uncles tends toward a certain monotony of contact. It also necessitates a good deal of delegation of responsibility, for youthful parents are time-consumed. The male is ambitious and many hold more than one job. He is also boyish and plays various games with cards and balls. Furthermore, he needs time to plan for his games, to get his equipment into shape, to develop theoretical principles, and to conduct seminars among his cronies on such enthralling subjects. The female has a house to keep, shopping and chauffeuring to attend to, perhaps a job of her own. She has also a time-consuming necessity to keep looking young and attractive, which requires not a small investment of time, money, and emotional energy. The housewife, concerned for the preservation of the home, knows her competition; the mass media constantly depict it and are increasingly explicit as to the points of competition.

In actuality, the American child has parents who are quite well informed about him, who are rather often too busy to give him much time, and who are too concerned with childish preoccupations to bring home a consistent adult image of themselves. The American parent is more jealous of his parental prerogatives than encumbered by responsibility toward his children. Grandparents and relatives may be reproved for "spoiling" children with gifts and attention, but they are effectively ruled out as far as responsible family participation in decision-making is concerned.

Busy American parents, jealous of their sole right to their children, are amazingly generous in delegating responsibility to a variety of agents. Television is foremost in point of time; other children (including siblings and the backyard gang) and baby-sitters, who are usually children too, also play their roles, as do nursery schools and laissez-faire neighborhood supervision consisting largely of intervention to prevent mayhem.

In the foregoing comments the preoccupation with youth on the part of the American adult is apparent. This preoccupation is considerably greater than a concern to retain good appearance and physical vigor. It is a continuing refusal to grow up. Jean Piaget[2] identifies the characteristics of childish thought, including egocentrism, the consideration of all matters with reference purely to self-concern; the inability to depersonalize; the inability to see cause and effect or to admit it; the confusion of reality and fantasy; and the justification of all action and choices. These characteristics also define the behavioral mode of too many parents.

The American dreads aging so considerably that a consequence may be that he rejects maturity. European and Asian visitors often comment on the rejection of the aged in our society. Social security and the so-called science of geriatrics attend to the senior citizens and then segregate them into social and psychic ghettoes of their own.

What are some of the educational consequences of the foregoing?

1. The children who come to school have scant contact with adult authority that is exercised with maturity and objectivity.

2 Jean Piaget, *The Language and Thought of the Child* (Cleveland: Meridian, 1955).

2. The child's general expectation of adult motivation is that it is like his own except that the adult possesses special powers of physical strength to get his way.

3. The child generally expects to make his way with adults by cajolery, favor-seeking, emotional indirectness, and manipulation rather than by reasonable direct communication.

4. The child, therefore, often mistakes unwillingness to be coerced emotionally as hostility and inability to achieve favored status as rejection.

These consequences often adversely affect the child's adjustment to the new environment of the school.

Frontiers of Learning

Starting to school is a formidable exploration. For some children it is a chilling, tension-making experience; for others it is a joyful adventure. It is a life frontier like being weaned, housebroken, learning to walk, and saying first words, but it is more complex than any of these. It requires adjustment to a whole new institutional framework: Strange adults in lieu of parents who are something more and less than parents, peers who afford company and pleasure but who are unpredictable and demanding, routines, new expectations, responsibilities, and opportunities.

Preparation for the school experience is important. A good nursery school for the three- and four-year-old children may be very valuable, but it is still within the reach of only a minority. In the late 1960s only 20 percent of the children who enter first grade will have been lucky enough to have attended kindergarten.

Preparation need not have been institutional. Parents can do much to prepare the child for a happy exploration of his first school frontier. They can develop informal peer group situations. They can find nursery groups in churches or social organizations. They can speak positively of the school. They can love without overindulgence. They can develop responsibility without pressure. They can guard against planting seeds of bias, which are instructions in fear and insecurity. They can familiarize children with the tools of school, which are the tools of civilization—books, songs, constructive toys, colors, games. Above all, they can encourage the child's native curiosity by delighting in learning things with him and by dealing with his questions in seriousness and respect. In fact, if parents did these things, the schools would find children significant months ahead in early learnings.

A fixed curriculum for the elementary school is a matter of some necessity and more impossibility. A rigid stratification of grade norms is a near absurdity; organizational dictates force some arbitrary standards and groups, but good teaching presses always for flexibility and the individualized standard.

More than anywhere else in the schools, at the elementary level the teacher is the key to the curriculum. The elementary schoolteacher must be skilled in such highly professionalized jobs as the teaching of reading and the imparting of concepts of number. In the intermediate grades he must have effective knowledge in a half dozen substantive fields. His administrative talents must equal those of the most responsible. Effective managements of groups and subgroups, attention to individual differences, seeing a number of children through the routine of the day, and getting his own work done are no mean administrative accomplishments. In addition, he will need a developed talent in human relations. Requisite, of course, is real knowledge of child growth and development and a deep-rooted love of humanity.

In respect to methods, the most enlightened attitude for administration and supervision to support is that of confidence in the teacher. Not only should they exercise such confidence, but they should actively develop it. Supervision should abstain from imposing rigid models of methods and procedures. The teacher's own initiative should constantly be encouraged. The activities and the goals of instruction must be worked out in a continuing process of planning and reappraisal in light of what the teacher is learning about the students, and what they are learning about themselves.

Finally, successful explanation of the frontiers of learning in the elementary school depends upon these factors, among others:

185

1. Intelligent preschool direction of the child

2. A congenial institutional environment for learning (and that beautiful elementary schools are an excellent investment)

3. A recognition that real learning and accomplishment are the goals of the elementary school. (Far from being an either–or relationship, happy childhood development and successful learning are mutually dependent.)

4. Highly professionalized, well-educated teachers

Basic Premises for Elementary-Learning Experiences

The success of curriculum in the elementary school depends upon its relationships with certain basic realities. The elementary school is not universally successful. Sometimes children develop an aversion to learning and a repudiation of the schools. Some eighth graders cannot read at second-grade standards, while others cannot add, subtract, multiply, or divide dependably. Some students enter and leave the high school devoid of value patterns or in advanced stages of antisociality; some know only what they have absorbed from the common culture. In these cases the school has sometimes failed, though usually not in the ways harped upon in the public press. More often in these failures the school has simply been unable to overcome the antieducational influences of home and community.

Successful elementary learning begins, of course, with respect for every child. This means regard for him as a human being. He is no vessel to be filled, nor is he any more fit object for human engineering or manipulation than is his teacher. Value judgments, choice, and decision-making are the most important lessons that he can be taught. Gesell and others have observed his developmental phases closely and nicely reported them. This is important knowledge for the teacher, but the child cannot be regarded as less than complete in his human essence because of his phases. Adults go

186

through phases, too. *The complete humanity of the child is the basic premise for success in the elementary school.*

Our second premise is: *The concept of readiness is of prime significance.* School-readiness is of prime importance, and such other notions of readiness as reading-readiness have even entered the common vocabulary. Because schools are conducted in groups (with ill effect when the number exceeds fifteen to twenty in the primary grades), a good deal of teaching must be directed at the mean. Group-readiness must be judged and acted upon in terms of its central tendency, but individuals must be taken into account too. It is well to remember that to delay acting in the case of early readiness is as bad as to force premature learning challenges upon the unready.

A third premise is: *The child in school not only lives and learns in and for that living and learning but also for the future.* Young children not only can and do store skills, knowledge, and attitudes for their future utility, but they do so willingly. Educational philosophies and methods that deny this fact have been largely a reaction to an extreme emphasis on deferred utility, extrinsic motivations, and so-called preparation for life.

Premise four holds: *Motivation is not signally improved by devices of extrinsic reward, by contest, or by invidious comparisons.* Many devices and uses of grading and reporting must be viewed with severe skepticism. Evaluation and reporting should be precisely related to undertaken learnings. A list of ten spelling words learned for a piece of candy, or a quarter, or an "A," or in fear of punishment, of a scolding, or of a bad report, is not a lesson in spelling. It is a lesson in how to receive a reward or avoid a punishment. Those who try to teach by this method usually become as frustrated as the child, because the method simply does not work. Method and goal cannot be separated from meaning; they must be part of an educational whole.

Premise five holds: *The briefly characterized democratic climate is the appropriate environment for all learning experiences.* The school exists for learning, and a democratic climate repeatedly has been shown to be the most effective for promoting learning. This climate is a matter of active values, not necessarily the arrangement of chairs, though such arrangement may indeed reflect a democratic rationale. Democracy is not a free-for-all; it bespeaks attention to discipline. Undemocratic classrooms tend to be preoccupied with evidences of discipline or lack of it and may mistakenly pride themselves on either score. A democratic environment will exist to promote learning and human development, which are the goals of education.

Premise six states: *Elementary education can be so effective that children entering secondary school can know a great deal.* Upon completion of elementary education children *can* be good readers, effective arithmeticians, and knowledgeable of the world about them. They can be socially well-adjusted, free of prejudice, communicative, expecting and giving of love. They can like school and be eager for more learning. Society should expect no less, but it will have to support a truly good school to realize this expectation.

The elementary school is, at best, an unnatural intrusion on the life of a child. It places numerous strictures on him. While at school the child is subject to instruction and authority from persons whom he has not chosen, from whom he has small, if any, approved channels of escape, and against whose errors and injustices he has little chance of redress.

School imposes long hours of quiescent, passive behavior upon him. His very "exercises" are often regimented; his recesses are brief and heavily supervised. The way he seats himself on a chair, itself inflexible enough, is a favorite object of academic pressure; the traditional schoolteacher equates "good posture" as a prime symbol of decency, an evidence of "attention," and a tangible about which something can be done. It is also something that supervisors can observe readily and stands at precisely the level of educational significance from which supervisory suggestions are most likely to be forthcoming. As a matter of fact, "good postures" vary from culture to culture, and relationships between posture and morality or attentiveness have yet to be established. General health, out-of-school physical activity, and personal morale seem to have the most bearing on the matter.

The school chops up the clock and the calendar into meaningless segments. It arbitrarily says "go" at stated intervals to experiences that may or may not be meaningful, welcome, or necessary. It shouts "stop" whether or not the experience is at the point of diminishing returns or maximum involvement or within a minute or two of climax. Particularly by its apparent willingness to assign time equivalence to anything and its disposition to shelve all urgency "until tomorrow at this time," the school implicitly teaches the child that it has no scales of importance. By calling off its own motivations, it clearly instructs that it does not really believe that any experience it happens to generate is very important after all. Consequently, the events of time that are of consequence to the child as far as the school is concerned are mainly these, in order of increasing significance: the time of daily dismissal, the day of dismissal for weekends or special holidays, the long-anticipated hour of dismissal for summer vacation. This view of the clock and the calendar is not unlike the one that conscripts and convicts hold.

School deprives the child of opportunities to make meaningful communication with his friends and avoid his adversaries. Talking to schoolmates, even "whispering," is a veritable sin in the classroom. The school does not hesitate to intrude on the child's privacy; it eavesdrops, intercepts and reads his notes, and makes his personal matters its institutional business, to no effect other than to teach him distrust and evasiveness.

These points are enough to establish the case. This is not to say that the school can easily change its institutional patterns. It is to suggest that the school is something less than graceful in its bearing upon the life of the child. In this context, the school is often a fairly restricted classroom with forty students, more or less, and one teacher trying his best to establish learning situations within the directives of the system and under the eyes of numerous critics. However, our basic assumptions are that learning is important, that the school need not be simply ritualistic, and that good faith is essential in the relationships which exist in sound institutions.

Great detachment from the going concern in the school is needed in curriculum study and reconstruction is necessary. Reconstruction will not begin from scratch; institutional inertia and normal social process will assure that. But reconstruction will remain in the fringes unless a long perspective is sought, unless the reasons for considerable discontent are discovered.

The reasons for discontent can be discovered deep in the literature of serious learning. Would Socrates have interrupted a discourse at the ringing of a buzzer? Rousseau found it necessary to protect the child from social corruption. Emerson and Thoreau inveighed against pressure toward conformity and sought to bolster the morale of youth toward self-reliance and individuality. Unlike in many respects, Froebel, Pestalozzi, Dewey, and Montessori agreed on a fundamental necessity: respect and concern for the child. And to none of them was the "whole child" a mawkish or sentimental cliché. The school that a bureaucratic and frightened society will reconstruct will seek its sanctions in its own purposes and its own fears. That reconstruction may indeed be taking place now. If so, harder days are ahead for the children, whose wait for a new Dickens to expose their educational plight may be a long one.

The Ungraded Primary Years

Regardless of earlier formal training, when the child enters primary school he has important learnings ahead. He must learn the institutional realities of the school. These include finding his way about; adjusting to adults who exercise authority and show concern in some measure like parents but with greater objectivity; adjusting to the necessities of group life; and confronting new dimensions of challenge, expectations, and even demands upon himself.

The first grader will learn the mechanics of civilization. His encounter with these will already have taken place in some depth, thanks to the intrusion of the media upon childhood and to the increased educational background of the American home. It is important for the school to assess the depth of this encounter. It can err considerably, even to the extent of deadening curiosity, if it underestimates the child. To assume that it is starting from scratch, to begin by teaching the child what he already knows, is to get off to a discouraging start. Usually the child will not read yet, though some may be very ready to learn. Arithmetic skill may be undevelóped, but many will have some sense of number, and a few will already be performing basic computations. To some the tools of the school will be utterly strange: the books, pictures, crayons, paints, paper, scissors, pencils, chalk, and erasers and the doing of tasks.

The child will have much to learn of systematization. Some will already have encountered it, and they will know that it is well to assemble all useful materials before beginning a task. They will know that there are rewards in laying out tomorrow's clothes at bedtime and keeping their toys in some order. *Systematization* is the key, not routine and formality. Routine and formality are often invoked for their own sake or for the convenience of others. They are not persuasive in their motivations. But *system* is purposive; its rewards are intrinsic and personal. It makes sense because it improves life in some tangible respect. True system is a matter of form following function. In a very real sense, children come to school disorganized. The school may unwisely seek to organize them and to press down the model of routine upon them. These extrinsic controls regiment but do not teach organization. The educational goal should be to develop awareness in the child of the need for and utility in system and to help him learn to systematize.

In the majority of schools the primary experience will be spoken of in grades: first, second, and third. Beyond this lies a more formidable structuring of learning into clearly defined areas, or subjects. The school becomes cumulative in its demands. The content of these forthcoming years will have a larger quotient of deferred utility. If well conceived, it will be immediately satisfying and intrinsically worth learning, but a good part of its consequence will be a foundation for future learning. It will be built upon; it will be useful, even essential, to subsequent learning. Clearly, the primary phase must accomplish its work to the point of mastery, or the child will enter the intermediate phase of elementary education with a handicap load.

The graded school has encountered real dilemma at this point. It has not been unaware of the problem. Some of its children have mastered primary targets rapidly. Expedients such as "skipping" grades are as old as graded schools. Leaving friends and entering groups of larger and older children often caused second thoughts as to the wisdom of this choice. Too often, skipping amounted to just that; the child was sometimes advanced untaught in some areas though precocious in others. The skippers were sometimes regarded as winners in a speed contest. The others sometimes felt left behind.

Conversely, the school has often been aware that three years of school have not readied the child for the more structured learning at the intermediate level. Then the school has another type of problem, whether or not to hold over, to fail, the student. To what avail will repetition be for the child?

"Social promotion" as a doctrine rose to resist coercive detainment or advancement. The need of the child to learn in a compatible group was invoked under this doctrine. The research on retaking grades tended to bolster the case; retaking third grade tended to reproduce similar patterns of strengths and weaknesses a second time round. The grade simply was too gross a term for diagnostic use. Learnings gained, or learnings lacking, were not precisely and usefully identified. The protagonists of social promotion were also sensitive (and not merely sentimentally so) to the development of the concept of "failure." A sense of failure rarely motivated renewed application. More often it induced deep traumas of guilt and inadequacy and such adjustments as withdrawal, defiance, avoidance, or covering up (including hitchhiking on the work of others, "cheating" in a word). People do *fail*, countered the hard-nosed, and the child might as well learn his limitations.

But the unexamined school, it may be paraphrased, is not worth keeping. Too often when the child *has been* failed he has in no precise sense of the term failed. He has been bewildered more often by being brought to tasks whose dimensions and demands were not made clear to him. He has been set chores but left uninstructed in the skills or tools essential for doing them. He has confronted tasks for which he is unready, not big or strong enough, or sure enough, afraid either to go forward or to speak of his insecurity. "Go milk the cow," a farmer might say, thrusting the milk pail at a city nephew and pointing to the barn. Can the luckless lad be called a *failure* when he returns embarrassed with empty pail and perhaps a few bruises? The farmer will know that the boy has not failed but has been the victim of a practical joke or been given a lesson in humility. But, though playing practical jokes on children is a time-honored function for uncles, it is not the job of the schools.

The grades of the primary school set up a trap for failure. They constitute a public announcement that if a child takes more than three years to cover them, he has either failed or is somehow lacking. Ungrading the primary years announces a more sensible and educationally defensible expectation. It says, in effect, that the children of this community come to a basic phase of school in which they are prepared for a second, more formal phase. Children at these years, five or six to eight or nine, have considerable similarities. Many of them will proceed on similar courses with similar achievement patterns. These are years, however, of great diversities and irregularities in development. Home interests and backgrounds of the children also variously affect their adjustment to the tasks of the schools.

How long will the child remain in the primary phase? The answer is until he has mastered its necessities. But how long will that be? It will not be for just a few weeks, and it will not be for many years. Including considerations of age and size, some will stay for two years and most for three. This is the central tendency on which the program is based. However, some will stay for four years—not that they will have failed, but they will simply take longer to master the course.

The Primary Block

The ungraded primary school is an eminently sensible development. Studious curriculum planning can, of course, make the best sense of it. The *primary block* stands in the curriculum continuum between the kindergarten and the intermediate grades. It represents the educational period ordinarily thought of as the first, second, and third grades. It is well, however, to try to stop thinking of the primary block in such terms. To ascertain its functions, one must be aware of where the student has come from and where he is headed.

If the child has been to kindergarten, he will come to the primary block with an acquaintance of the fact of school, knowledge of simple rules, some sense of schedule, and a loose acceptance of flexible routine. He will be aware that there are many children of his own and other ages; he will be aware of both their similarities to and differences from himself; and he will have begun to make exploratory and tentative peer group contacts. He will be aware of some of the school's function in transmitting culture in games, stories, and songs to him and in developing his skills in working with the materials of civilization. He will have begun, however unevenly, to conceptualize in areas of the school's fundamental learning enterprises. If the child has had no kindergarten, however, the school will have to spend some time in the early stages of the primary block in simply helping him to define and understand what it is all about.

Whether the child comes to the primary block from kindergarten or straight from home, he will be encountering the school for the first time, and he will spend his next twelve years there. Part of the work of these early years will be that of inducting him into the educational program. We shall now consider the most important aspects of his induction.

Increasing confidence in his ability to solve problems. Learning is problem-solving, and the child has been learning for several years. If he worked with other children to build a block house in kindergarten, he probably was unaware that he was learning and solving problems. Now he will be much more conscious that making sense of the printed page or putting his own pencil to lined paper to make marks that others can make sense of is a problem. Again readiness is of greatest importance because success is necessary in his early attempts to solve these problems. His tasks must be geared to his abilities so that his accomplishments may be his own and he can understand that he has learned something. The child is ready to do things for himself and can get much pleasure from success, pleasure that makes him willing and eager to attack new problems.

Ability to work in a group. In kindergarten or at home the child takes part in group activities, but he still looks mostly to teacher or mother for encouragement, direction, or comfort when things go wrong. His friendships with other children will usually be momentary, on a one-to-one basis, and shifting with circumstance. In the early days of his primary education he will seek and need much individual attention from the teacher, but slowly he will see himself as part of a group, all of whom are engaged in common efforts. This is the time for him to discover what he can offer to his peer group small or large, to share experiences, to divide tasks, to gain satisfaction from group effort. A happy and successful classroom at this level will be one in which the children enjoy each other, together and as individuals.

Development of longer spans of concentration. Set the child to work on something that is meaningful to him and he seemingly can work forever. Because a child's interests will vary, his attention and concern will likewise vary. Therefore, it is necessary that the program be colorful and inviting and reach out in many directions. There still must be much time, as in kindergarten, to play, to wiggle, to chatter, to dawdle, and to do anything or nothing. Space and material are very important in these early years. A well-equipped art room, a room big enough to dance in with the familiar rhythm instruments and piano, a gymnasium with balls and things to climb, and a playground with swings and slides and monkey-bars are virtual necessities. Trips and planning for them add much excitement to what can become long and tedious hours and days of confinement. The more opportunity there is for the child to move about and find his own interests, the easier it will become for him to sit still when it is necessary and to apply himself for increasingly longer periods to accomplishing his tasks. Most programs today, however, are so fragmented that a child is often stopped in the middle of something in which he is interested.

Expanding interest in the world about him. Most children ask questions. Their early questions are often asked to test verbal ability and to test the willingness of others to pay attention. Now children will be asking questions for information and insight. A child in kindergarten will probably plant a seed and watch it grow. He may or may not wonder aloud about it. By the time he

195

reaches the primary block, he is almost certain to be asking why and how. If he is not, it is probably because he has no confidence that others will answer him. Questions must be encouraged and built upon. Simple scientific experiments can be brought to the classroom. Children can share experiences about trips and their fathers' jobs. They will want to know, if given the chance, about how things work and how people live—and why. A teacher must be very skilled and understanding to know how to help find answers that are satisfying and understandable and that open the doors for increasingly complex knowledge.

One thing the primary block must not do is undermine what has been developed by the kindergarten or the home. The child must continue to enjoy what he does, to think of himself as important, and to feel cherished.

To the Intermediate Grades

After the primary block the student will enter fourth grade. Because the school, as an orderly institution, has some trouble adjusting to an ungraded primary, it will probably hold to traditional grade levels in the later years for some time to come. (This is noted simply as an attempt to hold to the tempo of reality.)

At this point the student should be readied for more structured learning—systematic studies with both immediate and deferred substantive consequence. This is not to say that the function of the primary block is to "housebreak" the learner for the acceptance of a deadly formalistic enterprise, but that it is to ready him for the enhanced conceptual challenges for which his maturity and acquired competence now suit him. When he leaves the primary block, he should be competent in four areas.

Understanding of the relationship of symbol to reality. The child must know how to read, write, and work with numbers. To do this with competence and understanding, he must be able to work with increasingly difficult symbols. He will have to be able to see more on the printed page than nouns and verbs. Even if he does not often read by choice, he should not now find reading a chore and should have found some kinds of reading that are pleasurable. Literacy is a necessity in the modern world, and it is up to the school to see that the foundation of reading competence is laid in these early years. By the time the child is eight or nine, he must be able to obtain meaning from what he reads. Because each child has his own interests and his own experiences, the school must make a wide selection of reading material available and help him to find books that he can understand and enjoy. Free access to a library that is attractive, well stocked, and not bogged down with restrictions and rigamarole is mandatory.

The child also must be able to write legibly and with ease. What system he uses is unimportant. His vocabulary should be large enough to meet his needs for expression, and this means he should also be able to spell fairly well. He should be aware that effective communication rests both on what he has to say and how well he is able to say it. He will learn best how to write when he has something to say; therefore many opportunities must be provided for him to say something.

Arithmetic competency is similar to reading competency. Numbers and what can be done with them must have meaning. Every time a shortcut is used, such as the memorization of multiplication tables or the idea of borrowing in subtractions, the how and why must be clear and meaningful. To give numbers meaning, they must be related to other areas of knowledge. It is not necessary to think up word problems when the class is working with weights, measures, weather and temperature, geography and population, or space travel. The understanding of the numbers involved in these areas is necessary to an understanding of the whole area of study. If the young child has early experience with numbers as meaningful symbols, he will never find "higher" mathematics a trauma.

Ability to express himself. The child must learn to raise his hand or take his turn in classroom discussion, but he must also have the opportunity to be spontaneous and involved. Talking is not the only way he will express himself. He will also write, and he will build and paint and make things and daydream and wonder about the world and its meaning. He will learn how to get along with other people, older, younger, and his own age. He will best express himself fully, creatively, thoughtfully, and responsibly in the classroom, on the playground, at home, and in the workshop, or by himself, if the atmosphere in which he lives and moves is one of acceptance and respect.

Knowledge of the world, its peoples, and its problems. In the primary block the children will develop a sense of history as they study cavemen, or American Indians, or the Pilgrims. They will also begin to see that man has always had certain needs for survival and for self-expression. However, they will learn only a part of man's history if they see only the Indians' feathers, dances, wigwams, and canoes, and interesting customs. In order to lay the foundation for understanding the problems of today's world, they must be made aware of the conflicts between primitive and industrial societies; they must learn that man also acts with hostility and injustice. While studying history and geography, the headlines of the newspaper and the news broadcasts should not be ignored.

The world, of course, is not just people and their problems. Young children are as curious about birds, trees, rocks, the sea, and the sky as they are about the other people with whom they share this world. They will want to know how houses are built, where milk comes from, what makes a car go, how a television set works, and on through an endless exploration of everything about them. Those early years of school should be full of questions, field trips, sharing of experiences, and learning about things in general.

Acquaintance with ways of finding things out. The first thing that the children will discover is how much they know from their own experience. The effective primary teacher will help the children find much meaning in their existence, and they will respond by being ever more alert, alive, aware, and perceptive. But the children will also be introduced to ways of getting information. They will invite people to come to talk with them; they will read newspapers, magazines, and books, look at television and movies, and listen to records; they will go for walks and to museums where available; they will ask questions of librarians, parents, and people

198

in the neighborhood; they will conduct simple experiments. Such children will enter the intermediate grades already equipped with the basic tools for research and understanding.

The Intermediate Block

In many ways the intermediate block will be like the primary block, but more sophisticated. Knowledge and skills will be more meaningful when they are part of the solution of large problems rather than when taught in isolated fragments. Children still need to be active and participative.

Arithmetic in these years should lead the child to mastery of the processes of numerical problem-solving. It should also lead the child into the community of man disciplined by quantitative cause and effect and sensitive to some degree to the moral, aesthetic, and ethical implications of finite relationships in an infinite universe. Because his mathematics is increasingly likely to be "new," the child in the intermediate block will be at home with the concepts of sets, probabilities, algebraic language, and the relation of symbol to reality.

Communication arts and skills will overlap with arithmetic, for the modern curriculum will be at one with the modern mind, searching for the relationships that will supply binders for the many-multiplied aspects of present knowledge. So, too, what some call "language arts" will establish fundamental concepts relating symbol to reality.

In the intermediate grades the student will have an increased need for communication skill. He will need it in school because of the demands of his studies and the expectations of his teachers and because he is in process of qualifying for secondary education. In other words, an *academic need* for skill exists. Academic need, however, has very limited power to reach all the children. It seldom reflects a need alive in the child, but there is *real* need that supports academic purpose. Children have real, enlarged, and relatively complex needs to communicate.

Questions and the need to understand himself and his place in the world grow no less as the child grows, and his feelings about these questions grow even more complex. He urgently needs the words, the phrases, the power to articulate his quandaries and to put himself into communication with the rest of humanity. The child will also have social needs for communication skills. He will want to write to friends who have moved, to relatives who live far away. In and out of school he will need to know how to recount experience to others and to know the techniques of argumentation, persuasion, apology, and reconciliation. He must learn responsibility with his developing skill; being human he is prone to employ communicative skills for devious, self-seeking purposes. He will need to learn to reveal, not to sell, himself.

When the intermediate child reads, he should be developing new skills. He will read faster and be more able to pick out the important words and meanings in a paragraph or on a page. He should be able to understand some words that express ideas as well as things, and he should be more susceptible to mood, feeling, and tone as he reads. It becomes increasingly important that the child be able to select some reading simply for pleasure, that he occasionally enjoy reading for its own sake.

Music, art, games, and physical education are still of prime importance. The child may be playing an instrument by this time; he may even belong to the school band or orchestra. His art projects will be more complex, and he will be able to sustain interest over a longer period of time. New tools and materials will be introduced as his skill in construction increases, but he will still probably like to work with clay and paints. He will be ready to learn more sports with simple rules and enjoy some competition in team sports. The child will delight in spending long hours developing a single skill; girls may play jacks for hours, boys may bat balls. At home most of these children will climb trees, ride bicycles, roller skate, and spend much time with friends in physical activity. One thing that they will not need at all is a lot of homework to intrude upon their opportunities to grow in these areas.

Science will be much more tightly constructed as the children are capable of closer and more discerning observation. Besides simple, prepared experiments they will probably be able to think up a lot on their own. (Nine-year-olds still try their own experiments with only a dog, a piece of string, and some tin cans.) At this age children will go off for treks in the park or woods and pick up insects, toads, snakes, and poison ivy. They can use a lot of information about nature. All the old curiosity is still there, and a lot of new knowledge can be made meaningful.

Social learnings are likely to remain a continuing headache for those who wish to make sense of the curriculum. The odds are high that there will be mandatory study of American history and some local history or government at the intermediate level. Geography will be taught in more depth. The best social studies programs will be "full-bodied." The following characteristics will justify the term:

> *Social learnings will be established in meaningful integrations of history and geography, sometimes with literature, other times with science.* The intermediate-grade teacher must know how to double the value of time and to escape the silly and rigid strictures of the thirty- or forty-minute period by building integrated units of instruction.

> *Social learnings will be the outcome of every day's methodology.* The classroom will be a microcosm of democracy in action: of mutual respect, of open and understood purposes, of full and candid communication, of group enterprises *and* individual undertakings, of cooperation, of competition in the better doing of worthwhile things for the advantage of all, of applying the methods of free and scientific inquiry, of majority rule in decision-making, and of the rule of ascertained facts in arriving at conceptualization. Not just the social studies "period" but the whole schoolday should be a workshop in ideas.

> *The human experience (whether systematized under the rubrics of history or geography) should be sought in full dimensions.* Shall the child go around the world once with a political geographer, again with an economic geographer, then back again with an anthropologist, back through time with an historian, around again with a sociologist, and, if time and money hold out, once more with a political scientist? It is better that he go once, carefully, in full company of the well-informed.

The social studies program is in a state of confusion for lack of distinction between the "disciplines," the *social sciences,* and the function of their findings and methods in the schools. Academic competition is just one of the causes. This is how the school can make sense of the confusion:

> *The social sciences represent a division of labor among scholars in searching out meanings in the complex of human experience.* To some degree, they also represent distinctive techniques for arriving at knowledge. They are in sad want of intercommunication and synthesis. They sometimes obscure reality rather than enhance it by the insularity of their perspective and the preciousness of their concerns. But the several social sciences have discovered a great deal that man needs to know about himself and his world.

> *The social studies are best understood as a branch of the profession of teaching.* Its concern is to be aware of the most useful findings of the social sciences, to know what learners of varied ages can perceive and conceptualize, and to make judgments as to what is most valuable to be taught at a particular time and place. Social studies professionals are in a position to be educational statesmen; representatives of the social sciences, if put together to make curriculum, are ordinarily mere academic politicians pulling and hauling to serve their own constituents and interests.

Education at the elementary level must assert the necessity for autonomous control of curriculum. This would be good at the secondary level, but the realities of academic and collegiate influence make the cause quixotic there. But no compromise with curriculum and child development should be tolerated, for compromise here is betrayal of our best chance to make learning effective. In sum, education through its professional agent, the social studies specialist, goes to the social sciences to find out what has been learned. What essence of it shall be taught, to whom, at what level, in what arrangements, and by what methods are the business of education.

In this context further sense can be made through deep respect for the social sciences. First, the school can utilize them all, not in perfect perspective but better than any one of them alone will provide (or than all in town meeting would achieve) to give the child a better conceptualization of complex human realities. The

202

social sciences themselves should see a persuasive reason for supporting the educator's role in curriculum building at this point. In
truth, most of the newer social sciences receive short shrift in the
schools; history, geography, and government hold the fort. Psychology, anthropology, sociology, and their combinations and derivatives have seldom crossed the moat, let alone breached the outer
walls. Secondly, in their wisdom, educators are increasingly agreed
that acquaintance with the *methods* of the several social sciences
shall be part of the *content* of the social studies program in the
schools.

Reconstruction of the Elementary School

The negative reconstruction that may be taking place could be
compounded of the following elements:

1. *A propaganda campaign against the good but vulnerable phrases
of modern education.* This includes such phrases as the child-
centered school, the self-contained classroom, the needs of the child,
felt needs, and the whole child. (Unlike Solomon, who bowed to the
wisdom of love, many "reconstructors" today would not hesitate to
slice the child when they send him to school.)

2. *A rebuilt program of teacher education that will minimize the
study of the history and literature of good teaching.* This would
deride methodology, proscribe the study of the child and of human
development, defer exposure of the prospective teacher to serious
thoughts on the school and children in classrooms as long as possible, and concentrate on the academic respectability of courses
taken.

3. *Semantic miracles.* These resemble the public-relations consultants for big brother who give such perverse meanings to good
words as "slavery is freedom" or "black is white." Psychological
bribery becomes reinforcement, canned tasks offer intrinsic motivation, the instruments for the school's further depersonalization
become the means of attention to the individual.

203

4. *A drive toward selectivity.* This is the categorization of human ability and worth by academic standards (determined by standardized tests) and results in the development of meritocracies.

5. *An anti-intellectual confidence in gadgetry.* This takes the form of television sets, teaching machines, and organizational patterns with newly prescribed syllabuses and team teaching.

6. *A compulsive sense that what can be done must be done.* Thus a three year old may be taught to read, a crop of seventeen-year-old college graduates may be created, the *N* (statistical symbol for "number") of thirteen-year-old mothers may be significantly increased. (Much can be done, including blowing up the world, but is it all worthwhile? The negative reconstructionist fails to ask.)

This regressive blueprint is not an idle dream. It exists and operates in reality. It must be rejected. A reconstruction of education could take place that would be fundamental to the health of society. Such a reconstruction would have to be deeply thoughtful, philosophically and boldly experimental, and operational within the discipline and limitation of humane purposes.

Not as a blueprint, but as a corrective to acceptance of conventional practice and to the noisy propaganda of regressive reconstruction, study should be made of the great radical educators who urged reconstruction of education on behalf of the children: Rousseau, Froebel, Pestalozzi, Montessori, Dewey. All these held to no party line; the unity among them was not in method but in spirit and concern. To this list must be added another, A. S. Neill. His *Summerhill, A Radical Approach to Child Rearing*[3] is based on a lifetime of teaching and of running an exceptional school on rare premises. The book gives important evidence that *alternatives do exist.* Summerhill is not a Utopian alternative. It is the story of a school that existed and did a job, many think well, for over forty years.

In considering the elementary school, it is necessary to speak of arrangements. If the school comes first, arrangements seem logical—

[3] A. S. Neill, *Summerhill, A Radical Approach to Child Rearing* (New York: Hart, 1960) .

even sensible. If the child comes first, the question may paraphrase the poet and ask "What are arrangements for?"

The elementary school is the place where the child lives half his waking hours for half the days of the year. No less than one quarter of his childhood is spent in school, and is enough time to take seriously. Whatever the concern for school and society, some seriousness ought to be expended on behalf of the child in relation to time.

A sound philosophy for the elementary school lies not in child-centeredness but in human concern. The context of decision-making for the school may be dangerous if it includes only the realm of childhood. On the one hand, if it is sentimentally biased, it may incapacitate the child for reality; on the other hand, if it is indifferent to the fact of the child, it may prepare the child only as material for manipulation. Thus, an effort to analyze the context of the elementary school in somewhat fuller terms than that of childhood is essential. Five elements in this situation must be considered.

Life is prolonged in general expectation. If the youth turns to bread-winning at twenty, he will have every likelihood of forty-five years of more or less well-earned paychecks—and the increasing expectancy of five, ten, or fifteen years of retirement to enjoy (or years with which the geriatricians may be concerned for him) .

Life is blessed with leisure. This fact is becoming increasingly so; when joined with life expectancy, it carries weight for decision-making. Life is also easier and free time more abundant. Adults know this fact; they have created the condition. They rejoice in it and take substantial advantage of it. Never have so many played so much.

Leisure requires developed individuality. Regimented or scheduled time demands much less of the person than does free time. Free time is a time of forced choice. It discovers who the person is, the quality of his choices, the character of his interests.

205

Axiomatically, the uses of leisure are not to be learned in drudgery or within conditioned routines.

Much more exists to be learned. The necessity for learning bears more heavily by the hour. Thus, the foregoing elements should not be misused as a dictate toward hedonism. They point to the qualities in which the person must be reared. Knowledge explodes within our era, but the abundance of new knowns is ever overweighed by the obsolescence of yesterday's assumptions and data.

Storehouses for knowledge must be kept. They must be extended and made efficient and accessible. Archives, shelves, and filing cases are old-style storehouses. They are being supplemented and made modern by electronics and invention: microfilm, tapes, computers. The storehouses must be well organized and well used. But the human mind must not be mistaken as primarily a storehouse.

The earlier progressives fought the notion of the mind as a storehouse for knowledge on grounds of methodology and higher uses of the mind than for memorization and recollection. Now reality takes the issue away from the realm of rhetoric. The mind *does* store and memory *is* an index of its health among other things, but for education today to dwell primarily on this potential is no less than folly. First, there are better instruments for storing knowledge than the human mind. Second, because knowledge advances so fast and much recent knowledge rapidly becomes rubbish, the hazard of making children's minds mere factual ash bins is great.

When machines can store, compute, and sort so effectively, the special character of the mind takes on new significance. Values are enhanced, not diminished, in a world of choice and leisure. Values are enhanced, not diminished, in a roomful of computers that may sort out who will go to college or who must go to war or where a button spells *nay* to human survival. The qualities of mind that long life, leisure, and automation can release could bring the great humane breakthrough for which history and the prevailing human condition cry in unison. Creativity, imagination, joy, compassion, confidence—these transform the person and move the human condition from suffering, past the merely endurable, into the very transcendence of life.

Are these elements that relate to the whole human condition too far extended for the context of the elementary school? To establish the possibility of central relevance, several considerations should be made.

The adult world takes these realities very much to its bosom. It likes long life, supports efforts to extend it, endeavors to live it out—preferably in the sun. It likes its leisure and spends lavishly on it. It agonizes for individuality and often makes best sellers of books that deal with threats to the person. The adult world is convinced that it is as well to know where to find facts as to know the facts. It is quite mature in this respect. For on the first four points, adults are quite at home, even content, with the realities of their time. If they are somewhat alive in the fifth element, there is yet hope.

If the foregoing elements are realities, and they appear to be, they would seem to make sense as educational dictates. If they are the sense of our time, they apply both to adults and to children. They are the sense to which humanity must accommodate. Let them then be applied to the elementary school for their bearing on such questions as these:

> If life is to be long, what is the hurry? What is the bearing of reality on the education speed-up?
>
> If leisure is to be abundant, shall the child be left out of its abundance? Even the Puritans who dreaded the fruits of idleness were indulgent toward the play of children. How can modern parents who go out for a night of play instruct baby-sitters in the enforcement of the child's homework?
>
> If time is to be abundant, shall the school not seek to make children resourceful in the use of time? Must they not learn to create their own routines and schedules? Do not too many people flounder already in the very abundance of time that is now at their disposal?
>
> Will not the school do well to seek its curriculum for the child among the realities of the age—and not from the patterned notions of rusty academic conventions or the new exploiters of children?[4]

[4] See John Hersey, *The Child Buyers* (New York: Alfred A. Knopf, 1960).

Arrangements in the School

In the context of the foregoing realities and questions, we may now ponder on certain arrangements of the school. We will set forth vignettes of related or contending practices, discuss them, and appraise them.

The self-contained classroom. The classroom as a home for learning and a secure base for individual development within a sustaining group is part of the sanction for this institution. The security of relationship with one adult—the teacher—well known and trusted, is emphasized. The sense of containment, of proprietorship, of owning, of belonging, is further justification. The favorable climate for studying and using individual differences over long periods of time in varied situations is very real. The responsibility, competence, and versatility of the teacher are also essential attributes.

The departmentalized elementary school. Attempts to push departmentalization downward sometimes extend as far as the fourth grade. This is based on assumptions that subject-matter competence of teachers requires academic division of labor, that the variety of teachers and learning situations motivates students, contrary to some observations of child study that the students are ready for it, and that departmentalization prepares students for taking responsibilities, diminishes coddling, and prepares them for junior high school.

Team teaching. Simply stated, this device represents an effort to redeploy teachers in more functional arrangements. It seeks to loosen inflexible arrangements of class size and scheduling. It respects the idea of academic division of labor, not merely in terms of subject matter but also on methodological grounds. For example, a team member's specialized competence might be a special talent for conducting a discussion, or making a field trip live and rewarding, or making sociometric observations on group behavior, in addition to knowledge of his subject matter.

As arrangements, each of these approaches is mutually exclusive. They force choice, and the consequences of choice are real and are worth taking seriously. But this consideration deals with choice among *arrangements,* and arrangements are not nearly as significant as *arrangers* believe they are. Not one of these arrangements teaches. Not one is capable of redeeming incompetent or unconcerned teaching. Any one of them can be vibrantly educational in good hands, directed with profound values. Only in this context, then, are the problems of arrangement important as advanced.

An attempted resolution. What shall be a theoretical or basic resolution of this minor but relatively important matter of arrangements? The humanized school that we have set forth can best be built upon these elements: (1) the reality of the child in the setting of human reality, (2) concern for individual development, (3) a sophisticated and complex view of intelligence, (4) a view of learning as the development of full potential, and (5) a professionalized and responsible view of the teacher.

As we apply these elements, they seem to lead toward resolution in this manner. The self-contained classroom is a good basic institution for the child. He needs a home, especially when he is only likely to find one at school. If it turns out to be a graded prison, the self-contained classroom can be turned into an anachronistic absurdity. Self-contained classrooms can be shut off, overprotective, and exclusive. When they are, they share the psychic disadvantages of all ethnocentrisms. Nor are they perfect or without hazards.

The responsibility of the teacher in the self-contained classroom is great. No other arrangement nurtures or demands such professionalism. The teacher is crucial. If one entertains doubts that teachers can rise to this demand, schools should be visited and real teachers observed at work. The self-contained classroom is a going concern; despite its hazards and limitations it is much more proved than its contenders.

Limitations are real, however. One teacher all day in one classroom is worked inhumanly. Furthermore, one adult in the course of a day may not necessarily be in good accord with all of the children. When human relations are bad for a student, this arrangement can be a consistent obstacle at best and an unrelieved horror at worst. Moreover, the cumulative demands upon academic versatility become greater, until at some point (not the same for any two teachers) they become simply absurd. Again, however, before we jump to the necessity for specialization or academic division of labor among teachers, we must note what is expected of the child. He is not allowed to specialize in the lower grades and is expected to learn "the works." But perhaps teaching is more complex than learning and thus justifies some compassion for the teacher here.

Departmentalization as an alternative seems self-defeating. Its division of labor is purely academic. Its one device for giving the students a base for social entity and security, the homeroom, is one of the most disappointing and generally discredited devices in recent educational history. A pale modification of departmentalization, the special teacher, is a helpful expedient. A special teacher is helpful only if he knows his field and teaches it professionally. He is most helpful when he fully takes on the burden of instruction, for often the best help to be given the teacher is a chance to rest. Instructional television is often used as an electronic, supplementary special teacher. The medium has no research-proven magic and is severely limited in the range of its methodology; however, it can extend the academic competence of the classroom. It can also give the teacher a chance to sit down, not an inconsiderable contribution.

The most promising resolution of arrangements seems to be a combination of the self-contained classroom and the nondoctrinaire version of team teaching. As practiced in the elementary schools of Cedar Rapids, Iowa, it works something like this: Two sections of a fourth grade spend alternate half-days in two classrooms with two different teachers. For each classroom the general assumptions are the same as for a standard self-contained classroom, except that it happens *twice* each day for each child, with two classrooms and two different teachers. The self-containment is psychologically complete in each case, but academically it is partial. One teacher and one classroom may function in the areas of social learnings and linguistic and communication arts and skills; the other, in mathematics and sciences, for example. The division of labor is flexible and related to the varied interests and capabilities of the cooperating teachers. While the classrooms and teachers are varied, however, the learning group (the class) remains intact.

There are advantages that seem to commend this scheme: (1) The variation itself, moving once a day, and the chance to build learning environment for groups of learnings provide an atmosphere conducive to learning. (2) The demands upon teacher versatility are reduced to sane proportions; conversely, the time and opportunity for real preparation is exactly doubled. (3) The motivational impact on teachers is good. Furthermore, preparation is now less than a matter of academic frenzy, and a larger part of preparation can be methodological rather than simply reading ahead. (4) It is psychologically sound for the students. It discourages overdependence upon one teacher. If, by chance, one teacher is a man and the other is a woman, the balance may be a fortunate parallel to family or real life. In cases of personality conflict between student and teacher, the chances are improved that a student will find more rapport for at least half his school day. (5) The fact that two teachers are professionally involved with two groups of students makes possible a sharing of judgments for purposes of development, guidance, and evaluation. On the other hand, the fact that they work independently rather than together in the same room diminishes the likelihood of inbred, conspiratorial appraisals of students and invidious judgments of one another. Most important, the principles of professional responsibility are clearly maintained.

Some large cities have started using part-time assistant teachers in the lower grades to help with paper work, to do specialized chores such as conducting reading groups, or to supply a readily available substitute in an emergency. In time, it may be possible to develop a truly professional part-time teacher, particularly as more educated women look for meaningful work when their home responsibilities decrease. At the moment, however, the assistant teacher is usually much less than professional, in terms of qualification and commitment. The job is viewed as temporary, and there is a marked tendency to quit when the going gets rough. The best atmosphere for the children, if their time is to be shared by more than one teacher, is one where the teachers are fully professional and responsible.

Commentary: Always the Children

In this chapter the school for the child has been our focus. The concern for the child is profound but not in the usual sense of child-centeredness. The child is prized not because of his tender years, but because he is a human. He embraces the full human potential; he carries the promise of adult life. The school has boundaries. The elementary school comes to an end. The child, the human person, has few boundaries; he may even travel to the moon. The school terminates; the person goes on. We therefore direct this commentary and our subsequent work most appropriately to thoughts on the child.

The fault in a child-centered environment may be that it underrates the child. So often the adult world fails to realize what real people children are. European children after World War II were often left homeless—homeless, but not helpless. In their children's gangs they re-created a social order. They made sense, they took care of themselves, they survived. A former colonel in the Hungarian army spoke to us of his amazement at the exploits of the schoolboy freedom fighters in Budapest. He said: "I could not believe it. I am a regular army man and have little regard for amateur soldiers. But these boys, these twelve-year-olds, they were magnificent. They were brave; they were resourceful; they were effective. They were like professionals; they were not reckless; they took care of themselves. It was unbelievable."

Children of tender nurture are often distrusted. Even their

212

ability to choose their clothing or to plan their lessons is doubted in our culture. Yet we have have seen second graders give a profound dramatization of a United Nations session with sense and sound feelings. We have seen second graders race for the morning paper to read of the day's events on a civil-rights issue because the entire second-grade class was concerned with such matters. These children are convinced that they will be able to run the world better than is being done now. They are probably right; they are making a fine society of their culturally pluralistic classroom. They are not afraid of one another or themselves.

In 1950, we were taking coffee in a sidewalk cafe along the Boulevard Anspach in Brussels. A gentle tap on the table brought to our attention a thin child in a faded dress, a child with enormous serious eyes and a cigar-box tray of little things to sell. Matchbox pill containers, pipe cleaner poodle dogs, pin cushions, tiny pencils, and one dainty cluster of violets were her wares. We handed her five francs and reached toward the violets. Her eyes widened; apprehension tensed her mouth. She had hoped the violets would remain unsold. We quickly took a poodle. *"Merci,"* and she was gone. We returned to our coffee. Then again, a light tap: *"S'il vous plait,"* and the cluster of violets was thrust on the table. One meeting of eyes and the child moved quickly on.

In Pittsburgh, there is a big fountain near the University of Pittsburgh and Forbes Field. On hot summer days it gets good use as a swimming pool. On such a Sunday, a handful of boys were splashing riotously. One of them, twelve or so, yelled in delight, "Man, this is really living."

With such incidents in mind, we ask "What may the school know of its children?" It is true that they are brave, competent, and resourceful beyond any use or demand that we make of them. In love, no one would send them into battle, but it is not love that underestimates their potential. They can be involved in life, engaged in life's great concepts. They are also responsive to sensitivity and concern; they more than repay any little gestures of respect that adults can bring themselves to give. They want to find adults kind and fair. And they are pleased with so little. A splash of cool water on a hot day and the world is all right. Little may well be less than a child's desert, but how do we manage to allow so many children so much less even than a little?

The direction of the elementary school must be related to the greatest potential achievements of education. These will subsequently be dealt with in full conceptual scale; here we will simply identify them. The school can begin performing several functions for the child, that will add depth to the individual:

> The school can build and increase the intelligence of the child.
>
> The school can motivate or remotivate the human person toward human growth and fulfillment.
>
> The school can support the child in his quest to discover himself and can help to build a secure personality, to build the indomitable ego.

The person comes to the elementary school. He comes as a child, to be sure. But as a person, he is real and significant, as real and significant as he will ever be. If planning of the educational experience is not consonant with this reality, it will be bad planning. The person continues; from elementary school he proceeds to the secondary school. Therefore, what has been basic in our consideration here will be basic and essential matter for our next consideration—the secondary school. It is the common base of conceptual undergirding that gives real meaning to the idea of the educational continuum.

Chapter VII

The
School
for Teen-Agers

As I have already stated, I am convinced American secondary education can be made satisfactory without any radical changes in the basic pattern. This can only be done, however, if the citizens in many localities display sufficient interest in their schools and are willing to support them. The improvements must come school by school and be made with due regard for the nature of the community. Therefore, I conclude by addressing this final word to citizens who are concerned with public education: avoid generalizations, recognize the necessity of diversity, get the facts about your local situation, elect a good school board, and support the efforts of the board to improve the schools.[1]

—James B. Conant

What Is the American High School?

The high school is frequently said to be a unique American institution. Unique in what way? For a time it was unique in that it provided secondary education at public expense for "all the chil-

[1] James Bryant Conant, *The American High School Today* (New York: McGraw-Hill, 1959), p. 96.

215

dren of all the people." The Soviet Union now also has mass secondary education and joins company with us in this dimension. However, the high school remains distinctively American in its comprehensive quality, a characteristic toward which others, notably the British, are beginning to move.

What does *comprehensive* mean? Conant identifies three functions of the comprehensive high school: (1) to provide a good general education for all the pupils as future citizens of a democracy, (2) to provide elective programs for the majority to develop useful skills, and (3) to educate adequately the college-preparatory group.[2] This text extends the definition: the high school serves as a center for intellectual development; it also assumes a large institutional obligation for youth development on a broad scale. Like the home, it is concerned with the healthy social and emotional development of youth. Unlike the Soviet system, which is comprehensive in the academic and universal sense, it does not leave youth development out of the curriculum or develop a separate youth movement to nurture it. Significantly, the American high school is closer to the home because of its very comprehensiveness. More than the Soviet school, the United States school trusts the home, finds reciprocity and complementation at many points between its objectives for the child and those of the home, and counts indeed on value reinforcements in two-way communication. Therefore, in a basically unsentimental sense, the American school is *homelike* in its acceptance of a total concern for youth at home in the school. Obviously, certain clearly educational functions are delegated for the school to perform. It is bound to systematization and institutional modes; it is objective and professional in its work with youth rather than subjective and personal, as is the home. However, this distinction does not imply that the school is necessarily cold and depersonalized. No, its profession is to mobilize its concern fairly and effectively for *all* and to make viable as far as its resources allow the principle of the greatest good for the greatest number.

The high school has certain common meanings. Very probably

---

2 James Bryant Conant, *The Comprehensive High School* (New York: McGraw-Hill, 1967), p. 23.

the matters that afford a common denominator of experience among American youth in secondary schools exceed the factors that distinguish one school from another. One student may attend a school along with 3,000 other students, that boasts a magnificent plant with the broadest of curriculum choices, excellent laboratories, and superior libraries. Another may attend a high school in a country town, with perhaps 90 others in a four-year program, with severely limited facilities, and a graduating class of 17. The differences of experience are real and extensive; yet again, the common denominator is large.

Even at such extremes, these youth share an American educational culture. They are adolescent in a modern industrial society, which delays their assumption of adult roles past the time of their physical and mental maturity. They are common consumers; television programs in Manhattan are much the same as those in Cedar Rapids, Iowa, and the same magazines are read in both places. They are targets of advertising (like the rest of us), of multiple hidden persuaders. The things that count high among peers may differ in rank from school to school but remain much the same. Proportionately more country students will own cars than their urban peers, but accessibility of an automobile is a social asset in either place. Girls will be considerably on the minds of boys in town and country, and girls in neither place will be considerably unconcerned over the fact.

The schools in both instances will do a job. Either of them on close professional scrutiny may be doing it well or badly. Neither consequence is inevitable for either. Big school, small school—neither functions in an educational vacuum. In both schools the teachers will be college graduates; in both state certification requirements will presumably have been met. In the small school the curriculum may be surprisingly comprehensive. It will come out of the teachers' "backs"; four, five, or even six daily preparations will be a normal load. In any school there is a large opportunity to educate. The question is: Will the school use this opportunity wisely and well?

The American secondary school is divided, more or less willy-nilly, into junior and senior high school. To the extent that it

217

remains a reasoned choice, and largely it does not, the junior high school's raison d'être is based on biological maturity. Today, the junior high school tends to be simply an earlier high school, and an administrative convenience. We shall examine it, however, in somewhat narrow and specific terms of utility.

The Junior High School

The junior high school was established for good reasons and for high purposes. The reasons for the most part remain good, but many of the institutional purposes have been obscured or distorted.

The eight-year grade school and the four-year high school belonged to a period when secondary education was available to a minority of American youth. At the beginning of this century an eighth-grade diploma was the certificate of a good education and marked a level of formal education not reached by even half of the adult community. As secondary education became the normal anticipation of most youth in the 1920s and its completion achieved by a full half of them in the next decade, the traditional 8–4 division of the elementary and secondary phases was challenged by a new rationale and affected by the growth of a new institution or educational phase—the junior high school.

The junior high school evolved from such premises as these: The children tended to outgrow the elementary school in terms of social and biological maturity. By the sixth and seventh grades many of the students had become big boys and girls. By the eighth grade most were in stages of puberty; some thirteen-year-olds and certainly the fourteen- and fifteen-year-olds were often well-grown adolescents. In terms of social development these children were past the point of needing or even accepting a fully dependent relationship with one teacher. The fact that the teacher was then almost always a woman increased the likelihood of rejection by the boys or, at least, deterioration of teacher relationships with the boys. At this phase culturally, boys are self-consciously manly in their interests and quests for models and heroes; biologically, they are intermittently avid in their sexual curiosity about girls and at the same time chauvinistically antifeminist. Scouting, boys' clubs, and gangs institutionalize many of the attributes that characterize male youth at this age.

The sex interests, curiosities, and explorations of children begin with infancy. For students in junior high school, sex is not a new reality, but an enhanced one, linked with a new capacity and a growing drive for expression and fulfillment. Education at this level needs special professional competence in knowledge of the students' ranges and degrees of biological preoccupations and tensions. Teachers do not err in being overconscious of this reality. Actually, even at this date, well after Freud, the most valid warnings to the school must be levied against academic obliviousness, psychological ignorance, or tight-lipped prudery with respect to sex.

Our purpose for education is moral. We want boys who accept themselves as boys, girls who accept themselves as girls. We want them to arrive in adulthood with a developing capacity for love and a degree of responsibility that will fit them for enduring human relationships. We want them to grow emotionally, and we hope that they will grow with as little injury to their emotions and psyches as possible. But growing up without hazard and without hurt is not possible. The school or the home may shelter itself from knowledge about youth, but it cannot arrange a sheltered life for youth, particularly one that ignores the presence of sex. (We are not discussing programs of sex education here, of which there are effective and ineffective, intelligent and half-baked programs.) Our point is that the school itself must not be fugitive from the reality of sex and must not underestimate the significance of that reality as a factor influencing the education of youth. The school has been called on to adapt its curriculum to the reality of this "life adjustment." This term has been rejected or deliberately misunderstood by many; in our discussion we shall refer to *educational adjustment* as a more appropriate term.

Children in grades seven through nine, or in the junior high school, have sex fantasies. Sometimes when a young female teacher gets a glassy stare in response to a question addressed to a fourteen-year-old boy, it is because, however awkwardly, he is having such a fantasy. These children often masturbate, sometimes in school hours on school premises. Homosexual phases may be leading to homo-

219

sexual practices. Some children fall victim to aberrant, confused, and socially unfortunate emotional lives at this stage. Heterosexual secondary sex play and sexual exploration also begin to emerge at this stage, while sexual intercourse is neither common nor socially acceptable. Students in junior high school are entering one of life's most confusing, troublesome, rewarding, and exciting dimensions. They make mistakes; they get hurt. If the adult world, including the school, is ignorant, unguiding, vindictive, Victorian, uncommunicative, the consequences may be lifelong. Adult patterns are then cast in the mold of youthful mistakes and the injuries may become fatalities. Included in the reality of the youth's world are sex crimes, suicides, murders, and madness. An ignorant era charged these to the evil of sex. While these are not consequences for most children, sex *is* a reality for all of them, and the potential for ignorance to betray is universal.

If these things are true in the junior high school, they continue as realities in the next phase of formal education—the senior high school.

The Adolescent at School

The high school is the teen-age school. If it were to be considerably responsive to teen-agers' needs, what would its nature be?

The Purdue Studies of the Teenager, reported by Remmers and Radler,[3] furnish some challenging evidence. Obviously, the teen-ager has problems. How does he identify them? A nationwide sample of 15,000 teen-agers revealed "clear-cut indications that about 10 percent of the nation's teen-agers may have relatively serious personality difficulties."[4] Of those surveyed, 35 percent worried about little things; half of them worried about gaining or losing weight; a third worried about pimples; sex and dating were on their minds in a broad range of particulars. Such returns are not surprising. What is surprising is that they are so often ignored. That boy with the preoccupied frown in the second row—is he

[3] H. H. Remmers and D. H. Radler, *The American Teenager* (New York: Bobbs-Merrill, 1957).

[4] *Ibid.*, p. 57.

worried about the hydrogen bomb or entrance to the right college? Perhaps, but the odds are better that he is fretting over a pimple on his nose. That girl who is staring into space, who failed to hear the teacher's question—is she pondering Hamlet's tragic flaw or her future in the feminine mystique? As a matter of fact, her boyfriend made "improper advances" last night, and she is wondering whether he will tell his friends about it and what is next. (She is, as any John O'Hara reader knows, not necessarily from a socially inferior home.)

The teen-ager spends more of his waking time in school than in any other institution. How considerably does the school influence him? Evidently not too appreciably. James S. Coleman finds that in a hypothetical choice situation teen-agers report parents' disapproval "hardest to take" in about 53 percent of his sample, "breaking with a friend" hardest in the view of about 43 percent, while only about 3 percent rated teachers' disapproval as hardest to take.[5] The weight of peer group judgment is clearly affirmed, but not to the degree of negation of parental influence as is sometimes feared. On the other hand, even in terms of the opinion of a favorite teacher, the weight of the school is barely discernible. Does the school seek no major influence, even on matters within its province? (The hypothetical choice had to do with joining a club in school.) If the school would like to have a major influence and is somehow failing, how shall the failure be accounted for?

Several considerations brook large among the relevant factors. *The program of the school may be predominantly focused on the academic ladder,* that is the taking of courses so that subsequent courses may be taken. Conversely, it may be that learnings are not articulated in terms relevant to the choices with which the teen-ager is presently concerned. The school program may not be reaching the students' viscera.

As a corollary, it follows *that the classroom may be devoted to the compilation and study of subject matter without turning it to educational consequence.* In our terms, this is conceptualizing subject matter into content. The affective weight of the peer group

[5] James S. Coleman, *The Adolescent Society* (New York: Free Press, 1961), p. 5.

221

and, perhaps surprisingly, the family indicates that the adolescent is actually being educated primarily away from the school. He acquires *content* from his family and friends.

That family and friends have a superior methodology becomes the next derivative factor. How can this be true? The major variables between the effectives in affecting choice (home and peer group) and the ineffective (the school) sort out as *concern* and *respect*. Parents and friends really care what the adolescent does. Does the school, or its teacher agent, really care about the choices students make as long as they behave themselves in class and do their lessons faithfully? How do parents and friends influence choice? They get down on the mat with the decision: they argue, cajole, persuade, threaten, shout, weep, pressure. *They provide human encounter.* They show respect; they act as though the concerns and choices of the adolescent have a real and present meaning. The real and present meanings of the school are often none too apparent to students. If the school possesses such meaning in its academic arsenal, perhaps it had better study the process of humanizing itself and personalizing its relationships with students to bring home the real and present meanings that it now seems both to hoard and to obscure.

It may be that students wait to allow the school a place of influence in their lives until they find friends there. It may be that the 3 percent of students who found the teachers' disapproval hardest to take had somehow encountered that effective minority of teachers who put people ahead of programs. The real teachers, the school's *effectual* agents, are those who maintain human roles, along with and beyond the academic, and secure a status somewhere between parent and friend in their encounter with youth.

An Alternative View

Another proposition has always attracted some support. It holds the school to be the agent of "life-deferred." Contemporaneously, the proposition has glossed upon its antique rationale. The school disciplines; the school's business is intellectual preparation; the school must hurry to keep up with the explosion of knowledge; the school must discover so-called excellence. No fault accrues to these goals, except that in the minds of their protagonists they constitute a blueprint of the school as it must be. Youth will recognize these as legitimate goals in a sensible context; but, being always more human than students (while being less human than teacher is so often the educator's fault), they will refuse to live by so small a view of life.

To guard youth in terms of present capacity and future fulfillment, they must be kept in school. Yet, this casual phrasing is misleading. Merely to keep them in institutional confinement is rewarding neither to the person nor to the school. What *is* essential is that presence be real, both physical and psychic. A good many dropouts from education, precisely speaking, have very good records of attendance at school. Coercive assignments and extrinsic motivations have a good deal to do with the phenomenon of uninvolved presence at school, which is the closest thing to actual dropout. This uninvolved presence can, indeed, have a very busy day. This bears directly on our discussion and emphasizes the quest for intrinsic motivation. A school principal boasted that he had "challenged the abilities" of all his able students by forcing them to "take" *six* or *seven* courses. In the survey report it was noted: "This confuses frenzied scheduling with intellectual challenge."

For example, Coleman provided sociological insight on the oft-debated issue of homework. He compared television viewing and homework, and naturally he found that students do a good deal of both. But the *patterns* varied. Homework represented a graphically revealed unimodal distribution and indicated a process of conforming to a norm (namely, assignments backed by coercion). Few students did none; most did the normal (assigned) amount; few went past requirements. Television viewing, comparatively unguided and uncoerced, showed many who viewed a lot, a few who viewed a little, and many who simply did other things. Some had their interests captivated, and they became deeply involved.[6]

These two different patterns raise an important question for education. Is it best to have intellectual activity among adolescents

6 *Ibid.,* pp. 17–19.

compressed to a mean by setting "requirements" that call out energy enough to meet, but never greatly exceed, these requirements? Or is it better to have a distribution of energy more like that in television viewing, with greater freedom to put it aside or carry it to extreme lengths? Our educational system through high school is predicated upon the former strategy; but the latter merits serious consideration as well. *It would require, of course, a better educational system than does the first, for scholastic activity would have to compete for adolescent attention, without the present use of compulsion.*[7]

The Meaning of the Dropout

At this stage a definition of *dropout* may seem gratuitous but is necessary. A dropout is a person who quits school before he should, or before someone else thinks he should, or before he gets his diploma. This defines him from a community perspective. From another perspective, that of the dropout himself, he is a person to whom it makes better sense to stop going to school than to continue. But we will not labor the point. Everyone knows what the term means, at least in a limited sense.

Opinion exists that the dropout is better off out of school. Some believe that the "pre-dropout" (or student) is detrimental to the school. Others such as Edgar Friedenberg and Paul Goodman believe this because the school has been detrimental or at least useless to the person. We will examine this alternative after we examine the great supplier of school dropouts to the market (or more precisely, to the streets). This institution is the *dropout-prone school* (or DOPS, for fashion and convenience).

The social scientist has a ready definition of the dropout-prone school: an educational institution in which a tendency exists for a considerable number of students to leave (to depart or to withdraw), before completing the intended program. An educator might define it as a school that quite a few students quit. Social

7 *Ibid.*, p. 19. [Italics added.]

scientific evidence also reveals that, although some schools are more dropout-prone than others, all schools to a degree are dropout-prone; thus, the typical American high school is dropout-prone. Whether this constitutes a problem, whether it is a "good thing" or a "bad thing," science cannot tell. The moment we go beyond finding facts either in the realm of meaning or of decision, we must go by means of judgment, which is an intense effort to achieve a basic relation to reality. In the 1960s common educational and public judgment has tended to make dropouts a problem, or a "bad thing," especially in the social sense. Before we echo this judgment, let us analytically examine the characteristics of a DOPS.

The DOPS is located in an area characterized by social and economic change. In other words, because we are speaking of American education, it is located somewhere in the United States of America. The forces of change are intense, and for practical purposes, universal. Interestingly enough, it is not uncommon for communities to feel that history has singled them out for special abuse, as though they have some unique burden in the common predicament of the twentieth century. Administrators or teachers will often try to explain their school by such remarks as: "Oh, but this used to be such a nice community," or "We have a different class of people going to school here nowadays," or "You wouldn't know this school from when I went here," or "This community is undergoing a sweeping sociocultural transition." Such comments scarcely distinguish any school, except in a provincial perspective, but they characterize the twentieth century rather well.

The DOPS has a completely conventional view of the curriculum. It works hard at being a good school, but its programs are sand castles. The bedrock of reality and the brick and mortar of profound human analysis are missing. Curriculum across the country seems to say that man's vocations are encompassed either by going to college, quitting school, pounding a typewriter, or operating a machine.

Among the very real matters to which the school may never turn its serious attention are such questions as:

Why will a sizable fraction of this class become mentally ill, become alcoholics, or experience divorce in the years ahead?

Why is there a fair chance that some of this graduating class will die in war on the other side of the world?

Why does the nation's military budget exceed its total expenditure for constructive public works?

Why does the school so seldom take a profound critical look at the *why* of anything? On all the foregoing questions the school supplies so-called reasons. Its instruction is replete with superficial and comforting pap. The only trouble is that the questions are profound, and the easy reasons by means of which the school skirts true encounter simply do not satisfy modern man.

The DOPS *ignores its learners.* This is not to say that it fails to exploit them or to heckle them insistently. It is also quick to advertise its students' achievements; today scholarship rates are becoming newsworthy along with athletic prowess. The school is forever assessing its next tasks in terms of what its students do *not* know. This is a legitimate part of the job, but only part of it. But why does the school for the adolescent, for the young adult, not focus a good part of its attention on what the student knows? Why, in other words, does it not acknowledge his presence? Only when he marks up attendance by means other than a check on the roster does the school ascertain whether the person is really on hand or is a dropout who is still attending school. To the ritual response, "present," the humanized school must reply: "Yes, Orville Schmidt. And who are you? What is all this to you? How does it seem to you today and tomorrow?" Without this attempt to penetrate the identities of the students, all the yesterdays of school life will light their way to a drawer full of dusty report cards.

What these students know something of is life and death, and they are anxious to probe their meanings. They have rich knowledge of emotion, of joy and frustration. They can, if respectfully invited to do so, parallel their experience with that of the characters they are asked to consider in history and literature. They know about work. They know more than adults think, and less than they themselves think they do about sex. They are consumers and spenders. They hold full ranges of attitudes, of good function and sorry ineptitude. There is not a student who will leave the school or sit inattentively if his encounter there consistently addresses itself to an active concern for his presence. The way the school does this is to root its curriculum in the student's incompleted knowledge of himself; it does this by asking, in every vocabulary and with every nuance of phrasing: "Who are you? What do you know about this? What does it mean to you? Does this make any sense to you? How does your experience relate to this matter? Why does it seem this way to you?"

Involvement is the key. To be sure, this brings pain into the classroom—but it also brings growth. In the depersonalized institution that the school too often is there is also pain. For many it is a general aching; for some, a sharp and bitter agony. It is the pain of being ignored.

A Look at the Student

An educator was recently accused by an amateur critic for being interested in people, not programs. The dichotomy suggested is absurd, of course. As far as education is concerned one might well ask if programs are not for people, what are they for?

The student *is* the school. Realizing his unique quality and potential is the point of education. There are some who insist that the differences are the individual's own concern, not the school's. The curriculum to such people is an essential codification of what ought to be learned and what the individual, if he be fit for school, ought to be able to learn, and ought to have sense enough to realize that it is in his best interest to learn. The more humane of this breed will allow the school certain attempts at motivation, will often applaud prizes, merit systems, exterior awards as well as grade-threats, test-scares, and college-entrance coercions. Essentially, however, the curriculum in this view represents a standard, a measure of worth. The student must measure up—or else.

227

If so, what of such a student as this one? Robert is bright. His I.Q. has never been measured as less than 176, but he is known at school as an "underachiever." Some teachers have given him Bs and Cs, even when he led the class in comparative achievement "because he was not working up to capacity." The "tough" subjects are easy for him; he did all the final examination problems in advanced algebra in his head. He is a clown and a persistent disciplinary nuisance. He led fights to abolish freshman hazing and to make the dramatics club open to all rather than keep it a closed group that was open at election only; he refused to take the trip to Washington, D.C., for "Honors" students because he said it was "undemocratic." He has earned punitive Ds in English for not handing in book reports. He reads two books a day (one during school, one in the evening) and more on weekends. Among the hundreds consumed since he became an omnivorous reader at age ten are many of the classics. The best way to make sure he will not read a book is to assign it. He was an outsider in social life until his junior year, though regarded as a rather decent bookworm. Over that summer he grew up and is now active socially. He has many friends, and the girls he likes best are always going steady with someone else; this "bugs" him. He is a regular on the basketball team, is popular with his peer group, and generally is regarded as a troublemaker by the faculty. He intends to go to college but gives it no particular thought. He refuses advanced-placement courses; "might interfere with my reading," he says. He identifies no vocational ambitions: "time enough to decide later."

There is much more to this youth that the school will never know, although it may not know very much about him at that. It knows that his parents are intelligent, middle-class, permissive toward his rearing, supportive of his choice-making. It does not know how much his parents fight at home. It does not know that he has gone to several adults in the community (among them a judge, a doctor, a minister, a mortician) raising questions about the meaning of life (in just such words) and has come away feeling that he had been handed a stone when he asked for bread.

What shall the school do? Shall it force him to measure up? Shall it mark up his "underachievement" to laziness? Shall it enroll him in five or six courses "to take up the slack" in his time? Shall it discover the tension in his home and thus discover his "psychological problem" and make a big deal over it? Shall it try to create *drive* by manipulating him into an early vocational choice? Shall it put him in a special program for the gifted to challenge him? The questions are legitimate; affirmatives to all of them have been tried.

The school often carries concern to a destructive degree: it feels that it must do something *to* everyone. The school, however, in some respects can often behave most responsibly by not *doing,* but by *being.* Robert happens to be a rarity: a self-determining, seeking person. He accepts his Bs in courses where he is highest in achievement because he accepts the institution, but he does not accept the teacher's right to change his way of life. He does not brood over his folks' fighting. He tries to mediate as a responsible third party on occasion, but he accepts life and does not try to live his parents' lives for them. Actually, his school is too small for "ability grouping." If it did have such a setup, he would prefer the C group; the teachers regard most of his best friends as dumbbells but he happens to know that the teachers are wrong.

What resources have affected Robert? The library, and it is unfortunate that the librarian is untrained, for her very association with books gives prestige with Robert. He has taken her advice about books less critically than he has ever taken adult advice. Next to the coach, she holds status in his eyes. Too bad neither the coach nor the librarian is in a position to encounter him fully. He uses them as resources, but they do not contribute to his development. His courses? The school assigned him *Silas Marner* when he had already read *Daniel Deronda.* He had read more American history than the teacher on the day he entered the class. He would have mastered calculus as easily as algebra had the curriculum offered it—but he has never considered being a mathematician.

His need, however, is *not* to be left alone. Laissez faire is not responsible behavior. He needs acceptance and respect. He needs a serious, seeking adult to discover him and to give him some time, to talk seriously about life with him. He will not starve for ideas; books see to that. And if the school is to share deliberately in his development, it will have to do so through communication. It will have to enter his life. This could be an important thing to do. There is a void in his experience. The school cannot do this, of course; a person—a teacher—will have to encounter Robert. If the school cannot provide the encounter, it can at least do one thing: It can cease to heckle this sometimes serious young man.

Let us take another example. What should we make of Ben? He is everybody's favorite. His father is a laborer and Ben is not too eager to invite friends to his home. Such an invitation is a mark of trust rarely given. Ben studies conscientiously. His grades are generally Cs; his Ds in mathematics are balanced by a few Bs received from teachers who like him. Ben dates confidently and well. He works after school and spends money on dates. Parents trust him and commend him as a young gentleman. There are no books in his home; he reads only what is assigned. He is going steady with a bright girl from a good family. He achieves particularly well in the eyes of his peers. He is football captain and class president. He played the juvenile lead in his class play. In the store where he works, and in class affairs, he often holds money. He is known to be scrupulously honest.

Ben may go to college. It seems unlikely that his career at the small undemanding institution that has awarded him a football scholarship will be strikingly different from high school. Yet, all along, there has been a joker in the deck that could have been played against him. His school, a primitive one, does not place much concern on I.Q. But on a card, well filed away, is Ben's—82. Is it an educational misfire that this significant information has never been examined and used clinically?

The meaning of the high school cannot be plumbed by studying vignettes of the two students described here. But the study of students holds part of the method for discovering the meaning of the school. The method is derived from sociology and psychology, of aggregates and types. But the social sciences, like society, can call no student by name. The school must redeem the student from anonymity. By the same token, subjects must be encountered existentially; they must be looked at afresh, beyond their own claims and assumptions.

An Illustrative Look at a Field of Study

For purpose of illustration we shall examine one important curricular area, the social studies program. Many have asserted that this area needs a complete revamping, although it is not likely to get it. Current directions of change are generally regressive and represent gains in collegiate domination of the curricula from the earlier schools. No area is more important, and no area is more torn by internecine feuding of the several related academic disciplines than the social studies. Legislative intrusion on educational planning is most presumptuous in this field, adding to the difficulty in establishing rational curriculum building. Observe some of the conditions obtaining in this area, and the patent absurdities involved.

In a period when historical mindedness was never so necessary, the only nonnational history in the high school is the streamlined hybrid known as world history or world culture. Before the United States had entered even one world war, in a time when America's isolationism was partly based on reality, before the United Nations and the cold war and American involvement in every corner of every continent, then, as far back as 1910, the high school offered *three times as much history as it does today.* Today the social studies profession gives abundant lip service to the notion that world history must be more than Western European history; thus the world history or cultures package includes units on Latin America, perhaps Asia, and most recently Africa. Yes, the subject matter makes sense, but the curriculum design is absurd.

What kind of learning is encouraged by a course that even after rigorous selection necessitates such teaching as this?

One week for early man. This includes not only prehistoric man, but primitive peoples, as well as the Egyptians, Sumerians, Babylonians, Indians, Chinese, Hebrews, and assorted others.

Three weeks to cover the Greeks and Romans. Which way shall it be, two weeks for the Greeks and one for the Romans, or vice versa?

231

This cavalier and patronizing organization encourages such a barbarian view of man's heritage that it might be better to restore the study of classic languages to the curriculum.

A week for the Industrial Revolution. Fine for the students briefly to get Arkwright and Cartwright straight. How profound will be their grasp on this central dynamic of the modern epoch?

And what of the twentieth century? Too bad, here it is June 1 and Miss Grundy has just gotten the class to the Opium War. But there has been so much to learn: Napoleonic wars and the French Revolution, Chinese dynasties and Indian spiritual geniuses, kings and treaties, potentates and plagues—all history, all worth studying. Why say more and risk appearing indecisive? The point is: world history per se is just *too* encompassing.

We are not unappreciative of work done by the National Council for Social Studies in this field. One of their yearbooks[8] was a landmark in the substantive and methodological consideration of the educational problems in the teaching of world history. But neither this nor subsequent works by the Council make a case for world history courses as such. Neither the yearbook editor nor any contributor seems to state flatly that the course itself is meritorious or defensible. We take it that this fact implies reservations. The very substantive weight of this yearbook and others constitutes an indictment of the course. That there is much to be done and well worth doing is demonstrated, but clearly what is to be done cannot be covered in a single year's course. Our best professional estimate would demand a minimum of three years, at least until subliminal methods of instruction are perfected. Edith West stated the problem modestly and succinctly: "Teaching world history becomes more complicated with each passing year."[9]

We are approaching the three-quarter mark of the twentieth century, but what of the fate of twentieth-century knowledge in the schools? In this century the fields of inquiry known as the social sciences have burgeoned: psychology, sociology, anthropology, and

---

[8] Shirley H. Engle (ed.), *New Perspectives in World History*, Thirty-fourth Yearbook (Washington, D.C.: National Council for Social Studies, 1964).

[9] *Ibid.*, p. 585.

the subsequent hybrids, social psychology, cultural anthropology, *et al.*

Just where do the tremendous insights on human behavior, social institutions, and patterns of culture that are products of these inquiries enter the curriculum? Generally speaking they do not. The social studies program is made up of American history (three years of it), other history, geography, smatterings of government and economics, and a good deal of superficial discussion called "current events."

Is there too much history, geography, government, and economics in the program? Far from it! The problem will not be solved by more academic juggling and wheeling and dealing. Should the graduates of American high schools in the 1960s be ignorant of Sigmund Freud, William Graham Sumner, Thorstein Veblen, Franz Boas, Elton Mayo, Kurt Lewin, Erich Fromm, Jean Paul Sartre, and Gardner Murphy, for example? They go to school in a social class and graduate into it. Should they not be instructed in its analysis? They live in community. Should they not learn to study community in somewhat sophisticated terms? They graduate into society riven with bias and discrimination. Should they not be taught some ways of objectifying their views of persons and issues? In the common culture gross and slanderous generalizations about man and his nature run rife. Should the school not make way for a more solid report on man? The social sciences can bring much evidence to bear on these matters.

The solution? There is one: Have two tracks through the curriculum for this area—one for history, geography, economics, and political science; and paralleling it, another for the newer social sciences. If there be a priority for earnest endeavor, this is it. The school that pioneers such a double program will make the one advance that the curriculum needs most.

In the field of social studies conceptualization is a major necessity but it is a necessity generally ignored. Argument about the teaching of facts and dates is common, and the question itself is bootless. An illustrative conceptual necessity is the development of time sense. This is not relatively easy to accomplish.

"When?" "How long?" These are questions that people encounter in reality throughout life. Beyond the measurable depth of these concepts are the unfathomable and unthinkable dimensions of time. Chronometers, calendars, sun dials, and the semantics of time measurement (months, centuries, millennia) bear the same insignificant relationship to eternity as meters, miles, and leagues do to infinity. The measures of time and space meet in the incomprehensible astronomical unit called the *light year*. "Columbus sailed the ocean blue in fourteen hundred and ninety-two," as many first graders are likely to know. Do they know *when* this was or *how long ago* by *knowing* a date? They do not. And the time sense, the historical sense, of many adults is inadequate because they too lack real comprehension of this "simple fact."

Several years ago the author was trying to teach a university class in social studies methods the meaning of time sense. Ten of the twenty prospective teachers expressed confidence in teaching "dates."

"All right," I said. "How many of you know the date of the fall of Constantinople to the Turks? It's considered to be a key point in Western history."

Six students raised their hands. Another raised her hand very tentatively, then lowered it in slow retreat. "1453!" chorused the six when I raised my eyebrows. "Right," I confirmed. "Matter of fact, I looked it up before class to be sure. But," I added, "Myrna, why did you back down—didn't you really know?"

The half-decided student hesitated then offered, "Well, no—I guess I didn't really know. I was going to say 1454 or 1455. You see, I figured it had to be about then because. . . ." She went on with considerable disquisition on internal politics, external pressures, trade and commercial rivalries, dynastic affairs, cultural and religious forces, and ambitions all affecting fortunes in the Eastern Mediterranean of the fifteenth century. She concluded, "So I thought it must have happened about that time."

The class was impressed; so was the teacher. I asked, "Could any of the six who had said '1453' have given us such an explanation?"

They smiled their negative. "Nor could I," I conceded. "Well, here is the point," I said, turning didactic. "Seven of us, including me, knew the date, but in the real sense we didn't know much about *when* Constantinople fell to the Turks. Twelve of us didn't even know *that* date. But only one of us, who *didn't quite* have the date right, had a significant knowledge of the *when*. Maybe *when* is not a concept that often stands alone; perhaps it is closely related to the *why* and *wherefore*."

An Approach to Curricular Criticism

The proper place for development of the content of the subjects is in the hands of those who know most about them, and the presumption or pretense of omniscience by curriculum specialists can only work harm in the school. When the curriculum specialist or general educator realizes his mortal limitations, in the defensiveness of his insecurity he may turn to an equal and opposite error: he may cover his sense of inadequacy by turning blatantly anti-intellectual. In a blind rejection of the subjects he may even discard the concept of useful knowledge. In either posture he becomes a hazard to education. When he believes he possesses omniscience he becomes either a ubiquitous nuisance or a preposterous character, an umpire or a coach who knows the name of the game but little of its rules or techniques. In his retreat to anti-intellectualism he makes war on curriculum in the name of reforming it.

What then is the role of the curriculum specialist? In brief, it is to be an educator and to assist all others within the school to take the educator's view, that is, to hold in an educational perspective the special matters that are best known. The administrator administrates, but not in an institutional vacuum nor with any omniscience of "administrative science." A great naval captain might be a disaster as a commander of a regiment; the president of General Popcorn, Limited, "America's Liveliest Corporation," might be utterly baffled in charge of an ordinary high school. To be an educator is to understand the complete human potential and to see and guide the school toward its most universal fulfillment. The teacher's special province is his subject, but it is in educational perspective that he must hold it.

History, for example, except by some historians and *aficionados* is not well held as an end in itself. Few things in life are. Horses are marvels in many respects: in exhibiting the skills of horsemanship, in running races, in hauling drays (a somewhat outmoded function), and likewise in pulling plows. Indeed, about the only way a horse constitutes an end in itself is as an item of diet. With horses, as with history, functional utilization is preferable. The man who thinks otherwise may make the best historian, or enjoy the most delightful evenings in his study over Thomas Macauley or William Prescott, but he will not make the best teacher. This argument is not presented to diminish the scholarship of teachers. Quite the contrary, but the teacher is obligated to exercise his scholarship in behalf of his students. Educational perspective insists that as teacher he must be more than grudgingly aware of their presence; he must study their persons and their identities and concern himself with making his subject consequential to the realization of their potential.

To shatter the pose of omniscience is not to deny the intellectual demands upon the educator. It would be well for him to understand that the schools will only flourish as educational institutions in the hands of the most broadly and profoundly well educated. The educator should live as fully in the lively realms of the arts and the mind as time, energy, and budget allow. The greater his knowledge, the less likely the educator is to become a meddlesome nuisance or an anti-intellectual bore.

A proper intellectual humility is the outcome of much learning. Such modesty does not deny the necessity for the educator to assume an appropriate educational responsibility. This responsibility is to keep the school educational, not merely an aggregate of disjunctive academic hobbies, games, and exercises. Two means are available to the educator: (1) ever to instruct in the meaning of education as it is profoundly understood and (2) to exercise the function of educational criticism on varied substantive enterprises within the school. The first lends purpose and coordination to the institution; the second initiates and keeps alive the process of institutional change.

To point up a distinction the educator should certainly be more than merely aware of the work and implications of such curricular ventures as the Biological Curriculum Study, the Physical Sciences Study Committee, the School Mathematics Study Group, Project English, and Project Social Studies. His knowledge is functional to retain his view of the scene and to facilitate reasonable communication. He should scrutinize the claims of advocates and enthusiasts in the light of research and comparative claims. He should then neither presume to judge beyond the limits of his special competence nor to intrude within the bounds where the special competence of others far exceeds his own. If these words impose some discipline of restraint upon the educator, the other responsibilities that we assigned him throughout this book still point to an almost unspeakably formidable professional burden of essential competence. In this critique on subjects, which in this chapter we have related specially to the secondary school, the purpose is simply to suggest the function of educational criticism and its exercise without any pretense of exhausting it. To recognize the existence of the subjects is not to sanction; it is to keep our text reality-oriented, for as curricular entities the subjects are nothing if not realities. Our illustration is simply that and assumes no special bias or vulnerability, and the languages have been used illustratively because they enjoy a tremendous current vogue while their best case is seldom made.

The languages. These make ideal subject matter as an example of an exercise in educational criticism. The educator assumes on professional faith and credit that language teachers want to teach language and know how. Even when bitter factional disputes break out and some of the qualified are universally disqualified by the well-qualified judgments of others who are qualified, the educator must keep his peace, for his lack of qualification surely constitutes no qualification to calm the Donnybrook. When enthusiasts press for such major expenditures as language laboratories, he may press for cost accounting or even cite some of the less exhilarating re-

237

search findings. However, his most responsible role with respect to any subject is not with respect to the *how* but to the *why*.

Because the languages have left themselves most vulnerable to the *why*, they are particularly easy to criticize. Their reasons have been flimsy indeed, though educator–teachers' classrooms like those described in Chapter IV furnish their own vindications. The languages, for example, press their cases as a necessity for modern communication. It is true that time and distance have been erased in the jet age of modern travel. But can we thus justify the case for languages within the American school? If we do, it is only in the most slippery of terms. With a $300 excursion flight and a $100 Eurailpass, many teachers may take a month's holiday in such countries as Sweden, Denmark, Norway, Germany, Austria, Belgium, Holland, Switzerland, Luxembourg, France, Italy, Spain, and Portugal. We immediately recognize certain familial utilities among the Scandinavians, or the Dutch and Flemish, or Spanish, French, and Italian. Nonetheless, which of these languages will the time-and-distance-shattered-argument justify for the American school curriculum on the grounds of demands for such a holiday? Rather, does not the tourist thank his stars for the friendly English-speaking services of international travel agencies and the fact that European secondary schools do a better than passable job of teaching English as a second, third, or even a fourth language as in the case of Switzerland? Mind you, we are not holding a brief for travel at such a frenetic pace but are merely pushing a certain justification for language instruction to the very hilt of penetrating effect.

Or, what of the assertion that the knowledge of language helps to understand other cultures? To be sure, it does. But at what relative cost in time and other resources? To understand the Soviet Union seems a fair necessity in this hour of history. Shall the high school then offer a couple years of the Russian language? If it does, a few students may achieve language mastery at something better than an "Ivan saw the bear" level. The class may even sing a few folk songs to a balalaika accompaniment. But these accomplishments will be the measure of two years of class time. If the justification is to learn about the Soviet Union, the time can be better spent. The geography of the Soviet Union can be richly explored. Its history could be solidly studied. Its culture and political science could be penetrated. In place of a few short stories badly read in Russian, several pillars of Russian literature could be examined with some profundity, in translation to be sure. Nominated for attention might well be such classics as *Crime and Punishment, Anna Karenina, War and Peace, Quiet Flows the Don,* and *Dr. Zhivago.* If there be time for two years of language "to further international understanding," there is also time for this alternative. Which more profoundly fills the bill?

The case for utility is also made in terms of the exigencies of modern commerce and politics. Adult life may well take a man to Germany, Argentina, or Vietnam. This seems to argue a deferred utility in the learning of German, Spanish, or French. Since it has not yet been insisted that the student learn them all, what if business takes the student who studied German to France, the one who learned Spanish to Brazil, the one who took French to Japan? The curriculum cannot anticipate Babel. Important concerns are now held by our fellow citizens in residence where Hindi, Swahili, and Arabic are large assets to communication. Does this fact argue inclusion in the curriculum? Utility of language is unpredictable in a world so fluid. If the exigencies of career, public or private, call for such competence, why not learn the skill as public servants or businessmen do—under intensive instruction before departure or on the scene?

The American is culture-bound to English, more or less well spoken. This has not ceased to be an embarrassment, but it is not so general an embarrassment as to be worthy of avoidance at large public cost even if it were possible.

The American school, a Pennsylvania schoolman averred, has done a magnificent job in teaching languages. It has taken its polyglot population and given it a common tongue. Switzerland and India might indeed hold this enviable. Languages to the traveler are a convenience and to the person who seeks a rare cultivation, a rare reward. The opportunity for their study might well be more broadened within the schools. It is not their intrinsic worth that is under criticism but the pattern of collegiate coercion and specious rationale by which they are imposed upon the curriculum.

As a matter of fact, the case can be made seriously that the rigorous inquiry into language (in this case English) and the study of languages—linguistics—is the proper role for general education and the course that most broadly anticipates the kaleidoscopic demands of communication in the modern world. The high-school graduate who knows the structure, the power, the capacity of his own language and the technical bases for the development of languages surely stands better prepared to make his way with the tongues of men than the one who makes a narrow cultural bet upon the one that his school happens to offer or the one that the college of his choice requires. If such words cause anguish among vocational educators who teach languages, let them better define their vocation and justify it.

At this point serious educational concern dictates that we turn our attention to the activity within the school which receives more public interest than all other curriculum combined—the athletic program.

Fun and Games

High-school athletics afford an opportunity for good clean fun on the part of the educational critic; even the best efforts to make sense on this subject are unlikely to have the slightest influence on the scene. The games of the school are too deep in the culture to be much affected by intelligence or discussion. Common educational discussions on this subject are themselves a part of the games, an educator's hot-stove league, as it were. Decision-making ostensibly resides somewhere among the coaches, the athletic associations, and the principals. That is where the formal articulations are made, where the so-called regulations are set forth. The real decision-making is lost in the common culture: it is a vector analysis of factors that cannot be defined or identified. Hullaballoo and ballyhoo and rah-rah-rah express the matter. The games and their attendant rites are tribal; they are not beyond reproach, but they are beyond reach of the mind. The games, however, satisfy.

Yet momentarily, though undeluded by hope of serious impact, let us make an intellectual attempt at something more than inno-cent merriment. In terms of testimonial the critic can have his cake or eat it. Thorstein Veblen once observed that football has the same relationship to physical education as bullfighting has to agriculture. On the other hand, Albert Camus baldly stated that most of what he knew of ethics, he learned from sports.

Americans take sports seriously. Not more than other people, however. No one who has seen the soccer fans of Guayaquil or Quito performing mass mayhem on one another in the stands will claim an American monopoly on game-oriented madness. And in view of things that men take seriously, where lies the fault in games? Was not Sandy Koufax better occupied and more socially productive than Wernher von Braun, or Willie Mays as much an artist at his trade as William Burroughs?

Is it not sadly but often so that the best things which go on in a school are its games? Here is found consummate human accomplish-ment, a boy who handles a basketball like a wizard, a baton twirler who juggles as shrewdly as any ever presented by Ringling or Barnum. In games the school presents people who are really good at something. Teachers who bemoan the attractions of sports might try to become as accomplished at their trade as the varsity team; who knows, they might attract an audience of their own. Making major moral or educational issue in this realm is not merely ineffective but risks detracting from the intensity of more serious aspects of educa-tional criticism.

Certainly physical education deserves a universal role in serious education. This is not less than a classic educational bias. In not all measures of man did the ancient Greeks exceed the modern Ameri-can. To be sure, music played a more central part in their curricu-lum, and while the Greeks took physical education seriously they did so no more than American moderns.

As a matter of fact, doctors of philosophy in physical education now plan programs in this field, and through their researches they assure that its advances parallel the other arts and sciences. To illustrate the vitality of inquiry in this area an example of research done at a prominent midwestern university will suffice. A degree candidate in physical education found himself pondering nice questions of relationships and decided to test one for his thesis. Therewith, he set forth this hypothesis: "that success in putting the shot is positively correlated with the strength of the shot-putter." After refining his purposes and methods with the advice of his professors, he arrived at his research design. He found a population of 100 shot-putters (defined as boys who engage in putting the shot). As the statistician would have it, $N = 100$. To these he administered a battery of strength tests on the basis of which he established two equal groups of 50 boys. He defined Group A as *the stronger boys,* the boys who scored in ranks 1 through 50 on the battery of strength tests. He defined Group B as the *less strong boys,* the boys who scored in ranks 51 through 100 on the battery of strength tests. Thus, he distinguished the two groups by the variable of strength.

He then had each of his boys put the shot three times, carefully tabulating results. After computing results and applying appropriate tests of significance, he established that a high correlation between strength and putting the shot did appear to exist. The utility of such a finding for the selection of shot-putters can scarcely be exaggerated. He later said, perhaps apocryphally, that one of the members of his committee was dissatisfied with his design for the study. Lacking demographic, academic, and socioeconomic data, he suggested that some other variable such as religion, political affiliation of parents, or ethnic origin might be used. The suggestion intrigues but is probably a matter for another study as the candidate himself remarked.

There is no justification for academic snobbery with regard either to athletics or to physical education. Whether we like it or not, the games have a cultural sanction quite as deep as the school itself. Physical education, sometimes on the defensive, may scarcely know its own strength, sanctioned as it is both by classic tradition and modern research. As with all matters educational, the job of constructive criticism is to employ the method of intelligence.

The High School and the College

The high school apparently serves its college-preparatory function well enough. At any rate, it serves to populate the American campus with such an annual flood of reasonably acceptable freshmen as to make dormitory construction a constant race with necessity. The colleges, to be sure, define "acceptable" quite variously; but the more austere among them who pride themselves on steadily advancing admissions standards nonetheless, do find themselves swamped with applications that allow them the pleasure and the headaches attendant on selecting from among the qualified. Excellence made commonplace through educational abundance permits some institutions to pursue their sometimes highly admired elite admissions policies. Of course, the colleges continue to voice their perennial complaint that the high schools are not doing their job or are doing it badly. This has had and will continue to have germs of truth within it. However, in the main, it represents simply one of the conditioned reflexes within the educational culture. In effect it is a knee jerk stimulated by the shock of instructional necessity that causes the toe of the academic boot to launch out at all prior teaching efforts. So, too, do first-grade teachers comfort themselves by denigrating the efforts of home and kindergarten.

The press of this work is that schools prepare best for subsequent schooling when they attend to the matter at hand by giving the student the best education they can conceive at the time and place they encounter him. Since the person who is schooled resides in a continuum of time, it is altogether appropriate to speak of "an educational continuum." These good words should not be allowed to sanction the pressing down of a regimented lock-step upon the curriculum. Conceptual continuity is not furthered but denied by such a process. Curriculum planning must proceed at any level well informed in regard to what has gone before and what lies ahead. It must also proceed with a decent respect for the judgment and integrity of the educational custodians of adjacent segments of the continuum.

The comprehensive high school is not exclusively a college-preparatory school. Nor is it often argued to be; that assumption would be setting up a true straw man. The comprehensive high school is, however, sometimes taken to be a catchall, one of whose better purposes is to run a discrete college-preparatory program within its walls. We insist that the obligation of the school at any level (until occupational specialization has become its avowed and limited aim) is to provide strong incentive and opportunity for complete human development. In our categorization this is a four-dimensioned task, each one of which involves the person in both his cognitive and his affective dispositions. Whether for special or constricted academic purposes, whoever invites or coerces a lesser commitment upon the schools tampers with the educative process and worse, interferes with maximum human development.

The college is not at its best when it ritualizes its own educational dilemmas and problems into a generalized complaint about the inadequacies of the secondary school. Nor is it engaging in a very serious educational enterprise when it sets down its coercive curriculum terms in such quantitative terms as so many units of this or that for admission. These are bookkeepers' terms. Of course an increasing number of students are going to college, and they will have to pay the price. Because the school is concerned with these students, it will help them to pay the price. But it may do so knowing that it is conspiring to meet terms that lack sense.

The college is at its best when it ponders how to give something more than honorific connotation to the term "higher education." Presently it is largely content to let the term say *more*. The college is situated to dwell upon and to develop its advantages. It resides in a fortress of intellectual freedom from which it can, if it will, attack absurdity, bias, injustice, corruption, and spurious values. Because of the advantage of its more genial working conditions, the college faculty can live at the very frontiers of the developing modern mind. Because it has more time and freedom, the college faculty can dwell in scholarship and bring its pressure to bear toward exciting a full-blown curiosity and an appetite for being where the action is in the world of the mind. The college has some advantages and somewhat capitalizes with respect to its stu-

244

dents, not so much because of the selective process for entry but because its students are older, away from home, ready and demanding to be adult.

On the other hand, when invidious comments are made with respect to the college, they would resemble these: Under the mantle of liberal education, the college functions in an atmosphere of furious vocationalism. Most of the major educational advances, especially in methodology and curriculum reform, arrive tardily if at all upon the campus. For many of the students who do find the campus a new and rare intellectual oasis, the classroom is not a primary source of the life-giving waters. Such points are merely a reminder that the college has business of its own to attend to.

The high school can concentrate upon its own business and supply the colleges with students who will succeed in college-defined terms. Even if success is defined academically and the high school has employed its time in a considerably progressive direction, this can be true. Such was the lesson of the classic Eight-Year Study.[10]

The school and college have much in common. They have the student. With the present condition of the market the college can present its case to the school in the most anti-intellectual terms. If the school will not bend itself sufficiently to academic conspiracy, cram schools can be counted on to do the job. It is no major educational accomplishment to take the ordinary, lethargic student, scare him half to death about the rigors of the freshman course, and even more with respect to various consequences of not making it in college, and fit him out with the skills of a respectable pass enterpriser for the college venture. Give him a dose of Calvinistic character education in the form of arbitrarily assigned chores, a handful of prescriptive moralisms to stand in lieu of developing self-discipline, and a preview of a new set of academic courtesies and protective devices; teach him two dozen sure-fire handy "authorities" to quote (the "in terms" of academic vogue) ; show him how to make meticulous footnotes and bibliographical citations (coach him on "sprinkling" techniques) ; give him the facts of life about proofreading and neatness. Thus, he may be assured success in

[10] Wilford Merton Aikin, *The Story of the Eight-Year Study* (New York: Harper, 1942) .

college of a common order. For those sufficiently motivated by fear and dread this is about a two-month job.

The educational approach is different but simple. Let the high school and college direct their separate but related efforts toward educating the person. In their times and places and circumstances let them do the best they know toward building mature and responsible individuals who know, cherish, and use the willed intelligence to the full. Let them pursue this enterprise in mutual respect. Let them study the differences of condition under which they operate and derive from their study a functional understanding of the other's educational role and problems. And let them vastly enhance the commonality of their professional association in meetings and the general enlargement of communication. But let them keep strings and hands off one another. The product of such professionalized behavior will be its own vindication.

Commentary: Frontiers for Comprehension and Behavior

Modern man would like to believe that his confidence in human intelligence has been vindicated. Surely, the mind and ingenuity of man have created formidable wonders. In the 1960s man sent his cameras on picture-taking expeditions around the moon, and he himself ventured a few miles (very few indeed in astronomical terms) into space. The businessman in Chicago can pick up his telephone and converse with an office in New York, London, or Stockholm. In flights from East to West time appears literally to be erased. A person can board a jet in New York and arrive in Chicago at approximately the same hour as his departure. Indeed a legitimate speculation of the modern mind must be whether time is an illusion rather than a reality. However, if one has ever waited in traffic court, one realizes that the dimension of time still retains a very considerable reality.

Science has worked its marvels not alone in space and time. Closer to the earth, indeed close to the prayers of mothers around the world, it has affected the very essence of life. The scourges of man, diseases and plagues, have in large numbers been abolished or controlled. The diseases that no longer need afflict and kill the children of man constitute a roster of great humane achievement: malaria, yellow fever, poliomyelitis, smallpox, diphtheria, typhoid, typhus. These cripplers and killers have all bowed to the discipline of the scientifically trained mind.

Man obviously need not apologize for his mind. It only fails him when he refuses to use it; it only betrays him when he puts it at the service of his prejudices, his base emotions, and his selfish ambitions. Not because mind has failed, but because man has failed to use his intelligence do the Four Horsemen of the Apocalypse still ride rampage and wreak their havoc in the human community.

It is good for teachers to know that science and research have bulwarked our humane art with useful and sure knowledge. Many teachers are already employing this knowledge for the improvement of their craft. Regrettably too many others still plod along the paths of antique practice and ignore the modern highways to learning. Let us examine some of the significant and useful knowledge now at the disposal of those who would teach in a new and modern spirit.

Humane rather than punitive discipline is most effective in sustaining learning. The birch rod, the ferule, the harsh word, and the sarcastic phrase throughout history have been the traditional motivational devices of schoolmasters. Of course the greatest teachers, among them Quintilian, Vittorino de Feltre, Comenius, Pestalozzi, Froebel, Montessori, Dewey have always favored kindness and concern over the paddle. Today, this choice is not merely a matter of humane preference but of scientific evidence. The researches of B. F. Skinner and others show clearly that learning is reinforced better by positive than by negative methods. That is, praise and reward receive better returns in achievement than do scolding and punishment. Humane teachers, therefore, have science as well as sentiment on their side.

The tools of modern education, the products of educational technology, are no better than the skill of the teacher who employs them. Tools forever have always had a dual potential: they may be used to create or to destroy. In the hands of the malicious a hammer

247

becomes a weapon of murder; in the hands of the inept it becomes a hazard to the fingers of its user. The tools of instruction similarly have a dual purpose. What use then may we expect an inept teacher to make of the most ingenious instruments of instruction? Will a shop full of expensive tools make a good carpenter or a classroom full of gadgets make a good teacher? No more, of course, than a nursery full of expensive toys will make a happy child. Tools are only useful in the hands of the skilled and the discriminating and are no better than the purposes to which they are put.

And what of *emotional* tools? The school seems to have great difficulty in developing emotional maturity. Surely the philosophical and humanistic goals of education must encompass this purpose. What is the idiom of the schools with respect to the models of human behavior it sets forth? What of its heroes and hero worship?

Let us consider one of its heroes here. *With Napoleon in Russia*,[11] written by one of his youthful aides, is literally a text on the hazards of wishful thinking. It reveals the self-delusions of those whose egos become so demented that they count their will and ambition as beyond mortal bounds. The book reveals that Napoleon even refused to believe weather reports. So convinced was he of his special destiny that he was confident that some special dispensation would spare him the inevitable rigors of the Russian winter. Yet most of his Grand Army perished in the cold and snow, and the few thousand emaciated scarecrows who tottered into Paris served only as living relics to his dreams, to his megalomania. Despite this and much more, Napoleon receives a hero's treatment at home and abroad.

How do we teach historical wisdom? Most schoolboys know the axiom: "Those who live by the sword shall perish by the sword." Do we teach them the broader psychological corollary that the emotions by which men live, which can give so much to self-expression, if not understood and if not reined by intellect can as surely destroy as they can create? Does not the emotional quality of the classroom have a bearing on this matter? Think, for instance, of contrasting

11 A. A. L. Gaulaincourt, *Memoirs: With Napoleon in Russia* (New York: Morrow, 1935).

classroom environments. How do we take emotional conflict into account in the learning situation?

We know what can be done. But how? First, the conflicts must be taken into account. They must be recognized and turned to use. They must at least be talked about. The psychologist speaks of catharsis; there is also the institution of the confessional.

There is no work, no learning, outside of the human condition, and the human condition for ourselves *and for our students* is complex and contradictory. So what of this matter in our schools?

The school must become real. It must comprehend that the obstacles to learning are more than a matter of intellectual difficulties. There are more problems to learning than matters of understanding difficult concepts, of putting subject matter in order, of memorizing facts and data. There is the more profound matter of understanding what goes on in and around the learners.

In respect to the complexity of circumstance and feeling, the willed intelligence is important, but it cannot do the job of learning *against* the emotions. Conflicts are not overcome; they are resolved. What can the school do when it is profoundly concerned with learning, if it is not concerned with the problems of the learner? It can in a sense do what each of us must do in order to work.

It can legitimatize the problem. It can let the real question be raised: What is getting in the way of learning?

It can open up the question to an examination of the factors involved. It can assist the learner to self-knowledge by inviting him, as it seldom does, to conduct a more searching inquiry into circumstances. The school is accustomed to giving some attention to the problem in purely academic terms such as: What is difficult (intellectually) about the problem? What don't you understand (in terms of formulas and methods)? But seldom does the teacher encourage the student to ask: What feelings interfere with my work? What circumstances beyond the school are getting in my way? It is important to understand that these questions are not courtesies to the student; they are necessities. There is no discipline that can compel reality to disappear, and these matters are real.

249

The school may open up its channels of communication. Even in the classroom, such matters may become the substance of discussion and comment. In teacher–student conferences the scope of what is relevant to a discussion of a student's learning problems must be enlarged. But the school, the modern school, can do more than this. It can institutionalize and give professional sanction and professional leadership to the matter of seeking self-knowledge. This means building into the life of the school the guidance and counseling function. This means providing professional staff to give special help to students, and it means in-service education for teachers so that they may properly complement efforts both in classroom methodology and in their work with individual students.

The view of curriculum must be extended so that in every class it is possible to take our feelings and our life circumstances into account. That is, the inquiry into self becomes the proper subject for *all* learning enterprises. These feelings and conflicts are *not* hazards to be overridden or ignored (which cannot be done); they are a part of motivation and purpose. In sum, the whole person is mobilized and is now not merely taken into account but is put to work.

The school's error in failing fully to regard the real complexity of the learner is to set man against himself. The failure to accomplish attainable academic goals is but a small consequence of this error. *Man against himself* is the most tragic circumstance of the human tragedy, both personal and social; it speaks of poems unwritten, discoveries unmade, breakdowns, insanities, suicides, broken laws, shattered treaties, and war. Finally, the schools' errors are but the errors of humanity. The schools are built in an attempt to diminish human error, not perpetuate it.

PART THREE

LEARNING RESOURCES AND THE HUMAN POTENTIAL

Chapter VIII

The Humanistic-Ethical Dimension

One generation passeth away, and another generation cometh; but the earth abideth forever. . . . To every thing there is a season, and a time to every purpose under the heaven: a time to be born, and a time to die; a time to plant, and a time to pluck up that which is planted; a time to kill, and a time to heal; a time to break down, and a time to build up; a time to weep, and a time to laugh; a time to mourn, and a time to dance; a time to cast away stones, and a time to gather stones together; a time to embrace, and a time to refrain from embracing; a time to get, and a time to lose; a time to keep, and a time to cast away; a time to rend, a time to sew; a time to keep silence, a time to speak; a time to love, and a time to hate; a time of war, and a time of peace.[1]

—Ecclesiastes

We might add that there is also a time to pay the price for the errors and follies of history. In the humanistic–ethical dimension the schools of America pay a most peculiar price.

1 Ecclesiastes 1:4, 3:1–8.

By the ruling of the highest court of the United States the public schools are forbidden to use some of the greatest sources of wisdom and inspiration. The Supreme Court dicta on Bible reading and prayer are at once products of historical necessity and historical irony. Consummate indeed is the irony. The public school was born as an act of conscience, an act of Puritanical conscience, to be sure. The school was designed to create a universal literacy, not as an end in itself but to assure access to the source of religious authority, the Scriptures.

The School and Conscience

The Puritanical conscience was a two-edged sword; it could be both coercive and liberative. Under the Massachusetts theocracy it did indeed indulge itself in the complete repertoire of meanness of spirit. It drove good men and women into exile; it cruelly persecuted minorities. It elevated dogmas above justice; it wrote Blue Laws. It codified its superstitions and killed to sanctify them. At the same time this conscience served as a wellspring of dissent, inspired great documents of religious tolerance, insisted upon civic responsibility, and served as a major fountainhead of the democratic spirit. It even gave rise, during the troubled history of the seventeenth century, to major inventions in democratic political science.

Further irony lies in the fact that American civilization rests proudly in the current of Western civilization itself. A major directive of Western civilization is surely the Judaic-Christian heritage. Yet, the school in a very real sense is forced to deny its heritage. The denial is an historical necessity. But why?

Because man has a memory, and because memories of meanness and persecution in the name of conscience have not yet been erased by good works in the same name. Catholic parents can recall that the nineteenth-century school was often in essence a Protestant school, and they often saw it function in a deliberate effort at cultural coercion. And Jewish parents? A good man of small sense of history can say in simple spirit: "But the words of Jesus are good and it can hurt no one to hear them." History, however, has more to say than this.

To be sure, there are no teachings of Jesus that could be used undistorted to incite pogroms, persecution, and genocide. But when a people has suffered all this at the hands of those who called themselves Christian, what degree of present sensitivity would be surprising? Who could expect many Jews not to resist compulsory exposure of their children to teachings that have historically signi-fied the cruelest of injuries to them?

Cultural sensitivities are nothing peculiar. Therefore, we should like to give an exercise in historical mindedness to the well-intended critics of Supreme Court rulings concerning school religious exercises. Catholics, Jews, Protestants, atheists, and others all send their children to school together. Children get along remark-ably well, and as adults they will create better harmony in the common community than their fathers have done. Still, it has not been long, not long at all historically speaking, since each of these has been done great harm by coercive majorities acting in the very name of conscience.

As families once torn by feud and fratricide come back to-gether, so come the children of many creeds to school. Some words, though true enough, are by common consent left unsaid. Spoken, they may open old wounds, stir up ancient fears and animosities. Later generations may speak more confidently, but only after trust has been well restored. A great and a rare day will dawn when all the children of humanity can come to school, unscarred by painful memories and inevitable suspicions, and bring with them all their great texts for common use and mutual enrichment. No spirit of pessimism dictates this assertion: that fair day is *not* hard upon us. Neither is it forever distant if the school and society pursue their humanizing quest intelligently, patiently, and without remission.

The ecumenical spirit in Western civilization is real and hopeful. Even more hopeful is the expansion of this existential understanding: that whatever differences abide in the minds of men they are linked inextricably in one world-wide predicament, the human condition, and that the great resource is human responsi-bility. Ecumenism and existential accord are only hopeful au-

255

guries; they are, sadly to say, far from pervasive disciplines upon the mind and temper of man.

In the imperfectly functioning consensus as to the necessity for the separation of church and state, the school advances within a rudely defined value structure. The public, the parochial, and the private school, which have in the rather recent past operated with grave contentions among them, now perform and are more or less commonly perceived as interrelated parts of the American educational system. The legal knowledge that none of them can somehow contrive the destruction or the subversion of purpose of the others gives all a sense of institutional security that diminishes suspicion and notably enhances works of educational cooperation among them. This growing trust and cooperation is well worth concessions and compromises. Magnanimity, in effect, seems to do more to bring men together than conscience has ever done. The fabric of common purpose is real but still fragile. It could easily be torn should aggressive zealotry indulge in its age-old disposition to cram dogmas and rituals down the throats of others, even with the very best of motives.

The conscience-ridden appear on occasion to hold the common school in dread. Reason may scarcely touch this dread when it derives from primordial ethnocentrism. But mistaken apprehensions can be eased. The distinction between secular and atheistic is sometimes not understood. The conscience of America is not forbidden to the school. The school does not attack religion. By leaving religion out of the curriculum the school manages to avoid repeating the old errors of psychic and cultural imposition that have worked such harm.

Frequently the hope is expressed that the curriculum can include teaching *about* religion in the historical or comparative sense. This is a worthy though probably unrealistic thought. Efforts to be genuinely scholarly and objective, let alone critical, are likely to strike the old raw nerves of denominational or creedal sensitivities. Such efforts, as commonly observed, consist of academic walking on eggs, pious platitudes, and evasions of central issues. These characteristics are essential, but they scarcely conduce toward vigorous content for learning. It is quite apparent that the subject matter of religion, considered in the creedal or scholarly sense, has little access to the public school. Its study in the creedal sense seems inevitably to be the concern of home, church, and parochial schools; in the scholarly sense, it seems likely to remain reserved for the realm of private inquiry and for the tougher-minded inquiries and forums of higher education. Whatever the other results, this latter circumstance practically assures that the teen-age student is in for some intellectual surprises either when he begins to explore the library beyond his assignments or goes away to college.

One comment can be made with fair certainty: those persons who express the deepest dismay over court decisions denying religious exercise and practice to the school would generally be the last to urge a vigorous, full-blooded historical and comparative study of religion and religious institutions according to the ground rules of critical scholarship as applied to other institutions and bodies of knowledge. Pragmatically speaking, the best curricular sense for us now seems to urge this discipline: In intercultural matters, if you can't speak favorably, say nothing.

Value Confusion and the Student

The fact remains that the student must lay hold of values that endure. He needs some solid generalizations that will serve him well for a lifetime. It seems reasonable to expect the school to help students grasp these sustaining verities.

At this point, the educator is confronted with a hard choice: to laze or to get to work. There are codes, prescriptions, and pronunciamentos galore. Or, he can take his ease negatively but sensationally in a general and superficial iconoclasm. It must be noted that good words are not hard to come by. In fact, by this time, any reasonably articulate person blessed either with a good memory or sound human instincts can find words of almost unexceptionable merit on almost any subject. Sermons seem not to be in short supply; working concepts do.

We will now set forth some assumptions, including some that it

257

would be easier to ignore. First, however, let us note that these assumptions express confidence—confidence not that the school is doing a splendid job with respect to values but that it *can*. Nevertheless, with respect to the school's role in assisting the students' value search, the assumptions from which we proceed are painful to assert. They are of such matter as that which follows.

The school has little notion of what it is up against. Its program is vastly unrelated to the primary needs of its students in this area. Let us stop with just this much to chew on: To get excessive mouthfuls of words is very easy when the problem of value is the matter.

What is the school up against? A basic problem is the confusion and unrelatedness of its own purposes. Easy simplification will not commend itself as solution to any educational problem, and that is not our intent. The school is a complex institution in a complex world. Its purpose surely must be to help the person to find his way around and amid complexity, not to compound confusion. But it does just that.

Let us get down to some of the signs of this confusion. But again, do not mistake the mood. The signs of confusion are a matter for diagnosis and reconstruction of sense and meaning. They should occasion neither diatribe nor pity.

Consider the wrongly worked concept of value itself. A value nourishes a universal need. A value, therefore, works in common throughout the human condition. If a concept does not have this potential, it is no value; it is either a notion, or a cultural preference, or a destructive antivalue. Cultural relativism overstated sometimes denies reality or exaggerates cultural distinctions into what it chooses to call differing sets of values. But euphemisms do not alter circumstances; "one-party democracy" sounds better than "age-old tyranny" or "dictatorship," but it smells no sweeter. Whatever the name, the dissenters are in the same places: dead, hiding, or in exile, under house arrest, or in prison. All people need nourishment; it is a value that mankind be fed. Starvation has no euphemisms. The fact of dietary differences and preferences is an interesting phenomenon, worthy of study. The traveler who is culture-bound in this respect is in trouble. But hunger, except for reasons of diet or fasting, serves man ill.

The term *value* is not merely diminished by adjectives, it is destroyed. The adjectives are largely derived from ethnocentric preferences. To refuse meat is not a vegetarian value; it is a dietary principle. It is not uncommon to speak of democratic, socialistic, or communistic values. Here the word is quickly shorn of essence. If a political system serves *values* and differs from another, it simply seeks them by varied means. But it cannot deny man his heritage and call this value.

The vocabulary of education is preoccupied with such social class terms in this context as middle-class values or lower-class values, for example. The school will clean up some of its practice if it cleans up its concepts in this field. Values know no class distinctions. A certain degree of cleanliness has a bearing upon value: in this case, human health and survival. A daily shower and the possession of two or three bathrooms do not indicate a stronger middle-class value for cleanliness: they are products of opportunity, affluence, and habit, sometimes tinged with neuroses of guilt and fear.

The values have all to do with human well-being. They function whether or not they are known. Bad sanitation brings typhoid to those who have never heard of germs. That in ignorance some may resist improvement does not make disease a value.

The student might find some assurance in the school if he found a large measure of institutional consistency in the realm of value. Furthermore, his confusion might be diminished if the school gave evidence of some priority in these matters. With respect to such behavioral matters as those listed here, most schools are making their institutional position quite clear to the students.

1. Necessity for punctuality.
2. Virtue in neatness.
3. Penalties for cheating.
4. Approved lengths for skirts and haircuts.
5. Conventions of acceptable public vocabulary.

On what other matters is the school as clear and explicit? Does it as clearly articulate, codify, and exert its pressure on such matters as these?

1. The necessity for respect toward every person, regardless of family, color, dress, or manner.

2. Its opposition to all snobberies—class, social, and intellectual.

3. Its position with respect to the necessity for integrity in all public roles.

4. Its eagerness to have its own institutional shortcomings brought to light by honest criticism.

Our contention is that the school is articulate in moralizing and penalizing in areas where *values* are hardly at all involved or implied. It is confident and assertive about matters that apply not universally but only within academic confines, and there the application is far from being demonstrably valuable. On the other hand, in respect to questions where values are certainly involved, the school plays a mute or negative role. The school in this realm is schoolteacherish as in no other. If the students turn in dismay simply to peer-group consensus for their value structures, why be surprised? But it seems a little cruel, a little casual, to turn them back upon their own congenial but uninstructed resources when there is a whole civilization that might be brought to bear upon their quest.

The Democratic Value

The classic language of democracy has been sparingly employed on this point. The intent has been neither to disregard nor to neglect. A review and scrutiny of earlier chapters will reveal no concept inconsistent with the democratic view of society or education. Nor will many elements be marginally supportive or irrelevant to democratic education. We are firmly committed to democracy and securely rooted in its concepts. Nor is our commitment limited or qualified. We have stated our conviction that the historical meaning of American civilization lies in a commitment to democracy; the American educational system is unique in the degree to which it is a product of that commitment. The primary responsibility of the school is to make democracy meaningful and to exert its intellectual and affective force toward creating a society more profoundly democratic than ever before.

The burden of this assertion is levied without restraint. Its weight is placed upon the school in the most naked terms. *Nothing that is democratic is irrelevant or unimportant to the school; nothing that is undemocratic has any business or should be tolerated within the school.*

Why then have we been chary of using the standard and ready vocabulary of democracy? Partly as a matter of impact—to put these words close together and to strike out with every force at our disposal. Second (and this is a candid report of deliberate intent), the previous restraint has been strategic.

Our strategy has been to disarm and presently to confound those critics and educators to whom democratic criteria have become outmoded, irrelevant, or weakly sentimental. Educators have very considerably abandoned the use of their traditional democratic vocabulary. Many books about education have recently been written that give either passing or patronizing mention to democracy. Unless these have been narrowly technical, treatises upon the construction of school privies or the care and cleaning of chalkboards, mark it up that they will not have been good books.

The neglect of the essential phrasing of democracy in these volumes deserves some comment. Knowing educators and living among them as we do, our assessment of cause depends upon no apprehension of lack of good intent. Children are a prime concern of educators. The infection of humane spirit reflected in an embarrassment with its best vocabulary has not yet led to an abandonment of the child as an educational concern, but it could be a consequence within a short period of time. Students of education must take the world into account, and to do this it is necessary that the discipline and burden of democracy be vividly imprinted upon their work. The world observed demonstrates that where democracy prospers and improves so does the lot of its children; where democracy is honored in empty words or is vehemently denied, the children are neglected, exploited, abused, sick, and hungry.

The abuse of children where democracy is shyly practiced or rejected is not a phrase of sentiment or rhetoric. It is a plain ugly fact. The bitter cries of the children brought warm response during this century, but only to the extent that the combined drive of the democratic-humanitarian essence has worked its change. "I tell what I have seen" was the common preface of persuasion from one of the most effective people in American history. So spoke Dorothea Dix as she carried her fight for reform in the care of the insane to numerous committees and to the legislatures of state after state. Any person who has lost faith in the efficacy of dedicated individual effort should study her career. She trusted communication to do its work; she had confidence in the minds and hearts of decent men to work well when once informed.

That is our confidence, too. American educators working hard and in good will and intent abound overseas. They too are generous in report when they return. They speak of technical assistance, of project gains, of political and academic obstacles to be overcome or to be borne in frustration. The reports are couched in terms of progress; they have charts, graphs, and pictures to demonstrate their gains. Yet we wonder why they do not speak more generously of what they have seen, for the picture in every so-called underdeveloped land is the same: the children hungry, neglected, and abused. It is of what we have seen that we will speak. This is done not to share our travels but because of its trenchant meaning in revitalizing an articulate confidence in the essential nexus between democracy and education. American educators do know the fabulous record of the schools in democratic attainment. Still, sheltered by their affluence and history, they may forget the consequences of a lack of humanitarian democracy. America learned, not overnight nor readily, what to do about it. It learned against deepest biases and grudging purses to send all its children to school and to keep them there. The consequence of a lack of democracy is an agony to behold. This would also be the consequence of the loss of it.

There is more to it than this; but this is the essence. At a time when educators seem embarrassed to use the essential terms of the vocabulary of democracy confidently and frequently, we deem it a necessary utterance. We have attempted to present the concept in the bedrock of necessity.

Democracy derives from recognition of the fundamental reality of human equality. How the centuries of exposure to the mystique and institutions of inequality have conditioned man to fear this most essential fact of life. How the timid and weak-spirited and the vestigial aristocrats fuss and shy at the word. This word is *equality*.

The phrase "equality of opportunity" though representing an unrealized goal of our decent society is a weaseling evasion of the educational necessity. For, what is the sense and justice of equality of opportunity unless all men are indeed created equal?

"Equal in what sense?" is the familiar caviling inquiry. "Equal in every significant sense of being" is the essential response. With what sophistries of sentimental evasiveness this assertion of reality is greeted. Once, squirming on the barbed hook of this proposition, a student whom we knew to be devoutly religious asked, "Isn't this concept of equality necessarily a limited one?"

"How so?" it was necessary to inquire.

"Doesn't it simply mean equality in the eyes of God?" he queried—as though we could authoritatively respond.

"Well," we answered, "God is, I take it, a very meaningful reality to you. In that case, I can only marvel. Where do you get such magnificent eyesight to perceive distinctions among men that God himself cannot see?"

Other theological considerations aside, few can object to "the eyes of God" as symbolizing an utterly unobscured view of reality. The perception of inequality among men is due not from acuity of sight but from blurred or astigmatic vision.

Consider the historical conditioning of modern man. An operational assumption of the centuries has been that of *inequality*. The agony of Western civilization has been its effort to install another proposition. The effort was not political or rhetorical in origin. The rejection of the assumption of inequality was the result of the demonstrated inability of humanity to suffer and abide the abomi-

263

nable weight of hunger and injustice that accompanied the supporting luxury of this illusion. The reality of equality has won effective though cautious and limited acceptance in some societies. But nowhere has the yoke of the past, particularly of its elitist and aristocratic nations, been completely lifted.

We are not so patronizing as to assume a general historical illiteracy, nor shall we presume to recite the conflicting records of one assumption against the other. But with history in mind, we would direct this question to those who squirm and cavil at the thought of putting the egalitarian assumption thoroughly to work. Where do you get your historical evidence for a confidence in the institutions of inequality, and who are your prophets?

A spurious argument of the inegalitarians is that devotion to equality somehow obscures appreciation of and impedes development of special talents. This is a repetition of the familiar canard that democracy conduces to a common uplift but also to a general mediocrity.

Notwithstanding, democracy affords the only institutionalization of political science. To speak of democratic "ideals" is a well-intentioned error, but a dangerous one. It summons up images of the remote, the visionary, the unattainable. In fact, the assumptions of democracy represent historical learnings, hard-learned realities, the very necessities for human society and intercourse. For example, having learned that conscience makes tyrants as well as cowards of us all, democracy has learned the necessity to divide religion from politics. Having learned that power surely does corrupt, democracy has learned to divide its grants of power and to put limits of time and circumstance upon them. Having realized that the only alternative to rule by the many is rule by the few, democracy opts for majority rule; but having discovered that majorities, like minorities, can be coercive, democracy has learned to institutionalize the defenses of minority rights. These learnings were forged in the hard crucible of history. They are not visionary constructs fresh from some Utopian's drawing board.

Never in class does someone fail to ask, "What is democracy?" and no doubt someone is raising the question now. This is no question to be answered by glib definition or a few easy sentences.

Democracy is not to be reduced to an *ism*. But the reluctance to formulate does not mean an unwillingness to talk about it. Although our entire text is a conceptual disquisition on democracy in educational terms, at this juncture we would make a very direct point.

Democracy is reality-oriented. It derives its tenets from the way things are, a condition that holds whether the essential reality is perceived as "natural law" or a high degree of observable probability. Although a "democratic faith" is commonly spoken of and usually with favorable intent, democracy actually depends less on faith than on any other view of man and society. Fascism is servile before a mystique of the state; communism is dependent upon a myth of historical process. Democracy, open to all experience, is a matter-of-fact view of man and affairs. It imposes few constrictive myths. Because its arts and letters are free, it nurtures the richest of humane symbolisms and retains as fully as cultural memory will permit the total legacy of mythologies for its humanistic edification and entertainment. Its mystique is not official and prescriptive; mysticism abounds as an attribute from the identities of its varied multitudes as they realize their creative potential.

In pursuit of this fact, temptation exists to call democracy scientific. Great theorists—among them John Dewey, George Counts, John Childs, Boyd Bode—have strongly asserted the democratic–scientific nexus. But independence is the characteristic of democracy. Its basic characteristic is openness to all the evidence; it dreads no tokens of reality whether they be products of *objectivity* or of *science*. No one, to be sure, would associate "scientific" with the frightened tribalism and institutional defensiveness that is fascism. But "scientific" has become a term reducible to the pejorative in the semantics of dogmatic Marxists.

Democracy does not seek security in the bands of protective certainties whether sanctified by antique rituals or contemporary modern hocus-pocus. The virtue of democracy, then, is not that it is scientific, but that it is open to science and hospitable to all its findings.

265

The Method of Objectivity

Objectivity might seem logically to belong in our scientific–quantitative category, but to do so would be faulty categorization. Objectivity is not involved in matters of weighing, counting, and measuring. Objectivity involves the diminishing of subjectivity in matters of judgment and in decision-making. Weighing, counting, and measuring are qualified by precision and accuracy. They can be expressed with certainty in finite terms. The length of a running course can be expressed as 100 meters; the time in which a man has run it may be measured precisely to fractions of seconds. No objectivity is involved; the course is either measured accurately or in error, and the same holds for the time of the race. This also applies to objects; if the butcher weighs out two pounds of meat and charges for two pounds, three ounces, he is not unobjective; he is a cheat.

Academic fashion speaks now and again of the "objective social sciences." The fault lies not with the term but in the association. Sociology and psychology, among others, like to regard themselves as objective when they most nearly ape the techniques and methods of the sciences. The cliché echoes in the corridors of academe: "Whatever exists can be quantified, and whatever can be quantified can be measured." Among those who think this to be true, there can be no objectivity. The only question is whether they can count straight.

Objectivity belongs to such larger exercises of intellect as the humanities, law, scholarship, refereeing, and stating the conclusions of research. The criticism of a book, the determination of facts in a lawsuit, the saying of guilt or innocence, the evaluation of causes in an historical movement, the decision on a close play at home plate or the goal line, or the delineation of the meaning of measurements are all acts of judgment, of discretion, of person. And in every case they acquire a greater degree of justice even as they gain in objectivity.

266

Perfect objectivity is not possible. How can perfection be reached in matters of judgment, discretion, and person? These all function within cultures; objectivity is affected by culture. Reality *is*, but is functionally, as it is perceived. "The phenomenological spread" in perception of an event or circumstance even among products of the same culture is considerable. Sartre speaks of "intersubjectivity," and of objectivity. This is an uncommon although perhaps preferable manner of speaking of the same thing. At any rate, to be objective may be called a method of reducing "the phenomenological spread."

We would therefore define objectivity as a method, not as a quality. This distinguishes objectivity from science; it also puts the two in parallel. This distinction and parallel should cut through a great deal of emotion and confusion in dialogue. The normative element is largely diminished. Seldom does one speak of a "bad scientist," and when one does, the odds are that the reference is to method rather than his personal quality. If the scientist cheats on his wife, there are words for him; if he falsifies his findings, he is a charlatan and a fraud.

Name-calling has greatly corrupted the dialogue between "the two cultures." Partly this was due to the lack of clear distinction between the scientific and the nonscientific. Sir Charles Snow and Hannah Arendt are, of course, right in positing large difficulties of communication, but this difficulty can be eased if not obviated. That the scientific–quantitative realm has its own discipline of inquiry, a system of intellectual integrity, is axiomatic. This is sometimes called "scientific method," but the phrase is redundant. Science *is* method. It is the method of disciplined inquiry that pertains to the measuring, counting, and weighing of those things which can be quantified. Name-calling sometimes results from the naïve notion that this is the only method available for perceiving a more sharply defined reality. A social scientist who speaks judgmentally in the manner of C. Wright Mills, Robert Lynd, or John Kenneth Galbraith may be charged with speaking "unscientifically." The charge is irrelevant because the method that should be in question is not science but objectivity. To charge a man with speaking untheologically while he is discussing baseball would be no more irrelevant. But name-calling also goes in the other direction. Dr. Edward Teller has been called "unscientific" because of certain judgments he has expressed with respect to public policy involving atomic energy. Dr. Teller's scientific findings have been scrutinized by his qualified colleagues and little fault has been found with his science. In his judgments upon public policy, his scientific method is not in question; his method is questionable, but it is his *objectivity* if anything that is defective, not his science.

The intellectual world has been addled by the fairly common assumption that there is only one real method of inquiry—the scientific method. The serious-minded have either warred on this assumption or accepted it. But this is not the choice. Neither is the choice between the naturalistic method and the metaphysical method. Both science and objectivity are methods available to man for seeking a more valid and reliable appraisal of reality, which is quite as much as man can aspire to. Science helps to achieve this by measuring and describing the things that can be perceived in precisely definitive terms; objectivity reduces "the phenomenological spread" and furnishes a basis for decisions and circumstances that the method of science cannot reach.

Science as method has been well and often exposed. We are not likely to improve significantly on the exposition. Objectivity, on the other hand, has been talked of as a goal or quality rather than as a method. This method was greatly obscured by the pragmatists, who most generally (perhaps because of intellectual fashion) spoke of scientific method while they actually talked of objectivity.

There is, again, no perfect objectivity. To the absolutist this says, of course, *no* objectivity. It must also be said, but not as one of Veblen's "invidious comparisons," that there is no perfect science. The sands of the seas may someday be counted; not sooner, however, than will have been achieved a perfect justice. No, objectivity will not achieve perfection, but it will in many circumstances significantly improve the validity and reliability of human perception. The fans in the boxes behind first base may be in practically as good a position to see the close play at the bag as is the umpire. This is not to say that they are in as good a position to *judge* it.

The difference is in their *objectivity*, in their method. These are elements of method in such an example:

1. Objectivity is supported by sensory mobilization. The umpire brings his eyes and ears to bear in determining the question of "safe" or "out." The partisan fan brings his emotions into focus to support his hopes for his own team. That the first method reduces phenomenological spread is indicated by the fact that four umpires focusing on the same close play usually see it the same way. However, 100 fans equally divided by team loyalty are practically certain to reveal a 50–50 split in their perceptions of the event.

2. Objectivity is supported by deliberate emotional divorcement from the attendant circumstances. The umpire is literally quarantined from fraternization with ballplayers.

3. Objectivity is enhanced by well-defined roles and special training. The umpire is taught his profession; his definition of self, his satisfactions, and his rewards are linked to successful exercise of method.

4. Objectivity is improved by technique. The first-base fan who thinks he sees and hears well probably does not know the umpire's elementary technique on a close play. The umpire has been taught that he cannot see foot on base and ball in glove at the same moment. The umpire *watches* the foot and *listens* for the impact of ball on glove. If the foot is first, his hands spread and he shouts "safe." If sound of ball precedes foot, he glances up to make sure ball is held, then up goes the peremptory thumb signaling "Out!"

5. Objectivity is increased by independence. Hometown officials locally paid have notoriously poor eyesight on crucial decisions. Justice rendered by politically dependent judges often assumes strange configurations. Critics are fallible mortals, but their judgments on literary works are likely to be closer to the mark than are publishers' blurbs.

Because both science and objectivity are attempts to get at what is real, they obviously have no inevitable conflict. In fact, occasionally the development or adaptation of new instruments makes possible moving from judgment (a function of objectivity) to measurement (a function of science). Photo finishes at the race

269

course are now measured rather than judged, and without doubt a higher truth is served.

Even as discovery is the forward thrust of science, so is justice the forward thrust of objectivity. Both are concerned with the opening of the avenues to new perceptions of reality. The courts speak of the administration of justice; it is more precise to say that the courts seek justice through objectivity. Earlier we asserted that the schools should study justice. At this point it becomes more precise to assert that the schools should both study and apply the methods of objectivity.

The Use of the Best

Were some things not better than others, choice would be meaningless. If choice had no varied consequences, instruction in judgment would be nonsense.

The school must develop its program in awareness of the best, and in apprehension of its uses. The concept of the best holds hazards that must be exposed before its use is sanctioned. The school in its *academic* way has too often exemplified the hazards instead of employing the concept rationally. Among the hazards are the following:

An uninstructed confidence in identifying the best. Says the philistine, "I know what I like." So too the curriculum builder often makes judgments from his biases, his inexperience, his moralities, his ethnocentricities. Then the best becomes what tickles him most, what frightens him least. But the judgment in identifying the best must derive from knowledge of the art, the craft, the game. Ignorance seldom recognizes the best and often builds fences to shut it out.

An identification of the best with the traditional. Tradition is not conscience but has long made cowards of many teachers. Where is the dynamite to blast the junk from the anthologies? Not even tradition sanctifies much of the school's standard literature. Enshrined is the bad judgment and execrable tastes of the first anthologists. Tradition is at fault in what it keeps out as well as what it keeps in. Dickens' *Christmas Carol* need never depart to suit us; but who can say that Dylan Thomas' *A Child's Christmas in Wales* is not equally fit to enter the tradition—and the curriculum?

A turning of judgment against creativity. The forms of the past were often part of the disciplines of greatness, but greatness ever demands breaking old molds and recreating its forms. A child's verse or story may never enter the lists of qualified greatness, yet he should be nurtured in the aspiration that his work may someday exceed today's best.

The use of the object as a measure of human worth. The most common disposition of the school is to define the best, then to misuse it as a measuring rod. Take Shakespeare as an instance of the best; if Shakespeare does not by consensus qualify, then there be no best, and if some other dramatist be nominated as his peer or better we do not assume the burden of proof. The typical practice of the school is *to teach* Shakespeare and judge the students by their reaction. To teach here means to expose, to set the student against, to measure the student by. It is, in a word, the *antiteaching* that passes so often for reality in academic institutions.

Now let us examine the real *use* of the best. Simply, it is the most appropriate focus for teaching. In literature as in all of life the best is the most considerably human, the most largely universal. In these qualities it is there for all. It is an object, something created, something extant and active. But another "best" is significant for education, the best in the human potential. The best derives from universal human experience, and humanity is fit for the best. Fit for it, but not always ready for it. The job of education is vastly to enhance reality for students whose best has been developed and who have been brought into the community of the best.

Again we turn to Shakespeare and will use *Hamlet* as our illustration. *Hamlet* is in the school, bids fair to remain, and it would not be our wont to dismiss this classic.

271

How typically doth the school make use of all the hazards of the best in its uses of the Dane! With uninstructed confidence it makes nonsense by making "one-sense" of the character. Let the variations of John Gielgud's, Richard Burton's, and Lawrence Olivier's readings of the role illustrate the silliness of academic linearity. The living theater and cinema have given new dimensions to the character. How often does the school ever treat the character apart from the confines of the original Globe theater? As for elite notions, Hamlet is often regarded as caviar for the student and is too often reserved for the college-preparatory track. Even there it is used as a measure of aptitude rather than as a focus for instruction. The point that we wish to stress is that *Hamlet* is an achievement of the best, the best in drama. Students have in them the potential for association with the best. They deserve to be brought to it. However, it is necessary to be realistic. In a class of thirty students, for example, only a few will be able "to read" *Hamlet.* If we throw the book at them, even in a school in a fashionable area, a good many will just not get with it.

What happens to Hamlet in a culturally deprived setting? Consider the reality. Some of these students have heard of Shakespeare. He is worse than square. He is impossible. These students dig the Beatles. They read—comic books. They see a lot of drama: on TV—twenty, thirty, maybe forty hours a week, mostly junk (because that is what there mostly is). These students (read their themes if you doubt it) can't write, are stingy in willingness to communicate, spell abominably, and punctuate as though deliberately to obfuscate the reader. They recite and write in the barest conformity to the minimum levels of academic requirement. They have learned to reveal and to give as little of themselves as possible.

These people have also lived sixteen, seventeen, eighteen years. The teacher is unaware who knows them only by their stingy little themes and their grudging responses to the questions in class. They hunger. They fear. They lust. They know jealousy. They laugh and weep over drama; however spurious television may be, they respond. They learn: they are rich in the lore of the subculture. They have "practical knowledge," much of it as false as astrology and as illusory as alchemy, some of it as dangerous as the hard-learned

272

codes of the children's gangs who dwelt amid the rubble of their elders' global war.

They are here in the classroom, and Hamlet is far away. He represents one form of the best. They are culturally deprived—cut off from the best. That is what the term means. Here they are; there is the best, far distant. So far? No, not so far. Only as far as an act of teaching.

The act of teaching must move toward their experience. Ask them what they know of murder. What kinds of feelings move a man toward it? Have they things to say of jealousy? What power do they think sex has to excite human behavior? What do they know and think of suicide? What do they know and think of ghosts?

The teacher could talk of other things by way of introduction—the Elizabethan theater or Shakespeare's biography. But this is not the way to engage the student with the play, and high sanction holds the play itself to be the thing.

When the teacher tells students who are involved with views of self and murder and lust and suicide that this is some of the stuff of *Hamlet,* he is "telling them true." He can then push their experience a little more particularly with questions: Did you ever think you wanted to do something, but couldn't bring yourself to do it? Did you ever know you had to make some choice, but couldn't quite see what it was? Did you ever find yourself with a lot of good reasons for doing something—and a lot of good reasons for not doing it? What did this do to you?

These questions do get at some phrasings of Hamlet's dilemma, but the purpose should be to get at authentic expressions of the students' experience that they can relate to *Hamlet* in due course. We are not preparing them to "measure up" to Shakespeare; we are bringing the best to them by bringing them toward the best.

Questions that involve their own experience move them in this direction: Ask them if they ever knew a person who was full of good advice and silly behavior. Ask them what things combine to make a good television play or a good movie. Put their list just as they give it on the board and explain that they have named elements in *Hamlet* that will measure up. What are the next steps?

First, be assured that the foregoing has been part of learning,

273

not a preparation for it. If one takes the universality of great art seriously, one realizes that the authentication of personal experience in universal terms is the most essential learning. The students will now be ready and pressing for the play. Give it to them intact. Best of all, show them the film: in this day of affluence, both the Olivier and the Burton versions are available. If not, regrettably, the film, use a recording, the Gielgud for clarity of reading, if you share our view. But let them have it whole. If your school resources are so impoverished that you possess only handsome stadia and resplendent laboratories, then the play must be read without other introduction; join with your best readers and bring it to the classroom with all the verve at your command. The play will carry itself if you talk it out good and clear.

Then the students should begin to wrestle with the play and its complexities and problems; this will happen not as an academic exercise, but because the students will not let go of it. These students will among themselves talk of *Goldfinger* for days; and *Hamlet* is to good talk as *Goldfinger* is to mutton. Before the class is through, every helpful annotation in their texts will have been turned to in excitement: these very footnotes that the teacher cannot beg or coerce students to consult. Such a teacher has helped to put *Hamlet* into the students' lives permanently. These are the same students who groaned when Shakespeare was first mentioned. They will go the whole route. If the teacher is lucky he can go the whole route with them. If they were introduced by way of Olivier, they can conclude with Burton. Let them discover what a different reading can do to the same drama. They will see for themselves how much an exuberant ear for comedy can uncover beyond routine comic relief in this tragedy.

The route to the best is methodological. But that method is humanistically and ethically rooted. It takes the best seriously by taking humanity—the student—seriously. Modern education does not provide universal education by abdicating from the best or denying its existence; it recognizes that the potential for the best is in every person and *exerts itself* to provide authentic encounter between the best in the person and the best there is.

The Subjects of Learning

The academic custodians of humane learning have not been lacking in good intent. Still, the humanistic–ethical potential has not flourished too noticeably in the schools. The clue to the slippage between intent and performance is a semantic one. The treasures of knowledge have been customarily called "the subjects." This miscalling is not a simple error in nomenclature. It imposes a conceptual distortion that renders education, human learning, next to impossible. Its first derivative is the notion that "the subjects" are to be taught. But no profit accrues to spinning out dubious and well-known illogic.

The *subjects* of education are the *students*. If attempts at education are addressed in any other direction, they are focused toward futility. The fact that learning of sorts does take place in schools that focus on everything but the person does not commend the choice. Such learning takes place only because the true subjects have the human capacity to put themselves into the picture, to contrive meaningful experience for themselves out of the well-intentioned but blundering enterprises of the academicians. In precise terms, the willed intelligence of the natural learners (the students, the true subjects of education) often redeems antilearning efforts of the school; the willed intelligence effects this change by developing its own methods for translating subject matter into content. Thus, to some degree the students manage to transcend imposed absurdities and to derive meaningful experience from a welter of chaos and indirection. Commonly, the notably learned but unschooled have been spoken of as "self-educated." The term might as appropriately apply to those numerous students who somehow continue to subjectify the mysteries of the school and derive nourishment for their human development from it. But the school is conceived and supported in its intent to assist in education. It can scarcely justify itself as a laboratory of proof that the person has considerable capacity for human development against whatever odds are imposed.

In this chapter we have directed our efforts toward clarifying certain humanistic and ethical dilemmas in the schools and toward effecting means of reducing the slippage between good intention and poor performance. Here, if anywhere, a considerable austerity of demand appears in order. In a sense the creative–aesthetic potential is highly individualistic in its motivations; the scientific–quantitative measures in its own special terms; the vocational–utilitarian derives many if not its best motivations from the acquisitiveness nurtured in our peculiarly competitive society. The humanistic–ethical dimension, divorced from none of these in a well-conceived education, nonetheless has its special obligations. In this area of development the person learns not only something of what humanity expects of him but also what it expects of itself. These are not the most clearly inscribed lessons. The voices of history and literature are many; the tongues of creedal and tribal loyalties dispute all matters. But unless all be madness, and no sense can come from such a postulate, then humanity itself must be capable of speaking something coherent of itself. The school must help the student to seek this common sense of man, not to put new dogmas and tribalisms into ferment.

The Guidance Function as Value Application

In the dual field of guidance and counseling the humanistic–ethical element goes directly to work. If the school has a functional value system, its presence will be especially discernible in the exercise of these related practices. But this is not all. Through the exercise of this function the school must also *help the student to understand who he is and what he is becoming.*

Notice that we ascribe the function to the *school,* not to the guidance department. Professionally trained persons who are hired to lead and develop this function in the schools are valuable resources. Sometimes the school exercises these functions in the absence of specially trained personnel. The advantages of professionalizing the function are obvious; it fixes responsibility and brings special skills and knowledge to the institution. It also creates the hazard that the teaching faculty may then feel that its personal obligations to its students have been assigned to other specific persons who will henceforth fully and exclusively discharge them.

We will now distinguish broadly between guidance and counseling. Guidance matters are such things as these: giving educational information and data, assisting in vocational decision-making, and administering tests of aptitudes, interests, and intelligence to assist in the foregoing. These concerns vary greatly from school to school. For example, in a given suburban locality as many as 92 percent of the high-school graduates may proceed to higher education. The guidance process in such a school is devoted almost exclusively to helping the student decide on an appropriate college or university and to helping him gain admission to the institution of his first, second, or third choice. In a nearby school only 25 percent of the students may pursue further education. In this case guidance is practically concerned with finding jobs for girls in offices and stores, giving boys information about military draft and varied opportunities in the armed services, and helping them find placement in semiskilled occupations.

Obviously, evidence of interests and abilities becomes essential for all these purposes. That is where tests come in. If a boy thinks he wants to become an engineer, some indication of his mathematical and technical abilities is important. If a boy is considering medicine as a career but he scores low in scientific subjects and his personality ratings in such qualities as persistence and systematic effort are low, then surely he should be made aware of the contradiction between his ambition and his qualifications *up to this point*. The phrase "up to this point" is important. Testing should never be regarded as *conclusive* evidence. The evidence of tests is useful to give the student an appraisal of the *present condition* of his aptitudes and abilities in relation to his goals. But the capacity for decision-making does not reside in the tests; this remains both the right and the burden of the individual. Many cases exist where new purposes and motivations have overcome bad previous records;

277

persistence and hard work will truly overcome many obstacles; dedication and effort have often upset the odds in many contests.

In fact, the person trustworthy in guidance has three special areas of knowledge about tests: (1) *their uses,* which are primarily *diagnostic;* (2) their *limitations,* which lie mainly in the fact that they reveal, however significantly, only identifiable aspects of the person, but *never the total person;* and (3) their *abuses,* which lie principally in the areas of *coercion* and *prediction.* The tests, we reiterate, give the evidence only "up to this point." It is well to beware of statistical studies that presume predictive value because of correlations established between test scores and later performance. These have only the same limited and dangerous value as "tout sheets" at the race tracks and merely give bettor's odds. But 20 to 1 shots sometimes win sweepstakes. Indeed, a man who nearly failed his college course in Mathematics of Finance later became the competent and trusted comptroller for a manufacturing concern that was the wealthiest in its field.

In practice, the administration of tests, which is relatively simple, is much less important than their interpretation. In the limited area of academic testing, what shall we think of the boy, for example, who breaks all records in his standardized history examinations? Shall we prophesy a great career as an historian for him? Perhaps, but not on such limited evidence. Possibly his interests direct him to the law or, for that matter, to physics. Perhaps he easily acquires historical knowledge. But does he have the patience to spend years of research in musty archives, and is his judgment so balanced as to assure wise interpretation of events?

Testing is merely a beginning; its meaning lies in perceptive *interpretation.* Some tests, for example, gain their meaning largely through interpretation. Such psychological assessments as the Rorschach and Thematic Apperception tests (ink blots and pictures, respectively) gain meaning only through interpretation. The respondent is given opportunity to reveal rather specific, limited, and perhaps hidden aspects of self by saying what he *sees* and feels in response to certain visual stimuli.

In one picture of the Thematic Apperception Test (TAT) a

person stands looking from a window. If the respondent says, "The window overlooks a high cliff; he is getting ready to jump," what shall the interpreter conclude? Nothing, of course, on the basis of one response, if he is wise. In the presence of other consistent evidence, this might be one indication of a self-destructive tendency. Of course, it might merely be an expression of a melodramatic flair or it might be a rather generally morbid sense of life that is acute in adolescence but is not even then always associated with the suicidal.

Bad testers, and they exceed in numbers the good, abuse tests consistently; they err in their interpretations by being overconfident, dogmatic, overgeneralized, and coercive. In such tests as the Rorschach and TAT the weight upon the tester's wisdom is such that we might well say that the wise tester would be well off without the instrument, and surely the unwise one would be less dangerous without it.

It is through *interpretation* that the gap between the *objective* and the *subjective* aspects of guidance is bridged, for the function is not simply to guide the student into wise educational and vocational choice. It is to assist in the student's process of self-realization and life adjustment. In classic terms, it serves to assist the student "to know himself and to live the good life."

Obviously, the person is a great deal more than the sum total of what the tests say about him. Not more—a great deal more. And this is true despite the fact that now there exist literally hundreds of tests, either more or less valid and reliable, to which the individual may be subjected.

The second and more challenging related area is *counseling*. Counseling is concerned with the attempt of the trained and objective worker to meet and respond to the *whole* person of the student. In a sense, the objective area is the realm of "guidance"; the subjective area, of "counseling."

The world of the student is a great deal more than a matter of education and work. The student lives in a vast complex of human relations, some satisfying, some producing discontent; some helpful, some hurtful. Many students ride the crosscurrents and conflicts of life with fair success. They have problems, but they handle them.

Others some of the time and some much of the time encounter such anxieties, conflicts, and problems that they are less than fully effective as persons. They become "tied up in knots."

Often they would like help, someone to talk to, but they have no one to turn to. That is what the counselor is for: to give the student someone to turn to. Even more, he is qualified to respond to the student's need. In brief, his qualifications should be these:

1. He is *available*. He has time and this is what he has been hired for.

2. He is *trustworthy*. Students can trust him because he has been taught to receive confidence and to keep it. Wise school administration supports him in this role, for it knows that if the counselor's knowledge about a student becomes "official" knowledge, the effectiveness of the counseling function is destroyed.

3. Therefore, and for other reasons, he is *not to be feared*. We all know the fear of those who have knowledge about us that may be used against us. The counselor is effective to the degree that he is not feared. Paradoxically, he is effective in the subjective area because of our next qualification.

4. He is *objective*. Unlike the parent, the teacher, the school principal, even the spiritual adviser, the counselor should have nothing that he wants to do *to* the student. His goals for the student are intrinsically the student's own goals. The counselor only wants to assist the student to a *greater degree of self-awareness and a fuller realization of the student's state of being*. He is more fully qualified in these respects because of the next qualification.

5. He is *nonjudgmental*. "Judge not that ye be not judged" is an ancient admonition, but who can listen to an intimate revelation from a person with whom one is personally and emotionally involved without leaping to judgment? We want to say, and too often do: "Oh, that is terrible," or "Why did you do that?" or "That was very good—or bad, or very wise—or foolish of you." Thus, generally, we put an end to communication. These statements lead only to guilt, to denial, to self-justification, to self-defense, or simply to argument. But the counselor wants to hear the matter out, he wants the student to find out all that he knows about himself. Therefore, he is trained to say, "Well," or "So?"—or simply to sit quietly and wait for more. In a word, he is "accepting."

Because these are qualifications that all mature adults should possess, why hire specialists for the schools? Unfortunately, there are fewer mature persons than the world needs. But more to the point, the school is busy with its other purposes; unless someone qualified is given the time to respond to the student's personal needs, perhaps no one else will find the time.

Now, clearly, there is another distinction to be marked between guidance and counseling. The *guidance* aspect of this program is for all the students. It is related to the academic function of the school—to prepare for further education and for a place in the work-a-day world. The fulfillment of this function is necessarily a part of the official knowledge of the school. All students share in the guidance program because all students share in the need for it.

The *counseling* aspect is different. The availability and qualifications of the counseling service should be known to all. But its services should be imposed upon no one. Respect for the individual demands that he surrender his privacy only voluntarily. Believe this, however, that such are the problems of youth (or of man) that if these services are known to exist, the counselor will soon be one of the busiest persons on the premises.

One illustration may point up this distinction. Discipline is an important educational problem. This fact sometimes leads to unwise use of the counselor. In effect, he is made the disciplinary officer and is therefore forced to negate his qualifications. His knowledge becomes official; he is feared; he is coerced into judgments; he becomes an *institutional* rather than a *personal* figure. Therefore, he might be better unqualified because he is forced to deny his qualifications.

But, with respect to discipline, if the counselor is allowed to retain his professional mantle, he has a large contribution to make. Most disciplinary cases are with students who are first of all in trouble with themselves. Counseling affects discipline directly as it relates to the real source of disciplinary problems: conflicts within the students themselves. Nonetheless, ever recall that not always is the "disciplinary case" a student "who is wrong and needs to see it." Sometimes the school is wrong, not through its intent but because it is busy and impersonal. The student in trouble sometimes personalizes the school's intent toward him, when really the fault is that the school simply does not see him. Through personal communication this may be exactly what the student comes to see; thus, blind rebellion is translated into an awareness that allows him to function. It allows him to function with his critical faculty still alive. He knows it would be better if the school could see him, but he responds to his awareness without action that is socially unacceptable and that is most damaging to himself. He responds better not because he submits to authority, but because he sees the whole picture.

Surely, it cannot be pointed out too strongly that the jobs of guidance and counseling should be made and kept professional. There are residual hazards in the guidance function. The guidance movement is the country cousin of the discipline of psychology. The basic discipline of the guidance worker or counselor is psychology— and a rather too-exclusive one. The immature counselor is likely to be a half-baked Freudian, a psychoanalyst manqué. Though performing in the most taxing of humanistic roles, because of this strictured education, he may be ill educated in the humanistic sense.

Too often the student is attracted to this field because of hopes—quite legitimate, indeed—for finding solutions to his own psychological problems. It is quite likely that a boy who has suffered polio in his youth might be motivated to do research on this virus. However, the medical profession has never regarded the sickness of an individual as a qualification for the practice of medicine. The psychological professions, on the other hand, have often either failed to grasp this distinction or have inadequately guarded against the hazard.

What should be the preparation of the counselor? Maturity, for one thing: it is not a profession for boys and girls. Though the trend is away from this, teaching experience should be a requirement; for it is in the classroom that the counselor learns about students *as* students. It is in the classroom that he learns about the roles and problems of his colleagues, the other teachers. In a word, without teaching experience which is axiomatically only to be gained by teaching, he may be an institutional illiterate. Further, and this is a lesson the young often need, in teaching as perhaps in no other job, he will learn the meaning of a good day's work.

The counselor should study psychology, to be sure, but it should not be either the exclusive or primary base of his preparation. Clearly the counsequence of this narrow preparation has led to professional narrowness and dangerous dogmatisms. The basic preparation must be philosophical in the broad sense. History, literature, anthropology, sociology are as necessary to the preparation of the counselor as psychology. Psychological doctrines derive from historical, cultural, and sociological settings. It is a credit to psychological research that it has established this fact. It has, however, rather jealously guarded against the professional implications of the fact.

The counselor who is narrowly prepared is dangerous to his clientele. No matter what his avowed techniques, the attraction for the psychologically insecure in this profession is the chance to play Jehovah, to manipulate and to guide children in directions that suit his own fantasies. The broadly prepared counselor through exercise of his special skills serves as a useful agent of the school's complete purpose: to help every student make the most of his educational opportunities and to help him develop to the utmost his human capacities.

Commentary: Toward a Responsible Profession

The teaching profession must either reaffirm its commitment to man or abdicate its humanistic pretensions. It must demonstrate either its strength or its docility. Is ours, after all, a docile profession? Who knows? The question that any of us can answer is narrower: "Am I docile?" The answer may or may not content us. But, after all, it is with oneself that a man must primarily come to terms. In solid nineteenth-century language, conscience can be more terrible than any institutional force.

The better question is: "Am I responsible?" Thus, we cannot inquire *"Have we a responsible profession?"* We can, however,

283

assess our qualities, can decide *alone*—as all moral decisions must be made—what stuff we have to support us. Then, when a crucial issue arises, we can ask, "Who will be responsible?" Then responsible men can step forward and be counted. Even so, we do not know anything about an abstract profession—for a profession is not a single organism; it is an aggregate of men. It is not unimportant, however, that we have a count of the men about us who take stock of themselves and judge themselves ready for responsibility.

No sophistication of institutional analysis, no rationalized procedure for adjustment to the irrational, can ever reverse the meaning of words (not even in *1984*). If I lack courage, it does not mean that I am wise, simply that I am cowardly. If I will not be responsible, I am by definition irresponsible. In the name of charity, it may be fine for me to forgive myself all manner of faults; *but,* I had better not, in the name of truth, create structures which make it appear that my very vices lead to virtues, which, as a matter of fact, I do not possess.

But who needs palaver on this question? We all know, because we are expensively educated in the tradition of the West, all that we need know on this subject. We know the real question and all its implications—*"Am I a free man?"*

This question does not ask whether someone or some institution is trying to limit or discourage my freedom. It is a most searching question as to one's own quality. In this civilized institution of the school, where literally the assurances to free exercise are better than almost anywhere else, if a teacher cannot assert calmly, "Yes, I am free," and behave that way, what is the prospect for man?

Lack of trust in others, lack of confidence in the process of open communication, and self-doubt may lead us to question our capacity to be free. Yet, I judge from what I see in men around me that if I can summon up the stuff to say, "Yes, I will be responsible," and take one step forward, I will find myself in good company. These are such old learnings, but they are not *tired* words—merely ancient ones.

Chapter IX

The Creative-
Aesthetic
Dimension

So, where our culture is concerned we are a fat gaseous aggregation; too much of everything; no good digestion of anything wholesome.

Too much education, mostly the wrong kind in the wrong places.

Too much money, most of it in the wrong places.

Too much food, most of that in the wrong places at the moment.

Too much machinery, the right kind in wrong.

Too much science, even in the right places.

Too much salesmanship of mechanical artifice in the name of art.[1]

—*Frank Lloyd Wright*

Discovery and reflection. How much opportunity do the schools give for *discovery;* how much time do they give for *reflection?*

The schools are our great hope. This belief is in keeping with the deep discontent concerning the performance of the school in

[1] Frank Lloyd Wright, *On Architecture* (New York: Duell, Sloan, and Pearce, 1941), p. 207.

285

releasing human potential. The schools, which should and could do much in this area, too often do much to discourage it. The human potential is to create, to invent, to be joyful, to sing, to dance, to love, to speculate, to know wonder and amazement. To be surprised by life, to feel its sadness, to endure in its tragedy, to revel in its comedy, and to be at one with all men in these things are all inherent in the human potential. And this potential the school so often leaves untouched.

The great distinction between a good school and a bad school can be readily identified and is this: whether children enter it eagerly and purposefully, laughing and happy, or enter it glum and sober, as scourged to their tasks as children once were who lined up to enter the mills, mines, and sweatshops. We have seen them often on the playground, dreading the first school bell. We have seen them at closing time, pushing their way out of doors, again laughing and chattering. It is as though they were leaving prison. But these are creatures made for learning; learning is the activity that makes them most human, most alive. And schools are said to *be* for learning. Should going to and coming from the school be like this?

In the good schools it is different. There is a distinct difference between the typical school and the excellent one. Excellent schools do exist, and they do nurture the traits that we have specified. Two schools, used illustratively, function conspicuously to draw out these traits in their students. Both of them are public schools; neither of them is a rich school. We observed Fairmont Heights High School, a Negro school near Washington, D.C. in the 1950s and compared it with a steel-mill town school in Weirton, West Virginia. Money is a necessity in running a school, but the difference between an ordinary school and a great one comes not from money. It comes from educational vision.

What characterizes good schools? "We trust the students," said the assistant superintendent of the Weirton schools. "We believe that they *must* have freedom to learn how to appreciate and use it."

In the high school at Weirton there are no bells announcing the beginning and ending of classes. There are clocks, and teachers and students alike know their schedules. When a student has no class, he is free: he may go to a laboratory, the library, a gymnasium, a conversation room, or simply outside and lounge on the campus. An important feature of the program is *independent study:* each student spends a large block of time on a special project. These include scientific experiments, research papers, construction in shops, building an automobile, even training a gaited horse. Respect for the interests and talents of all is the keynote.

Does this freedom of choice lower academic standards? Far from it—many more graduates now qualify for college from this school than formerly. In fact, the school has the atmosphere of a serious intellectual institution rather than a mere academic treadmill. The most active places in this school are its library and laboratories. The library, though well-equipped, is so crowded that students often must sit on the floor to read. At Weirton they say, "We have wall-to-wall kids in here."

What about discipline? These students represent all social classes, all races, many religions. Few of them come from what are called "privileged homes." Most schools in similar communities have elaborate systems of control, policelike codes of rules and punishments, and plenty of disciplinary problems. But at Weirton there seem to be no disciplinary problems. With the pressure off, students exert their own controls like responsible human beings. The assertion is neither romantic nor idealistic. That is the way freedom works. When we observed the school, 1,400 students were enrolled there, yet when classes are passing you would estimate the figure at less than 500. There is no crowding, only normal conversational noise. (We observed this prior to recent changes.)

What is the atmosphere at Fairmont Heights High School, the other school? Dr. James Gholson, the great educator who was its principal, told the author: "I like to believe that everyone in this school, teachers, students, and custodians, knows the philosophy that is at work here."

Observation found this to be true. Some of the best statements about the school were heard from the students. "Everybody is treated fairly." "Teachers respect the students." "You get to learn what you need to know." "Nobody is more important than anybody else." "The teachers know their stuff." "We are learning how to live and to be good citizens."

What may be said of the morale of most schools? Too many of them are full of complaints and whining, from students and teachers alike—but not in Fairmont Heights. This school was a happy place. The conversation among the faculty was about education, which they found an exciting subject, not a depressing one. The students were glad to be in school. They were learning, and they liked it.

Thus, we confirm that the educator *can* be confident, both from research and from observation, that learning can be pleasurable and school a happy place. The school can bring to life the axiom of Anatole France, "One learns while one is being amused." Grim teachers proudly state, "My classroom is not a place of amusement." Perhaps what they are inadvertently boasting is that it is not a place of learning either.

What are the requisites for releasing human potential in the classroom? There must be belief in each student's potential and confidence in the natural inclination of the human creature to learn. "Trust the students," we were told. Second, the educator must know and apply the best research on the development of desirable characteristics. Without this knowledge the efforts of the school may be self-defeating. The school may state profound objectives, yet in lack of knowledge it may work toward quite opposite goals. Third, the school must establish itself as an institution that knows and practices the discipline of freedom. If self-reliance and responsibility are desirable characteristics (and who says that they are not), then they will only be learned where it is possible to rely upon self and where one is entrusted with responsibility.

Finally, teachers must realize their responsibility. The school must be taught by persons who trust children, love life, and are themselves at home in an environment of learning. The great teacher not only teaches, but he is the most eager *learner* in the classroom.

The Conditions for Creativity

The hardest premises for the schools to accept about creativity are the conditions for its nurture. To avoid frustrating and stifling creativity, to cease destroying it, would require drastic changes in the school. Actively to encourage and to nourish it would require no less than revolutionary change. The choices are hard, and policymakers in the public eye tend to shun hard choices. The road to creativity in the schools would involve the school intensively in the process of social change. This would increase the tension of the school vis-à-vis conventional child-rearing practices, unexamined value structures, conservative social forces, and the keepers of the keys of academic respectability. Creativity may well be a good thing, but how likely is its nurture in the school if the price be no less than hard choice and leadership in social change? Has not the school been more often than not a haven of conventional child-rearing practices, a neutral element in the value struggle, a bulwark of conservative social forces, and a veritable keeper of those keys of academic respectability?

False fronts in this arena are now hard to maintain. A decade of research in the 1950s may not have adequately defined creativity, but it somewhat established its nature and the conditions that either stultify or encourage its development. The odds, we contend, are heavily against the schools in doing anything about creativity. Anything, we add in haste, except to talk about it.

Could something be done? Yes, indeed! Aesthetic theory, research on creativity, the technical development of the arts are quite as far advanced as comparable elements in the field of physical education, and for example, the schools are not without tangible memorials of decision-making in this field.

Perhaps, then, the price is too high. If the school is strong in all else, then to reverse its nature could cause gain in one dimension at the expense of loss in several, a patent bad bargain. *But that is not the case.* The case that the school is doing well is largely an aca-

289

demic one. It is doing well in what has little consequence *outside* the school. The conditions for creativity are the conditions for self-realization, the conditions for living a full life. Creativity could infuse the whole school and translate it into a *real* institution, a place where live people learn, and are, and create.

What are the school's conditions and verities? Routines, schedules, order—it is a clock-ordered establishment. Railroads and airlines hesitate less to alter their schedules than do the schools. Values! A good deal was said about values in one of our graduate classes one evening. The class waxed eloquent on values, moral and spiritual ones at that. Now, one likes to be "agin" sin, so eventually we pressed for clarification: "What," we asked, "is one of these values that the school should represent and develop?" The question seemed fair and relevant. The response was disappointing. Eloquence vanished; except for little nervous shifts and shuffling, silence abounded. But professional resourcefulness was not altogether lacking. A solid man, whom we knew to be a competent curriculum coordinator, after reviewing in his mind the whole great tradition of the Western world, raised his hand, took his stand alongside Socrates, Augustine, Aquinas, and Einstein, and proposed "punctuality." *Punctuality,* and we could almost hear a reedy schoolteacherish "Yes, punctuality, punctuality, and don't chew gum, don't chew gum!"

The creative potential on which the school so often lays its heavy hand is a very delicate thing.

The British novelist, Joyce Cary, who was also a fine educator, wrote this in a wonderful novel about childhood called *Charley Is My Darling:* "The Child is a born creator. He has to be, for though in sympathy he is one with those he loves, in mind he is alone. He has to do his own learning and thinking. . . . Anyone can see how children enjoy discovery and reflection. But also how soon they are bored with what is known."[2]

From his analysis of the research on *creativity* Gaston Lebois[3]

[2] Joyce Cary, *Charley Is My Darling,* from the Prefatory Essay to the Carfax Edition (New York: Harper, n.d.), p. 348.

[3] Gaston Lebois, "An Analysis and Synthesis of the Concept of Creativity" (Ph.D. dissertation, University of Pittsburgh, 1963).

summarizes the personality traits of the creative individual under two headings, cognitive traits and noncognitive (or affective) traits. From his lists (32 characteristics in the first instance, 48 in the second) we incorporate and select the following:

> *Cognitive traits:* sensitivity to problems; fluency and flexibility of thinking; ability to form rich syntheses of ideas, ability to sense one's own ignorance or gaps in knowledge; "childlike perceptiveness combined with a sophisticated mind" and "the capacity to be puzzled, to wonder, and to be surprised"; openness to experience.
>
> *Noncognitive traits:* freedom from persistence; unconventionality; tolerance for ambiguity; interest in the meanings and implications of facts rather than the small details sometimes related to facts; acute self-awareness, openness to inner life, and a distinct sense of independence; maturity, forcefulness, strength, self-reliance, self-assertion; being at home in complexity; need for recognition, variety, autonomy, and ultimate closure; "a willingness to take a larger calculated risk than the average person"; "a lack of fear of the unknown, the mysterious, and the puzzling"; internal locus of evaluation; the tendency to withdraw and to be quiescent; and "a willingness to be born every day."

The school has three potential models, which we will indicate only for purposes of reminder. In the forthcoming analysis we shall point out that only *one* of the three choices represents activation of the principles of creativity; the other two choices *deny* them.

> 1. *The ordinary school.* Its characteristics are well known. They simply comprise the standard, common practices of contemporary "schooling."
>
> 2. *The neobehavioristic, mechanized, programed curriculum.* This model is promoted *ad nauseam* in the "literature."
>
> 3. *The new model.* This is the school that is the legitimate progeny of the best educational thought and research of our century. For instructional practice it modernizes and adapts the Morrison Unit Method, common learnings, and democratic classroom procedures with ample opportunity for self-direction and individual study.

The analysis in Chart 9.1 clearly makes its own case. If creativity is to be nurtured by the school (and what educator would deny that it should be?) the choice is obvious.

Chart 9.1

Creativity: Affinities and Contradictions

Selected Traits of the Creative*	Characteristics of the Ordinary School	Characteristics of Neo-behaviorists in Programed or Mechanized Teaching	Characteristics of the New Model Conceptual Learning
Sensitivity to problems	Resistant to problems —	Problems solved by programer —	Problem directed, problem-solving +
Fluency and flexibility of thinking	Prescribed directions and limits on inquiry —	Jerky structural patterns —	Developmental, conceptual growth +
Ability to form rich synthesis	Compartmentalized learning, atomized programing —	Predigested synthesis —	Synthesis search built in as goal and procedure +
Ability to sense own ignorance or gaps in knowledge	Exterior judgmental view, ignorance as a fault rather than a fact —	Gaps anticipated —	Exploration and inquiry to serve +
Capacity to be puzzled, to wonder, and to be surprised	A priori judgments, cocksureness —	Built-in boredom —	Goals include unknown and unanticipated +
Freedom from persistence	Persistence synonymous with virtue —	Persistence required —	Achievement valued ahead of schedules, programs, and protocols +
Unconventionality	Conformity rewarded —	Conformity required —	Rooted in experimental, premium on inventiveness, uniqueness of contribution +
Tolerance for ambiguity	Much inadvertent ambiguity + or —	Ambiguity synonymous with evil —	Scientific in suspended judgments, mature in avoidance of dogmatism +

Interest in meanings and implications of facts	— Small details enshrined —	Facts as steps to more facts —	Meanings and uses of facts consistently stressed +
Acute self-awareness	— Depersonalized environment —	Depersonalized instrumentality —	Respect for and utilization of *presence* of the whole person +
Openness to inner life	— Outer-directed atmosphere —	The person as object of manipulation —	Conceptualization dependent on internalization +
Distinct sense of independence	— Valuelessness —	Subservience to the instrument —	Constant use of independent judgment in planning, searching, appraising, evaluating, and generalizing +
At home in complexity	— Rich in confusion —	Studied oversimplification —	Makes learning at home in complexity +
Risk-taking willingness	— Always plays it safe —	Rules out risk-taking —	Utilizes and teaches probabilities +
Tendency to withdraw and become quiescent	— No place to hide —	Enforced activity —	Room for every person and every mood +
Willingness to be born every day	— The same yesterday, today, and tomorrow —	Willingness to bore every day —	Continually drawing up new goals, constant reappraisal, and evaluation +

+ equals supportive or nurturant.

— equals frustrating or destructive.

* Excerpted from Gaston Lebois, "An Analysis and Synthesis of the Concept of Creativity" (Ph.D. dissertation, University of Pittsburgh, 1963).

Toward Nurture of the Creative

Creativity builds new realities. The artist himself may in a sense merely paint. To say this does not patronize him. Rather it accepts him. He is what he is—an artist. The verb *paint* is active and observable of what he does. The noun, *the work,* is present and discernible of what he creates. But in essence he has given the human environment a new complexity. Something new, in his case a painting, is in the world to be encountered or experienced. At the very least someone may have to step aside to avoid bumping the easel. But much more, the experience of the object adds the qualifiers, the appraisals, the judgments as to how the artist has worked, what his effort means and evokes, and what it is worth. The adverbs and adjectives may move the artist deeply or leave him unconcerned. Usually he is not unaffected by at least someone's critique. The point is that having made an addition to the environment, he adds to the sum of potential human experience; something new is there to evoke response, both cognitive and affective. Consequently, human communication is enriched. There is something else to be talked about. Obviously what the artist has experienced in the act of painting, even his intent, is not covered in this comment. This is a good deal harder to get at, but we will not altogether avoid the subject.

Creativity labors for originality, yearns for the unique. Men's motivations are too complex to write off in invidious or competitive terms. However, creators ordinarily do not seek merely to do some things better; they try to do what has not been done before.

To create is to participate in the universal. Each human is a product of the creative. He was created; he is creating; he has potential for further creation. Conversely, creativity is universal in the human potential. It is both a condition and an attribute of man. Education, therefore, if its program is to be responsive to the complete quality of man, must recognize this common element and provide opportunity, nurture, encouragement, and discipline to its development.

The school, one is tempted to say, has done rather badly for creativity in comparison with other aspects of its enterprise. The statement would only be true, however, in comparison to the academic (or unreal) aspects of the program, the largely inconsequential purposes that it has so considerably realized. But this comparative disadvantage the creative shares with the other real dimensions of experience: the humanistic, the scientific, the vocational. The unreal alone—in our terms, the academic—can profit at the expense of the real. But if any dimension of reality is neglected the total of reality is thereby diminished. This seems axiomatic, and it seems so terribly obvious as to be not worth stating, except that in curriculum making it is so generally ignored.

Creativity, and, therefore, the whole curriculum, have suffered in the school as a consequence of certain *false assumptions.*

Creativity is a scarcity item in the human make-up. It will be found rarely and unpredictably; therefore, the school can scarcely be expected to make itself broadly competent to meet it. Then either of two choices follow: (1) its encouragement is better left to parents or philanthropy, or (2) the school puts creativity into a curricular quarantine befitting its rarity. It is either isolated on the basis of special subjects, especially the arts, or entrusted to the general custodians of the peculiar, often called "special" educators.

Creativity is to be regarded as unrelated, or at least peripheral, to the central purposes of the school. If it be so rare and the function of the school be to serve the many, its neglect may bring only negligible deprivation, whereas a large concern for its nurture might well provide curricular distortions, exaggerate the "fads and frills," and even get to the state where the "tail wags the dog."

Therefore, it is possible to accomplish most of the worthwhile purposes of education for most students without deliberate concern for the creative dimension.

Another specious but common view obtains in a slightly different context from the foregoing. It derives not so much from the error of the scarcity assumption, but from an inadequate view of the real nature of creativity. After all, public education has given many hostages to the concept of self-expression. In developing opportunities for self-expression the schools have surprised themselves and the public by discovering that almost every child has something to express and can often develop a skill by which to express something quite well. This insight could be a window to the fundamental reality: the universality of creativity in the human condition and the human potential. But viewed partially or rejected as a basic insight, it leads to this specious assumption: The school serves creativity well when it provides multiple opportunities for students to develop the special skills of self-expression that come naturally or readily to them. Under the auspices of this partial view of the matter, the school is rare that leaves any Johnny or Susan without the chance to toot a horn, twirl a baton, write a poem, act a role, trip a light fantastic, cut a dress, build an end table, lead a cheer; these the school reckons as good works on behalf of the Muses—and such as they are, so they are.

The school needs to take a more fundamental look at the reality of the creative, not merely to respond to one more strident note from the educational bandwagon sounding "creativity." It is altogether possible to *do more* about creativity, either spuriously or partially perceived, and thereby actually to imperil basic curricular improvement. Special pitfalls abound in this area. To marry "creative programs" to certain popular elite ventures such as "special programs for the gifted" or "talent searches" is to instrumentalize the scarcity fallacy.

What is needed is a penetrating study of the complex attributes of creativity and the nature of creativity in the individual. The latter phrase more frequently reads, "the nature of the creative individual," but the rephrasing is deliberate and necessary. The "creative individual," as he has been studied, is well worth the recent flurry of research directed his way. Our assumption, however, is that from him we learn not the characteristics of a special breed but the nature of the person in whom creativity has not by dint of the blunderings of home, school, and society been blocked off, discouraged, beaten out, or scared away. In a word "the creative individual" is a person relatively undamaged in this major dimension of his human potential.

Patently, the creative–aesthetic dimension of experience must pervade the school and its program. True, certain subjects derive most directly from this area of experience and thereby contribute most directly to the appreciations, skills, attitudes, judgments, and accomplishments pertinent to the creative–aesthetic. However, the real target is creative living.

Like so many other works of the school, the pursuit of the creative will be much eased and its achievements enhanced if the home is mobilized toward similar goals. The school need not remain passive with respect to home influences; it cannot determine them, but it can affect them. In its public communication, in its meetings with parents and civic groups, the school can supply a creative–aesthetic press, even as it has learned to do in educating the public for the necessity to enlarge school budgets.

The home should furnish an early and continuing nurture to this potential for human growth. Parents can learn the rudiments of such nurture and adapt their ways to its requirements even as they somewhat have learned to respect the findings of child psychology and have disciplined their own behavior accordingly. Quite feasible ways of achievement, by which the home could be more supportive in this area, are easily recognizable. The budget could reflect an aesthetic bias: monies allotted to buy a real painting, to attend the cinema on a critically selective basis, and to purchase the materials for artistic expression. "Books instead of butter" might be an appropriate family slogan.

More important, the home should be alive in creative–aesthetic decision-making. A young housewife stated in class that she could hardly wait until she could afford to hire an interior decorator because she had no taste herself. Such an admission is not shameful, but sad, not only because "taste" is educable, but because of the default on life. Unless a person deliberately shapes out of his own needs, values, and experience the artifacts of his most immediate environment, he literally has no place to live. If he has some

297

central awareness of self and chooses "what he likes," that is, what relates meaningfully to his uses and his feelings, he need not fear the result. Form will surely follow function, and harmony will derive from the relation to the central awareness of self that is requisite to all satisfactory behavior. Form and harmony will, of course, be shattered if the person makes his choices with shifty glances right and left at the caprices of fashion, the ballyhoo of hucksters, and the invidious purposes of the neighborhood. Families can increase in cohesion and their homes can grow in beauty in no better way than by choosing together the rugs, chairs, pictures, lamps, and other tools among which they will live. They must only stubbornly and consistently apply simple criteria of how well it will serve us and how well do we like it. The family that grows in such confidence begins to abound in it and often discovers that it would rather build its own furniture and paint its own pictures; then a creative environment is really actualized.

If the home is imitative, conformist, timid, invidious in making its aesthetic choices, the children it sends to school will need to be not only instructed but "morale-built" to be human in the creative respect.

Why have we not spoken of the home "giving lessons"—in ballet, piano, fiddle, horn, voice, figure-skating, or juggling? Not because we underrate accomplishments in these fields, but because the matters we are stressing are educationally of greater significance.

On Aesthetic Restraint

Program- and policy-makers can be grateful for the research-produced clarifications and limitations to the term creativity. Many matters lie beyond the scope of such inquiry and definition. We can only assert a few and even those with less profundity than we would wish.

Surely creativity stems but little from meanness and the constriction of the human spirit. The assertions of genius have ever seemed to derive from an awful awareness of unique personal authenticity. One is even tempted to say that the authentic creator, the artist, asserts himself on behalf of man. However, such a thought probably confuses the *artist* with the *saint,* whose works, even his feats of supererogation, are truly in behalf of man.

Nonetheless, the artist is found at work, and while one must hesitate to cast him as a saint, it is hard to see him as one who works *against* man. If he goes for "hire" to tyrants or ambitious men, then one must suspect that his hand is not guided by creativity but only by a sort of craftiness. What do they sell who paint bold duchesses better than they are? Or when the brush and palette are employed to induce delusion of a political nature, does the artist's hand then take issue with his mind, or does it work in harmony delineating a delusion that the artist fondly shares?

Art does stand in prejudice when it goes to work for such causes as war. For one man's dream is ever another man's delusion. Who works without a reason? Now this were surely sufficient to reveal the complexity of this potential in which we expect the school to improve its efforts. It begins, however, to put teeth into the warning that when one speaks easily and generalizes confidently even from a plethora of little researches, one may be speaking and generalizing foolishly.

Let us lead further from our assertion: *Aesthetic theory must come to school as the stuff of curriculum, but the school must never arrogate to itself an aesthetic by which to select and reject, by which to judge, or by which to praise and condemn.* A good deal may be spun out from this. Explicit danger exists when the school takes the beginning of knowledge as completed wisdom. The work of the school is to explore and to release creativity, not to define and surely not to capture it.

That the school can thwart, frustrate, and stultify the creative has been well demonstrated. Even in its academic province, the school has passed over a large and exciting body of content. In the realm of aesthetic theory the subject matter that can be learned is abundant. In few areas of potential learning experience are the cognitive and the affective so closely joined.

The Aesthetic of Games

Let us now essay a creative exploration close to the heart of the school—its games. We assert that a considerable part of the affective attachment to these games by the whole audience of the school reflects a kind of aesthetic starvation. Let none assert that games fail to assuage this hunger. To the contrary: no one doubts that Athens sought and found aesthetic satisfaction in its games. The bullring is also evocative in this domain. If the discus thrower were a fit inspiration for statuary, so the *corrida* has inspired the sculptor, painter, poet, musician, and novelist. There must be art at the plaza de toros, for men will not sit long in the sun simply to see cattle slaughtered. If there be such force in such games, then doubt not the effect of the homely sports of Americans: football, basketball, and baseball, to name only the most popular.

The human perceptive system seems to have a "hankering" after the elements of what some call beauty—form, composition, harmony, and often these in motion. Whether this hankering is largely in the nature of the creative or more considerably a product of acculturation, it is as common as any other "universal."

Sports writers given to the trite and true phrase still do not blush to speak of the "poetry of motion." And bleacher fans who would indeed blush to be caught in the corridors of an art gallery yell out the aesthetic judgment of beautiful when a player makes a sensational catch. But beauty is ever in the eyes of the beholder. To fans of the winning team a flat-in-the-air, last-minute, diving-touchdown catch is a thing of beauty and a joy for some little time; to the losing fans stand, it is a horror.

The Music Man limned extravagantly the attraction of the quondam favorite dropout diversion: P.O.O.L. In appropriate Bible-Belt error its hold on boys was attributed to the allure of evil. But the smoky old pool hall attracted not so much with sin as with beauty. To be sure, the identity of these two was often suspected. But in the steady light only softened by tobacco smoke lay form, composition, sense, and order framed in a green baize setting. Any artistry compels respect, amounting to a sort of reverence. The hush of this esteem falls frequently among rude men, depending, of course, upon the artistry and dedication of those engaged in the game. The attendant lives of the men and boys who come to pool halls are often absurd, witless, unpredictable, formless, erratic—though not necessarily more so than those brought to polo grounds or golf courses. On the green-topped table, however, lie in focus precision and predictability. Cause and effect are visible and more closely related than in most human affairs. The science of ballistics, probably unmentioned but well applied, is in control. The staccato click of the balls, the shuffling feet, the spiraling smoke, the swift etching of lines and angles, the satisfying thud of the object disappearing in the pocket: these are the elements of art made, known, felt, and commented on.

Before dismissing the case as far-fetched, consider further. Baseball fans are patient folk. Do we attribute this virtue simply to patriotism? Surely not to a constant fever pitch of excitement? Try the factor of aesthetic appeal. This is the one constant that might induce a baseball spectator to sit attentively for three long hours. The moments of excitement are rare and hardly worth waiting for. But the pleasure in the setting is real. Now and then a dramatic tableau is enacted: runner sliding into base, shortstop palming the ball and swooping to the tag, umpire laying judgment, hands sweeping dramatically in the call. This is as photogenic as the raising of the flag on Iwo Jima—and unstaged.

The athletes themselves in pose, in posture, and in motion offer a stream of aesthetic satisfactions to the fan. An infielder crouched to move on the slightest cue in any direction; a pitcher poised at the peak of windup; a batter tense, alert, at the instant the bat draws back—all these enact the kinetic potential of man in form dynamic and complete, worthy of a Phidias. Fifty thousand fans (art lovers) crowded into Shea Stadium to revel in the creative wonder of the Mets may or may not document the point!

As for basketball, which was once a game before the boys outgrew the basket, how can we account for its continuing appeal? It is thoroughly stylized, altogether predictable—unless the teams are woefully mismatched, and then it is no game either. We would not put a bunch of muscle-bound hoofers on stage with the Royal Ballet. But when two teams of basketball artists really belong on the floor together, we have not a game but a dance: a dance familiar and lovely until almost the last four minutes. Graceful men race to and fro, they posture, pivot, leap, throw—they grimace, shout, enact their roles. They are not less practiced in technique nor more unconscious of their studied grace than ballerinas. At the point where the dance ends (four minutes before the end of the so-called game), the score will be even, or different in a nonstatistically significant sense (after all, with two groups not both can be "ahead"). At this point art lovers should in all logic leave. For now the comedy begins: the comedians, officials they are called in this variation of the theater of the absurd, take over. They spoil the dance, and in the name of what was once an athletic contest, in order to designate a "winner" they institute a free-throwing contest. Thus the home team always wins for the classic reason that black horses eat more than white horses—there are more of them. Yet, thanks to the yearning for aesthetic satisfaction, basketball survives as an art its demise as a competitive sport.

The purpose of this disquisition has been twofold: (1) to demonstrate the aesthetic hunger so rampant amid the school and its patrons and (2) to suggest content for the classroom. These matters will not fail to engage the students' minds or their emotions. Nothing in the total program of the schools will involve the total personalities of students, administrators, and some faculty more than do these games. Surely then, the school should offer the opportunity to study and explore the "why" of such total involvement. If such inquiry should find the motivation to lie in the aesthetic realm rather than in the cruder drives of atavistic demonstrations of prowess and tribal loyalties, it should gratify the *amour propre* of contemporary man, who likes to call himself civilized.

In Matters of Taste

If the yearning of the students for aesthetic satisfaction is great, the response of the school beyond the playing field is thin. Many high-school graduates have heard no better comment than the worn phrases of John Keats. (And rarely do they encounter a Grecian urn.) If they have a yearning, they also have a need—the need to develop taste. The school need not and should not abdicate from participation in the development of taste. We have already established that the school must not itself propose or inculcate an aesthetic. But that it should dwell richly and variously in the realm of the aesthetic is quite another matter.

We are not advocating that the school argue with the individual's taste or deplore his lack of it. We should be assertive at this point without being judgmental, and we believe there are certain strong observations with which teachers and students ought to contend. One manner of contention is to deal rudely and with immediate rejection, but this is tasteless. Another is first to consider, to reject on the basis of reasonable counterpropositions. This is the exercise of taste.

The contemporary American scene is a potpourri of bad taste. This comment should not be interpreted as intellectually snobbish or dyspeptic. By authority of the sentiment of a "first lady," to love this land is to deplore its man-made eyesores, its well-displayed junk heaps and billboards, all of which obscure its beauties. In association with these sentiments, the school should turn its scrutiny on other junk heaps piled high by tasteless and sometimes greedy men. Perhaps not by defining taste but at least by exposing tastelessness a generation will appear that knows to take offense at such barbarism, and to provide a poor climate for peddlers of such rubbish.

Unlike other tasks of education, this may not be Sisyphean. It may be almost insurmountable, but it may be accomplished. Insofar as the environment of taste is concerned, children in our schools dwell in a yowling madhouse. The execrable tunes of the peddlers have assailed their ears from the crib and stroller upward. The households of their dwelling, rich, poor, and intermediate, become less and less authentic. They have a common connection: if rich, the aspiration to fill their places with slick, synthetic, unknown, or misunderstood artifacts is fulfilled; if poor, they know the names, the prices, and where to get them when the day comes that their charge accounts will encompass them.

Not authentic? No, these children of America derive from numerous provincialisms and ethnocentrisms; their families are stubborn and conscientious in preserving their biases and bigotries. But they care not a fig for keeping a chair which great grandma rocked in. Of course, if they are on a colonial kick, they may pay a nice penny for an imitation of one somebody else's granny jiggled. They are running so afraid in the knowledge of their fundamental tastelessness that they will hide a picture which they cherish and which they could state good reasons for liking, to make room for an Art Club's prescription or the recommendation of a "decorator."

The cities, like so many homes, are aesthetic jungles. Most everywhere new building amounts not to construction in any philosophical sense, but to catastrophe. In St. Louis the crime lay in assuming a necessity to create a new architectural tradition when the city already had one. Pittsburgh lies beyond complaint; anything it did architecturally would be better than what went before. To build can be to create, to make better, to increase and not to diminish the aesthetic, to add to our neighbor's vista rather than to spoil his view. But in the main, our children are raised amid the raucous and the meaningless. In the abdication from taste, the "taste-makers" have moved in to peddle objects that are sought in spite of their sterility and ugliness.

What can the school do? It can undertake responsibility for development of the creative–aesthetic potential as seriously as it does the scientific–quantitative and the vocational–utilitarian.

One way to begin is by showing students the differences between the real and the counterfeit. In the elementary classroom this could be the comparison of a well-engraved postage stamp and a cheaply lithographed one, for example. Little children love to handle, to explore materials. They will respond to tactile experience in the varied feel of leathers and imitations, of gold and brass, of good cloth and shoddy, or well-finished woods and badly applied veneers. Taste, even in materials, is parallel to choice, in that it involves good, better, best appraisals.

The child is very much in the market. No use to argue or to deplore this fact. In all likelihood, barring war or depression, the children of tomorrow will spend even more money that they will call their own than do the children of today. The point is raised not to introduce the subject of consumer education, but to present another reason for the need to develop aesthetic judgment. That the toy market is a year-round business is to us a prime indication of the near decadence of the affluent society. That parents in our society wish to spoil their children rotten is a rather genial human disposition; it is only too bad that so many are able to do it. If an educator is not likely to influence parents to cut their children's allowances, he can influence the school to help them resist the purchase of outlandishly useless, ugly expensive junk.

Let the children bring their toys to school. Let them talk of what is real. The boys will have plenty of guns, and most of them will be broken. (Waste no emotional energy deploring their possession of guns. This is a culture of considerable bellicose proportions.) Let them talk about these toys. Why are they broken? Was it hard to break them? How do you feel when your toys break? Are a lot of broken toys nice to have around? Do they look pretty? Do they make you feel good? What materials are your broken toy guns made of? What is a real gun made of?

The point is not to glorify guns but to assert the aesthetic distinction between the real and the spurious. Poor little broken plastic rifle—stock, barrel, sights, and trigger are all cheaply constructed fakes. Let that little boy feel a real rifle (instruct him another day, in its care, its dangers, its uses, its responsibilities). Have him run his hand and eyes over that fine carved burnished walnut stock; heft that substance; study the imposing quality of that gun metal. Soon that very same boy will begin to comprehend the work and skill in the making of this real and lethal object. Before long the class will talk of the relation of form to function and that is where we wish to lead them. For even as in mathematics, we want them to abide in conceptual consistency from their first steps into the world of number, so in the creative–aesthetic will they dwell comfortably in the modern mind from childhood.

Our example of the gun illustrates the interrelated quality of the educational potential. The humanistic–ethical is seldom far removed from the aesthetic. The military would have its special approach to the problem of "The Gun." It would train in the assembling, firing, handling, and cleaning of the gun and would give explicit regulations in regard to the care and use of the weapon. Education would begin where training ended. Many of the questions that it would be involved with are not all possessed of definitive answers:

> What function does "The Gun" play in civilization?
>
> Under what circumstances is it right to employ "The Gun"?
>
> What regulation of firearms is necessary or justifiable?
>
> Why does the Bill of Rights assert the citizen's right to possess and bear arms?
>
> Is a home safer if a gun is available?
>
> Is an interest in guns a sign of manliness or of maturity?

The comparative ease of the first assignment is obvious. A sergeant may be trusted to carry successfully this burden of instruction. The questions raised by education are more profound and require a teaching beyond the ken of trainers.

The Academic Fate of the Creative

To dogmatize concerning creativity is contradictory in its very spirit. At the same time it is easy to sentimentalize over it. Our summation of research nonetheless comprises useful data in three respects: it furnishes working generalizations concerning conditions that nurture creativity; it delineates the conditions that sometimes thwart creativity, or at the very least irritate the more creatively disposed; it portrays by composite, if not in the definitive particular, the cognitive and affective disposition of the creative person.

If easy generalizations are dangerous in other fields, they are ruinous here, and some working principles are cautiously suggested. Surely the school can do more for its creative students than simply give them a bad time; it may also do the latter to its creative teachers. In a novel, Carolyn Glyn describes with poignant good humor the agony of an artistic English schoolgirl in a succession of ordinarily good and bad schools. In the end her sensible parents send her to art school. The girl's final words in the book are these: "It's all right, I thought. I do fit in. Art students still have their corners on. They've escaped. I've escaped. Everything's going to be all right after all."[4]

Creativity is a potential, it is not an accomplishment. Energy is a parallel; a waterfall possesses energy, but to be productive it must be harnessed, transformed, and transmitted. Creativity is a broadly distributed potential, a life force. The accomplishments of this life force are strangely distributed and difficult to assess.

For example, the educator has accomplished little in his attempts to define *genius*. At worst, he has made himself silly; at best, he has described the attributes of an extreme degree of academic aptitude. A genius then, in academic terms, might be one who accomplishes easily and exceptionally well the tasks the school sets for him. Or, in testing terms, a genius has an unusually high I.Q. In functional terms, such definitions have as much utility and make as much general sense as saying that a genius has a beard or a bald head.

"Genius" eludes definition. By its complexity it simply overwhelms the little definitions of the schools. Genius represents an extreme degree of talent and potential for accomplishment in some field of endeavor highly prized by some proportion of humanity. It is a highly selective term, but is exclusive of very little. It is amoral, unless qualified by a moral adjective. Because genius is so far from exclusive, it is one of the rare nouns in which meaning is strengthened by modifiers. "He is a genius" is practically a senseless

---

4 Carolyn Glyn, *Don't Knock the Corners Off* (London: Pan Books, 1966), p. 269.

comment. Statements that one is a business genius, a strategic genius, a literary genius leave plenty of room for ambiguity but begin to make some sense. But to work hard on its definition is a task from which we would warn the school away. Unless such a prize as the biggest genius of the junior class is about to be awarded, the school, like the society around it, will find little utility in semantic acrobatics around this word.

By now it should be apparent that the fate of the creative-aesthetic dimension of education is not merely its own. For the human person is one being indivisible; so too is the human potential an entity. Therefore, what stultifies one aspect of potential causes other aspects to wither and to decay. The school is institutionalized about concepts that attempt to divide being; it has devices that obscure this reality. Only in the academic sense, where learning is related to purely intrainstitutional criteria, is it reasonably possible to measure separated aspects of human development. It is ironically amusing that austere intellectual critics of progressive education, whose dedication to the classics constrained them to revere ritualistically the concept of the whole man, found it possible to heap scorn on the concept of the whole child.

Commentary: Toward a True Report

What can one say of a curriculum when one finds students taking a program of English, physics, American history, French, and economics? Where are music and the arts, for example? Or if this student's report card shows grades of A in English, history, and French, and Cs in physics and economics? To whom will such a report be relevant? College admissions officers and employers, possibly.

In this casual response, we may have stumbled upon a significant reality. The academic view of the person, fragmented and categorical as it is, resembles none other but the employer's view. From the vantage point of the school, this is the appropriate designation of the college. The college essentially screens candidates for admission as does any other employer: on criteria predictive of success in the chores that it will assign them. Obviously, an educational institution will be interested in an analysis of unrealized potentials toward which it can address itself in a program of development. The rather large probability that many will find this distinction obscure or absurd is merely evidence to the sorry reality that institutions of higher learning only employ grandiloquently the pious phrases of educational commitment, but practically (except for certain often despised institutions like public junior colleges) they behave toward applicants precisely like the personnel divisions of larger corporations.

In any situation that may fairly be called educational or lifelike, the person is regarded in a continuing total appraisal. The Peace Corps, for example, trains prospective volunteers in several aspects related to field purposes, but its most meaningful and crucial criterion for acceptance or rejection is a broad concept that it terms *suitability*. This resembles the condition of each partner's continuing appraisal in a healthy matrimonial relationship. At the very least, it would seem more schoolteacherish or employerlike than husbandly for a man to rate his wife periodically on such report-card elements as cookery, "bedmanship," constancy, companionability, diplomacy, but it is not uncommon for parents to call children to account as categorically as this.

No recourse to respectable educational theory will find sanction for turning the school into a vast personnel agency; Dewey and Hutchins among many others would be as one on this proposition. The sort of questions that are relevant to education are these:

What strength of self does the individual sustain?

In what balance are his capacities maintained?

Does his self-realization somewhat considerably match his potential?

What is his view of self, of the institution, of his claims upon the institution, and of his responsibilities to it?

What is his view of self, of his fellows, and of the obligations for communication and mutual support among them?

What is his peculiar phenomenology in perceiving the circumstances and events in which he lives?

What are his most considerable harmonies of circumstance?

What are his ungrudging gifts to the essential social consensus?

What are his dissonant traits? What are the cultural, the hereditary, and, most important, the *chosen* elements of integrity, his individuality—his apartness, his dissent, his discontent?

These are the questions that matter everywhere in life because they are lifelike, because they are what the person needs to know about himself, because they are what those whom he will live among need to know about him—because they are the very essence of creative living. That is, they matter everywhere except in the noneducational school and in the employment or admissions applications. These are none other than the central questions that all men, in whatever vocabulary, are constantly asking of themselves and of those with whom their lives are woven. It may be fanciful to envision them as the basis of a school's report. Beside them, nonetheless, the best report card seems a flimsy record.

However, be assured of two qualifications. First, these questions well answered will not leave lesser realities in doubt. He who lives well in response to such questions will, if a schoolboy, surely count well past ten; if husband, he will not betray his family; if farmer, he will not abandon his chores half done; if statesman, he will not shun a necessary unpopular public deed. The scores on lesser criteria are ancillary and subsidiary to performance on the major demands of life and may be safely subsumed or derived. However, the most elaborate profile of marks and test scores for a person unknown will not begin to give a glimmer of knowledge on the individual.

Second, these signal questions are the best, but not the only questions that may be asked. More penetrating questions could be asked, but these would be intrusive and perilously close to forbidden judgment. The questions that the school or the friend are permitted are those that are necessary to establish functional relationships. Even these must not be pushed to the point of intrusiveness or the invasion of privacy. It is not enough in the school that seeks to institutionalize human dignity to permit the student the right of refusal to answer, though it is an essential beginning. It must know when to cease to press the fair question. It must know the questions that it has no right to ask. These restraints should be binding equally upon all its personnel however disparate in function, from truant officer to guidance counselor.

The most sullied institutional practices of the school concern the types of records that they keep. The diploma of graduation from the humanized school will read:

> John, who has lived with us for some time, is found suitable, more or less ready to move on, to face life, to dwell happily, usefully, and responsibly somewhere among men. He will live in the development of universal potentials that he has already begun to perceive, realize, and fulfill. Whoever meets him, and abuses him little, need have no fear of him. He has learned much of his capacity to respect and to love; whatever is offered of these he can understand and respond to. He has learned of justice, and he will confront injustice. He has learned of mercy, and he will stand in the way of cruelty. He has learned of truth, and he will challenge the lie. He has lived well in this school; he will insist that he live in growing fulfillment. He has lived with others; he knows that he is one with all men. The good society will rejoice in his presence. But he has learned very well this latter lesson: that his life is linked with all humanity. Haters, corrupters, exploiters, take heed! There is no telling how far he will go to seek out the tormenters of man; there is no saying what trails he will walk barefoot in his quest for truth and justice.

Not less than this should be the diploma and record for every child. Moreover, if the school performs according to its mandate, it will be a true report. It will be evidence on the student; even more it will be evidence that the school is performing its creative function: the continuing creation of a responsible humanity.

Nothing is really relevant but this report. Let the colleges and the employers ask their lesser questions. If the foregoing be a true report, the student need not fear the examiners. But no matter how he pleases his inquisitors, if this not be a true report, he is ready to join not the body of humanity but the mass of wanderers, among whom men walk upright.

With this report made true and duly issued, school may mark another name upon its tablets and burn every other record. The school has no obligation to society or any of its institutions other than to complete its job and to certify it. That is its responsibility. It is not to be proud or unobliging that it should stand on this ground. The school simply must be too professional to offer anyone less than its most competent report on a student. Anytime that it cannot offer this diploma as a true report on a student it testifies to its own incompetence. Its job is to certify truly these things.

It should not need to be said, but before the day of graduation when all lesser documents should be *destroyed,* the school's records must be solely its own. It owes no dossiers to any agency, public or private. To cooperate with any other agency except in receiving their reports on matters germane to education or attendance is due to a false perception of communal responsibility. It is a betrayal of the school. It is a crime against the person.

Chapter X

The Scientific-Quantitative Dimension

Despite its spectacular successes, science is not yet firmly established in the human mind. Its increasing alienation from the problems which are of deepest concern for mankind might well transform the anti-utopian outbursts so characteristic of our time from a literary exercise into an antiscience crusade. In its mildest form, such a crusade will at least continue to clamor for a moratorium on science, under the pretext that knowledge is accumulating faster than it can be digested and therefore is becoming dangerous. In reality, of course, there cannot be any retreat from science. Rather, public apprehension and hostility point to the need for an enlargement of science. Scientists must take more to heart the questions which deeply concern human beings; they must learn to give greater prominence to large human values when formulating their problems and their results. Fortunately, this is probably easier than is commonly believed because . . . history shows that the broad implications of science can become integrated in the intellectual fabric of modern societies. Human cultures, like organisms and societies, depend for survival on their internal integration, an integration which can be achieved only to the extent that science remains meaningful to the living experience of man.[1]

—René Dubos

[1] René Dubos, "Science and Man's Nature," *Daedalus,* Journal of the American Academy of Arts and Sciences (Winter 1965), p. 244.

The Increase of Knowledge

The dramatic increase of knowledge in this century, often likened to an "explosion," has been invoked to some strange educational purposes. Western man has given many hostages to the pursuit of knowledge. In his enlightenment he has praised knowledge variously as power, as a fountain, and as great riches. The goal of liberation from ignorance and superstition through the quest for knowledge has been a pillar of many of his best hopes. "You shall know the truth and the truth shall set you free."

It appears now that there is an abundance of knowledge, or as seems implied in a favorite phrase on its increase, a hazardous superabundance. Instead of feeling enriched, eased in spirit, or set free by his increase, twentieth-century man acts fretful and embarrassed; he even stands in dread of it. Far from being grandly conscious of his enhanced power, he feels burdened, hag-ridden, and oppressed.

This makes no sense. Worse yet, it makes nonsense of a great and central commitment of Western civilization. The school must take note of this contradiction, this paradox, and it must resolve it. That the school can become an instrument for the perpetuation and propagation of dangerous nonsense the history of nations has demonstrated convincingly. To this perverse use the central educational purposes of the American people have never been bent. But educators too share in a common bewilderment regarding the disposition of new-found riches. It may be difficult to make sense of them; yet the sense must be made.

Overproduction of goods has been a novel paradox of the twentieth century. The Great Depression found the most modern nations wallowing in consternation amid surpluses. Somehow, their very capacity to produce had made them poor. There they were barefoot in bread lines standing in the shadows of silent factories and stacked-up untouchable abundance. Given to the rituals of words, they essayed to exorcise the paradox by clichés: "Prosperity is just around the corner." "It is not overproduction, it is under-consumption that afflicts us." "It is a problem of distribution." The clichés of easy hopes and the spelling out of the obvious seeming to drive out no demons, they fell upon certain expedients. To become prosperous again, they limited production and destroyed goods. And somehow they found themselves working and buying again. Whether they had found fundamental magic or not, history gave them little time to ascertain, for hard on the heels of depression came war. Its elixirs were more potent medicines. Production for the basic purpose of destruction put men and women to work and money in all their pockets. Meanwhile, the youngest and strongest went out to kill and to destroy the cities of man. There were dreadful deeds and dreadful things were said of them; there were bold deeds and proud things were said of them. The war put men to work; the war left work to be done. There was a great business of cleaning up the rubble, of paying wise men to tell one another what ought to be done, and of building more engines of destruction to assure most piously that such destruction should not occur again "in the time of our children or our children's children."

It is not an analogy that we are building. It is more than that. For war was finally punctuated by explosion of the atomic bomb: *period, the end.* Recollection of that event is central in the phrase "explosions of knowledge." That dread event is ever in our minds. The abundance of knowledge and the abundance of destructiveness coincident in our time demand no analogy; no conceptual bridges need be built. These things were annealed in the fury of atomic fission over Hiroshima.

But these things have been said before. And what of the school? The school must find frontier concepts and new directions for action. It must somehow disjoin the power to acquire knowledge from the capacity to destroy. It must again assert its knowledge and its quests for clearer perception of truth toward the uncorrupted ends of joyful living and constructive deeds.

Certain strange views of the educational implications of the explosion of knowledge have come forward. The strange quality derives from regarding this access of knowledge as a burden. Already this vast increase of information has evoked images of moun-

315

tains of materials to be assessed, classified, and learned. It has been cited as justification for teaching three-year-olds to read, for putting a disciplinary curriculum into the nursery school, for departmentalizing the elementary school, for an educational speed-up all along the educational continuum. It has all but taken the joy out of campus life, except for the unmotivated and the unregenerate. The assumed grim necessity of coping with this so-called burden of knowledge has turned up a crop of educational compulsives. The loss of the joys of childhood, the ulcers of eight-year-olds, the nervous breakdowns of high-school students, the "trips" and suicides of college youth—all these they have heard about and sometimes verbally regret. But compulsives never abate their efforts; to them, salvation requires its rigors. As they see it, Everests of information are not scaled by weaklings, and great enterprises are always won at the expense of heavy casualties.

If the matter were philosophical, the dispute in philosophical terms would well be worth undertaking. But the educators who so conscientiously strive for a regressive education are not, in the main, men who philosophically delight in grim regimentation. The fault with them is informational; they misunderstand the nature of an access of knowledge. The disqualification has deeper roots, of course, than functional illiteracy. Many who educatively abuse the concept of enhanced knowledge are well read. If there be a literacy that cannot read, the roots of that incapacity must be sought out.

In Western civilization the disposition to distrust the fruits of knowledge goes back to Eden and to the ancients. The Greeks, greedy for knowledge but wary of insolent intelligence, let Prometheus be bound and forever injured for his hubris. St. Augustine associated mundane learning with the "lust of the eyes," and modern man finds other ways to express his apprehension.

The writer a few years ago was urging a government official to initiate a vast literacy campaign for a Central American nation. An educator himself, the official listened fairly, then said, "Yes, I can see your point. But then we can go too fast in making people literate. They would just be able to read all that Communist propaganda that's floating around." Thus does dread of the apple persist.

But, what is now taking place? Those who talk about the explosion of knowledge (and do a lot about it too) are linked with traditions in the culture that actively fear and resist learning. How can this be? These educators preoccupy themselves with the image of the immensity of the informational mass because they have no appetite for the dictates of the new knowledge itself. Is it surprising that fear of reality should express itself in symbols of a frightful burden of fact?

It is no coincidence that those who advertise the explosion of knowledge so often have preoccupied themselves with the instruments of transmittal and classification and retrieval of information rather than with the identification and conceptualization of new vistas opened by this knowledge. Consistent with this is the fact that this view of knowledge is often linked with the most rigid and structured view of methodology and curriculum. It creates the most confining academic learning (without consequence beyond the school) in educational history. In certain programs it identifies as "behavioral goals" the most limited minor achievements in subject matter mastery. In the 1930s this could have been innocent; today it must be deliberate. Educational research and social psychology have made it clear. Imposed, structured, nonparticipating, inactive learning is not a road to behavioral consequence. The basis for the classic alliance against curriculum reform thus appears again. The social conservative and the psychologically insecure come together on common ground; they fear information because they fear its uses.

Let us next examine the reality of the explosion of knowledge. Its existence rests on no absurd rejection of that reality. It exists as liberator and easer of burdens. It deserves better fate than to have become the Abominable Snowman of educational thought.

But for the frightful memory of Hiroshima we might have evolved a less cosmic and better phrase to categorize our recent learning. Knowledge in less cosmic doses is explosive. The studies by Franz Boas and others have effectively blasted race mythology for those who would read and perceive their arguments. An *objective* look at segregated schools has destroyed the fiction of "separate but equal." The big lies of history have ever been vulnerable to, and ever fearful of, the tiniest dynamite cap of truth.

To take a bit of onus from those who have made an Abomi-

317

nable Snowman out of modern knowledge, let it be acknowledged that they probably have been more bemused than obscurant. Quite likely they have made mass of data, quantity of report, and ineptitude in communication the essence of the problem. Although they may have contributed a compulsive share to the welter, they may be forgiven for being lost in a confusion which in the making has been the product of many men's efforts.

In an affluent society it is even possible that a student of education may confuse the size of a research grant and the grandeur of the project's housing with its informational consequence. In a curriculum seminar recently a serious student was reporting on the first phase of a major educational research project on which he was a team member. This first phase encompassed the energies of several men over a year's time at a cost of approximately $60,000. The report, streamlined for an hour's presentation, was masterfully handled and bulwarked by an impressive array of charts, graphs, and tests of statistical significance. Since time was running short and the point had not been reached, the instructor intruded a question: "In brief, now, just how do you summarize your year's findings?" The response was readily forthcoming: "We think that we have demonstrated that in this elementary school the rate of learning varies significantly among the students along a broad continuum." To make sure that the point was clear, the instructor rephrased it, "You mean that you have found that some kids learn a good deal faster than others." The researcher nodded; the seminar sat silent, stunned perhaps by the explosive impact. The professor, no doubt presuming on instructional prerogative, editorialized: "Well, this is a very interesting finding. However, if time and money had been of any consequence, as clearly they were not, you could have readily established the point by a ten-cent telephone call to any primary teacher in the neighborhood."

Though the sheer volume of increased knowledge is staggering and without doubt demands technological resources for its storage and retrieval, there is an easing side to the development that seems altogether neglected. Additional knowledge sometimes simplifies even the storage problem. Half-knowledge has filled the stacks with competing disquisitions comprised largely of erroneous speculation on matters uneased by certain measurement or definitive research. Thus, before Drs. Jonas Salk and Albert Sabin, medical education had to acquaint the student with a large assortment of theories and approaches regarding the origins and often futile treatment of polio. The lore was tremendous and bulky. With their breakthrough, the preventative was explicit, definitive, effective, to the point, and all but eliminated treatment.

So too with the moon. Today we know a little about it. The green-cheese theory is held no more, nor are a thousand other speculations sustained. The real knowledge of the moon will extend and multiply; yet in time it will be relatively simple and explicit.

Such illustrations are not atypical. Much of the information in our repositories is comprised of the ramifications of speculation attendant on not knowing. A little learning may truly be not only dangerous, but bulky. A great truth may, indeed, be tiny, but explosive in consequence: witness $E = mc^2$.

Science and Public Responsibility

After Hiroshima the scientific profession underwent an amazing reversal of general attitude toward its public responsibility. Prior to that awful moment in which "modern man became obsolete," the scientist had primarily bound himself by the privilege and sanctuary of his laboratory in his search of pure inquiry. That the scientist had a public responsibility, a moral and ethical obligation to be involved in questions of consequent applications of discovery was a concept held in disdain as humanistic sentimentality. If others chose to use dynamite to destroy men and their works rather than to blow out stumps, well more fools they, but this was not the responsibility of the scientist nor a consequence of admitted concern.

Except for the rare scientist who was educated in a broad humanistic perspective, the culture-bound quality of pre-Hiroshima science was unknown. Yet the exuberant optimism of the post-Enlightenment Western world was a mood both nourished by science and at the same time encompassing it. The idea of progress

319

caught hold of the nineteenth-century mind, and sufficient historical evidence sustained it well into the twentieth century. Progress
was even suggested to be "a law of history." Then imports of dreadful twentieth-century events began to beat their way into conditioned consciousness. The generation shell-shocked by World War I
lived to experience a Great Depression and a second conflict prose-
cuted with terrible knowing under the conceptual rubric of total
war. The dawning new consciousness drew necessary and frightful
conclusions from the connotations of such places as Belsen, Dachau,
Auschwitz, Buchenwald, Hiroshima, Nagasaki. The twentieth century caught modern man by surprise; it included injuries of man
against man that were in scale and intent unmatched in the human
record. By its midpoint it had already placed itself in the running
for the worst century in history and had entertained the rare and
strange possibility that it might be the last.

After World War II the scientists furnished an edifying intellectual spectacle as they leaped over departmental barriers to
become the first social scientists and, indeed, the major public
missionaries of the atomic age. They descended upon the Congress
to defeat the May-Johnson Bill; they were effectively instrumental
in the political scientific invention of the Atomic Energy Act. They
founded the *Bulletin of Atomic Scientists;* they sought every platform and rostrum at every service club, PTA, adult education group,
and women's guild that would give them audience. They helped to
expose and to contain the nonsense of civil defense propaganda.
They bulwarked and helped lead the press of organized opinion
that enabled a reluctant Senate to ratify the Atomic Test-Ban
Treaty. Science educators like Hubert Evans and Will Burnett
joined their colleagues in preparing resource materials for the
schools on the implications of atomic energy for man and his future.

These public acts in the name of social responsibility were
certainly new in scope and dimension. This does not deny that
certain scientists always played a large public role, but that earlier
role had been almost exclusively an effort on behalf of science to
announce new discoveries and to urge public acceptance.

It was thus that John Tyndall spoke at Belfast in 1873; foregoing diplomacy, he asserted bluntly, in the face of conventional

Victorian belief, that the old notions of cosmogony would simply have to give way to revolutionary scientific findings. Thomas Huxley was more diplomatic, but the net effect of his argument was similar. In New York in 1876 Huxley delivered his three famous addresses reporting and interpreting the significance of Darwin's work. This was front page news and was textually reported in full in the New York *Tribune*. Immediately and for years thereafter, the letter columns of this and other papers around the country as well as the pages of a galaxy of opinion journals echoed with the repercussions of his utterance. The reaction ranged full spectrum from warm approval (mostly from fellow scientists) through "fair-minded" accommodation and compromise (including views of figures as disparate as John Fiske and Henry Ward Beecher) to rejection and outrage. One fundamentalist proposed the not illogical hypothesis that "God put the fossils in the rocks to test man's faith."

In the short span of history in which science has been of consequence to man both as pursuit and as producer, it has often lent instruments to enhance his *objectivity*. In all areas of human endeavor the tools of science have reinforced and certified judgment. Interestingly, the largest public controversy involving science and the common culture showed the reinforcement of *science* and *objectivity* to be a two-way street. In the Scopes Trial a man of science (a humble teacher, to be sure) was defendant. Laboring in his behalf, in behalf of scientific enlightenment no less, was no scientist but a man consummately disciplined in objectivity, Clarence Darrow. Thus, in controversy necessarily side by side were allied the two great methods of a closer hold upon reality, standing against the magnificent but weary rhetoric of the aggressive conventional knowledge voiced by the quondam "Boy Orator of the Platte," William Jennings Bryan.

Since Hiroshima and again since Sputnik science has come to the public with something new on its mind. Newly confident of acceptance, though still not fully free in every legislature or school board, science is outward-oriented in concern for the *saving* necessity within its knowledge. So it has most vigorously come to school. That it has come better subsidized through monies from the

321

National Science Foundation grants and United States Office of Education than other fields, is at this point no ground for invidious complaint. The fact is that the organized scientific professions have departed from the "trickle-down theory" of scholarship and have involved themselves intelligently in direct and massive efforts to effect a general enhancement of scientific competence through the instrument of the school curriculum. Of these, most noteworthy are the Physical Sciences Study Committee, the School Mathematics Study Group, and the Biological Sciences Curriculum Study.

These prestigious curricular enterprises have several constructive features in common. All have enlisted the energies of top scientists in their undertakings. Each has undertaken serious study and analysis of present practice. All have established teamwork arrangements among scientific specialists, curriculum workers, school administrators, and professional teachers. Each has devised and used special methods for teacher education (or teacher reeducation) including workshops, demonstrations, seminars, and institutes. The experimental preparation of new teaching materials has been common to their efforts. All have enjoyed considerable endowments of public and private support.

Such procedures are exceptionally well founded. The discovery of the necessity for method (the transmutation of subject matter into content, in our terms) was, of course, not quite the "bombshell" to educationists in these operations as to the subject matter specialists involved. The discovery of the intellectual excitement in teaching should, however, not be begrudged to anyone.

Although all these projects use constructive procedures and have brought new life to the curriculum, certain distinctive emphases of the Biological Sciences Curriculum Study (the BSCS) of the American Institute of Biological Sciences qualify it specially as a model of procedure. The BSCS got underway in 1959.[2] From the start its planning utilized the cooperative efforts of high-school, college,

---

[2] For a comprehensive summary report see Bentley Glass, "Renascent Biology: A Report on the AIBS Biological Sciences Curriculum Study," in Robert W. Heath (ed.), *New Curricula* (New York: Harper & Row, 1964), pp. 94–119. This report was originally published in *The School Review* (Spring 1962).

and university specialists in biological sciences and specialists in curriculum and methodology. The undergirdings of their work are notably strong in both scientific and educational realism; the analysis of the problem wastes little time in recrimination over the delinquencies of education or in messianic rhetoric. It states the problem as it is and undertakes to relate reconstruction to it.

In many areas of school study the subject matter of the classrooms has been seriously lagging, not merely behind the frontiers of inquiry, but well back of the body of what has become common knowledge among the well informed. The Steering Committee of the BSCS found this to be particularly true in the state of general instruction in biology. In viewing this condition, it revealed a sober apprehension regarding the potential for opposition deriving from the biases within the common culture. It firmly voiced the essential conviction for curriculum reform.

> We were unanimous in our resolve that no opposition on the part of well-meaning but uninformed persons and groups would prevent an appropriate scientific treatment of such supposedly controversial subjects as organic evolution, the nature of individuals and racial differences, sex and reproduction in the human species, and the problems of population growth and control.[3]

The same committee identified as a "prevalent sin" the teaching of these sciences as fixed, immutable, and established bodies of knowledge. Their educational sophistication was indicated, here as elsewhere, in identifying this as a common error of instruction. The way in which laboratory work has created a spurious facsimile of the method of inquiry was especially clear to them. "Cookbook experimentation" is the common cliché, more meaningful than most, which designates the academic ritualization that has so generally made mockery of experimentation and hollowed out the meaning from discovery.

The common denominator of all productive and relevant curriculum reform is its focus upon conceptualization, whatever the phrasing of the principle. BSCS early recognized that educational experimentation with organization of the high-school course would

3 *Ibid.,* pp. 95–96.

be a continuing necessity. The diversity of the scientific resources to be drawn upon and the quantitative bulk of the resource make the problem of selectivity no less formidable, for instance, than the task in teaching a one-year course in world history. (In fact, the explicit suggestion that the nature of science must be taught as a significant dimension of history tangibly relates these problems.) Whatever the experimental organization of the course, the conceptual framework must be identified and adhered to. In the committee's words:

> The principle means . . . that the biological themes of the inter-dependence of structure and function, regulation and homeostasis, the genetic continuity of life, its evolution, the diversity of type together with unity of pattern, the biological roots of behavior, and the relation of organism to environment must be treated at all levels of organization. . . .[4]

The committee was aware that the common mind has not clearly established its relation to science. Sometimes it stands in awe, other times in terror. It is inclined to a schizophrenia evidenced in reverence for scientific miracles and a dread of its essence as though it derived from witchcraft. The necessity for a method by which the student learns science by being scientific, by being a scientist no less, is an evident proposition to BSCS.

In remarkably clear terms the committee stated some of its purpose in the language of civic responsibility. "A sound biological understanding is the unalienable right of every child . . .," they say.[5] This right leads them to the tenth-grade placement of the school course for the simple reason of thereby attaining the most nearly universal enrollment. Conceptually, a sound biological education is explicitly associated with adult decision-making in respect to problems of health and nutrition, natural resource conservation, realities of nuclear energy, reproduction and parenthood, and government support of science.

The BSCS has moved far beyond these assumptions into preparation of materials and teacher education. Their works have been creditable, but the purpose of our analysis here has been to make

4 *Ibid.*, p. 97.
5 *Ibid.*, p. 98.

models of their methods and assumptions rather than to render special praise to their product. The contention herewith is that the utilization of these assumptions constitutes withal a very similar dictate for sound curriculum building, not just especially for the sciences, but with appropriate modifications of vocabulary for all subjects. Codified and generalized, the assumptions seem to be the following:

1. An advancing state of knowledge behind whose frontiers instruction must surely follow, but not in a lag simply induced by apathy, unawareness, and institutional statics.

2. A state of the common culture that is somewhat receptive to new concepts, but that may also be fearful and obstructive toward them, that must not be bowed to at the expense of depriving access to the student of what is well and truly known or of methods by which to extend and alter the pattern of the known.

3. The enhanced perception of the necessity for the school to be as firmly rooted in the institution of academic freedom as have been the halls of higher education. Sciences often press against the limits of common cultural acceptability, but the freedom of the school is an institutional necessity. Its battles are for the educator to fight. Sure, the sciences may discover even legislative bias against the challenge to antique views of the cosmos. But on another day the English teacher may find that the modern novels of Albert Camus or even J. D. Salinger have touched the nerve of local conventionality; or the social studies teacher, doing naught but teaching well-recorded history, may draw outrage from offended vested interest or chauvinism. The principal fault of the common culture when it comes excitedly to school is not so much in its intentions, which are often good, nor in its perception of its intent, which to its eyes is ever pure, but in the measure of its misapprehensions and sometimes ignorance. The authenticity of the community is neither denied, nor demeaned. It is there and deserves to be served. However, it is to be served, not catered to; and the service for which it pays is to be educated—that, and no less.

4. The common tendency to establish sacred cows for instruction to be replaced by the constant interchange of dynamic for static content.

325

5. The dictate of selectivity, not on the basis of arbitrary, capricious, or expedient judgment. This must be employed to the express function of serving and clarifying the basic and most essential concepts.

6. The vitalization of learning to be sought through participation and exercise of the learner in the intrinsic and appropriate methodology by which the content of an area is established and extended. Thus in the case at hand, the life sciences, the student functions as a scientist; in the case extended, the student of history becomes historian; of social problems, social scientist; of literature, writer and critic.

7. The recognition of fundamental life consequence in that what is learned shall be a constant concern.

Thus the essentials of modern curriculum construction as identified in this instance by hardworking scientists and science teachers might be summed up as (1) advancing knowledge, (2) recognition of obstacles, (3) freedom for learning, (4) dynamic content, (5) methodological participation by the learner, (6) selection by conceptual criteria, and (7) direction toward real consequence. These requisites of good, modernized education are identifiable in common functional terms. Their applicability to any field of instruction is both feasible and desirable. The educator bears then a dual responsibility: to help to make these conditions generally understood and more universally applied and to build an institutional environment and ethos conducive to their utilization and nurture.

Adequate Frameworks for Learning

The student of curriculum cannot prescribe sequences of study or write a course of study in a scientific or technical area on the basis of some general education biases. To do so would be a meddlesome brand of educational criticism and curriculum development that ends by destroying curriculum in the name of reforming it.

The involvement of highly competent scientists and mathematicians in curriculum work in recent years has led to some very beneficial effects. Through this process of involvement, these disciplined specialists have made their own discovery of the teaching-learning process. Though the process has amounted to genuine personal discovery, in a sense it has amounted to the rediscovery of most of the "knowns" of educational theory that were basically the *discoveries* of the progressive education movement, including: (1) the fact that understanding is the key to conceptualization; (2) that only conceptualized learning is retained, and therefore, is capable of being built upon; (3) that the learning of any subject must be conceptualized within an adequate framework; (4) that learning is a matter of involvement and participation, indeed, of discovery; (5) that one cannot teach without conscious attention to method—not that the knowledge of the subject makes the teacher competent in method, but that method is intrinsic to content. With no real teaching, there can be no learning.

In a very real sense the new mathematics, for example, is not so much a new subject matter but a new methodology grounded in modern curriculum theory to which Max Beberman has made large contributions. A good deal of reattention to curriculum theory has been due to the writing of Jerome Bruner. His *Process of Education*[6] is quite properly characterized as a long derivative footnote to John Dewey. Bruner's gift for graphic conceptualization as in the notion of "spiral curriculum" has drawn notice to certain programatic necessities. The spiral-curriculum concept shows dramatically, if not quite accurately, the basic necessity of curriculum continuity and development with a comprehensive conceptual schema.

The curriculum theorist, however, owes the students a vigilant regard for sound developmental learning that cannot be assigned by fiat to representatives of any subject field. Take for example the agreed principle "that the learning of any subject must be conceptualized within an adequate framework." These are good words and hard to quarrel with. But taken within the framework of common academic bias, they can support a generally regressive application. The notions of "structures of learning" or "subject matter integ-

---

[6] Jerome Bruner, *Process of Education* (Cambridge: Harvard University Press, 1960).

rity," for instance, can lend aid and comfort to antique concepts of the academic disciplines.

The development of adequate frameworks for learning has been obstructed academically by these biases throughout this century whose burgeoning knowledge has aptly been labeled an "explosion." The restructuring of learning experience has, nevertheless, progressively won the field. This advance in conceptualization has been due neither to the persuasive rhetoric of radical educationists nor to academic subversion, though the old guardians suspect this. It has been due to necessity.

The study of social phenomena, for example, has created new hybrids in academia: social psychology and cultural anthropology are cases in point. The necessities of medical education and research gave rise to biochemistry. The post-Einstein inquiries into the properties of matter have erased much of the boundary between physics and chemistry. Nor is modern mathematics merely a tool subject to the sciences as it was once regarded; it is part and parcel of the intrinsic content of the higher reaches of physics, chemistry, and, of course, astronomy and music.

"Adequate frameworks" have dictated not only functional hybrids, but also new composites of learning. To meet the demands of operational necessity within a shrunken global definition, the academic community, to the tune of the wailing of respectable guardians, has created frameworks of area studies and institutes of Latin American, Asian, African, and Soviet studies. This mobilization of learning resources deploys on common fronts geographers, anthropologists, linguists, educationists, historians, political scientists, and economists, among others.

Professional necessity has also forced a restructuring and redefinition of "adequate frameworks." When a school of journalism becomes a school of communication arts and skills, over the objections of the "who, what, when, where" advocates, its professional content enters the twentieth century. The ancient discipline of rhetoric may be drawn upon and revitalized. Statistical methods, survey techniques, media studies, and applications become the stuff of courses. New faces representing applications of twentieth-century inquiry appear: semanticists, linguistic analysts, sociologists, an-

328

thropologists, psychologists. And of course, unless the professional emphasis is to disappear into a new thin air of unrelated academia, the men who can teach the value of leg work, journalistic integrity, and clear expression in making a good news story will still be around.

What applies to one modern professional school applies to another. The new school of education, or of nursing, or of social work will follow a similar pattern. Interestingly enough, modern knowledge combined with modern necessity has brought a large common denominator of knowledge into the "adequate frameworks" of all these areas. The books, for instance, of Alfred Korzybski, Sigmund Freud, John Dewey, Erich Fromm, David Reisman, S. I. Hayakawa, Jerome Bruner, and Gardner Murphy will be quite as likely to appear on one reading list as another.

We place great stress on this curriculum trend at the level of higher education because it has a large bearing on matters of curriculum reform within the elementary and secondary school. The movement toward fusion, integration, common learnings, and core curriculum has often been misperceived as some notional invention of progressive education. The subject matter guardians in the colleges as well as lay critics often imputed its origins to anti-intellectualism or lack of respect for organized bodies of learning. Yet on the campus the same movement was going on, sadly out of communication to be sure. In neither instance was it notional, subversive, or deliberately maverick. The parallel movements were deeply responsive to the new ferments in inquiry and the new necessities for redeveloping adequate frameworks. It was not out of an unholy desire to upset academic applecarts that in the 1930s the secondary school began to develop new arrangements of learning materials into the forms of integrated or common learnings. The old carts were just not big enough for the new concepts; the new wines turned sour in the old bottles. No, educators are most often deadpan serious in their motivations; it would indeed relieve the scene were there more pure-bred mischief-makers among them.

For example, in this age of science it would seem difficult to argue against the importance of a student's knowing a good deal about the implications of atomic energy or the problems of conservation in a period of increasing pressure on our resources. Phrase these two as instructional inquiries at the high-school level, and then examine their validity as subjects for instruction. Are they relevant to the citizen? Are they pressing and continuing problems? Are they related to prevailing realities? Will the person be better off complacently unaware of the discomfiting facts involved? Do they have enough significance to compete for a place in the crowded program of the school? Are they, for example, as important as knowledge of the causes of the War of 1812, let alone the War of Jenkins' Ear? Are they worth as much time as the sonnets of Shakespeare, the short stories of O. Henry? If we find a month each to read *Silas Marner, The Tale of Two Cities, A Midsummer Night's Dream,* have we time for these matters? (This is not to propose invidious choices, but merely to test the matter of comparative significance.)

Suppose hypothetically there exists a consensus that these matters *are* worth their hour in school. How, then, shall they be arranged to be well taught? They are surely at first glance of a scientific nature. Science is involved in each. However, social studies teachers have on occasion claimed these topics and in courses in problems of democracy have taught them more than passably well. Take one at a time. What is involved in an adequate survey and analysis of the implications of atomic energy? Surely, the following, among other matters:

1. An understanding of the nature of the atom.

2. Knowledge of the theory of atomic fission and atomic fusion.

3. A basic knowledge of the technology of the atomic bomb.

4. A knowledge of the peacetime uses of atomic energy—atomic power, radio-active isotopes, for instance.

5. The history of atomic control—the political struggle for the development of the Atomic Energy Commission.

6. The struggle for international controls—the Atomic Test-Ban Treaty.

7. The potential for destruction; its bearing on international affairs —the Cuban confrontation, for example.

8. The literature of the atomic age, including such works as Norman Cousins, *Modern Man Is Obsolete;* David Bradley, *One World—Or None;* John Hersey, *Hiroshima;* Nevil Shute, *On the Beach;* Pope John, *Pacem in Terris;* the writings of Albert Schweitzer.

Reasonably complex, this subject, is it not? And reasonably important? Is it inappropriate to the high-school level? Do not attempt to hold this ground. Students and adults alike live within the age when strategies ever hold the unspoken (and sometimes spoken) atomic threat. For most of our citizenry high school still represents terminal education. And these citizens must one day vote and form opinions on matters derived from this subject, and they must live or die with their decisions. All men, informed on or ignorant of these implications, reside under the Damoclean threat of what Will Burnett called the two-edged sword of science.

Where does the context of this subject for inquiry lie? At the very least, among science, history, political science, international affairs, and literature. This list does not exhaust the possibilities. Will an adequate framework for conceptualization be found within one subject matter or one discipline? Will the student arrive at a more comprehensive view and a more reasonable set of generalizations if each subject in its own time and place deals with its share of the inquiry and leaves the putting together, the synthesis, up to each student? It would scarcely seem sensible so to assume.

The dictate, then, not for educational theory in some abstract form, but for the necessity of adequate learning, is to devise some new framework for instruction and learning. Among the feasible alternatives are these:

1. Cooperative or team teaching within a pattern of common learning
2. Integrated units taught by teachers specially educated to handle more significant aggregates of experience
3. Short-term fusion and integration of efforts on an interdepartmental basis.

Any of these devices properly administered may do the job, but it is rather difficult to see how conventional subject matter separation can even approach the task.

331

More economically, since the point is made illustratively, analyze similarly the conservation problem. Its components surely include:

1. Resource analysis
2. History of conservation efforts
3. Political factors in achieving conservation legislation
4. Economic issues involved
5. Scientific dimensions of conservation
6. The literature of men and resources
7. Geography and geology
8. International dimensions of the problem

The academic areas drawn upon are again several and include at least science, history, political science, literature, and geography. What subject alone encompasses an adequate framework? Does not the necessity of instruction compel some curricular rearrangement? It appears so clear a real and present dictate that we shall leave it as self-evident.

The General-Education Burden

Physicists and physics teachers are qualified and entitled to thresh out courses of study in their field or to choose from any of a number of ready-tailored alternatives. Again, the curriculum planner and critic has his obligation to the total development of the student's needs. The science department must settle whether to utilize the "chemical-bond" approach, and the mathematics department must debate the merits of incorporating calculus into the high-school program. But the student of education who weighs the necessities of general education can point out certain practical needs that have to be served in the quantitative–scientific dimension.

Now with professional respect for teachers of mathematics and science firmly in context, it is fair to observe certain occasional educational indispositions on their part. Along with many other teachers, they tend to share a somewhat social Darwinian view of their subjects. Either the student is fit to learn their subject or he is not. The ability to learn substantially unaided by teaching is too often their measure of academic virtue. Such teachers bemoan the fact that "half of my freshmen can't learn algebra." Yet another better teacher could, and has, taken that half of the class and proved that 90 percent of it *could* learn the subject. And exceptional teachers have even made surprising inroads on the remaining 10 percent of the algebra unteachables. Teachers of doubtful mind would have hooted at the possibility of teaching ordinary seven-year-olds algebraic concepts. But Dr. Max Beberman showed them how.

It would be uncharitable to put teachers of a certain bent into the squeeze of their own vise. Echoing the common collegiate antimethodological bias, they are prone to assert: "Command of subject is the key; if you know your subject, you can teach it." Maybe so; indeed, nothing in the educational commitment of this work quarrels substantially with this crudely expressed sentiment. Then in deepest respect for logic (the ancient kinsman of mathematics) does it not follow that where there is inability to teach, there may be lack of command of the subject? The bind of this *sequitur* might diminish at any rate the proud assertion of failure to instruct in learning.

In the contemporary frenzy of college preparation and competition for places in higher education, another bias of science and mathematics teachers is quite understandable. Actually, they merely share in a general contagion. These subjects, in particular, are academic hurdles for college acceptance. The intrinsic interest of these inquiries, moreover, tempts each teacher into a preprofessional stance. He may easily preoccupy himself with an annual talent search for the budding mathematicians or scientists among his students and direct his primary teaching energies toward grooming them for their futures.

This overemphasis not only distorts the purposes of secondary education but rests upon a beautiful mathematical irony. The assumption that a large and good crop of scientific talent will be assured by this kind of identification and selection reflects the old

333

mathematics of certainties instead of the new math of probabilities. To increase the activity in the whole field is the modern conceptualization of the way to assure a more frequent impact of the forces of ambition and motivation with the elements of personal ability and talent. In sum, it is the job in all fields both to develop all students in every aspect of their potential and to assist in the process of identifying and encouraging students into fields of special interest and promise. If modern rather than antique statistical assumptions are utilized, these two purposes are complementary, mutually supportive. If not, they compel and debilitate efforts toward achieving both purposes. The good program instructs all students in the ways of scientific thought and inquiry, gives them introduction to these methods, and acquaints them with the richness of the scientific contribution to the modern mind. From such programs the probabilities are enhanced that a fair proportion of lively, well-motivated students will find a continuing intellectual interest that may later mature into professional purpose. This assumption is better education, but it is also better mathematics.

The general educator is unqualified to tell the mathematics teacher how to teach math or the physicist how to teach physics. He is qualified and obligated to call to attention certain general-education necessities in the quantitative–scientific realm. The intent here is not to support the heresy that all of the science and mathematics programs should serve the purpose of general education. It is urged, however, that the modern world occasions quantitative judgments daily and that the school serves its clientele badly, even the academically talented, if it leaves untouched the active areas in the common culture where the student as citizen is often duped by his innocence. These are matters much more often discussed in faculty lounges, even of colleges and universities, than the theories of Darwin or Einstein. The school, not the science and mathematics departments, has the ultimate responsibility for the student's competence in this dimension.

Without advocacy of what is patronizingly offered in some schools as "consumer education," why should it not be urged that the school instruct the potentially gullible for participation in the great American market as a knowing and critical appraiser of the substances he is offered and their conditions of sale? Should the school's contribution to the marketplace be an annual increment of a new crop of suckers? If not, then the illustrations below will point up the opportunities for highly motivated learning and also the exciting possibilities for discovering the raw nerves of vested interest within the community. Approach these matters with scientific accuracy and objective judgment, and the school will find itself called upon and visited by persons who had never before shown any sign that they knew it existed.

For example, examine all the manners and methods by which credit is extended in the community: congenial finance companies, revolving-credit accounts, automobile loans, bank loans, credit cards, credit unions. Money and lending will concern most of the students perennially. The primary question in an era of competitive urgings to borrow is not where to get it, but what it will cost. Since lenders are shy only in advertising this matter in meaningful terms, the school can educate usefully without drawing too heavily on its mathematical competence. As a matter of fact, its curriculum in these affairs will be a better test of its gumption than of its arithmetic.

Then when the loan advertisement is stripped down and analyzed, the student—and his parent too—may ask, "How congenial are these folks who offer to lend me money at 30 percent interest?" The easy $67.37 per month (for three years) may make the new car it brings home seem just as good a buy when it is shown that part of the purchase price is money at 23 percent, and again it may not. The convenience of open accounts at "friendly" stores may even seem worth the revealed cost of 18 percent interest; the worth of four pairs of shoes to a family now may exceed the worth of five a year later, and again, maybe not.

At school there are many persons educated and skilled in quantification. The American market is free and competitive. Surely the merchants who serve the public by competing in offering it quality goods of infinite variety will especially welcome the vigorous preparation of customers to select wisely and judiciously from their shelves and counters. The school's laboratories can be used to make simple tests of substances and materials. Yardsticks

335

and measures for comparative shopping by fixed standards can be taught. The important questions about terms, services, deliveries, guarantees, and legal protection can be instructed upon. It is unlikely that the school will deny the relevance of such instruction to life as it is lived in contemporary America. Every adult involved will have learned these lessons and will have learned some of them hard, if not bitterly.

Ideally, the most enthusiastic support for such instruction should come from the business community itself. For the central responsibility of business is to the public, and *service* is the motto of business on every street and corner. Since such education in the long run can only improve the service business renders, it will ally the school with free enterprise in a most productive way. Schoolmen who introduce this subject at the weekly luncheon of the service clubs that they so loyally attend may be assured of an immediate interest and a very lively response.

The Appraisal of Educational Technology

Consumer education for the school itself may be urged in the same spirit upon the school. The subject matter for inquiry is coincidentally the product of the application of this very dimension of learning. Science has bred a vast technology; part of that technology offers itself as a boon, sometimes even as a panacea, to education. The school is a customer; surely of all institutions it should be a knowing one.

The school will persist as an educational institution. It will continue to develop ever more meaningful and purposive learning situations. Any tools which serve this purpose effectively and economically will be more than welcome. Unless the educator's judgment is corrupted by "easy" money or by glib salesmanship, these tools, like other instruments of education, will be brought to school as a result of careful scrutiny and professional decision-making.

The appraisal of any instruments proposed for utilization in the school should be conducted in relation to two ironclad criteria. The first states that the expenditure for the instrument must be weighed in terms of realistic cost-accounting. Distinctions between monies (hard and soft, local and federal, tax and foundation) can only lead to ethical deterioration and bad purchasing. It is the utility of the item that must be weighed in a critical and comparative balance; it surely cannot be measured simply against itself. The decisive question is not whether it does something well. Decision must follow the rigorous pressing of such questions as these: Is its educational contribution worth its price? Does it do something worth doing? Does it do it as well as some other instrument? At what cost are its additional increments, if any, in learning gained? The laws of diminishing returns and increasing costs are always relevant to any enterprise where resources are limited or finite, that is, where choices have to be made. Obviously this first criterion for appraisal will become a dead letter on the day when the public gives its schools an absolute blank check for any expenditure. Even then, however, other criteria would remain effective. Budgetary prudence is not the only factor in sound educational decision-making. For example, even with infinite resources, schoolmen might reject placing a jukebox and pinball machines in every classroom, despite their obvious though limited utility in teaching music appreciation and the laws of probability.

The second criterion states that the instrument must be appraised in terms of disinterested and comprehensive research. The objective citizen will probably think it wise to distinguish between the findings of the American Tobacco Institute and the United States Public Health Service in appraising the relationship between cigarette smoking and lung cancer. By the same token, school officials will be well-advised to scrutinize sales claims and research evidence when considering educational instruments for possible subliminal contamination due to an unusual proximity of the relationship between research and sales promotion. The identity of researcher and promoter does not ipso facto imply venality; it surely means an enhanced possibility of a diminished critical judgment and a larger necessity for exterior objective judgment. No inde-

337

pendent testing laboratories comparable to those of the Food and Drug Administration or the Public Health Service exist for the advice and protection of the educational customer. The research expenditures of the United States Office of Education exert this function to no considerable degree. Rather, in most instances they represent a very large investment in the support of *interested research*—that is, research where the enthusiasm and concern of the researcher in the product being tested are closely identified with his efforts at studying their effects. The Fund of Advancement of Education has often been charged with subsidizing *demonstration* rather than inquiry in its endowed studies of its pet enthusiasm, instructional television. Again, while this does not necessarily spell contamination, it does create an added potential for it. The government or a major foundation could at this moment perform no greater service to education than to establish just such an independent educational instruments testing laboratory. Its researchers would be disciplined strictly to inquiry and not to outcome. They would no more create their own criteria for appraisal than would a surveyor utilize a measuring system of his own invention. They would simply devise tests to answer questions raised by professional educators or utilize as standards those criteria that educational consumers ask them to apply.

Purveyors who find the schools behaving with the enlightened restraint of critical sales resistance are prone these days to inveigh against nineteenth-century mindedness and to cry superconservative whenever a new sales pitch is left unheeded. The school, however, is a good and sober consumer and a capable supporter of technology even as an educator, which latter role many conceive as its primary one.

A visit to meetings of the American Association of School Administrators is revealing. Here, the tremendous suppliers' exhibits of more or less useful goods resembles a Leipzig Fair for educators. The basic relationship is cordial, even convivial. The visible evidence of patronage and improved offerings over the years is at hand in hundreds of displays and exhibits of better books, better tools, better everything—desks, laboratory units, lighting, transportation, films, projectors, closed-circuit television, the works.

The interest of the conventioneers in school equipment is great, even though for most of them it comes second to the meetings where major issues in education, including the issues of technology in and for education, are threshed out. These schoolmen, ever prudent and ordinarily sober, one and all, are potential customers; but they are first of all (by training, bent, and public mandate) educators, and by educators' criteria they must be sold by them and likewise buy. (In Chapter XII, specific and more detailed attention is directed toward what might in this context be termed the conceptual basis for enlightened consumership of educational hardware.)

The conceptual preoccupations of the educator, diverse though they must be, and often utilitarian, must ever give priority to the question of meaning. Whatever utility there may be in a subject, however well an instrument may enhance this utility, the curriculum, the sum total of the impact of the school, can only be weighed by what occurs within the person and on that aggregate of persons that constitutes a student body. To the matter of meaning, agonizingly sought and profoundly realized, the concluding emphasis of this chapter is directed.

Commentary: The Meaning of One and One Million

Mathematics must attend to the meaning of the astonishing sums that it has presented to the modern mind. When confronted with enumerations in the measures of geological time, of astronomical distance, or such time-distance gauges as the light year, the human experience tends to reduce the quantification (to reduce the infinite to the mortal scale as it were), or to boggle at the fact and dismiss it before a baffled sanity abdicates the cranium. The astronomer, toughened to live with his perpetual amazement and wonder, often makes exquisite sense of it. Mathematicians could assist their contemporaries (teachers and students alike), to do this. The necessity to place conceptual meaning upon the bare bones of staggering figures may be a basic requirement for survival. The problem may be expressed as the determination of the meanings of one and one million.

Surely those citizens of the Western world are few who do not know this news of our century: that in the arsenals of certain great powers are hundreds of bombs, any one of which can exterminate a city. Sanity does truly balk at such facts; avoidance and denial are attractive defenses. They are also dangerous and delusive. Some men attend to these facts ambitiously; they seek to extend the strange capacity for "overkill." They make games of nuclear strategy. They make mathematical assumptions with human counters in deadlier detachment than the Olympian dieties brought to their machinations with human fate. In neat round figures, one such "accountant" set forth this calm assumption: "America could absorb an initial assault, suffer sixty million casualties, retaliate, and win the war."

The cheerful quality of this pronouncement could easily be exaggerated. Its substance depends on the meaning of the unit of quantification involved. Just what is one million? Few have occasion to count that far. Clearly to gain some grasp of the quantity it is first essential to fathom the meaning of *one*. One what? In this case, a person. To comprehend the meaning of "one person" is well within the experience of practically anyone. The meaning of *one* in personal terms is conceptualized by the degree to which a person holds a life in tender and profound regard. The public meaning of the loss of one might be exemplified by the names of John F. Kennedy or Martin Luther King. Sentiment would express the connotation of *one* in this sense in words of nearness and dearness. In the experience of each person, there is always one, at least himself, and happily usually more than himself to lend essence to the quantity: one, two, three, seven, eleven. Experience can count human meaning in intimate terms, though rarely to a hundred.

Thus a second grader will know the meaning of *one,* and can usually tell that a million is a million *ones.* It is important to remember that; but what *is* one million? Surely it is a lot. However, when a schoolbus is hit by a train and twenty children are killed, common human feeling calls that a lot. An air crash killing one hundred is accounted a disaster. Yet twenty plus one hundred comes nowhere near one million, as any third grader can also tell. Counting is not regarded as a high form of numerical manipulation, but the school must help the student to assess the meaning of simple counting on occasion.

A million? A million people? Think of this before you try multiplying by sixty to arrive at the sixty million dead. Let us see where we can find people so arranged that the number will become sensible to our experience. The automobile is a known. Suppose that a series of automobiles with five passengers each were driven into the Grand Canyon at the rate of one every ten seconds. The depth would assure that several were in the air simultaneously. Let us suppose this kept up at the rate of 360 cars an hour for a whole day, twenty-four solid hours.

Shall we count the dead who have gone over the cliff? But we are nowhere near a million; therefore, let us continue for a week. At the end of the week by our count we have disposed of less than one-third of our target: 302,400, to be exact. Yet as we surveyed the wreckage it did seem like a lot. To reach our goal of one million, let us go to sea and commence sinking *The Queen Elizabeth, The United States, The France, The Rotterdam.* But although all hands are lost, passengers and crew, we have added only 12,000 to our score. This is getting us nowhere. We must look elsewhere. Let us take to the air. Suppose 500 airliners are in the sky; all go down in flames, a hundred dead in each: 50,000 more. We shall never reach a million at this rate. Let us seek larger congregations of man: Radio City Music Hall; Lincoln Center; the Chicago Theater; Constitution Hall; and the largest public auditoriums in Pittsburgh, Denver, Boston, and San Francisco. And this gives us 50,000 more. And we have not counted half a million. So let's get outdoors; fill up Candlestick Park, Shea Stadium, Forbes Field, Chavez Ravine, and Wrigley Field with baseball fans. This gives us 250,000 more: time to add. This must surely make a million. No, only 664,400. So let's play football. Michigan Stadium holds 101,001 fans; kill them all. Then Kezar Stadium and Iowa Field and we have still about 130,000 to go; let us include Peoria, Illinois; then, we have *one million.*

Now our strategist was speaking of this number sixty times over. Quite a problem in arithmetic, is it not? This is not playful stuff, after all. This is the most important of higher mathematics for modern man. Still the school instructs its students in quadratic equations and avoids too often the questions of the more profound arithmetic.

Chapter XI

The Vocational-
Utilitarian
Dimension

In everything you do consider what comes first and what follows, and so approach it. Otherwise you will come to it with a
good heart at first because you have not reflected on any of the
consequences, and afterwards, when difficulties have appeared,
you will desist to your shame. Do you wish to win at Olympia?
So do I, by the gods, for it is a fine thing. But consider the first
steps to it, and the consequences, and so lay your hand to the
work. You must submit to discipline, eat to order, touch no
sweets, train under compulsion, at a fixed hour, in heat and
cold, drink no cold water, nor wine, except by order; you must
hand yourself over completely to your trainer as you would to
a physician, and then when the contest comes you must risk
getting hacked, and sometimes dislocate your hand, twist your
ankle, swallow plenty of sand, sometimes get a flogging, and
with all this suffer defeat. When you have considered all this
well, then enter on the athlete's course, if you still wish it. . . .
     Man, consider first what it is you are undertaking; then
look at your own powers and see if you can bear it. . . . This
is what you have to consider: whether you are willing to pay
this price for peace of mind, freedom, tranquillity. If not, do
not come near; do not be, like the children, first a philosopher,
then a tax-collector, then an orator, then one of Caesar's
procurators. These callings do not agree. You must be one

343

man, good or bad; you must develop either your Governing Principle, or your outward endowments; you must study either your inner man, or outward things—in a word, you must choose between the position of a philosopher and that of a mere outsider.[1]

—*Epictetus*

The vocational–utilitarian dimension of education is asserted for good reasons. Partly it is a matter of rescue emphasis. Vocationalism has too often been a sort of country cousin in educational thought. Liberal educators have usually been at least patronizing in their attitude toward it. But vocation simply refers to the basic human obligation to do one man's work in the world. Its broadest common denominator is the necessity of earning a living, though this by no means encompasses the proposition.

The Concept of Work

To reexamine the concept of work is an essential starting point. This reexamination involves the critical application of diverse conceptual sources: the Puritan ethic, the democratic doctrine, the idea of human dignity, and the realities of the modern productive world.

The morality of work provides a sanction beyond necessity. This supplementary sanction derives considerably from Puritanism. Except for those immersed in the Puritan heritage it holds both promise and hazard, for in its primitive sense the concept of morality of work derives as much from dread of the human potential as from confidence in man's productive capacity. "Satan," that same "old deluder" whom the first Massachusetts school laws were designed to foil, *will* find mischief for idle hands to do. Disregarding theological implications, this axiom is scarcely a rude observa-

1 Epictetus, "The Manual," 29, in Saxe Commins and Robert N. Linscott, *The Social Philosophers* (New York: Random House, 1947), pp. 262–264.

tion on human disposition. "Mischievous," indeed, are the hands of man, and playful as well. The Puritan, of course, tended to identify play with mischief. And mortal complexity is such that the psychologist, let alone the semanticist, has great trouble in sorting out the intent of the human gesture and in finding the precise word to communicate it.[2]

Work morality bears resemblance to occupational therapy in at least one respect: work is instrumental as a way out of something. For the Puritan it was an instrument of avoiding sin, or rather of attempting to avoid it. In such a philosophy, the total depravity of man is such that nothing surprises with regard to his ingenuity in finding the precious little time it takes to consummate appreciable mischief. A few minutes behind privy doors and the lad may masturbate; a tumble in the hay can be achieved while the horses pause to drink; a bauble disappears into the maid's pocket while mistress primps her hair. To another mind, such antics may have psychological or social explanations, even justifications. To the mind that defines them surely as evil, they simply pit ingenuity against ingenuity. The problem: how to keep the hands so busy that they have not time to wander.

The disciplinary value of work has a record of much historical application. Rigorous labor has long been used as an instrument of social control. The fourteen-hour workday for children probably kept many from mischief and surely from play. As a matter of fact, it kept many of them from growing up. But it did not so tire the men that they could not find time for mischief great and malicious in the minds of their pious employers: they found time to organize, to make unions, and to achieve with attendant risk to their character a shorter working day.

To suggest that the morality of work bore merely a negative aspect were to create a travesty. Work was also a necessity of life, a social obligation, and an opportunity to glorify God. It may remain all these, but the terms have become a bit elusive. "If you don't work, you don't eat," was once a most elemental fact of life. The frontier community had little patience with drones and incompetents. Man in his depravity might be incapable of works pleasing to

2 See Eric Berne, *The Games People Play* (New York: Grove Press, 1964) .

the eye of God, but he could try. The morality of work found its expression in sermons, in long hours spent in hammering out both doctrines of faith and laws of commonwealth, and also in building sturdy houses, well-tilled fields, schools, and hospitals.

For the school, the necessity appears to be to ground itself in a more austere definition of work. The school should face up to the charge that it has been thoughtless about this concept. Though truly it has been busy. Schools are very busy places, not second to factories. But with respect to work, should one press for a definition of what they are up to, the answer should generally be phrased in candor: "God knows what." This is also no doubt true but turns out to be a bit uncommunicative as a message to mortals.

Our proposition here is that the school must undertake to prepare its students to *work* in a most essential and limited sense. It must take its definition of work from the great workers among men: Horace Mann, Florence Nightingale, Albert Schweitzer, Pope John, Abraham Lincoln, and the anonymous—teachers, farmers, poets, mothers, doctors. The discussion here is exclusively of "work"—and not of making a living. We are not talking of the contracts by which men bind themselves to a dole or a pay check. We are not speaking of maintaining a standard of living. Rather, we are talking of what *deserves* to be called work.

Work qualifies in the educational sense, and this implies in the best sense of the Western heritage only if it does one of these: nourishes children, alleviates human suffering, or improves the human community. The meaning of these terms can be expanded to extend their sense. However, they cannot be so far extended as to take the sense out of them, for they do not include, by any means, all those matters to which men attend either to keep themselves busy or to make money.

Nourishment is clearly a matter of mind and spirit as well as of body. The children belong to the family of man, and we are all of that family. We are all in need of this nourishment. The child cries for food and needs love. There are no more elemental needs than these. If anyone thinks that modern technology has lessened the true work load of humanity, he should be instructed in the widespread hunger of man both for food and for love. As for suffering,

346

who can spell out its dimensions? But it is a universal, and the suffering must be cared for. In the human community, who doubts its need for improvement?

The tasks are real. There are many activities of man that qualify as work, even by this austere and limited definition. If a person chooses to qualify as one who works, however, should he not be instructed in the requirements, and should there not be some burden of proof upon his efforts?

To think critically on this subject, it is necessary to discipline the mind against two deeply conditioned errors: to be busy and still not to play is not necessarily to work; to be employed for pay, either low or high, is not necessarily to work. Consider these illustrations and satisfy your mind as to whether these active pursuits constitute an example of work defined austerely:

1. A mother feeds her child.

2. A man rearranges the hair of a woman to render her fashionable and aesthetically pleasing (to a particular taste).

3. A man and woman peddle lottery tickets on the streets.

4. A dozen men confer for a week on how to capture a larger market for a product no better or worse than ten other competing items presently for sale.

5. Fifty artists, salesmen, and television producers labor to induce millions to smoke more cigarettes—of a particular brand.

6. A team of medical researchers work an eighty-hour week studying the causes of cancer.

7. An army of functionaries build a wall of paper between the intent of the engineers and the building of roads, schools, sewers, and transit lines.

8. A teacher drills forty children on the multiplication tables.

9. Ten thousand men labor on an installation designed to build engines of war.

10. A ship's crew is busy loading unsalable farm surplus aboard to be dumped at sea.

In the ten examples, who is *working* by a precise and humane definition of the term? The answer is in this book, but it must be

347

found and applied. In the instances cited, all are busy, all are being paid. Are they all working? If not, what are they doing? What bearing has this upon this school?

The American is singularly at home amid a formidable matrix of technology. The contemporary American walks very confidently among the abundant applied devices of the scientific heritage. Occasionally he is himself surprised when technology, however briefly, lets him down. In 1965 on the Eastern seaboard he stood astounded in the company of millions when dramatic failure in the regional powergrid took place. The psychic shock exceeded the inconvenience of those remarkable hours. Something taken for granted was taken away. Something counted upon had proved unreliable. A source of security was transformed into a source of vulnerability. The effect was roughly comparable to that of an earthquake. When terra firma itself turns unstable, then the most basic underpinnings of man's confidence are shaken. And the urban American takes the reliability of his basic technology quite as much for granted as he does the ground he walks on.

This circumstance is a somewhat neglected aspect of curriculum. Quite possibly the teaching of conceptual matters involved belongs not to scientific subjects, but to humanities or social studies. It is, after all, a matter of historical and sociological appraisal of a scientific–quantitative phenomenon. If so, this illustrates again that no set of subjects can preempt totally or adequately any one of the four designated areas of human experience.

This is a concept that the school must instruct into the consciousness of contemporary youth: *The technological grid of twentieth-century America is a comparatively recent phenomenon; it is a work of man, not an attribute of nature.* It is comparatively dependable, but it has built into it—and forever will—not merely the potential for mechanical failure and material disintegrated, but also the fallibilities and unpredictabilities of its makers. In sum, while man amid technology is dependent upon it, and more or less happy in this considering the many attendant benefits, he is also essentially independent of it. For example, the hammer is convenient to a man's hand but not a part of it.

This conceptual understanding is not applied for curricular

consideration simply as an intellectual gloss upon a technological text. It is needed so that the student may walk about the modern world in conscious perception of its attributes and not simply as primitive man walked familiarly through an environment which he either failed to perceive or fundamentally though often quite poetically misinterpreted.

For example, most children are now born into television. Uninstructed they would surely misperceive the situation. They must surely take it for granted and assume that it is a constant and a universal. What is at fault here? A basically dangerous misconception—*that what things have become is the way things are or always were.*

The children will be like savages in their perception of television, in this instance, until they learn that it is an artifact and a comparatively recent one. They will be cheated emotionally and intellectually if they are deprived of the vicarious rediscovery of this instrument. Merely to re-create the sense of wonder? Well, that would be justification enough for the intellectually high-spirited. But let this also be said: The history and the sociology of science and technology are essential to the effective functioning of humanity. It is necessary that man know the relation of self to his works; it will at very least minimize his chances of getting hurt by his own artifacts.

Vocationalism Revisited

Although this chapter deals with vocational education, it does not enter into the special mystique of the vocational field. Its protagonists hold to some notions of educational mysteries that are peculiarly theirs to perpetuate. Nor does it move patronizingly in this direction as though it were a venture in educational slumming. The view of the vocational aspect of education is purely matter of fact, neither vulgar nor holy. It is a simple necessity.

The setting for the vocational is in the social and cultural context of the American school. The public bias in education, which is a large one, is basically a bias in favor of getting ahead in the world. This is not the view of education that we would prefer or seek to inculcate. Yet, there it is and it is a reality. People believe in their schools, and the essence of their belief is that it will assure their children of a good job and a good living.

Pursuing this further, not as a model of educational vision, but as a social reality, let us look at the relationship between the school and the American economy. The school prepares its students most directly for the organizational world. Its dreariest practices are extolled by some as "getting the kids ready for the way things really are." This is neither a high aspiration for education nor a noble view of vocation.

The general view of educators toward vocationalism is a composite of the uniformed and the hypocritical. The principal characteristic of the curriculum is its out-and-out vocational emphasis. The pose of the educator is that vocational education is quarantined, as it were, to a particular group of students. The air badly needs to be cleared of the smog of confusion that pervades this area of education, so let us have at it.

By and large the school reflects middle-class attitudes. This is no semantic bombshell; and it is said here diagnostically, not invidiously. The school as we speak of it has little to do with the upper classes; the school is little of their concern or they of the school. They are few, and schools for their children are likewise few. The middle class sets great store by its tangibles: its new churches, its community buildings, its automobiles, its houses, and of course its schools. It has confidence and solid evidence that the school is an instrument for perpetuating its claim to these tangibles. If the middle class came to doubt the efficacy of the school as an instrument of material achievement, the support of the schools would soon be in hazard. But should doubters arise, the work of the Metropolitan School Study Council could be mobilized to stun skepticism. As a matter of fact, the economic necessity of education becomes a tighter bind by every evidence with each passing year.

With respect to school and job, the vocationalism of the curriculum is all the more dominant because it remains unspoken. Why speak of the self-evident, of what everybody knows and feels? The dominant vocationalism of the curriculum is so deeply acculturated in the school and its public as to warrant no words. Nonetheless, we choose to examine it here.

The children of the public for whom the school basically functions do not talk much of the jobs they will get. These are the children of substantial people and who will in the order of things attend college. Go to college, succeed there, and all things within reason and a rather restricted philosophical view become possible.

This simple desire cloaks the entire curriculum. Mathematics receives great stress and is expanded in the school because the college demands it. English is taught as part of a vocational necessity, the necessity for succeeding in college. Foreign languages, not in their essence but in their utility, are the most vocational of all subjects. The study of language has intrinsic and humanistic worth, of course, but it thrives in the school today for one reason, the vocational necessity associated with going to college. All this is not to say that vocational purpose improves the learning of mathemathics, of English, or of language, as the case may be. It merely identifies the reality of the basic motivation behind the curriculum.

In this book vocationalism is not a word to be shunned. If vocationalism is overriding the curriculum, it is a distortion that is being identified, not a taint. And if along the way certain hypocrisies can be spotlighted and exposed, even the zealots will be well off should they choose to shed their shoddy mantles.

The one dimension of education which the general educators, the liberal arts champions, and the college-preparatory teachers shun to speak of is vocationalism. The one dimension of a complete education that they do not neglect is the vocational. They are the best job getters and the getters of the best jobs. To be well educated is the nearly absolute criterion for entering into the world of genial hours and working conditions, of necktied occupations, and at the minimum, of occasional expense-account travel. The custodians of the liberal educational mysteries guard the entry into his life most jealously. They do not make the pathway particularly hard or narrow. Theirs is no longer an aristocratic bias, and an affluent society imposes little necessity for quotas—at least, in terms of numbers. The only patent is upon the route. It is a broad highway.

351

Occasional tollgates dot its further reaches to be sure, but, for that matter, where the tollgates start, so does traveler's aid magnify. A benevolent public or a paternalistic government, as you will, even pays one to travel, merely reserving the right to direct one to its choice of exit gates. The only really discernible coercion lies in the choice of route. If one wants to get there, this is the road. And the conditions and specifications for traveling this exclusive highway are well laid out.

The vocational education program in the American school is not nearly as exclusively vocational as the nonvocational program. Perhaps this is to be accounted for by the fact that it could candidly assert its job-preparation purpose without guilt or without fear of its own intellectual snobbery. Such a statement is not intended to make educational heroes of vocational educators. We are simply establishing them as the least vocationally dominated group of educators. They have their distinguishing characteristics, some of which their critics might designate as faults.

Some of these characteristics are of considerable educational consequence. Vocational educators have been very successful in legislative relations. In other words, they have been consummate lobbyists. They realized many millions of dollars of direct federal aid to education a good three decades before federal aid to education became an acknowledged reality. They have been actively experimental in education since the turn of the century. Many of the excited verbal agitations of progressive education would have caused wry amusement among vocational educators had communication been open. For when progressive educational theorists began to talk of projects, field trips, integrated learnings, the world beyond the school, demonstrations, and group learnings, the Smith-Hughes teacher could sometimes recognize through the strange vocabulary of pedagese the devices of instruction that he had been practicing for years.

Our principal purpose in this chapter is to put the vocational–utilitarian dimension into a full perspective. However, the general educator's cavalier ignorance of the realities of vocational education necessitates a corrective purpose as well. Take, for example, this matter of federal aid to education. After Sputnik, when the climate of legislative opinion finally allowed Congress to hitch the wagon of educational need to the star of national defense, the administrative chaos and educational confusion were joys to anyone who reveled in kaleidoscopic patterns of fluid functions undisciplined by form.

Federal aid was shaped by several biases (not to mention those historical factors that long blocked its accomplishment). One was the pious and nonsensical ritualistic utterance, "federal aid but no federal control." Another was the public stance that such aid was temporary, emergency legislation. And a third was the amateur bias that was effected by a decade of noisy journalistic criticism of education, Ford Foundation influence, and the Washington–Ivy League nexus of the years since 1960. The consequence of these biases has been comic if not catastrophic. Other than the breaking of the legislative dam walling off a great volume of legitimate support for the schools, little as yet can be credited to the mainstream of American education as a consequence of the National Defense Education Act and the Elementary and Secondary Education Act.

The most visible outcomes of these acts has been to cause a Kafkalike proliferation of educational bureaucracy and a veritable dreamworld of administrative confusion. Such specific outcomes as the following can be enumerated:

1. An amazing degree of federal influence (in effect, control) upon curriculum through discriminatory support. The distortions in favor of vocational education, languages, science, and guidance are notable.

2. A plethora of funds for narrowly conceived and nonfunctional educational research, especially in the realm of educational technology.

3. A lowering of educational standards in certain fields due to confident amateurism.

Educators themselves admit these consequences even while they detail staff to study legislation and to write proposals for their share of the plunder. The looters in the cities have been scarcely more gleeful or grabby than schoolmen reaching through the shattered panes where federal funds are stored.

If the well-established and balanced relationship of local, state, and federal authority effected by the administration of the Smith-Hughes Act had been studied and followed, the breeching of the dam to federal funds could have more generally irrigated the arid fields of education, and with less flood damage.

Vocation in the Organization World

> Perhaps in the long run, the society that agrees to tolerate the tension between public and private worlds, that gives the individual a chance to create his own meaning in both these worlds, that provides him with the tools and symbols to understand the richness and complexity of the world around him without shallow myths and legends—perhaps *that* is the society that can evoke man's highest loyalties and deepest commitments. American education, we believe, ought to be dedicated to that possibility.[3]

The foregoing quotation states a concept with which we take no issue, yet its consonance with our intent here constitutes an irony. *Education and the New America* is an important book; its authors are serious, hard-working educators. They have produced a book that has been taken seriously. Its relevance to us here is that it constitutes the one contemporary work on education that we must not merely comment upon and relate to, but even attempt to override. It represents, in effect, another set of choices for American education from those on which our work is based. These choices are thoughtfully arrrived at, but they rest to a large degree on a fallacious analysis of the dynamics of modern society and the wellsprings of individual fulfillment.

Kimball and McClelland speak at least patronizingly of three sources of educational theory that the author holds in high esteem: progressive education; existentialism; and John Dewey. In fact, since "existentialism" does not even appear in their index, it took a bit of a search to locate the following particular citation in the text:

3 Solon T. Kimball and James C. McClelland, *Education and the New America* (New York: Random House, 1962) , p. 323.

"And this is why," say the authors in pressing a reality-oriented view of selfhood, "the currently frenetic search for autonomy, for selfhood-from-within, a search that is led by the many-striped existentialists and trailed by the bravado of *The Organization Man,* will be necessarily futile."[4]

The trouble with the school today lies in what these writers dub "The transitional function of the school." They say (p. 39), "*The perspective we hold is that of the school as a transitional institution in which the process of education gradually separates the young from family and locality and prepares them to join the great corporate systems and to establish their own independent nuclear families.*" It is not so much that they recognize this operative function (who can miss it?), but that they idealize it. As stated, it could more properly be called "the disintegrative function of the school."

It is a strange and inexact analogy for educators to assert (p. 15): "The school can no more stand apart and exert an independent leverage on society than can the tobacco industry, just to take a counter-case that is roughly comparable in size." Even if we disregard the appreciable impact of that industry on the death rate, this is a truly remarkable expression of disdain for the fundamental institution of the willed intelligence coming from men who consistently aver their scorn for anti-intellectualism.

Education and the New America is a critical essay. Since the whole work derives from a contrary view of most things educational, we shall not quarrel with the dim view of progressive education. But it is necessary to spend some words on the caricature of John Dewey. The authors seem to have read him. They cite his *Liberalism and Social Action* (p. 349) but from their summation of his social theory (pp. 113–114) it would appear that they might reread it to their benefit (and also Gerald Steibel's Teachers College dissertation on the same subject). To imply that John Dewey's limitations derive primarily from his Vermont village childhood is more than reasonably superficial. Dewey traveled as far from the village as did Sinclair Lewis and Thomas Wolfe. To try to make of him a rustic intellectual is as ludicrous as to give Robert Frost the image of a farm hand because of the hired man whose

4 *Ibid.*, p. 264.

death he memorialized. The "little" slanders on origins, however, do not constitute their basic misunderstanding of John Dewey's theoretical limitations. They say that, "In the final analysis his conservation overcame his devotion to change, growth, and process." His Marxist critics said similar things reminiscent of this non-Marxist canard. The informed view of Dewey's limitations lies in two elements: his practically deliberate ignoring of the Freudian impact on the modern mind and a lack of perception of the existential agony of modern man, a deficiency that these writers share generously.

The authors do make some striking insights about education in America that demand our respect. In pointing out that the American's goals are now largely internal rather than external, they say (pp. 166–167):

> Freed from the crushing burdens of material existence, we proclaim that man must now confront the obligation to fulfill himself as an individual personality. And yet we still hang back. Nor is it the demands of public duty that keep us from directly pursuing the ideal of self-fulfillment. It is rather a strange failure of nerve. We advertise ourselves into a hankering for yet more material objects. We propagandize ourselves into seeing the Russians or the Chinese as the prime threats to our corporate security. *And thus we artificially try to escape paying the price of being who we are and what we are at this historical moment.* [Emphasis added.]

We made particular note of the penetrating sentence, expecting surely to see it used as a springboard into an agonizing inquiry: *Who are we? What are we now?* But such was not to be. Instead, we have a hundred and fifty pages of a running start for an audacious secular leap of faith. Who are we? Simply said (p. 315), "In short, part of the price of being an American is *being* an organization man. Autonomy is not, as Whyte would have us believe, a viable alternative. On the contrary, the very attempt to discover an alternative is a form of mental and social illness, a denial of reality. The important question is not whether, but what kind of organization man."

Our competence not being theological, we cannot presume to criticize this creed. Perhaps, it may be possible to comment more or less reverently upon it. First, we are amazed to discover such theological competence in educators, perhaps because of a felt lack in this dimension. We have heard a little, however, of the historic quest for a defined deity, but just before the leap we find the summation clear: "God is a bureaucrat." (p. 314) If this be the father, what indeed shall the children be?

It is good that a new and precise theology buttress the ultimate dogmas of their work. The symbols of Christianity and Judaism, we are instructed (p. 312), are not making sense "within the larger structures of society and nature." So much for Isaiah and Samuel; so must be written off *Pacem in Terris*. Apparently, too, there is reason to believe that this economical view of God and man is adequate to the moral task. The striped existentialists, and other theologians, and even philosophers have obviously taken the human predicament much too seriously. It is comforting to read (p. 317), ". . . organized civil life would be impossible if truly difficult moral problems were the common experience of ordinary men." Here we shall grant Kimball and McClelland theological immunity. However, educational criticism and even skepticism might be in order. They say, for instance (p. 317), "For most of us, fortunately, in most of our actions, the right thing to do is not only very obvious, it is also the most natural, the easiest thing to do." We like the educational economy implied here: what is best? why, what is easy. Still, does such a comment derive from simple virtue, or simple-mindedness?

The serious trouble in this book is not the matter of the presumed necessity for education to mobilize itself to help the individual be the "right kind of organization man." This is not the central fault. A book that makes the moral dilemmas of modern man an easy matter is not one for educators to take seriously. This must follow, or else it would be necessary for us to judge, just for example, Albert Camus and C. P. Snow to be fools. Kimball and McClelland must map their primrose path to perfect adjustment, or "commitment," as they so strangely use the word, a good deal more explicitly before we are ready for that.

Sir Charles Snow has entertained most of the questions that

this pair have glossed upon. But he has labored in the vineyard rather than merely idled by to pick a few of the riper grapes. He is concerned with the dialogue of modern thought with traditional symbolism. He appreciates the tensions, the haulings and tuggings upon the person of the counterforces of public and private life. An organization man of sorts himself, he abjures playful Parkinsonian formulas as well as easy definitions of civil service ethics. In nine or ten novels, more or less, and a number of essays he delineates the many-faceted, kaleidoscopic intricacies of human relationships which go to make up a part of what may be in sum "reality." But he never prates confidently of what is real, and surely never suggests that profound moral choice is uncommon, or even far around another corner. In the myriad relationships of his hundreds of characters there is not a one to whom the dilemmas of choice were less than puzzling, and more often full of pain. Snow maintains an urbane psychic distance from the characters he draws, but he enters the scene now and again both with compassion and judgment. His acute distaste for the chauvinistic and demented atomic scientist of one of his later novels he gleefully reveals. He is scientist enough to allow his people to move without intrusion of his sentiments. He is no bleeding heart. Yet in the affairs of his many striped new men classic dilemmas are exercised and tested again and again. Loyalties are betrayed, and betrayals are cloaked by loyalties. Good men do hurt to other good men on behalf of men who seem less good. Family ties buttress strong decisions and cushion weak ones; family ties support and again put millstones round the necks of men who labor at things that sometimes hold meaning for them. Such a tiny sample indicates by contrast the superficiality of another view of the human predicament.

In *The Search,* a novel outside the plan of his major opus, Sir Charles illuminates his respect for science as tempered, as disciplined, by compassion and magnanimity. His protagonist is a scientist, a researcher, a man free of archaic symbols and values. Nevertheless, when his father suggests that the dead mother may be looking down upon them, the scientist son says in effect, maybe so. This was a little dishonesty on behalf of human feeling. Later this same scientist finds that he has used as support for his own research another man's efforts that on scrutiny do not hold up under rigorous scientific test. He knows his choice and makes it—but scarcely easily. He sets his career back by years by acting, painfully, upon his highest criteria of intellectual integrity. Yet, in a later and parallel case when it was his to expose another man even in a bit of possible scientific fraud, his choice was neither easy or sure. By the laws of scientific integrity and by natural vindictiveness, the choice should have been easy. This man had not merely flirted with charlatanry, he had stolen the protagonist's wife, whom he had loved and not surrendered lightly. Yet he did not expose the fraud. He let human considerations intrude. Of such complexities does one very literate scientist see the making of choice.

Such considerations do not prompt us to charge Kimball and McClelland with *talking nonsense* as they accuse Erich Fromm of doing (p. 372). But we happily borrow their invidious phrase "weak romanticism" that they apply to Chapter 8 of *The Sane Society*.[5] Weak romanticism is an apt, though charitable, designation for their thesis and much of its exposition.

Despite the ardent evangelism of these writers, education must deny that its function is to bring the souls of its seekers into the fold of the organization. The school will enrich their view of vocation; it will even labor to render them employable. Its central effort will be directed toward the enhancement of the person, the enlargement of his capacity to choose intelligently in the bewildering dilemmas that all men encounter. The outcome will be measured not in the degree of his acceptance of institutionally assigned roles, but in a sure sense of who and where he is, whether in the best of company, or enmeshed amid the absurd; in a word, the measure of man shall be his autonomy.

The Vocation Is Living

The school must study its definitions of work and utility in depth. It must strengthen competence in all its enterprises. It must ac-

[5] Erich Fromm, *The Sane Society* (New York: Reinhart, 1955).

knowledge its obligation to move all of its students along the road to vocational and economic productivity. It will only educate in the profound sense if it studies the implications of this reality—*the fundamental vocation of man is to live.*

We have at times lived in apartment hotels that were predominantly the residences of the elderly and the retired. These numbered both rich and poor, but except for the added worries deriving from inadequate pensions or family support, finance seemed not to be the major determinant of peace and contentment in their later years. "Involvement in living" is the best phrase to distinguish among the more and the less observably happy ones.

At evening in the lobbies this quality seemed to be put to test most severely. The days even of the aged have their occupations: dressing and grooming, the puttering little chores of putting and keeping things in order, appearances at meals, the greeting of friends and the chitchat, the medical appointments, the walks and easy exercises. After dinner, however, the supports of necessities and routines give way. For many the hours till bedtime yawned with anxiety and tedium.

Little old ladies appeared always to be coming and going, fretful, fussy, and uncomposed. Many seemed to welcome ailment as an engrossing preoccupation, a center of meaning. Lacking infirmity on which to focus, they seemed not to know what to do with themselves. To muster a table for bridge or canasta was often beyond the ingenuity of the heartier minority. To remain before the television screen for more than a few minutes was an unusual feat of concentration for some, a fact that did not in these instances denote a rejection of its inanities for more rewarding pastime—just more trips to the desk, the drug counter, the front windows, to pace a few turns in the corridors, to try another chair. The spectacle was pitiable and might have remained a generalized sadness over the vicissitudes of humanity's twilight years except for a dawning apprehension that became a conviction. These persons, for the most part, were living as they had always lived.

They had, it appeared, the more one observed and heard and learned of them, always been occupied in life rather than having been involved in it. Supported by busy schedules of household and family management, social engagements, travel, and energetic though empty expenditure, they had put in their years. Some had forgotten the necessity of self by putting themselves forever at the service of family, friends, and clubs. Now they were socially unemployed, lost, without the demands of tasks and sacrifices imposed by others. Others had obviously leaned hard upon their associates, demanding, exacting, and taking from them. Self-centered to the core, these had once possessed the tools of manipulation in good measure, charm, persuasion, position, managerial skill. With charm diminished and realms of control evaporated in time, petulance replaced imperiousness. With no one about to dominate, except briefly and indulgently or for hire, these too fussed about for lack of self-meaning.

Luckily for the human prospect, this was not the whole of it. Some, not always the least infirm or unlucky, held firm reins on existence. They engaged in sustained conversations, sometimes rich in old friendships or still possessed of the capacity to establish new ones. Some returned to long evenings at the card table where they pursued the continuing tournament with avid concentration—and now and then with piratical competitiveness. Not all of these, but a few held an eager interest in the doings of youth. A school of dance happened to occupy quarters off the lobby in what had been in the hotel's better days its ballroom. To the life-beaten oldsters, the going and coming of flashy-dressed and exuberant youth was a constant source of irritation and exasperation, of pinched mouths and slanderous judgments. The better-starred even ventured into the dance studios to watch, to smile, and to tap a foot, perhaps a bit behind the beat.

One man epitomized the objectives of successful geriatrics. He was in his ninety-second year. He was erect, active, frail. He had known wealth; he had family and was, it seemed, none too well used by them, for he was left lonely and was always short of cash the week before his monthly check. The cliché has it that to sustain connection with life one should "develop interests." That is wrong, as the author learned from this old man. The necessity is to *have interest.* Interest is a pervasive characteristic, a general quality that we earlier called *involvement in life.* This man sought us out, to sound us in terms of his interest. He lived in a constant and general awareness of the scene. Night after night his opening comment was, "I ran into an interesting thing today." The "thing" might be the opening of an amusement park, a change in governmental fiscal policy, an item about some Audubon prints, the launching of a new Atlantic liner, or a book that had come to his attention. Along with interest, he had fashioned *design* into his life. Each Sunday morning, he gave himself a consummately civilized treat. Dressed meticulously, cane in hand, he walked a steady slow pace some blocks to another hotel where he took his brunch in the quiet, white table-clothed dining room and read his New York *Times* cover to cover. After he learned that we were employed at the National Education Association, he found new bridges of communication. Many an evening, we would find clippings in our mail box concerning education, rather heavily loaded toward the more dyspeptic critics of our organizational ventures. Since he was fully alive in the world, we had no need to patronize him with indulgent agreement. He sought lively controversy; we had it, and enjoyed it with one another.

The ghost of this man stalks our thoughts of enduring education, along with better known examples of the same quality of tenacious involvement: Winston Churchill, Herbert Hoover, Eleanor Roosevelt, Margaret Rutherford, Bernard Baruch, to recount a few.

The vocational–utilitarian dimension of the human potential does demand that each person be shaped for useful occupation and that this task be largely defined and explicitly carried out. But the vocation of all is *life.* A trade, a profession, an occupation is a necessity, but occupation alone does not encompass life. And a life built on occupation, even if that occupation is the serving of others, cannot forever sustain on this. Sooner or later the routines crumble and if these have been the props of a person's interests, then the person tends to crumple. Interest sustains, but it must be outward in view. The sorriest of life consequences await the totally self-centered. Obviously, the science of geriatrics begins in the kindergarten.

Our intent is not to urge the school to direct the attention of students toward their retirement years. This would be a mean pre-occupation for the mind of youth. The teen-ager would not, if he could, choose to think as an octogenarian. No, there is no need for the curriculum to look ahead in this wise. The sobering fact is this: what the person has been, he is; what he is, he will be. The vocational dimension of education is but one aspect of attention to this fundamental state of being. What sustains well today nourishes well for tomorrow. The profound study of the best for today in building life-involvement promises the best for the many tomorrows.

Education would do well to dwell on the essence in the happy verse it teaches to all its children; and remember that these words of Robert Louis Stevenson were not from the pen of a silly mortal whose life was all ease and pleasure:

> The world is so full of a number of things,
> I am sure we should all be as happy as kings.[6]

Vocation and Social Waste

The vocational dimension needs intrusion in its substantive program no more than any other aspect of curriculum. Like the others it needs a more clearly conceptualized statement of its position in the whole scheme of things, and most particularly it requires some bulwarking against parochially conceived biases and practices with which it must often contend.

Commonest of complaints among teachers of the school's more immediately job-oriented efforts is that their courses are used as "academic dumping grounds." The slippage in such usage is somehow apparent: surely the community may more easily tolerate a few high-school graduates whose language is shoddy or whose grasp of Euclidean principles is hazy, than mechanics who foul up more than they fix or carpenters who construct things that quickly fall apart. Another perspective, simply of fairmindedness, suggests that

---

6 Robert Louis Stevenson, "Happy Thought," *A Child's Garden of Verses* (Chicago: Rand McNally, 1902), p. 55.

each branch of instruction and each teacher might be expected to share the burden of teaching the none too readily educable.

Rampant assumption has it that a sort of providential compensation affords nonacademic types, whatever they may be, an extra measure of practical competence. Research to the effect that manual dexterity correlates pronouncedly with low intelligence is hard to come by. Adjustment to circumstance and the acting out of rather essential motivations for survival have a good deal more relation to the development of other skills among those whom the academic program has tended to reject.

Force of circumstance or free personal choice now and then directs a girl with an I.Q. of 150 into a secretarial career or a boy similarly bright into a garage. Some deplore such outcomes as personal tragedy or social wastage. It need be no such thing. Such a view stems largely from an overdeveloped paternalism, occupational or academic snobbery, or a small view of the demands of life on native wit and education. The organizational world should welcome a share of talented office workers if only to bolster the efforts of employers of lesser endowments; and the world will find the road to an exceptional diagnostic mechanic as to any better mouse-trap maker. In whatever role, the person should find the job he takes, and life itself, to put the utmost demands upon his intelligence. The only legitimate educational apprehension is whether the school has affected the total range of human potential in its graduate or has merely turned him loose with a typewriter or tool kit that he has learned to use. But similar concern might equally be expressed for the completeness of education for atomic scientists or English teachers.

As far as social wastage is concerned, it is a grievous problem of society, and it is a problem to which society alone can attend. The school, for all its faults and misconceptions, has been offering the society an abundance of relatively well-educated persons, and beyond the school the college has done the same. This education has long concentrated on "the development of rich and many sided personalities." Society then takes this graduate, humanistically expanded by the school, and offers him its job. How many jobs then utilize the person in full? In what positions is the full nurture of human capacity so studiously attended to as in the school? A man of numerous talents often takes a job that requires the exercise of only a part of one talent; he may count himself fortunate if some premium is placed on two or three. Out of such frustrations of talent are conceived ulcers, illicit alliances, pointless hobbies, and great crops of proficient card players and low golf scorers. It is in the educator's province to point this out, but it is not a wastage that the school can eliminate.

Vocational and commercial educators can be urged to assert the full dignity of their enterprise within the school. Not only should they justifiably resist accommodating to the ineptitude of the school in its other dimensions, but more importantly they should bid forcefully in the academic market for a share of the most capable students. The ceilings on attainment in the practical arts are as high as in any other field of endeavor. Unless he is obstructed by nonsensical academic hurdles, the boy may find his way from vocational farming to botanical research, to large farm management, or to the presidency of a college; or he may find his way from the shop to his own factory or to an advanced degree and work in industrial design. It has already happened—and when male chauvinism has diminished it will happen more often—that the bright girl proceeds from typewriter to management and sometimes to partnership in an enterprise.

The explicit hazards in vocational programs that train narrowly, expensively, and well for last year's or last decade's occupations are real. They are also quite apparent to the leaders in vocational and commercial education. These subjects are in at least as good hands as the academic ones as far as modernization is concerned. The guidance movement also is applying its press toward living educationally with the modern constant of change. The general educator again need not instruct these competent colleagues in their profession. He *can* help them to conceptualize their efforts in larger terms, to assist them to a more generally accepted status as fully serious and significant participants in total education, and to beat down the impositions and derogations that are directed toward them by the academically snobbish or naïve.

365

Labor and Education

The curriculum has visited the labor movement superficially and gingerly. The attitude of the school has reflected the bias of ruralism, of the middle class, and of pre-Hoover Republicanism toward the organized works of labor. This has had a dual consequence: psychic neglect of the economic backgrounds of large segments of the school's population and neglect of important scholarship interpreting significant institutions of American life.

Those students whose families dwell in what some would call the working classes are the very ones on which the school has established its most tenuous hold. These are not the students whose poverty and aggravated social disadvantages have created the designation of the culturally deprived. They are, however, those who have most considerably gravitated toward the general, the commercial, and the vocational programs. They have moved at a disadvantage in the school's social life and with the exception of athletics in its activity programs. It has been abundantly demonstrated that the educational motivations of these students both within the school and toward higher education has been significantly less developed than among the children of the white-collar occupations. Because education effects its largest miracles when it turns its efforts toward morale building and identity building, the oversight of opportunities in this field is no less than reprehensible.

The drama of social mobility has been so tremendous in American life that it has quite legitimately become a primary focus of institutional interpretation. A significant segment of the teaching force is now constituted by the grandchildren and great grandchildren of the immigrants who came by the millions to take advantage of the opportunity to do hard work in attempts to better their lives. Yet social mobility by person, "the ladder of success," has been much less significant in its contribution to net social gain than social mobility by class, the aggregate advances of large, identifiable groups working to better wages, working conditions, and achieve social recognition. Overemphasis on the "poor boys who became famous" or rose to managerial levels has created the educational delusion that the only proper goal for a person with respect to physical work is to rise above it. Technology and automation may erase the total burden of toil. Prophecy has it so, and gives its advisory mention to youth in recommendation of technical operations and the service trades. Presently, it appears we shall all be husbanding computers or filling one another's gas tanks (and, of course, cutting and curling each other's hair) for a living. Thus, onward to Utopia.

Meanwhile, it appears that an interval remains in which work involving back and muscle will continue to be done: most of it not without tools and machines, to be sure. Trucks and tractors will not drive themselves for awhile yet. When America begins moving, as much of it does seasonally each year, the furniture that lifts and loads itself has yet to be invented. The agricultural revolution proceeds apace, with invention speculatively eying each manual process. Those fruits and vegetables on the tables of the affluent society, however, have still been touched and hefted by human hands over and over on their journey from the fields. Organized labor still enrolls millions; these and the millions of unorganized as yet remain an active and significant labor force—an institutional reality of the American scene.

If understanding who and where we are, and how we got here, is a defensible goal of enlightenment, then the neglect of certain institutional aspects of our evolution is difficult to understand. How then is it so? The mystery attended to unravels mightily. The inattention to the working man, his role and his organizations was first of all, perhaps, a matter of embarrassment. In the nineteenth century, where so much of curriculum and social thought still resides, in the pleasant phrasing of the time these were "the great unwashed." Beyond its need of them in mill, mine, and factory the nation had not much notion of how to deal with them, how to perceive them as neighbors. An inevitable consequence of inability to conceptualize a situation is to be reticent about it. In the course

367

of events the immigrants, the workers, made their own way. They conceptualized themselves; they became an ever-broadening and functioning part of the scene.

Paradoxically their way of doing this, and the institutions of social process that they utilized, further alienated them from the school even as it attempted to integrate them into the new America. Not content with advancing themselves by hard work, the laborers demanded not an end to toil but a lesser day of it for a fairer return. Their only effective instrument was to organize and to press their claim in united strength.

The children now in the school are far from the realities of breadlines. Even their younger teachers must learn from books and their elders the stories of the Great Depression and World War II. How little, then, will they know from personal experience the backgrounds of occupation and economic relationships in which they find themselves? Today when the right of collective bargaining has acquired a near constitutional force, how can they uninstructed believe that until recently every approach to the bargaining table was obstructed, contested, and enjoined against? How can they understand in this age of general consensus regarding an American's right to a decent living by a decently defined standard that not so long ago labor was commonly regarded as a commodity preferably to be bought in an unprotected market at the prevailing price occasioned by supply and demand? Unless they have been well instructed how can they understand the bitterness of the workers who organized to contest the hiring practices of such industrial captains as George Pullman, George F. Baer, and Henry C. Frick? It is not as though the books were closed to the accomplishments of economics in the social sphere; instead it seems as though they were opened on a partial basis. The accomplishments of inventive genius find their way readily to the texts, along with the benefactions of Andrew Carnegie and John D. Rockefeller. The precedent of the open door needs only to be more largely capitalized on. It is not mainly to assure a fair and balanced chronicle (though that were no mean target) that this is insisted; the basic necessity to seek and serve is a useful understanding of the fundamental institutions of American life.

It is no use objecting that such scholarship has political implications. So, too, does neglect of it, or its partial treatment. In a
democratic society almost everything worth considering has political
implications. The aim of free inquiry is, however, to serve the free
society. It is censored or restricted inquiry that is most vulnerable to
uses of partisanship narrowly conceived. We reiterate in order to
settle this fundamental decisively: the school cannot escape or evade
the fact that its instruction is inextricably bound with social, which
is to say political, consequence. The only way it can assure that the
political consequences of its curriculum serve the tenet of the
greatest good for the greatest number is that its inquiry be totally
devoted to the fullest evidence thoughtfully weighed—and altogether free.

How is one to explain the common partial treatment of institutions in the school? The history of the teaching profession has some
bearing. Two and three generations ago it was principally comprised of girls with rural and lower-middle-class backgrounds. These
antecedents furnished little support either for interest in or sympathy with working-class problems. Perhaps even more important
was the fact that these girls were badly educated. A normal course
of short duration or an exposure to genteel liberal education constituted the standard for teacher education. The administrators both
in self-concept and in practice identified themselves with business
management, as Raymond Callahan has documented so well.[7]

The irony of this professional stance endures, though the recruitment of teachers is now on a much widened social base and the
education of teachers has immeasurably improved. But the school-
child is seldom taught how profoundly indebted the public school is
to the labor movement. In the long decades when the National
Education Association (NEA) along with others sought vainly to
break the roadblock to Congressional approval of federal aid, its
most consistent lobbying antagonist was the United States Chamber
of Commerce. When organized business shifted its attitude toward
federal support, it was not so much a concern for education as a

---

[7] Raymond Callahan, *Education and the Cult of Efficiency* (Chicago:
University of Chicago Press, 1962).

revelation of the potential market in well-subsidized education that prompted it.

The attitude of the NEA toward the principle of unionization has long revealed an ingrained and articulate bias. Substantive grounds as well as organizational rivalries do partly account for the opposition of the NEA to the AFT (American Federation of Teachers). But in the continuing dialogue the class-oriented perception of the NEA is unmistakable: the union principle of organization automatically contaminates with unprofessionalism; the union is associated not with the whole but a partial interest in society; the union is not so much to be discussed on the issues as dismissed because of institutional defilement.

Fortunately for the working conditions of teachers, institutional competition between the great and little giants of their representation, the militance of the David has in this case not slain but inspired greater vigor in the Goliath. Since the elections in which the AFT won the right to represent New York City's teachers, the NEA has turned, however reluctantly, from purely public relations approaches to direct action in supporting teachers' economic claims. Long opposed to and disdainful toward the strike as "unprofessional," the NEA has developed the *sanction* as its weapon. The sanction is a formidable weapon of organizational compulsion and is a demonstrated and drastic force. The NEA, still frightened of the standard vocabulary of sound employer–employee relations, has contrived its own euphemism for collective bargaining, which it prefers to dub "professional negotiation."

Not fully admitting reality even under pressure, the NEA persists in acting out one great myth: that in salary negotiations the administration sits with the teachers in mutual cause and self-interest. The existence of the Loch Ness monster is no more negligible a statistical likelihood than this. In fact, the separate role of the chief administrator in collective bargaining or professional negotiations, as the case may be, is not so much a matter of his sympathies or alliances as a consequence of his unique professional position. In educational affairs he is a colleague: first among equals would be the ideal conception. He is, nonetheless, at the same time the agent designate of the community selected by its duly constituted authority to run the schools. His understood and often clearly defined obligation is to operate the schools as "efficiently and economically as possible." Typically, therefore, the superintendent of schools has been neither an impassioned crusader for better teaching salaries nor a Machiavellian conniver against teachers' interests, though both types have been known. In salary negotiations his most appropriate role is that of intermediary and objective communicator. If he has any undeniable sympathies they may be shown to a degree in his exercise of these functions, but his role will not be defined by his feelings. He will as a result be a happier administrator, if that matters, for his allegiances and motivations will not be brought into question and held suspect at each annual salary season.

The Tale of the Inarticulate Schoolboy

We are here attempting to offer a design for a complete and humane education, and our respect for the liberal tradition and even for the more traditional liberal arts is apparent. Furthermore, despite a deep and modern regard for science, particularly its mode of thought and inquiry, we do not hesitate to build from a humanistic bias. This we do in the name of objectivity, for in our judgment the humanities now lag seriously in the public dialogue between Snow's *Two Cultures,* and because many of the public works of so-called science are much more closely related to the worlds of Parkinson and Kafka than to the spirit of Galileo, Newton, and Einstein.

Despite the stubborn reiteration of Robert Hutchins and Mark Van Doren, the liberal arts are no longer a mere "seven." Nor were they so limited in the brief historical epoch when the *trivium* and *quadrivium* dominated the thought of the few educators who leavened the relatively sodden human community. Anything is a liberal art that induces the emancipation of the human being from the fetters of incapacities, awkwardnesses, ignorances, and fears and permits the person to develop and express his total human potential. This definition makes it necessary to strike critically at the

371

parochialism of those liberal educators who see their role more as the keepers of mysteries than as liberators of the human potential.

Surely rhetoric holds ancient sanction as a liberal art. Quintilian, classic schoolman of Rome, held oratory to be the consummate discipline and product of a good education. The modern school of communications arts and skills does not blush to build upon this ancient discipline, though communications in our time is a much broader and more profound discipline than the ancients ever knew. *Communications* is a discipline enriched by great social scientific insights: from psychology, sociology, and anthropology; from semantics and linguistics, and from the rich resources of multisensory aids and media.

Yet, the gist of the matter is that man has speech. That is, it is within his capacity to become magnificently articulate. Furthermore, since he has great capacity to perceive, he is somehow driven to express himself and is by these tokens somehow frustrated and thwarted, denied his potential, if he does not speak out his perception.

The requisites for this speaking out are three: that he have confident knowledge of an experience worth expressing; that he be assured of respect for his person and experience; that he have an audience aware of the need and competent in receptivity to hear what he has to say. These requirements being met, he will speak, and effectively; whatever his mortal limitations of tongue and person, he will assume the proportions of orator. Harrassed by an historical record of dramatic failures, a reputation for gross conservative errors, and a tongue none too nimble, Winston Churchill demonstrated this point fully. In a word, by his oratory, at a moment when his knowledge of necessity to express himself was certain, when respect for his person and character was at its zenith, when a nation was aware and in direst need to listen and to hear his words, he literally preserved the morale of the Western world and saved it by what he had to say. This is one of the most noble instances of the saving quality of speech in the annals of our century. And Churchill had once been a schoolboy whom the schools had held in no great esteem!

But our concern here *is* *with* the schools. If we are to bear upon the program of the schools, which deem themselves universal, we must prove ourselves with illustrations from more humble schoolboys. We must prove our points as applicable universally. Take these points as reference:

1. The liberal program, the college-preparatory course, presumes a peculiar competence in the liberal emancipation of man.

2. It is commonly agreed that effective speech is an important characteristic of the educated man.

3. It is a sad reflection on curriculum makers' knowledge that the school does little enough in the field of speech except for the few whom it deems to have talent.

Now let us tell the tale of one inarticulate schoolboy.

There appeared at high school, one September, this boy, call him Orville, who was big, blonde, shy, and on this day, scared. At any rate, he was lost in the crowd. There were nearly nine hundred students in one big brick building in Grades K through 14 (the public school system boasted a Junior College). It was a consolidated school, so upon beginning high school, the ninth grade suddenly had its numbers doubled. At this point, another twenty or so students came to town after graduating from an assortment of one-room rural schools flung about the county. The county seat and the big brick school seemed pretty formidable to some of these. Orville stumbled through the maze of registration and the paths to his several classes and studyhalls. On Friday he encountered speech class.

In this school, as in so many, speech was an adjunct of the English program. The topics were delightful: "Something I Did on Vacation," "A Book I Really Enjoyed," "My Favorite Hobby," or sometimes simply "Current Events." "Two-minute Talks," they were called. Some students, already glib, talked five. Orville? For weeks, when his name was called, he shook his head sadly, hung it, and passed his turn. The teacher quite as sadly marked his zero in her record book. Orville gained in confidence, however, and one day, not much later than some other classmates, rose at the invita-

373

tion and went to the front of the room, or near to it at least. Then he squared his shoulders, faced his classmates, and froze into a blushing catalepsy. The blush, which no doubt had stemmed from his very viscera, first appeared above his collar, climbed his visage, and soon shone upon his generous ears. His anguish flowered in a beautiful exhibit of pink skin bubbled with beads of sweat. Glassy eyed he stared at his classmates, turned hostile strangers to his view. In apparent pain he forced his jaw to open and uttered a strangulated, "Awgsh. . . ." Then he regained himself and stumbled to his seat. This occupied something less than two minutes. It was his first speech.

By his senior year, on Fridays, truth to tell, Orville could walk steadily up the aisle, actually put a few sentences together, and justify a charitable "C" in the record book. However, he never ceased to blush.

Orville was also a student in vocational agriculture (the Smith-Hughes program). The principal objective of this program is to make competent, modern farmers. The stuff of its curriculum is farm shop, crops and soils, animal husbandry, farm management. Adjunct to the academic program is a club called the Future Farmers of America.

In the August before the start of his senior year Orville went to the Great State Fair. Among the sights, one was memorable. The Future Farmers held a demonstration contest. In this event boys competed in displaying and explaining their projects in agriculture.

This same Orville took the platform before an audience of three hundred. He walked up confidently to speak for a solid thirty minutes to a group that included other students, farmers, newspapermen, teachers, and professors from the land-grant college. He moved about the stage among cages of poultry; with pointer in hand he indicated relevant statistics on graphs of his own making, turning flip charts as the occasion demanded. He commanded and informed this audience; and *he won the first prize.*

Yet the following year in English class his Friday performances remained shy, nondescript, and blushing.

Would it not be patronizing to spell out the educational, the curricular implications of this story? Is it really necessary?

Commentary: Toward a Complete Education

Clearly a complete education must draw upon the breadth of human experience to be responsive to the full dimension of the human potential. Although by no means ideally suited for this purpose, school subjects may serve well enough, but only if they are well taught and well conceptualized.

Well taught is, of course, a catchword phrase, for all too often it is awarded to the earnest pursuit of a duffer's model of instructional practice. But it is here intended as a professional designation, awarded only to teaching that consciously pursues a viable new model.

A complete education cannot be achieved by an elaborate construction of courses, no matter how broad in intentions or how heavy a burden be placed upon the energy and motivation of the learner. Let us take a curriculum class in which students analyzed the legitimate claims of varied subject areas upon their attention as an example. No less than *nine* subjects can and do make claims for a continuing block of time throughout the entire duration of secondary education. These at least may be enumerated and include (1) English (literature and composition); (2) languages; (3) sciences; (4) mathematics; (5) history (and government and geography); (6) social studies; (7) music and arts; (8) vocational subjects or practical arts; and (9) health, physical education, and related development.

To contrive a complete education by attempting to encompass all these "desirable" learnings is obviously a quantitative impossibility. Even if the academic speed-up were to impose a six-course load on the already staggered student, three tracks of legitimate subject matter would have to be denied. Thus, by working from this subject-centered model of curricular completeness, the most arduous application can achieve no better than a partial education. Yet it is apparent that a partial education constitutes a double betrayal: it robs the student of part of his human heritage; it denies him a portion of his opportunity for human development, a part of his life, no less.

Full-dimensioned conceptualization of whatever subjects are offered, or required, is the key. To attempt to rationalize curriculum by selectivity among subjects is a way to arrive at academic civil war, not at reform. For selection will not achieve completeness. Examine, for example, a six-course program of well-selected subjects: biology, geometry, English, French, world history, sociology. A "full load" most schools and all students might agree. It *only* omits the practical, the arts, the health and physical-development subjects. But it might omit more and be more humane, for if these subjects are ill-conceptualized, they are likely to teach scantily, regardless of the length of assignments and the rigors of homework imposed. Their only consequence can be academic, which in the broadened context of our work can now be read to mean "narrowly vocational," only related to the vocation of pursuing further academic study. The partiality, even the triviality, of such a conception of education should now be beyond dispute.

Some vessels are better than others, but our point is that the instruments, the subjects, are not so much ours to affect. Reason and educational criticism may affect their content and usage, but their curricular presence is the outcome of organized aggregates of academic power. To obtain changes in the educational power structure is possible; it is even intriguing to politicians and warriors. But the changes so effected bear little relation to better education except rhetorically. Our practical hope here is to achieve a profound revision of content and thereby a complete education for all students.

Let us assert that if conceptualization be profound and complete, the most unlikely assortment of subjects could carry the burden of a very complete learning program. (This is not to make a plea for oddly assorted carriers but to reassert the central relevance of content.) A very profound and complete education could be conceptualized out of such an economical and academically unlikely package as these four courses: Swahili, shop, poetry, and automobile, or substitute football or sewing for any one of these.

Not one of these subjects thoroughly conceptualized would lack its derivatives from and applications within the full four-dimensioned resource of the human experience and the human potential. To be sure, it is absurdly easy to suggest a more likely and appropriate set of courses by which to carry the curricular burden. Because this is true, it is about time that the subject area guardians and devotees cease to bring their empty baskets to school. These barely sustain their own weight. Although there are many who will still argue the point, these subjects do not justify themselves in themselves *alone*. They have to carry the educational burden; that is, each subject must fully nurture the total development of the person.

Each teacher should look at his work as though he had been shipwrecked with his students on a lonely isle; now though he had deeply preferred to teach discrete lessons in grammar or history or algebra, he must make what he knows serve, not merely so that students may pass tests but to sustain the burden of civilization and the development of the skills and morale necessary for human survival. This view of things is not fancy; this is the way it is! Each day the teaching encounter precisely takes this form. Human responsibility then faces its reality and its burden and assumes its total human task. Or it plays its games of academic pat-a-cake, awaits each payday and denies the possibilities of the deluge.

CURRENT DIRECTIONS: A CONCEPTUAL CRITIQUE

PART FOUR

CURRENT DIRECTIONS: A CONCEPTUAL CRITIQUE

Chapter XII

Technology, Media, and the Person

My work has accustomed me to the idea of being willing to allow imagination to roam freely, and my associates in science attribute a quotation to me which goes something like this: "Don't be ashamed to propose a ridiculous idea. Though worthless today, in 10 years it may be of no value whatsoever."[1]

—*Simon Ramo*

For man to fear technology is nonsense, but for man to be apprehensive of the uses some men would make of the tools and machines wrought by the mind and hand of humanity is utterly reasonable and necessary. To know history is to know such apprehensions. A knife is neutral; it may serve either as tool or weapon. So too is dynamite; it may serve to blow up stumps or to destroy a town. The efforts of the English weavers who attacked the machines of the early Industrial Revolution were pitifully futile; Canutelike they tried to stem a tide of history. A prophet among them might have seen, nonetheless, a degree of historical precocity in their angry resistance.

[1] Simon Ramo, "A New Technique in Education," in A. A. Lumsdaine and Robert Glaser (eds.), *Teaching Machines and Programmed Learning* (Washington, D.C.: National Education Association, 1960), p. 381.

Conventionally it is as necessary to be for progress as to be against sin, but the conditions of progress are elusive and hard to define. To oppose the uses of technology at Auschwitz and Buchenwald is not to be a Luddite. "To make a new machine" may suffice as a definition of technological progress. Humanity, though, has to make a more complex factor analysis. Of any instrument it must ask: What is it good for? What ways can it serve us? What potential hazards lie in its use? Will it do more harm than good? What are the costs in relation to consequences? Will other materials better serve the same purpose? Ordinarily, these are not questions that interest promoters. Educators, however, find it necessary to study such questions in depth.

Before we make critical comments on what have been called teaching machines, let us establish certain characteristics of two other resources brought to education by technology, namely, recorded material and communications devices.

Recorded materials. Photographs, films (sound and silent), filmstrips, phonograph records, and tape recordings come within this category. Recorded materials ordinarily capture experiences that are reexperienced in one or two sensory dimensions. (In *Brave New World,* Aldous Huxley carried it one sense further.) Sight and sound bulk so formidable in sensory perception that their achievement is not to be minimized. Audio-visual specialists are prone to speak of multisensory experience, which seems a bit thick since ordinarily their instruments are three senses (touch, taste, and smell) short of reality.

Two basic points must be made in reference to recorded materials. (1) *They are of proved instructional worth.* A teacher can scarcely claim professional competence who cannot use them in developing a learning enterprise; and, far from being in danger of overuse, they still are relatively unexploited and neglected among education's panoply of instruments. (2) *These materials are especially neglected in their fundamental essence—recorded experience, that is, recaptured reality.* The little didactic films and filmstrips that attempt to teach (and do it well enough, though other means do it as well) are not exemplary of the real educational force implicit in recordings. In the substantive sense, these materials have their great role in education not as *tools of instruction* but as the *stuff of curriculum*.

As the stuff of curriculum, it is possible to have through recording not educational tools but such magnificent realities as Arturo Toscanini conducting Beethoven's Ninth (captured by recording for generations of aesthetic experience); *I Can Hear It Now* bringing Franklin D. Roosevelt's "Fireside Chats" alive again, or reliving the horror of the last moments of the dirigible *Hindenburg;* Laurence Olivier and a fine company playing *Hamlet* or *Henry V* or *Richard III;* Dylan Thomas, T. S. Eliot, Robert Frost, and W. H. Auden reading their verse. Such things are not aids or tools. These and thousands of recordings of reality, of great creative experiences in history, literature, drama, art, and science are essences of life; they are great human events worth bringing to school to be studied as experiences in themselves. It is of this resource that neglect is largest.

Communications devices. Obviously to categorize one way is to deny another. A sound film and a television program seem very much alike in sensory terms; both project an audio-visual image effectively to a viewer–auditor. The intrinsic distinction seems to be that one serves uniquely as a recorder, while the other serves as a communications device. The recording (sound film, in this case) is by definition not "live"; television, even when transmitting a recorded program, is "live," that is, in transmitting a contemporary event (in this "impure" instance, the replaying of a film, kinescope, or video tape).

Communications devices offering utility to education include megaphones (largely limited to use by cheerleaders or desperate administrators), telephones, public address systems, radio, and television (closed circuit and open broadcast). The distinction between the types of television may be simply stated—a public address system is to radio as closed-circuit television is to open-broadcast television; which is to say, closed-circuit television constitutes an audio-visual public address system.

Obviously, television has educational uses. Any instrument that

383

communicates (one-way) simultaneous sight and sound has clear-cut instructional potential. The research pertinent to education was completed, in general, when television was made technologically marketable. So-called research as to its instructional potential has revealed nothing relevant either to its educational uses or its limitations that experienced educators could not have set forth from a description of the instrument.

Communications devices, then, may be distinguished from both recorded materials and teaching machines. In addition to the "live" aspect, communication devices are in themselves devoid of content. Their educational potential is altogether kinetic. They are ahistorical, neutral; essentially they are transmitters. To assert, as some do, that the "medium is the content," is simply picturesque nonsense. If this were true, then logic would dictate that all envelopes be cast away unopened and that cereal boxes and milk cartons be ingested.

As media, computers and electronic data-processing will come to school. Educators and technology will cooperate, even in the development of newer "systems" of instruction. These will necessarily be "systems" continued for developing the human, or they would have to be reckoned as antieducational. Since technology and media are neutral, they carry no intrinsic threat. The system, on the other hand, must always be evaluated philosophically because it is ever based upon philosophical abstractions. It is rooted as it were in a message. And a message may either liberate or enslave.

The Trouble with the Teaching Machine

In the curriculum for the kind of education postulated here (the education of human beings as human beings) there is simply *no place for teaching machines as presently understood.*

No issue in educational theory is so decisive as this one. The division is real. The issue involves sharp and clear-cut differences in the view of the learner, the learning process, and the objectives of education.

In a formidable anthology edited by A. A. Lumsdaine and Robert Glaser,[2] the essential positions of the proponents of these devices are comprehensively presented. The anthology should be closely studied (not for its intrinsic worth which is minimal in our opinion), but because decisions on the implicit issues raised are likely to shape considerably the direction of American education for some time. The student will find the anthology replete with grandiose claims, confident generalizations, considerable rhetoric, vivid prophecy, and surprisingly sparse empirical evidence. The abundant sophistries in the anthology will be quite surprising to the scholarly mind until it recalls the context of the work. These inventions are the by-product of behaviorism, the psychological fountainhead of conditioning, human engineering, animal training, the "hard sell," psychological warfare, and brainwashing. Thus, if these proponents seem to resemble salesmen and propagandists, the resemblance is familial rather than coincidental.

The behaviorists are of course specialists in animal learning. The patriarch Pavlov and his salivating canine hold classic significance in their lore. B. F. Skinner in his way has added some sophistication to the repute of the pigeon. Of rats, too, they know a good deal of what is to be known, though not more perhaps than sailors or housewives could have told them. Standard comments among "learning theorists" are these: "we know a good deal more about how animals learn than how people learn; we don't know much about how people learn; learning theory is in its infancy." As a confession of inadequacy, the statements could well elicit a good deal of compassion. They hardly constitute a platform for a vote of educational confidence. However, the student will not long mistake the basic attitude of teaching-machine advocates as an unseemly humility.

Students of animal learning may well be weary of hearing "pigeon" and "rat psychology" belabored. But if they have chosen unbecoming subjects in their search for insights into human learning, the consequences are in their choice. Their little findings are so unexciting to anyone who ever attended "The Greatest Show on

2 Lumsdaine and Glaser (eds.), *ibid.*

Earth." Long, long before Pavlov, dogs were taught to walk on their hind legs ("not," as Samuel Johnson said, "that they do it well"). We have seen seals play "My Country 'Tis of Thee" (and in Canada, "God Save the Queen") on toot-horns, though no one ever mistook it that the seal had learned music. For that matter, many doubt that parrots and mynah birds really talk. Horse handlers knew a good deal about conditioning well before the first text in behaviorism was ever written, including the knowledge that a lump of sugar is more effective reinforcement, under some conditions, than a kick in the flanks.

Were they students of history, conditioners would be less likely to think that they were explaining new dimensions of human behavior. When it comes to manipulation, they have embellished the techniques, but Machiavelli wrote the book. The feudal world or any authoritarian social community is loaded with devices of conditioning. "Clap, clap" go the master's hands, and the number-one boy comes running. These things being so, the modern educator must regard the theory as antique and moderately amusing. Both the circus and imperialism have seen their day.

As a matter of fact, behaviorists could afford to take animals more seriously than they do. It would be impressively manly if they would more often choose their subjects for observation from among the larger species. How our confidence in his findings would be accentuated if, like Clyde Beatty, an experimenter tested his hypothesis by sticking his own head in a lion's mouth, or ventured alone with nothing but his theories to sustain him into a year long adventure with the human adolescent in the maze called a classroom.

Animals are to be taken seriously and learned about. Scientists have learned a great deal about animals. The generic term for these scientists is naturalist. These are notably scientists rather than academicians. They go out and observe creature behavior on its own terms in its natural ecology. This knowledge is well worth its place in the curriculum. William Beebe went to the ocean's floor to bring us this subject matter. If the conquerors of the Himalayas ever do encounter the yeti, the scientific urge will be to observe it—the instinct of the carnival man and the animal psychologist no doubt to pester it. Beavers can no doubt be "taught" or conditioned to do things that no beaver in its right mind would think of doing. But if you really want to know about beavers at their best, do not put them in cages and heckle them with electrodes. Learn woodcraft. Train yourself to walk a quiet trail without snapping a twig. School yourself to virtue—in this case, patience and silence. Watch the beavers at work, and draw conclusions about their nature by what you see them do. A pigeon has a number of accomplishments, most impressive of which is to learn to fly. Watch this phenomenon and ponder on it and you may from animals derive something of significance for the curriculum.

Among strange assertions in behalf of the teaching machine is this by Lumsdaine: ". . . all of the devices that are currently called 'teaching machines' represent some form of variation on what can be called the tutorial or Socratic method of teaching."[3] Presumably, this writer has never witnessed a good tutorial and is unaware of the nature of the Socratic method, or he uses the phrase "some form of variation" with blithe latitude. Harry S. Broudy has made full and trenchant comment on this remarkable assumption.[4] The basic point is simply that no two methods could be more diametrically opposed: The one supplies a canned and predigested pattern of imposed response; the other (the Socratic) is the classic prototype of the genuine, open, inquiring dialogue.

The animism of the teaching-machine protagonists is likewise remarkable within a purportedly scientific context. Among the machine's virtues, as Lumsdaine sees it, is the fact that "slower students [are] being tutored as slowly as necessary, with indefinite patience to meet their special needs."[5] The anthropomorphic endowment of the machine with patience is a significant index to this fact: The mechanistic view of man is, of course, complementary to a vision of manlike machines.

Occasionally, the nineteenth-century curricular assumptions of the teaching-machine advocates are made painfully apparent. For

[3] Lumsdaine, *ibid.*, p. 5.
[4] Harry S. Broudy, "Socrates and the Teaching Machine," *Phi Delta Kappan* (March 1963).
[5] Lumsdaine, *loc. cit.*, p. 6.

example, B. F. Skinner said, "Even our best schools are under criticism for their inefficiency in the teaching of drill subjects such as arithmetic."[6] He might with some justification have spoken of "the drill aspects of such subjects as arithmetic," but to characterize arithmetic, without qualification, as a *drill subject*—especially in an era of attention to discovery and conceptualization—is a rather fatal revelation of the exact level of sophistication of his curricular views.

Not all assertions on behalf of teaching machines are unsophisticated; some are simply bizarre. Lloyd E. Homme enters the realm of prophecy under the guise of science to declare: "In fact, I will go so far as to predict that classrooms of the future, their walls lined with exotic machines, will resemble nothing so much as the emporiums of Las Vegas. I am even willing to bet that the players will be equally intense in their pursuit of reinforcements."[7] In this "brave new world" of mechanistic education, it appears certain that the compulsion of the players would be similar. An educator may be entitled to entertain the hope that the reinforcements would be more profitable than the choice of a con-man's model would seem to suggest.

Reduction of the Matter

In this section we shall summarize our reasons for rejecting the teaching machine as an instrument of curriculum. The attempts to apply the derivatives of animal learning via the teaching machine to human education simply do not work. This slippage in transfer is somehow not difficult to understand. If one were to apply for a research grant for the study of canine behavior and the subjects proposed for experiment and inquiry were a number of cats, the reviewers of the proposals would be astounded. Yet the zoological relationship between these creatures is somewhat nearer than between

6 B. F. Skinner, in Lumsdaine and Glaser, *op. cit.,* p. 106.
7 Lloyd E. Homme, in Lumsdaine and Glaser, *op. cit.,* p. 136.

birds and men. (How modern man avoids choking upon such absurdities constitutes a philosophical miracle of our age.)

Its roots in behaviorism afford an incomplete psychological foundation; education finds more productive insights among the gestalt, the field theory, social psychology, and phenomenological and humanistic approaches to psychology.

Such a view of man is philosophically unacceptable; the mechanistic view has too many affinities with authoritarianism to be a desirable choice. For choice it is, and such choices have long consequences. For the utter reduction of the conditioners' premises, one only need read Arthur Koestler's *The Age of Longing.*[8]

The curricular assumptions of the programers are, by and large, antique. The role of drill and memorization is exaggerated and distorted. Modern learning through conceptualization, discovery, and creativity is impossible to develop through these devices.

The programer is schoolteacherish in the narrowest sense of the word. His lessons are fragmentary and academic. Despite his claims of scientific advancement, his models for instruction are the hackneyed approaches of the most mediocre kinds of teaching, which it is the job of professional education to root out and reconstruct, not to reinforce.

The view of motivation is naïve. Oversimplified *reinforcement* devices are not a royal road to learning. Despite claims of *intrinsic motivation,* these devices rely completely on extrinsic devices. Canned answers to prearranged questions are about as intrinsic as candy-bar bribery.

The view of individual differences held by the proponents of teaching machines is simplistic, even primitive. Experienced teachers know that the speed in which an individual covers materials is one *and only one* of a vast complex of individual differences. Models for instruction that deal with and liberate many types of differences are known to education and are effectively used. The rhetoric of the machine sellers seems built on unawareness of this fact. (Our purpose in this summation is not to try to reeducate the "learning theorists." That would be an illusory hope. It is to re-

8 Arthur Koestler, *The Age of Longing* (New York: Macmillan, 1951).

389

mind educators and serious students of educational process of all the things that we have learned *about* human learning and that are relevant, which the teaching-machine advocates seem not to know or to dismiss as damaging to their cause.)

Finally, the educator who chooses to avoid the fundamental debate can still afford a basic skepticism on this account. The research is inconclusive; it does not bear out the grand claims.

Among assertions *not* borne out by research are the following:[9]

1. That the machine is essential to the effective presentation of the program.

2. That a feedback of right answers is indispensable.

3. That frame-by-frame, program-by-program *reinforcement* enhances motivation.

4. That differences in aptitude will be minimized by programing as factors in learning.

5. That proceeding at an individual rate rather than a group rate produces significant increments in learning.

6. That programing material gains learning results superior to straight narrative materials.

Insofar as classroom experiments have shown any superior gains in learning through programing, such gains appear to have been short lived. Their transiency seems to suggest that the Hawthorne and the novelty effects (known to parents at Christmas long before the Western Electric incident) are mainly active. The wishful notion that the problem of continuing motivation is solved seems blasted; most observers find, as did Robert Roth: "Most students initially liked this example of the programmed method, then grew restless with what they felt was its unceasing, impersonal, robot-like progression of minutiae, and finished up resenting and/or disliking their experience with the program."[10]

[9] For a fuller report, see John F. Feldhusen, "Taps for Teaching Machines," *Phi Delta Kappan*, Vol. 44 (March 1963).

[10] Robert Howard Roth, "Student Reactions to Programmed Learning," *Phi Delta Kappan* (March 1963). Note that every objection which we raise in this chapter is reflected in direct quotations from Roth's students; in fact, they make each point in greater detail, thus adding clarity and cogency.

All these negatives are apparent despite the fact that the research to date has been largely *interested,* that is, carried on by those already deeply involved in commitments to generalizations that they hope to prove. Furthermore, the literature of the protagonists is full of admission that "good" programs are few and far between. We believe that this limitation is built in and intrinsic. The form is, we think, a continuing strait jacket on the function in programed learning.

Certainly in the most limited terms of prudence educators can be chary of investment in these devices. A librarian would not, except in the strangest of new worlds, buy on confidence a lot of impressive book covers on the promise that exciting content would be forthcoming.

Once more, our basic position: even if the research to date bore out the extravagant claims for the teaching machines, and it does not, we would oppose their use in education. If the modern mind is right, and we think it is, the great hazard to man is loss of identity and communicative links through the depersonalization of society. Minor gains in the margins of academic learning, if achievable, would not be worth the price of making the school another agent of depersonalization.[11]

Feldhusen simply sums it up thus: "The logical questions to ask now are these: Is the teaching machine movement a failure? Is programmed learning in any way more effective than simpler narrative presentations by text, a teacher, or television? A growing tide of research evidence, classroom experience, and personal sentiment suggests a 'yes' to the first question, a 'no' to the second."[12]

Behavioristic Learning Theory

The foregoing disquisition on the so-called "teaching" machine is merely a springboard for a more fundamental inquiry into a nar-

---

11 We wish to apologize to any of our colleagues and readers who feel that our comments here have been too mild. This fault we do acknowledge, but we plead a tender regard for the sensibilities of other esteemed colleagues who have some regard for these devices as our extenuation.

12 Feldhusen, *op. cit.,* p. 265.

rowly based view of human action, whose limitations must be understood if any adequate view of curriculum is to be postulated. The learning theory to be examined at this point is *behaviorism*.

Years ago, when one of my children was in her crawling stage, our apartment had a dangerous electric outlet on the floor. One contact with it could have killed her. She was too young for reasoning or explanation. Trial and error would be no better for the purpose than in parachute jumping. The first lesson must be effective. And it must prevent, rather than use, experience.

So I applied a behavioristic principle. I *conditioned* her. I allowed her to crawl toward the object. Obviously, any object within reach was sure to attract an infant. I hovered like a vulture until the very moment that she reached out for the lethal object. Then in lightning succession, I slapped her hand, shouted "hot," and gave her a good spanking. The aim, of course, was to associate very unpleasant consequences with the act of reaching for this object. In writing this, I almost erred. I first wrote, "this dangerous object." But danger in the object had nothing to do with her reaction. The danger was in my experience; it was my knowledge. She had no concept of danger. Had she this concept, my method would have been unnecessary, even cruel. But I knew; and I was responsible for her.

Effective? Yes: she never went near the object again. If she looked at it, I merely had to say "hot" and she scuttled away as rapidly as possible. How effective? Well, years later, I have noticed the child unconsciously walk a wide detour around similar electric outlets. She did this without any conscious knowledge of doing it, and without any realization of why she did it. Yes, conditioning can be effective and powerful in affecting human behavior.

Psychology seeks basic knowledge about human behavior. It seeks to classify its knowledge. It seeks to generalize; it even seeks to find evidence of generalizations without exceptions so that it can assert *laws* of human behavior. It has moved to experimentation and laboratory method. In other words, it has used the scientific method to seek its evidence. It has gone further: it has claimed to be a science. Psychologists of one particular breed even claim to be scientists. These are the behaviorists. They place themselves as natural scientists, along with chemists and physicists. They do not accept the term *social scientist,* which would put them in a field with such lesser breeds (according to some) as sociologists, anthropologists, and *social* psychologists.

Historical efforts to explain man and his doings have been full of elements that the modern mind disdains: mythology, demonology and witchcraft, supernatural manipulations. Scientific psychology too holds these in disdain along with insight, will, introspection, observation, empathy, and reflection.

In order to be scientific, the behaviorist must regard the human organism as a machine. It is, to be sure. a complicated and flexible machine. It has a built-in communication system; it owes its potential for movement to its motor capacity and its complex motor controls.

It has intelligence. This the scientific psychologist does not like to deny. He is shy and embarrassed, however, about discussing intelligence in classical terms. In parlor conversation he may forget his discipline; he may even wax eloquent about imagination, creativity, and insight. But in his classes and in his research he avoids these concepts. He sees intelligence as a capacity to respond to stimuli and to accumulate patterns of responses (habit formation). He measures intelligence in simple terms—reflex timing and speed of learning.

The scientific psychologist seeks basic knowledge about the laws of the responses of organisms. Because it is difficult to put human subjects into conditions with laboratory control, he is prone to use animal subjects. The literature of scientific psychology is full of experiments with dogs, rats, hamsters, pigeons, and monkeys. Medical research does the same. However, medical research never asserts a specific fact in terms of human applicability until it has demonstrated the fact in terms of the response of human subjects. Scientific psychology in its youthful exuberance has yet to be so precise or so scrupulous.

True, many psychologists have been restrained and modest. They assert nothing beyond their desire to make scientific inquiry under suitable conditions. They hope that their findings about learning will have utility for education, but they do not make grandiose claims.

Humility is indeed the way of the scientist. In fact, we have learned that intellectual overconfidence is a clue to the pseudo-scientific. Witness the grandiose claims of the phrenologist and the astrologist, each of whom can tell us all we need to know either from bumps on our heads or from the positions of the stars.

Among contemporary scientific psychologists none has achieved more publicity than B. F. Skinner. His teaching theory (which he calls "learning theory") rests upon the techniques of *operant conditioning*. In operant conditioning the teacher decides upon desirable behavior for the students and then builds toward it.

At this point we must note that it is the teacher who decides. Let us suppose that the behaviorist teacher is working with pigeons and is going to teach a skill. Obviously, he could choose to teach the pigeon skills of soccer, baseball, or skin-diving, or ping pong. He decides on ping pong. But the teacher does not interest himself greatly in the *decision-making process*. Why not? Perhaps it is a bit complex for his method and experience. After all, pigeons have relatively few decisions to make. Or perhaps it is embarrassing. To teach the pigeon is desirable. This must be. For the only alternative is that it is undesirable. In that case, why do it? Or, the teacher decides that it is worthwhile to teach something undesirable. These considerations, which the scientist has given, are understandably embarrassing to him. He makes these considerations, for without them he could not act. But he does not talk about them, because they are cultural questions. They are not scientific. They raise moral, ethical, philosophical, questions. A decision to do something is a value judgment. To talk of it raises the question of value systems. The operant conditioner is the product of a century in which the scientific furnishes pervasive stimuli. These stimuli may result in this stimulistic syllogism:

Man is often a scientist.

I am a man.

Therefore, I am probably a scientist.

The stimuli of his century are *reinforced* by considerable rewards. Other men, in similar patterns of stimuli, buy books, give promotions, award research grants. These to academic men have the same reward effect as candy for children or carrots for burros. This does not suggest that the *ego* is involved. The concept of *ego* is alien and meaningless to the operant conditioner.

In sum then the operant conditioner, because he is conditioned against understanding, is by definition a man without understanding who behaves as he does because the stimuli that reach him force him to react as he does. In nonscientific parallel terms, he is a victim of circumstances.

The question at this point is addressed to teachers in nonbehavioristic terms. How much use can you make of a teaching theory that reduces you and your students to *victims of circumstance?*

In operation how does the operant conditioner behave?

1. He reduces learning to a step-by-step procedure.

2. He programs learning. Each step is identical.

3. He reinforces each correct step. He rewards the correct response.

4. He uses what he calls intrinsic motivation. The student is shown immediately when he has given the right response. This is supposed to be very rewarding.

The operant conditioner has a confidence in his method that, if we did not know him to be a scientist, would in another person be reason to hold him suspect of unscientific immodesty. No doubt because of the stimuli that have triggered the response, he is sure that he could condition mankind into a utopian society. He is not the first social scientist to feel this confidence. He assumes man to be completely subject to conditioning and manipulation. He gives the rational quality of man no considerable credit. The potential for self-direction is not an admissible point. Karl Marx, by contrast, sees only the forces of history as blind and somewhat mechanistic and opposes the alienation of man, his blind response to stimuli, as it were. Even Marx is Western and modern in his respect for intelligence and reason in the individual.

Skinner depicts his utopian vision in a book called *Walden Two*.[13] This is literary irony, though probably not to its author. *Walden* was the masterpiece of Henry David Thoreau, a supreme individualist. To Thoreau events were defined in the mind of the free, uncorrupted man. He composed his great "Essay on Civil Disobedience" while sitting in a small-town jail for refusing to obey what he regarded as an unjust law.

Skinner's Utopia is a society whose citizens are conditioned for their own good into a perfect society. Antisocial responses would be "extinguished" out of existence. The operant conditioners would replace the philosopher kings of classic Utopias. On what basis would they presume to rule? The scientific mind is reticent on such philosophic questions. One conclusion is apparent: they would rule confidently. The behaviorists turned utopian would obviously share this characteristic with all the ruling elites of history.

What of the educational contribution of the behaviorists? It is obviously a limited one. They choose to live in a sheltered world. They cultivate, quite legitimately since it is their own choosing, a small garden with high walls around it. They hold these things in confidence:

1. That human behavior can be made predictable.

2. That an individual can be taught to respond to any stimulus that is presented to him.

3. That a reward which is to the liking of the student will produce responses sought by the teacher—in order that the student receive the reward again.

4. That unpleasant rewards diminish response but not as much as pleasant ones enhance them.

5. That behavior can be *generalized*. That is, that behavior learned in one situation can be transferred to other situations as long as they are similar to the original learning situation.

6. That behavior patterns can be extinguished by long refusal of rewards or reinforcement.

[13] B. F. Skinner, *Walden Two* (New York: Macmillan, 1948).

Within limits, of what use are these things to the teacher? The conditioned response is economical in terms of response to school bells, disciplinary cues, reinforcing conformity to arbitrary rules and procedures. This is not exactly new knowledge for teachers, however. The conditioned response is useful in keeping small children or animals from danger, but parents or animal trainers would not regard this as a bombshell of new insight. Reward is a more useful incentive to behavior than punishment is a deterrent. It would probably embarrass these psychologists to find classic sanctions for these "research findings"—that certain knowledges may be systematically analyzed and as systematically taught and that the learning process is worthy of scientific study and inquiry. Nor is it an arguable point that a continuing function of the school should be an examination and appraisal of its goals and methods and of its methods in relation to those goals.

Behaviorism then is worthy of a teacher's time in study. It does not offer a complete learning theory. Some behaviorists, not all, think that it does. Behaviorism does offer a limited set of tools and insights for teaching. These are worth application. Some technological applications of presumed scientific principles do not work. Behaviorists try to study human behavior as a science, but psychology in any form still has far to go to vindicate itself as a science. In some respects behaviorism is not merely limited with respect to modern education; it is, in fact, inimical to it in ways that we have set forth. The roots of the limitations lie in its inadequate view of man, of intelligence, of scientific method, and of knowledge itself.

Technology and the Mass-Education Error

Educational thought and technology may come into a conflict so basic that it demands particular perusal. This conflict has less to do with opposing concepts of method and learning than with the characteristics of technological devices offered to education and the unique assumptions of democratic educational philosophy.

Technology generally serves and is utilized as a mass medium. Not uncommonly, instruments are alluded to as aids for *mass* education. This, in American educational terms, is an erroneous and dangerous concept. The fact that television not only comes to school but also occupies almost as much of the child's time as does school itself is of large and necessary concern for education.

American public education is *not* based upon a mass-education theory. The term "masses," as applied to people, has connotations of inchoate throngs or unreasoning herds, of aggregates of people who must be trained and conditioned in groups and who, by definition, should they panic or turn suddenly, easily become a howling mob.

Mass as applied to the broad reach of media is appropriate. Applied to education, however, it implies either wrong purposes or misconceptions of educational goals. The distinction is significant. When television comes to education, it comes to an institution deeply rooted in history, philosophy, and social theory. Therefore, unless the communications assumptions that television carries to education make sense with educational theory, its acceptance will be reluctant, grudging, and even impossible.

American education deals with more students than any system in the world. "All the children of all the people" is its great boast. This means large numbers, not masses.

Mass education is based on a conditioning theory. The controllers of mass education have clearly defined behavioral goals for their pupils. The purpose of education is to indoctrinate, to train, to housebreak, as it were, the masses to these ends. The constant reiteration of the clichés of Nazism that pounded German radio audiences was of this order of education. The Soviet radio and television broadcast are wedded to the same principle.

American education deals not with masses to be conditioned but with great numbers of individuals to be enlightened and liberated to free, intelligent choice. Its aim is to create a society of free men, who will weigh issues and evidence and make their choices in primary regard for their own purposes and interests, self-disciplined to choose with respect for the rights of others and the good of the commonweal.

398

The infant institution of educational television must study this point. When television comes to education, it becomes part of education. It will share its glories, its responsibilities, its rewards— and its headaches. Unintelligent or ill-informed criticism is one of these headaches. One of the great canards about American education derives from the notion that it is a mass operation, an assembly line that turns out millions of identical and mediocre products. Television is sure to have a particular vulnerability to this slander because it is a mass medium associated with just such mass operations.

As a result of the lack of either strong positive or negative consequences among children who view television, it is possible to judge its use to be simply a pastime. Something further needs to be considered, however, in the context of this observation. Television does command a great deal of the average child's time. Within a year he spends time before the TV set nearly equal to that which he spends in school. If no particular harm is done (and society may be thankful if this is indeed the case), may one be content? Could home or school, for example, content themselves by demonstrating that at any rate they had done the children no particular injury?

But if television, with all it purveys of what is tawdry, trivial, and inconsequential, can command 20 to 30 hours per week of child and family time, interpretations must be attempted. Clearly these viewers for whom the act is an uncoerced choice can find nothing or think there is nothing better to do with their time. It is not that values are adversely affected, for apparently there is no particular set of values to be disturbed. There is simply a vacuum of time and values to be entered. In view of the known properties of a vacuum, it is no great wonder or no great achievement of television that it could make so considerable an entry. If man is simply a ruminant among the pastures of existence, the harmless killing of time is a good enough end for institutional activity. This, however, is not an accepted criterion among the higher arts nor even those of entertainment. It is certainly not a postulate of education nor of any who hold high respect for the human entity or who cherish philosophically a concept of civilization.

Americans, not unlike other people, express a great concern for

399

the welfare of their children. A glaring contrast exists between this active and discriminating concern in regard to some things as opposed to others. Since World War II we have witnessed striking improvements in the concept of elementary education, reflected in improvements in methods, instruments, and school architecture. Children's literature has been a new focus for creative effort in the publishing industry; the results at best have been no less than beautiful. But with reference to the media, especially television, there has been a strange attitude of laissez faire, and the results have been depressing.

For example, on two consecutive nights the author saw television programs that drew large family audiences. In both programs a parent killed a son in cold blood. In each program the son was also a murderer; in each case the surviving parent's action was portrayed as a desirable substitute for legal procedure. The clear inference was that a lynching was all right if administered by a parent. In neither program was there any suggestion of the destructive social consequence of such arbitrary personal justice, no note made of its fundamental immorality or illegality.

A publication of the Foundation for Character Education supplied a splendid analysis of the characteristics of children's programs:

> Nearly half of these programs are "action drama." This includes the classic Western, the crime mystery, and science fiction. Much of the remaining time is variously devoted to puppet shows, circus programs, children's talent programs, quiz contests, comedy, family situation drama, and sports. There are a few serious assaults upon the child's curiosity in such programs as those whose subject matter is news, travel, religion, animals at a zoo, or elementary science. But at the most, these provide but one-fifth of his available television fare. Without benefit of expert psychological advice, and largely depending on pragmatic observation, television program managers are capturing the young audience with programs in which *aggression* is the central ingredient.[14]

[14] Foundation for Character Education, *Television for Children* (Boston, n.d.), Chap. II, p. 11. This booklet, based on a conference held in 1954, is to date the most thoughtful consideration of the subject in print.

The analysis further states: "The basic characteristic is physical action and violence in an oversimplified moral situation."[15] Thus, the motivating forces suggested in children's viewing are those of fear, curiosity, and achievement.

Apologists for common television often appeal to the lack of evidence of direct harm as a justification for their unwillingness to effect direct good. It may even be that the instance of consecutive instruction in immorality cited earlier was purely coincidental. Instruction in bad doctrine, however, does not have to be a daily occurrence to be wrong.

Children are, in a sense, innocent. Adults are aware of certain realities of the world of which the child is not. They know that they cannot preserve the innocence of the child indefinitely, but they seek to guide and direct the exposure of the infant to reality. Neither in conversation nor in education do they immerse or surround the child with repeated and constant exposure to all of the seamier attributes of human society. They do not wish evil to appear as commonplace or the norm. Nor would many parents long tolerate instruction by a teacher who, however effectively, taught children lessons that wrong is right and right is wrong. Television consistently manages to do exactly this without incurring justifiable wrath, though now and then it earns intellectual criticism, which it appears to resent deeply.

Television does make the sordid, the tawdry, and the evil commonplace. In the name of acquainting their children with reality, few parents would introduce and expose them to the company of bawds, gunmen, tin-horn gamblers, sadists, or psychopaths. As a matter of fact, not too many discriminating parents would encourage their children to see the world through the eyes of either a superman Western vigilante or a socially anarchistic private eye. Yet they do all these things every day and for hours at a time through television.

Quite a difference exists between good men, as defined by the long record of Western civilization, and "good guys" as they are depicted in common television. Good men do not maintain that the

[15] *Ibid.*, p. 12.

ends justify the means; "good guys" often do. Good men do not maintain that might makes right; "good guys" act out the proof that right is on the side of the faster draw. Good men take no delight in inflicting pain in equal and opposite measure to that which sadistic and criminal minds are compelled; "good guys" seem to. Good men seldom kick a man when he is down or get in extra "licks" on a beaten foe; "good guys" are increasingly disposed to do just this.

This is television's essential content and is stated here not as an argument for censorship. It is stated as an argument for the creation of better canons of choice so the school can bulwark efforts of those parents who are discriminating and affect those who are not.

Television cannot be let off the indictment for its usual errors on its accustomed defense. It can and does make the following claims, which are specious in the main:

1. *That it entertains, which is its job and its justification.* This is a bad premise. Gladiatorial shows entertained, and effectively. Bear-baiting and public executions were once part of the common amusement. Civilized taste eventually ruled them beyond the pale, though individuals who would enjoy each are by no means nonexistent. Entertainment is a good word. Marjorie Rawlings' *The Yearling,* Charles Dickens' *David Copperfield,* and dozens of good children's books are entertaining *and* civilized too.

2. *That realism is important to the arts, that reality cannot be sugar-coated, and that ignorance is not innocence.* This is an exceptionally sound point when used by artists of integrity. Who would care to defend the common television diet, however, as a high expression of reality? *Dragnet* and Marshall Dillon move in a comic-strip world, not in the world of creative, realistic drama. *Gunsmoke, Wild, Wild West,* and *Hondo* bear little relation to the West of history, the West of Francis Parkman, of Ole Rolvaag, or of A. B. Guthrie.

3. *That art cannot be censored but at the expense of creativity.* The television producer is on the defensive; therefore, he associates criticism with censorship. The critic and educator seek to expose him or to instruct the audience, not to cut him off. They would have him earn his living honestly as an artist, not as a con man. Common television is routinized, stylized, and imitative. *High Noon* was the

creative prototype of the adult western. But how many creative experiences can be derived from one simple conflict of good and evil in a simple frontier setting?

4. *That the conflict of good and evil is a reality and that common television is essentially moral because it always shows that crime does not pay.* Even on the lowest level, television fails to justify itself. Its general and obvious influence is that crime *does* pay. The "bad guys" live well, and they endure happily to all outward appearances. Because they are the men to whom the television writer has given his stamp of approval, the viewer will associate with them and call them good. These men get away with all kinds of deeds including implied illicit sexual affairs, explicit breaking and entering, detailed mayhem, and frequent murder. In one respect only, cowboy heroes, antique and modern, are morally consistent: they are never horse thieves, and this establishes a clear-cut distinction between riders of virtue and villainy.

Good and evil are not historically and philosophically simple terms. Art can claim a defense for the fullest, most incisive, and candid examination of moral problems or human error. Art must stand free from censorship. When it is deeply honest, it will often evoke criticism on its behalf. It will have affirmation from the intelligent and discriminating when it is both creative and constructive. Madame Bovary and Anna Karenina did not find the fruits of adultery bitter because they were caught, but because of their deeply rooted human, social, and psychological conflicts, and even of conscience. The complexity of the forces that pursue the criminal, seldom even suggested in common television, is illustrated at its best perhaps in *Crime and Punishment.*

The elementary schools' humanistic concern with the media must be specially sensitive. At this stage the value structures are peculiarly in the making; the target, peculiarly vulnerable. The school cannot, even if it would, keep the child from TV, but the school is obligated to try to provide an intellectual and emotional insurance against its larger depredations. All children, being human, have certain attributes in common. In the effort to effect convenient categorization, this has often been overlooked. As a matter of fact, the institutional rigidity of the divisions of the educational structure have intruded excessively upon the continuity of human development in the view of many educators. The bridges between the elementary school, the junior high school, the high school, and college have their hazards, and the crossings are on occasion unduly traumatic. At every stage, the child is growing, developing, acquiring habits, predispositions, tastes, knowledges, and preferences. At every stage he is a complex of physical, emotional, and intellectual needs, though the patterns of these continuously change. There is no stage in the development of the child, however, where the fundamental postulates of our society with reference to the human being do not totally apply: each person, each child is unique; his individuality is priceless; attention to his differences is an obligation of education; each child has dignity in his own right and must participate in the community of respect because his human quality demands it. Furthermore, within the limits only of his ability, the child is entitled to develop his capacities and pursue his interests in equal opportunity with all others.

This reprise of basic democratic doctrine is not an idle exercise. In the first place, it furnishes a base for critical analysis of much of what broadcasting does *for* children. Appeals to a low common denominator of excitement and of violent emotional approaches do not begin to respect the total human quality of the child. Children have fine emotional, intellectual, and aesthetic capacities. They respond to literature of great emotional depth. They learn to love poetry and often to create it. They paint, they dance, they sing, they dream. Children can learn to laugh with hostility, but it is more natural for them to laugh with joy. They can feel concern over suffering and injustice; they can learn to weep for a hurt to another who would be remote but for the bonds of empathy. Children can become ethnocentric and provincial, but this should be neither the task nor the way of American schools. Our children are learning to reach out and to know the world and should continue to do so.

Those who believe that to produce television for children means that programing must be innocuous, trivial, narrow in scope, shallow in emotional and intellectual substance, devoid of philosophy, or just silly, simply know little about the quality of education and less of children. A few exceptions point the way: *Misterogers'*

Neighborhood, The Children's Film Festival, and, above all, *Captain Kangaroo.* In fact, each of the Captain's programs is a model of the four-dimensional experience.

Finally, respect for the child denies that his innocence be engineered for commercial advantage. Bluntly, this means there should be no commercials on children's programs. They are a plain psychological crime against the child. There is no more justification for them than to allow teachers to hawk wares on the playground at recess.

Multisensory Approaches to Education

Because we are rooted in the modern mind and respectful toward science, we welcome any tools that technology can provide which have a real potential for educational utilization. These tools must be developed and their uses assessed in educational terms. Axiomatically, the more of the student's senses that are involved in learning, the more complete is the learning situation. Ironically, the term "multisensory" has been preempted for those instruments of education that stimulate only two senses—the audio-visual tools.

Where may we find complete multisensory education? Not in the ordinary classroom where most often only the ear is assailed with talk, talk, talk. Probably the kitchen or chemistry laboratory furnish the fullest instances. The cook and the chemist give close visual attention to their concoctions and blendings; by touch they identify tools and materials; they listen for the sounds of vaporization or other chemical action; the cook often, the chemist rather seldom, checks the outcome of his efforts by taste; and both the cook and the chemist are fully aware of meaningful odors.

When a girl learns to cook, which situation is preferable for her: actual experience in a fairly well-equipped kitchen or an educational film in full color of the most elaborate kitchen in the world? Our answer is obvious and reaffirms our thesis: the complete learning situation exists where the total stimulation of reality is accessible to the whole sensory equipment of the person. This is not to say, however, that *only* the total learning situation is effective or even the most desirable. Most would obviously prefer that children learn of war by reading about it rather than by experiencing its multisensory horror.

Nor is the full life of meaningful adventure given to us all. Some few have climbed mountains, and they know them best. For most men it is better to conquer Mount Everest with Sir Edmund Hillary and Tensing by watching the film of their exploit than never to scale its heights at all.

Though modern technology provides many of the instruments or potential tools of audio-visual devices, the teacher–blackboard combination dates far back into preindustrial times. What can the tools of technology bring to our classrooms that may make their use a good investment? As we ponder this question, we might consider various pictures, maps, recordings, films, and television, for example. Basically, these are the contributions that such tools may make:

1. They may supply clear visual representation or symbolization where only verbal abstractions exist without them.

2. They may bring recorded life into the classroom: poets reading their poems, statesmen delivering orations, drama as spoken on recordings or more fully recorded on film.

3. They may bring demonstrations of expensive or unavailable equipment before the student.

4. They may extend the child's experience in the classroom: take him to far-away places, bring him into contact with the best, give him windows on the world, as it were.

5. They may enhance scholarship by bringing great teachers and authorities into the classroom in a limited role.

6. In areas of educational deprivation, they may afford a desirable substitute for no-teaching. Again, they do not justify the claim that they constitute a substitute *for* teaching.

These constitute a formidable potential. Obviously, the best education will avail itself of such resources.

On the other hand, what are the limitations of these technical aids?

406

1. They are limited in their sensory approach. They lack the touch, the smell, the taste of actual events. For the fan, football on radio or television is surely better than no football; but how does it compare with presence at the event?

2. They lack an actual human encounter. A parade, a legislative session, a game may be faithfully reported on television. But how does viewing compare with being there? In the real human encounter we are crowded and jostled; we feel and smell the emotions about us, the joys, angers, passions of those who participate in the event with us.

3. They tend toward depersonalization. This is a very real hazard. Their very excellence constitutes a trap. They tempt modern man to believe that his synthetic experience is real. And this has been too long the ordinary fault of education: that by its abstractions and symbols and representations it rendered life synthetic. Pictures will not do. Let pictures substitute for reality long enough, and in place of compassion we shall have crocodile tears; St. Francis did not kiss a *picture* of beggars. Let pictures substitute often enough for love, and man must lose his virility.

What has been outlined are the *fundamental limitations,* not the mere technical ones. Now, let us consider the basic educational matter of *visualization.* Like a great deal of illustration, much visualization is purely ornamental. To show a picture may be either educationally useful or meaningless. To what effect would we show a student in Southampton a picture of a ship, in Pittsburgh a picture of a steel mill, or in Iowa a picture of a corn field?

There must be an intrinsic necessity or function for visualization. If the student's experience gives him a clear hold on an aspect of the real world, one word will evoke it. Say "plough" to a farmer, "gun" to a soldier, "child" to a mother and the image, three-dimensioned, leaps to mind. A two-dimensional picture would reduce, not extend, the image.

The best visualizations extend perception. They do not merely repeat or limit it. Visualization may extend perception in two ways: (1) by enlarging upon the minute so that it may register upon our limited powers of perception and (2) by reducing the immense and overwhelming to a perceivable scale.

407

In the first instance, the microscope and the microscopic photograph may serve to illustrate the point. Man's marvelous sensory apparatus needs tools provided by human intelligence to experience some areas of perception. To make visible what cannot be seen is a consummate act of visualization.

In the second case, the problem is that sometimes things are too big to be perceived. One can, for example, only come to *understand* Ecuador by much living and by many explorations. Yet to *comprehend* Ecuador, or any major geographic area, is too grand a job for raw sensory reaction. A map is better; it is far from reality, but the reality is too much for us. Therefore, a symbolic representation carefully drawn to scale enables us to see more of the whole geographic essence of Ecuador than the reality itself. From the symbolic representation, we would proceed to the particular.

Now let us reexamine certain specific instruments. First and most modern is television. In its purest application—bringing remote events near for audio-visual perception—it is superb. As a transmitter of canned material, it is less impressive. What of its capacity for transmitting a learning situation? It can transmit that part of a learning situation which is limited to one-way audio-visual communication, no more, no less. Television is a marvel, but as far as instruction goes, it has no magic beyond this one-way communication.

Much use is being made of television in schools and universities. It can compete adequately with teachers who simply talk at students and do it as well. But the students weary of its impersonality. Indeed, with many vaunted "innovations," once novelty has worn off, students appear to languish in a progressive disenchantment.

Most of us know that one-way communication is not enough in a classroom. The television class cannot question its teacher; the teacher cannot appraise his class's reaction nor react to its moods. The television class cannot pause for discussion nor interact among itself. The class must limit its response as it would to an audio-visual public address system in one-way communication.

But television can enrich the classroom by bringing in resources not otherwise available. It can also bring instruction to areas where none would otherwise exist. We have seen mathematics and science instruction brought by television to small rural high schools that could not acquire teachers for these subjects. Classes of adult illiterates for whom there were no schools have been taught to read by television. The enrichment of learning and the extending of educational opportunity into areas of deprivation are the uses of television that ought to be explored.

The sound film is a very useful asset. It is more flexible than TV inasmuch as it conforms to the school's schedule rather than vice versa. In using a film or the cheaper filmstrip in the classroom, the teacher should be reminded of certain guidelines:

1. There should be a definite purpose in using the film. It should not be used as a time-killer.

2. The selection of a film should not be made on the basis of anyone's recommendation. The teacher himself should preview it. Titles and catalog descriptions are notoriously unreliable, as many of us have learned to our regret.

3. Students should be given a viewing guide. They should be directed on what to look for and be told the purposes for using the particular film.

4. Sufficient time must be allowed for discussion. The educational purpose of the film should be related to the students' other study and experience.

5. A second showing might be valuable for clarification, further understandings, or review.

Basic premises apply to all devices that serve as a tool for education. Whether one uses a sound film, a sketch on the board, a map, or a television set, these rules of educational sense apply:

1. The *visualization* must be functional, not merely decorative.

2. The purpose of the tool's use must be known not only to the teacher but also to the students.

3. The students should be instructed in the limitations of the device. With maps, for example, they should be taught the distortions of various projections. With graphs, they should learn how some lend themselves to statistical misrepresentation. With films, they should

409

learn how selective photography is as an art, and how it can be used to shape as well as to report a scene.

4. If the effort is to visualize, every student must be able to see it. This simple rule is often ignored. The student also needs time to perceive and to conceptualize. One picture fully explored is probably worth ten merely glanced at.

5. This, the best rule of all, is no rule at all. Teachers should not allow themselves to be victimized by devices. They are education's servants and are best used as educational judgment dictates. They should not be used unless one is sure of his reasons for so doing.

In conclusion, let us return to the broad concept of multisensory education. Instruments will not provide this, nor will the classroom unless its doors to the community and the world are opened wide. The field trip, the project, the excursion all invite learning to come out of the classroom into the world. None can question whether a boy will develop more of character and capacity by climbing an Andean foothill than by seeing a film of the scaling of Everest. He will learn more of the sea by rowing a boat on a small stream than by seeing the greatest naval epic in a movie. *This* is the point: he will be educated in the multisensory manner not by the devices brought before him. Noise does not teach him to hear, nor do pictures teach him to see.

Multisensory education is a job for instruction. Since antiquity, there have been those with eyes that see not; with ears that hear not. The school's job is to help students to see clearly not by showing them pictures, to listen with care and discrimination not just by smothering their ears with words, to know the touch of quality, to learn that smell is not only physical but that there is a stench in evil and injustice, and to learn that one can taste delight. That is truly a multisensory education!

Commentary: The Excitement in Educational Technology

The most debilitating effect on the constructive development of educational technology has resulted from considerable infiltration of the movement by the neobehaviorists. The nexus between teaching machines and Skinnerian psychology has been so noisily established that the uncritical might easily be led to think that a machine or device which instructs must derive from behavioristic premises. *This is not at all the case.* The sophisticated teacher distrusted Skinnerian approaches and articulated his distrust. In a shrewd defensive ruse, the behaviorists shifted their semantics from "teaching machines" to "programed learning." It is a testimonial to skillful propaganda that they made this move from solid to weaker ground appear to be a concession to educational responsibility. They seemed to abandon the machine as uninformative and irrelevant.

As a matter of fact, the utility of machines that can instruct is very important. Their promise has been fully vindicated, and vast frontiers remain to be explored and developed. It was programed learning that constituted the millstone, not the machine. (It has been less than edifying in the recent educational dialogue to hear the cry of "Luddite" issue from those who under pressure first scuttled the machine in favor of a woefully antiquated and schoolteacherish approach to instruction.)

The best friends of educational technology are those who wish to see inventive genius and educational imagination wedded to the most modern learning theories and to the most effective and exciting methodologies. *Simulation,* for instance, has produced the most realistic instructional machines. The Link trainer surely derives from the *gestalt;* it re-creates as much of the total flying situation as possible while removing the actual hazards of flying from initial flight instruction. Electronic photographic devices for gunnery instruction have proved their worth; adaptations have found their way to amusement parks and entertainment parlors. Driver education is the beneficiary of similar devices that place the driver in a large *field* of simulated traffic conditions, including a wide and typical assortment of hazards, obstructions, and distractions, without exposing the novice to the lethal risks of city streets or turnpikes. Trap-shooting equipment and baseball-pitching devices are also teaching–learning machines.

All of these devices are *programed,* that is, they have built-in

411

teaching–learning purposes of a deliberate, planned, and systematic nature. But they are programed from a progressive approach to the total learning situation. *Feedback* is immediate: the prospective gunner sees when his electronic gun is off the target; the tyro aviator feels himself go into a spin; the would-be driver gets instant demonstration that he has run a traffic light, made a wrong turn, hit a parked car, or nearly run down a careless child. The *reinforcements* are real and total, not verbal, academic, or piecemeal. The learning situations are rooted in situational reality. These are action-oriented learnings, to be sure. So much the better. The consequence intended for all learning is behavioral change. The great vindication of *these* teaching–learning machines lies in this: if the principles of learning underlying them were more generally applied in the classroom, the learning even of verbal conceptualizations would be improved.

There is a deliberate semantic distinction here. The teaching–learning machine derives from larger concepts of learning theory; it leaves the learner free, allows personal rather than imposed choice, induces full initiating participation rather than simple responses. Above all, it allows for the full panoply of individual differences and includes but is not restricted to speeds of learning.

Not all effective teaching–learning machines are devices on the grand scale. For an interesting contrast in a somewhat nonacademic area of content, we invite a comparison between the Auto-bridge device for teaching contract bridge and the Tutor-text, or programed-learning approach. The first device is a handy means of participating fully in a vicarious four-hand bridge situation. The second is presented in the garbled unbook manner of "tutor texts." This is not an attempt to wax profound on such matters, but the former learning device is simply a lot more fun to use. Nor is this to reflect an invidious and amateur judgment on actual teaching or on learning from a master such as Charles Goren. His genius simply does not function within the strait jacket of conventional programing.

The teaching–learning machine played its part in saving Western civilization during World War II and continues to play large roles in training and education. It deserves no slander; as a matter of fact, it wants some reconstitution of its repute. It should not suffer from guilt by association with the pedagogical monstrosities conceived as the illegitimate progeny of technology. Not merely will these machines survive, but their future variety and utility will be extended beyond present limitations.

Speculation on the future may partly suggest their promise. The social studies, for example, have long been fair customers in educational technology, but such trade has largely been in the respectable and conventional area of audio-visual devices: long-playing-recordings, filmstrips, sound films, and tape recordings.

Think of what teaching–learning machine resources might be developed to enliven the social studies laboratory. For example, imagine a large electronic map of the United States. Its first feature would be a locator system similar in principle to the maps that detail local points of interest found in motel and hotel lobbies. A panel of buttons could illuminate the state capitols simultaneously or in whatever sequence was desired. The regions and sections could appear in various functional arrangements. Historical movements could come alive perhaps with a synchronized accompaniment of taped words and music or appropriate imagery on a closed-circuit television screen.

The great future in the schools for the inventive genius of industry lies in creating effective linkages of media with sound curricular objectives. In a word, let the technologist seek from the professional teacher a measure of that professional's needs. At the point of real action, the production of a true educational tool, an effective dialogue begins. It is this approach that has been so generally ignored.

The *NEA Journal* devoted a considerable section of its February 1967 issue to the topic "How Will Computers Affect the Schools?" The *Phi Delta Kappan* devoted its entire January 1967 issue to the subject "Big Business Discovers the Education Market." In the latter views were advanced on such topics as controls, educational engineering, the systems approach, satellites and schools, the future of educational technology. The tone and substance of all such presentations has become altogether predictable. The excitement over the technological adventure is very real. The gap be-

413

tween the language of the educational engineer and technologist and the educator–teacher is large. The petulance in the utterance of the former was a complaint against a communications barrier.

Only one obstacle stands between the educator and the technologist. The educator stands ready and qualified to talk educational sense with the technologist. He is quite capable of excitement over an educational "breakthrough" and has seen a number of them created. He has also seen the broken bubbles of many promised panaceas. The educator's excitement over technology will necessarily be derivative. It will not be a matter of childish glee over new toys but a deeply seasoned joy in new instruments that help him in his work. The current obstacle to communication is the naïveté of most utterances from the educational technologists. The educator has really no place to begin, except to say: "After you have learned a little about education, we can perhaps begin to talk."

There is some temptation, even some invitation, to take hold of the arguments of the technologists and rip them apart analytically. It would not be difficult to rip them apart, but it would be pointless. The educator has no quarrel with technology and no malice toward the engineer. He is eager to enter into a dialogue with the engineer to further the role of the school.

Unfortunately, the educational technologists are so unsophisticated in educational theory that they have linked both their criticism and their aspirations in education to a duffer's model of educational practice. They need to find out what modern education is all about. Presently they are programing for *parcheesi* when the name of the game is *school.* Sense can be made when communication becomes recognized as a two-way street, when technology concerns itself to provide instruments for educational needs in a modern construct, and when the primacy of substance, the message over the medium, is clearly recognized.

Chapter XIII

Education
for Urban
America

And it has always seemed to me that every ordinary child is by nature a delinquent, that the only difference between us as children was the extent of our delinquency, whether we were found out in it and how we were punished for it.

. . . And boredom and confusion are surely the two prime sources of childish wickedness. . . .

Just as the grown-up world is for ever [sic] seeking new arts, new ideas, so children want change; and just as grown-ups who are bored take to gambling or mere destructiveness, for the kick, so bored children get up a fight, or a dare, or steal, or smash. These too are novelties, adventures, and also explorations.

. . .

Knowledge, in short, the experience of the mind, is just as important to a child's happiness and "goodness" as affection, adventure; above all, the knowledge of his own moral position. And the last is often most difficult for him to come by, not because he could not grasp a complex situation ("this is a grand deed but a bad one"), but because grown-ups do not trust the power of his imagination to form a picture in more than one dimension.[1]

—*Joyce Cary*

[1] Joyce Cary, *Charley Is My Darling* (New York: Harper, n.d.), pp. 345–350.

American education has begun, but only begun, to live somewhat in its present and has barely taken any measure of its future. The American present is urban; the significant abode of the school is the city. That is where the people are. Long decades have elapsed since William Jennings Bryan declared, "Burn down your cities and leave our farms, and your cities will spring up again as if by magic; but destroy our farms and the grass will grow in the streets of every city in the country."[2] Gone since the 1930s is the gold standard against which the Silver-Tongued Orator of the Platte inveighed; gone too is much of the validity of his rhetoric.

Anachronistic Ruralism

It is difficult for the nation to rid itself of its agrarian image, to divest itself of romantic retrospection about a way of life that never was. Historical research shattered Frederick Jackson Turner's thesis in the 1940s, yet the notion persists that somehow the frontier was the decisive factor in building American civilization. Political stability was reputed to have its roots in an abundance of free land. Frontier opportunity by this thesis served as a safety valve for urban discontent. But as Fred Shannon showed in *The Farmer's Last Frontier,* from 1860 to 1900, for every city worker who forsook the town for the country, twenty farmers deserted the fields for the city. As Shannon drily remarked, "This is not the way that safety-valves are supposed to operate."[3]

America was and is a land of opportunity. But where did Americans find opportunity? Hundreds of thousands found it on the soil, to be sure; but millions found it in the city. The American has lived in town for a long time. But only lately has he begun educationally to discover his whereabouts. It is about time; 200 million Americans are now fed substantially by 1.5 million farms. The remainder of our enterprise is mainly urban.

2 William Jennings Bryan, "Cross of Gold," in Henry Steele Commager, *Documents of American History,* Vol. II (New York: Appleton, 1958), p. 177.

3 Fred A. Shannon, *The Farmer's Last Frontier* (New York: Farrar and Rinehart, 1945), pp. 55, 356–357.

The curriculum cannot make sense until this anachronistic bias with respect to American civilization is straightened out. Our streams are polluted and our water supply is in hazard, but this is treated as though it were a rural problem. But it is the industries of the cities that spoil the rivers; it is the people of the towns who consume the water. It is from the direction of the cities that our problems must be faced. The highways of the country are crowded. Why? Not principally by traffic moving from farm to farm or farm to village; they are crowded with the traffic between cities, with the trucks that move to keep the cities alive, with the restless and businesslike folk who roll at seventy miles an hour from city to city.

Even the culture of the farm and village is urbanized. New York City is indeed in Iowa. The mass media, television, radio, motion pictures, and magazines originate in town. Even in TV's two operatic styles, soap and horse, an urban sophistication and corruption is brought both to the tales of cowboys and Indians and of home and fireside. The adolescents of Ogallala, Nebraska, and Tipton, Iowa, dance in the same concatenations as the teen-agers of Chicago and San Francisco.

The tunes of fashion are the same in Des Moines, Dallas, Seattle, and New Haven. The girls look pretty good—and pretty much the same up and down the land. If in a given year they all look silly, it is no miracle of coincidence; all of their tastes are conditioned by Madison Avenue. Playboys and mademoiselles alike —all are urban types, whether they reside in Squirrel Hill (in the heart of a great city), or in Sheldon, Illinois (which is not).

Why in the face of such reality does America's view of itself, reflected in the curriculum of its schools, reside so stubbornly in an agrarian past? The best response we can propose is in humanistic terms. The fact is that the nation's poets and novelists often have dwelt in the narrow dimension. In the main, the literature of the city has been a literature of hate. The muckrakers shamed it; the social novelists excoriated it; the poets butchered it. The new literature and the newly perceived reality finds the city not hateful but dreadful. And dreadful too have been its schools!

417

The State of the Urban School

Before we attempt to analyze the causes of the "state" of the urban school, let us consider the condition. Among our major cities there is scarcely a school system of distinction. For schools of distinctive reputation and quality it is necessary to turn to the suburbs, the small cities, and the towns. Perhaps at present only Denver and San Francisco provide the encouraging evidence that public education can indeed not merely survive but even flourish in the modern city. If this be true, then it is not by accident. These cities have had not only the good fortune to acquire rare educational leadership but to a considerable extent constitute exceptions to some of the conditions afflicting the course of public education in most cities.

The merits of special programs and experimental efforts at improvement of urban education should not be minimized or ignored. They are considerable and we will treat them in due course. But neither should educators overlook several central facts about education in our cities. (1) Urban education is characterized by a *general mediocrity,* and exceptions are hard to come by. To name the worst would be to choose arbitrarily among a wide field. (2) The *problems* of urban education *are central,* not peripheral, and they will not be affected by attacks at the periphery. Overcrowded classrooms; low-moraled teaching forces, antique physical structures, hag-ridden bureaucracies, and stagnant curricula are the central problems and most common phenomena of education within the cities. (3) Urban education is affected by the *flight from the city to the suburb, inadequate taxing structures,* and, of course, by almost universal *statewide political rigging* that starves the cities in the legislatures.

But worst of all, the schools of the cities muddle along as a consequence of an abominable lack of civic statesmanship. St. Louis, for example, built a triumphal arch when it could have chosen to build twenty new elementary schools. Pittsburgh celebrated its renaissance by continuing to overlook the fact that it owns scarcely any but second-rate elementary schools and not a truly modern high

418

school. For the price of several great high schools, or perhaps twenty-five elementary schools, it chose to build a baseball stadium. Consequence exists in human affairs. Knowledge of consequence is sometimes terrible. Our hopes would be easier if progress demanded no antecedents. The consequence of choosing civic monuments in the manner of the Pharaohs or decadent Caesars is damning. Such choices assure not merely that the schools will get no better; they are likely to get worse.

Our function here is not to induce pessimism. A grim analysis does not necessarily derive from pessimism. No city is beyond hope. Not all are totally dominated by folly. At least in one arena the school is somewhat its own master: the curriculum. So, the redemption of the schools of the city may necessarily begin with a concept of urban education.

Educators in recent years have written or orated lively words on this popular subject. But they have seldom come to terms with fundamentals. They have been apt in semantic invention of names for peripheral projects to qualify for foundation or federal funds and prolific in press releases. The rationale for all such projects has been the assumption that certain groups of students are suffering educational neglect. This is not so much erroneous as a misleading assumption. The fact is only too obvious that the urban school neglects some children more than others. An elementary principle of constructing social scientific survey instruments, however, is that the question must be inclusive enough to encompass the data sought. The question urban schools should use to institute self-appraisal and reconstruction is not, therefore, "Which groups are being neglected in our education program?" The adequate question would read: "How many *children* are receiving an inadequate education in our schools?" This would encompass the data in most American cities. And whether computerized or hand-tabulated the answer would simply be: *All of them.*

Therefore, before we proceed, we shall establish certain basic requirements of good urban education. The first of these: to make the urban complex comprehensible. To do this, it is necessary to become matter of fact. Or, even more to the issue: to get the facts. This does not say that anyone is deliberately hiding the facts, but

419

there is a smog from the mystiques that becloud the cities. There is, for example, all this proud pronouncement about renaissance and urban renewal. The best that these phrases mean anywhere is that efforts at reconstruction are beginning to rival the erosions of deterioration. What perverse concept of progress can prompt a city to make civic boast of the fact that a decade or two ago it instituted smoke control? The significant fact is that it befouled itself for so long.

Learning in Simplistic Societies

Because the city is so complex and in a sense so modern, it may defy analysis. Yet the city has ancient roots and remains considerably tribal. This analysis of the simplistic society is then not an exercise in anthropology but an essential leverage to be exerted toward comprehending the city.

A simplistic society may be identified by several characteristics: (1) it lacks cultural pluralism; (2) it occupies a clearly defined and limited geographical resort; (3) it possesses a common body of traditions, mythology, and taboos; (4) it has little contamination through social intercourse or communication with other cultures; and (5) it holds to established patterns of governmental and social obligations without active or adequate consideration for rebellion and change.

The foregoing are axiomatic. Corollary premises are that simplistic societies ordinarily hold intrusion as a hazard to their state of being (and a consideration of history by no means dictates that this apprehension be adjudged as false), that neighbors are viewed with a combination of disinterest and dread, that one's own difference is translated into perception of special virtue and superiority. In effect, this states a reasonably adequate analysis of the primary attributes of ethnocentrism.

In contemporary consequence the simplistic society is obviously an anachronism. Modern communication and transportation, the effects of wars and commerce, and the building of nations and supernations have practically eliminated societal isolation and have destroyed both the reality and potentiality for undefiled cultural autonomy (except in the minds of the most stubbornly ethnocentric elders and the paranoid fantasies of the most culturally chauvinistic youth).

Wherever the relationship of education to civic development is significant, the persistences of the simplistic society's ways and attitudes are anachronistic. This does not say that cultural distinctiveness and integrity are either anachronistic or valueless. It merely states an undeniable state of human affairs that history appears unlikely to alter.

To comprehend the dimensions and complexities of the modern world and to assess the immeasurable intricacies of the reality of common and world-wide social interdependence is a formidable necessity for modern man. But it is a necessity and presents a mandate for adequate education. If this be true, is there any point in looking at questions of learning within an historically nonexistent and abstract context? Such observations serve two functions. First, the principles involved in social learning are likely to be more clearly visible where the society is simply defined and where the relation of the individual to the society is understood and "uncomplex." Second, since tribal isolation is no longer a viable proposition in human affairs, but its attitudes (the archaic propositions of ethnocentrism) do persist, such an analysis may also point out an essential adversary with which a truly effective modern educational system must contend.

If the educator does not see this proposition clearly, his curriculum will be at least confused: that is, it will tend to mix the historically viable with the historically obsolete. Education thus will serve mainly to confuse the mind of man; at worst, it will perpetuate the destructive and fearful myths that make the larger human community and intercourse with it hazardous rather than a joyful enterprise for human life.

The typical American city encompasses a wide scope of cultural pluralism. The components differ from city to city but in many respects are similar. Everywhere the modern and the complex rub elbows with the old and the simple. Cosmopolitanism vies with tribalism. America is still less than two centuries away from its

421

colonial period. Many of our great cities are barely a century away from their village origins. Not so long ago all Americans lived the ways of simple cultures.

With this proximity of old and new in mind, what does a simple society do to instruct its youth? First, *it makes a realistic and pragmatic analysis of the skills that the tribe needs to perpetuate for its survival.* Usually, a first principle after this analysis is to effect such a rough division of labor between men and women as this: women work in and around the house and in the fields and serve considerably as intelligent beasts of burden; men hunt, fish, make war (which they always call defending the village no matter how far from home the defensive action takes place), and make plans, policies, and high strategies. This latter is, of course, the most important function of the male in simple societies: namely, *to be wise;* it necessitates that the male be free from vulgar exertion except in pursuit of animals, other men, or women (for purposes of procreation or essential pleasure), and in training for these pursuits. Of course, to be wise the male must act wisely. In simple societies this means that he must often close his eyes for considerable periods of time, an exercise in contemplation that the envious and unwise female is wont to slander by calling sleep. To be wise, he must also take counsel. This means that he must have abundant time for palaver. The women, being less wise, are sure to confuse these talkative hours with their own silly sessions of gossip and idle chatter. They cannot know better, to be sure, for by division of labor they are forbidden these counsels, which would naturally be beyond their understanding. The men carry out heavy responsibilities; they sit long and tirelessly making great palaver, their wise and dreadful talk.

Lessons from the simple culture run deep. One of the fountainheads of Western educational attitudes is ancient Greece. Indeed, Greece in all its glory *was* tribal. It was as ethnocentric as a human community can manage to be. Its xenophobia was extreme. Its education severely differentiated between men and women. The women were kept in their place (though the pursuit of Helen led to one of the most celebrated wars in all literature). In the *Odyssey* most special respect is given the woman who for decades remained constant while her husband fought, explored, dallied, palavered, and philandered among the islands of the Mediterranean.

The ancient Hebrews too were a simple and ethnocentric people. They cherished their ways and knew their special merit. The men dominated their counsels, spoke their prophecies, wrote their psalms, enunciated the meaning of their laws. Yet they too confused the matter by making heroines not merely of Ruth, who proudly bent her will to the course of her man, but also glorified Esther and Judith, who bent their wills to no man.

The rule of the simple society in this matter was to effect a simple division of labor. *But,* significantly, the reality of the matter, even among simple tribes, was too complex to hold humanity in such exclusive matrices.

Thus these are the axioms for education among simple tribes: the skills and abilities of men and women are different. To the women, lesser in strength and mind, shall be given the easier and less taxing chores of cooking and plowing and harvesting and carrying; to the man, the playing of games, the chase, and important talk. How appropriate then that the woman should walk with back inclined, proof of her toils and symbol of her submission; how appropriate, too, that the man should walk unencumbered, shoulders back, head erect, proof of his strength, his dignity, even his majesty as a male.

The second matter that distinguishes the simple tribe is its upbringing of youth. *The tribe knows how to instill in its youth the special limitations and ignorances that it deems to be its particular virtues.* In other words, the tribe knows how to develop and perpetuate its value system. It is even willing to cripple its young to fit the pattern, and continues into twentieth-century simplistic societies.

Whether the culture prizes bellicosity and aggressiveness, as do the Kwakiutl of British Columbia, or cooperation and submissiveness as do the Zuni of New Mexico, the methods of indoctrination are the same. All of the community's resources are enlisted: elders, leaders, family, and peers. The whole cultural press must be toward the same virtues, the same verities. The community must put its weight of approval behind every desired act; it must show its disapproval of every act of nonconformity and every word of dissent. It

423

must diminish the chance of contagion. It has a special vocabulary for naming foreigners. Among the ancient Greeks, the label was "barbarians." All ethnocentric peoples have labels for outsiders, and these are never complimentary terms.

But *reality* is everywhere the same. The children everywhere have five senses. What can the tribe do about maverick individualism, the stubborn disposition of the person to see, feel, touch, smell, and hear, and his inclination then to make his beliefs and behavior correspond to what he perceives? What if he even decides to make public report on these matters?

The tribe has its resources. *It can limit the field of perception.* That is, it can deny the experience of that which is different. It can try to limit reality to the tribe's own report. Therefore, it attempts to make its legends, songs, stories into the whole matter of the child's experience. The tribe writes its own history and tries to assure that the children hear no other.

It can make it painful to look beyond prescribed knowledge. It can reward the unseeing. It can elevate eloquent conformists to positions of leadership. It can, has, and does sometimes tear out the tongues of those who report too much of their strange perceptions on matters. It can banish and kill. These things often have been done in the name of virtue, the virtue of tribal *verities.*

It can invoke magic and mysteries and the terror of symbols to promote its beliefs. It is difficult to refrain from saying "to promote or to keep its ignorance." That would be unscientific, would it not? That would sound as though one had never heard of "cultural relativism," would it not?

There must be something to be learned from these matters. Surely, the lesson is not how to protect and nurture tribalism and ethnocentrism. Yet, despite the lessons of history there are still those who seem to have some hope of doing the impossible, of educating the child in a provincial view of the world. They still try the devils of indoctrination, of thought control, of secret police, of banishment, and even of torture. Why? The answers surely do not lie in good educational theory.

It would appear that man must learn that there is no refuge from the world. It seems that value systems must be broad enough to encompass all humanity. The mysteries of the universe, of space and infinity, can unite men around their wonder; the mysteries of tribal medicinemen can only tear humanity apart.

A sound educational theory can only be rooted in an encompassing view of man. It can only be sound and educational if it is ecumenical to large degrees. Education will be nothing but tribal witchcraft unless it is rooted in a very large veiw of the world.

Of Cultural Deprivation

With every advance of educational opportunity, a lesson is relearned. The talents and abilities of humanity are very broadly distributed. And genius lurks in places once deemed most unlikely.

In the United States we have learned that true equality is not easy to achieve. It begins with the opening of the school doors, both the elementary and secondary school, to all children. But it only begins there. Some students are much better prepared to succeed in school than others, not simply in "natural intelligence" but also in broad experience, in acquaintance with the tools of learning, and in knowledge of schools and their purposes.

Educators and the public recently have begun to take note of an old and common phenomenon—*cultural deprivation*. Some children come to school richly prepared. They have had books at home. They have been read to. They have been taken to plays, to museums, to zoos. They have even traveled. Others have scarcely any experience beyond the rooms in which they live and the streets on which they play. They are rarely noticed by their parents except to be punished. When these children come to school, what do they make of it? Their more fortunate peers have vocabularies of thousands of words; theirs are numbered in scanty hundreds. The teachers and some classmates speak familiarly of things of which they have never heard.

In the past the school has usually held a laissez-faire attitude toward these children. Some of them by luck or effort have managed to catch up. Others have become more and more lost in school. Because the school makes little sense to them, they resist it. They

425

become disciplinary cases. This, at least, is a hopeful sign of spirit. More sad are those who quietly accept circumstance, who neither learn nor rebel. They simply wait for the day when this confinement is ended. But when it is ended, what place is there for them in the modern world? Can our societies afford this waste of humanity?

The phenomenon of cultural deprivation affects all schools, even the universities. If education is serious in purpose, it cannot take a laissez-faire attitude toward this. It cannot leave the outcome to chance. It *must* take deliberate action.

We are not now discussing those students whose handicaps are physical or who are mentally retarded. The hard of hearing, the blind, the brain-damaged are subjects for special education. The field of special education has done wonders for them. We are discussing those students who are normal children but are handicapped simply by living in conditions far below the norm of the society.

The first thing that the school must do is recognize the problem of cultural deprivation. Then it must go to its source. It cannot ignore it. Yet sometimes, the school does worse than ignore the problem. It often comes up with a wrong diagnosis. It labels these children stupid or uneducable. This is the common defense of the school that does not want to take the trouble to become an educational institution. Thus, by trying to avoid trouble, it stores up trouble for itself and for society. Worst of all, it builds trouble into the lives of these children. It conditions them to low self-esteem and to an expectation of failure.

Yet, the basic premise of good teaching is ever *to take the students from where they are.* If this accepted principle of education be applied, the problem of cultural deprivation can be attacked. For the children who are its victims it is a matter of learning that they do not know what they need to know. With this diagnosis successful teaching can begin.

From the recognition and analysis of the phenomenon of cultural deprivation has evolved a new and useful concept—the concept of *compensatory education.* Compensatory education means a systematic effort, either in the school or beyond the school, to attack the problem of cultural deprivation. It represents an effort to narrow the experience gap between the privileged and the under-privileged.

In 1965, for example, the federal government began a program called Head Start in many cities. This program was directed toward the problem of cultural deprivation. It sought out the children in those areas where such deprivation was common. It established special classes under specially qualified teachers for preschool children. The purpose was to try to prepare these children for school so that they could enter it on terms of more nearly equal readiness with others.

Teachers in these classes often found that the first problem was a psychological one. It was a matter of overcoming the children's fear. Their fear was first of adults. These children often had little experience with adults who came to them in a friendly and helpful role. Who were the adults they had known? Parents? Often there was only one, and that one was harried with worry and resented life and unwanted children. The most fortunate relationship for many of these children with parents was neglect. Attention often meant hostility. Other adults were the police and neighborhood merchants whose attention was mainly directed at preventing their petty thefts. Sometimes they knew young neighborhood adults whose attention was to bully, to exploit, or to seduce them. The teacher's first job then was to develop knowledge and confidence with an adult in a new role, in friendly and responsible support. It is no surprise that this confidence was sometimes won slowly.

Beyond this factor of fear of adults but always in its presence comes the matter of expanding experience. The schoolroom and its equipment must become familiar. Crayons and paper are discovered for their uses. Beginnings of a realization of self begin with self-expression. Children learn to mold clay, to paint with water colors. They are surprised with themselves; they find themselves singing together. They are amazed, the teacher smiles, she approves. She actually seems to enjoy them.

Then the world begins to expand. They have never ridden in an automobile. One day a bus comes for them. They are subdued, quiet. They are a little frightened and terribly excited. The world had been their block; now they are to see a city. They are told they are going to a zoo. They wonder what this means. They are told they will see strange animals. The promise has no meaning. The meaning waits for experience. Animals to them mean dogs, cats, and rats. In other parts of the city there are birds and squirrels, but not where they live. The zoo! Strange animals! They see them. They learn their names. Tomorrow they will talk of them. Not today. Today their eyes and indeed their mouths are open wider than ever before. Tomorrow they will draw pictures. And they will ask the teacher questions. By now they know that she will have much to tell them that they are eager to hear.

Another day it will be a museum. Another day a picnic. A picnic? They have not heard the word before. But a picnic is not a word. It is a glorious happy event for children. It is grass and swings and games and running fast and free. And not all happiness, because these are children whose cultural deprivation means not merely that they do not know the word for picnic. It means that they do not know their own capacity for joy. Some of them will stand aside, bewildered and wary. Inner excitement will prompt others to the expression they know best: aggression. They will fight one another. They may throw sticks and even stones at the teacher. And because she knows her job, she will stand patiently, watch and wait, and only interfere to prevent injury. She knows the need, and she can recognize learning when she sees it. Learning, real learning, has in it sometimes the agony of birth. And to watch the process of birth is both beautiful and agonizing.

These children are like you and me, the children of God and of man. The world is theirs. They can come to fear and to hate it, or they can come to know and to love it. That is what compensatory education is all about. It is to introduce the good dimensions of life that some children share so fully to the children whose circumstance of birth has denied them these things.

Wherefore the Blackboard Jungle?

The first observable impact of cultural deprivation is on and in the elementary school. Here the consequences are pathetic. When the culturally deprived are kept in school but never really educated, never personally affected, the consequences are terrible. Evan Hunter wrote *The Blackboard Jungle* in 1954.[4] At the time some educators regarded this novel, which was later made into a film, as sensational muckraking. The truth is that the blackboard jungle existed and still exists. Its location in any metropolitan school system is an open secret. Teachers in any city, not necessarily a large one, can state its location and its attendant characteristics.

The blackboard jungle in most American cities lies within boundaries of socioeconomic and ethnic ghettoes. Its limits are more widespread in some cities, diminished in others. A disillusioned school principal in one city responded to the question in these words: "Where is our blackboard jungle? The whole damned school system here is a jungle. The kids and the teachers are lost in it, and the administration keeps itself shut up in its compound at the Board of Education building. Yes, it's *all* a jungle."

The blackboard jungle is the result of incompetent educational practice, the abandonment of the schools by the citizenry, and a failure of civic responsibility. Why not say once more that the jungles are the result of severe social and economic problems? Because to say that merely locates the problem within the context of other unsolved problems. The problem of the poor school in the poor neighborhood has *been* located, both geographically and sociologically. Talking in a circle, no matter how spritely the vocabulary, is not going to get at the real problem, which is to do something about it.

Something surely will be done about it because the crisis in urban education is so evident and the consequences of the imminent disaster are so frightening that the only apparent alternative to chaos is effective action. These are necessary words and easy to say. The requisites for effective action are not easy at all. These requisites are the content for our discussion here and are basically editorial. But the *public* discussion of this subject must be improved; it must be rooted in more profound concepts, and it must

4 Evan Hunter, *The Blackboard Jungle* (New York: Simon and Schuster, 1954).

explore the practical with a great deal more mental effort than has yet been applied.

Incompetent educational practice is a basic cause here. The human disposition to cite all the excuses for failure before getting down to our own blunders and incompetence is universal and understandable. The teachers and administrators in our blackboard jungles like to exonerate themselves from responsibility for the bad schools they are running by citing all their headaches: depressing community conditions, failure of public support and appreciation, damaged humanity that comes to them. But this will not do. We maintain that education is a profession. If this is true, then the first determinant of success or failure is within our professional competence.

In the novel that may serve to springboard consideration, Evan Hunter, who knew what he was talking about, described a number of the incapacities of those who worked in his particular jungle. Among them he included these: bureaucratic irresponsibility and time-serving attitudes, cynical disdain and general disinterest in students as significant persons, a tendency to underrate or to ridicule the biological preoccupations and drives of students, forlorn efforts to appeal to students in terms of the teacher's personal enthusiasms rather than the students' own experiences and motivations. Above all, the beaten and fugitive teachers lacked an adequate psychic reserve of persistence, stubbornness, and patience. And they dwelt almost universally in a climate of deep-rooted fear of their students.

It takes no gift of prophecy to anticipate raised eyebrows or voices at this point. In tough schools there are things to be reasonably afraid of in specific instances—for example, students with drawn knives or guns and psychotic youths with deep aggressions and paranoid perceptions and motivations. It remains a fact, however, that the *fear of students* is a professional incapacity; it is a corollary to *fear of humanity*. The person who is incapacitated by this fear is ill-equipped to walk around in the world, let alone to assume responsible social roles. Plenty of teachers, like all humans, are afraid. The profession can tolerate the knowledge of these fears (which is significant self-knowledge), but it cannot allow teachers to make a virtue or an excuse of their cowardice. If we offer pap on important issues for fear of community reaction or avoid encounters with our students through fear, we are behaving unprofessionally. Doctors, lawyers, soldiers, statesmen walk sometimes in hazard. They are not foolishly unaware of danger. But if out of fear they fail to perform their duties they do not appeal to the name of their profession as excuse. Nor must we. A teacher afraid may have our sympathy, but he must face the fact that his fear makes him less a teacher.

The foregoing incapacities are summarized from fiction, but they sum up many realities. They are compounded in the dramatically bad schools that are a common denominator in most of our urban school systems. Professional incompetence is not the only cause of bad schools; it is named first because it belongs to the teaching profession. This is the fault we can find with ourselves, and it is also the one we can do something about. It is not easy to assert our professional responsibility as our first premise because there is a kind of defensiveness that equates a tough-minded or even critical self-appraisal with disloyalty to the group.

Teachers, like other professionals, reside among a complex of loyalties. Like the doctor whose first obligation is to his patient, and after that to his colleagues, and to society, the teacher owes first obligation to his students. That obligation is professional competence. In a not uncommon public stance (not so much we think derived from hypocrisy as from self-delusion) the organized educational professional says: "Yes, we know all about these bad schools. They are not our fault, you know. If you would give us fine new plants and good equipment and give us incentive pay in these areas, we will make good schools where there are bad ones." Such gains will affect the performance of competent educators positively, but they will not affect the pattern of incapacities previously cited.

That administrative practice compounds the problem is common knowledge. Schools in areas where bad schools abound are often used as educational Siberias. Teachers are sent there for disciplinary reasons, to learn the consequences of nonconformity or of rocking the boat. Out of perverse logic and as a result of stultifying seniority privileges, they are also used as training grounds for beginning teachers or for teachers new to the system who come in without special contracts or influence.

Could you have a good school where a bad school now exists simply by changing a single variable, *professional competence?* Well, there are undistinguished schools in very privileged communities that are beautifully housed and have comparatively good salaries. The material variables alone will obviously not of themselves produce an excellent school. In bad environments not all schools are equally bad and some are surprisingly good: the variables seem to be *professional competence* and *human concern*. Even in the worst schools in the poorest conditions of environment and support, classrooms exist where teaching and learning take place of such quality that they would lend luster to the repute of any school. Other variables, of course, bear upon the situation. The best schools do not simply leave good and earnest staff at the mercy of the winds of adversity.

When real education is found in unlikely circumstance, it is reasonably certain that the aforesaid bill of incapacities is turned squarely around into a catalog of assets which are so significant that we shall relist them in their positive form. Teachers see responsibility not simply in terms of filing reports and keeping the record clean but in terms of obligation to achieve a learning situation by standards that they will not hold obscure. They concern themselves with the life and person of all their students generally and with as many as their emotional energies will allow personally. They live with teen-agers with the friendly knowledge of all their own adolescent drives and interests—biological, psychological, social, cultural. They subordinate their peculiarly sophisticated perception of meaning in an attempt to enter into the students' phenomenology and by intersubjective communication they attempt to find grounds for common appraisals of reality as take-off points for conceptual expansion. They exercise tolerant self-discipline in attempting to increase their capacity for continued effort, lack of dismay, and constant patience.

To Escape the Jungle

What would it take to make a good school out of a blackboard jungle? Many teachers of the blackboard jungles have easy answers: expel all problem students from school, enforce rigid academic standards, stratify classes by complex ability groupings, send the academically untalented to work or to special schools, and of course raise teachers' salaries. In the main, the American community and the educational profession recognize these easy answers as self-serving abdications of educational responsibility. These answers will not be allowed. We do not originate the rejection, but we join it.

Good teachers, free to do the job needed and led by administrators who know education and have stubborn vision, can make a good school in any circumstance found in America given the very ordinary support that the almost universal bad schools now claim. There are conditions in this statement—an austere and realistic definition of good teaching, freedom that is functional rather than nominal, administrators concerned with learning rather than with careerism, and courage. This conceptualization is practical and workable. It is not a utopian vision; it does not demand more of educators than they can give. Rather, it is built upon the motivations that bring people to education and so often betray them. When the school does not proceed from this conceptual stance, the good people who would like to be good teachers have three alternatives: (1) they may succumb to the low level of organizational survival attributes of the system with an attendant growth of apathy and cynicism; (2) they may gamble on a move to another system, or (3) they may leave education. Only two things prevent the immediate broad-scale application of these premises—their necessity has not been clearly set forth, and they would compel a drastic reform of the bureaucratic structure of the American school system (not so much structurally, but, as in Denver and San Francisco, in the motivations of administration from self-oriened, prudent, civil service careerism to exciting, risk-taking, educational commitment).

Of these obstacles, we can do little to affect the latter but dwell in hope of remedying the former.

The reform that can be effected will begin and will practically be consummated through teacher selection. It can begin, as the Peace Corps phrases it, by "selection out." First, out will go the teachers who accept the general and cordial invitation to transfer away from the school. Second, close on the heels of the first group, will depart those whose records are replete with student conflict, whose achievements are measured in terms of high ratios of failure and large contributions to the dropout rate. Third, after a more careful screening, will exit a number of marginally successful teachers. Their records will be characterized by faint praises in such words as these: "always here on time," "never brings problems to the office," "gets all his reports in on time," "has good discipline."

With a little bit of luck, after the selection-out process, a hard core of teachers will remain from the original roster. These will provide a nucleus to build with and a pool of experience to utilize in the cooperative teacher-education program that must be constructed in the school. It is quite likely that this nucleus will be small indeed.

The "selection-in" process will be more arduous. The first criteria will be motivational. Just as the first out were those who wanted out, so the first consideration for these jobs will be those wanting in. This alone will *not* qualify. Back of the wish, the "why" must be scrutinized. In sum, the motivation sought would be similar to what we may generalize as "Peace Corps" motivations. (This term is used unofficially, of course, but not in unawareness.) After having worked as director of a Peace Corps Training Project, the author would sum up the significance of such motivations in these terms: Peace Corps volunteers appear as a group, with some exceptions, not unlike a typical collegiate cross section. At least, they are not distinguishable from typical college students by externals. Nor will they be markedly different in academic ability or intellectual power. They are a representative cross section as far as academic achievement is concerned. They are not a crop of intellectual superstudents.

How are they different? Two distinctive characteristics, not common to all, are nonetheless uncommonly apparent among them. One, the umbilical cord has really been cut for these people. They are capable of going away from home and feeling secure about it. This does not mean that they are in rebellion against their homes (though some of them are). It simply means that they are comfortable about growing up and quite capable of being away from home—farm, village, or city—and on their own in the big wide world. That, though true of some potential teachers, is not one of their more noteworthy characteristics. Second, these volunteers, in a manner of speaking, really seem to have taken "Sunday School" seriously. This does not mean that there is unusual piety or devotion to religious observances among them (although both are to be found). It simply means that very largely characteristic of this group is the conviction that there is something more important to life than serving self. They are viscerally convinced that the idea, or the belief, dictates action. Having somehow become aware of the great needs within the human condition, they feel a necessity as responsible adults to do something about it. Nor can they be content with relatively indirect involvement. Their response must be direct, immediate, and most of all, personal. The teaching profession, especially for its more demanding roles, can use a large infusion of just such motivation.

An Essential for Reconstruction

The hard qualifications for educational reform that our schools require are stated here in confidence, not in pessimism. The professional opinion herewith is that such motivations are sufficiently abundant and are to be counted upon. At present, they are neither being recognized as necessities nor are they being used. Nor will this essential reform necessarily occur. Under contemporary governing assumptions, it is scarcely taking place at all. Unless such motivations do exist in sufficient quantity and are mobilized, or unless they can to such effect be developed, the necessary reconstitution of the urban problem school will not take place. There is, after all, no sure winner in the grim race between education and catastrophe.

435

The reconstruction will begin by a drastic shifting of forces. The principal characteristics of bad urban schools are not the beaten-up physical plants, and some are housed quite well. Our main concerns are with the emotionally beaten, frightened people who go through the motions of teaching there. Many of these teachers, principally those who will leave with the first wave, not merely fear but hate and despise their students. The students in the jungle schools are nearly all poor. This in itself is a frightening and despicable phenomenon to teachers whose ideas of decency and aspirations are fully middle class and who reside economically dispersed along its lower fringes. In different localities the ethnic make-up of students will differ, but rest assured they will be considerably comprise of groups whom "decent," timid souls easily scorn. The amount of virulent race bias among faculty in the ghetto schools is one of their distinguishing characteristics. In fact, conversation in teachers' rooms lends substance to apprehension that the public policy of the school is to serve as an instrument to punish students for belonging to despised subgroups.

Make no mistake about this. Culling of the actively race-biased teachers from the ghetto schools is an essential step toward their reconstruction, but it will take radical reform to get at this infection. The virus already exists, and not just marginally. Race bias is a dominant social attitude among faculties of ghetto schools. School authorities do not acknowledge this to be a problem nor do they publicize it as they do overcrowded classrooms or low salary schedules. On the contrary, the most flagrant instances of discrimination or prejudice will be ascribed publicly to any cause other than the true one. Around this primary debilitating attitude the bureaucracies within the schools have woven a sheltering silk screen of evasiveness.

The organizational characteristic of the machine has something to do with it, to be sure. But principally it is due to the fact that the board of education, whatever its address, generally feels exactly the way the teachers in the jungle high school do. They too know that there is something basically wrong with being poor, with being black, or with speaking a foreign language in the home. Not that the board knows so clearly how it does feel. Its members are sheltered from such daily trials to their psyches as having to face forty aggressive, bewildered, frustrated children of deprivation. Encounters that bring racial epithets roaring to the consciousness if not to the tongue are to them not a matter of daily incidents, but this fails to increase understanding. Profound administrative loyalty to teachers is shown in few other areas. The board will support its teachers in no strong attitude of religious prejudice; it will often allow them little political candor, but race bias links with a very fraternal hand.

Such talk is reasonably ugly. This is only a small part of the message that radical black leaders and more moderate spokesmen have tried to get across. Such talk shocks because it seeks out reality with an existential impact. In effect, it says to the whole community: Of course, you all are biased against the black and the poor. If you are not, why do you keep on pretending that racial discrimination is something other than what it is? If you are not, why do you not really do something about racial injustice *now?*

Sometimes we question the capacity of existential reality to make any impact on comfortably situated middle-class Americans. The present urban crisis is severely testing this capacity. Upon the undecided question of whether the middle class can divest itself of complacency and surrender some of its illusions and biases the future of the American community considerably depends.

The teachers who will reconstruct the school will be nobody's party liners. They *will* be solid in self-knowledge and strongly motivated, and their recruitment will be based on a wide range of academic and professional commitments.

Commentary: Education as Existential Exercise

Education is a great public enterprise. Indeed, it is *the* great public enterprise. It is worth taking seriously. Yet, for all the expenditure of wind and dialectic on this subject since 1960, the signs of profound educational serious-mindedness are few. The single-purposed dedication to the issues of multisorted pronunciamentos has been to themselves. In characteristic fashion the establishment finds it easy

437

to phrase verbal commitment to large purposes and great enterprises but can enlist effort only from the self-seeking.

The morale that will perhaps rebuild the schools of the cities must derive from a tremendous zest for the joyful task of putting genuine life opportunity at the disposal of all youth. To characterize the essential *élan vital* from which future deeds of great accomplishment will thrust themselves, it is necessary to find and speak the words of a grand concept that prudent little men, rank opportunists, and those seriously dedicated to their own aggrandizement will quail before or will transform them into emboldened seekers of noble visions. This public enterprise must become the transcendent existential exercise for modern man.

In due time the makers of isolated and useless small projects begin to feel seriously useful. They will be healthier if not happier when their messianic dreams of educational salvation by *project* have been shattered. *Projectitis* is becoming the affliction of the body educational in our time. Many small matters, well worth exploring as limited utensils, have been blown up in the minds and press releases of their makers into educational panaceas. Small wonder, for the great purposes that can teach the most ambitious careerists humble commitment have been hesitatingly and falteringly phrased.

Team teaching, programed learnings, searches of talent, guidance for all, ungraded schools—all these and others in grand mosaic will find their place. The city that first truly educates its youth will not have been won by educational salvationists nor by a handful of academic supermen. It will be won, and somewhere that may be soon, by an aggregate of honest professionals who allow themselves to see the real task and set about doing it. It will be done by a host of knowledgeable men and women who are content with a view of self that exacts from them simply one man's work from each, and that defined by an austere and high standard. The city that truly educates its youth will have learned that it can make no monuments of its achievements. The first metropolis to erect a dozen magnificent "educational parks" or superschools is not the city of which we speak. These edifices are likely to become our Pyramids memorializing the paralysis and death of the human view of learning. It is boys and girls and the teaching of them on which the school must center its mind and spirit. Our society has already built structures so glossy, so formidable, so inhuman in dimension that men and women wander around in them wondering who they are, whither they wander, and what manner of folk they encounter.

The city of true education will not stand bewildered in its own presence because it will have re-created itself to the uses of its only reality: its inhabitants. It will stand in no dread of its works because it will have studied them in view of their purposes and will await their completion, not to stand in awe, but to move in and go to work. This city will be modern in dress, design, and surely in technology. But it will be modern in a more centered sense than in its tools. Our calendar reads 1968, 1970, or 1971, tomorrow, 2000, but no date spells "modern." Civilization itself has cowered in our time before barbarians well equipped with the deadliest products of machines. The modern city will grow from a studied perception of who man is, what his condition is and, where he is heading. It will undertake to define its directions and will be captive to the waking nightmares of neither determinists nor conditioners.

The city that first truly educates its youth will have no delusions of standing completed or secure. Its very vitality will be inspired by its knowledge that it ever shares the risks of life, and in its most humbly satisfying moments of achievement it knows that it must be said "this too shall pass away." The morale that needs surety, or even lasting achievement, is "fools' gold" of the spirit. In its perversions it has spoken gruesome words of "final solutions."

The achievement in nonrhetorical terms of school systems that liberate the many-faceted human potential will be made. The willed intelligence of contemporary man is stirring. It is becoming more critical of the fools' errands to which it has been so often mobilized. It is about ready to define its own works and to cease to play the role of Lepidus.

This is the mind, for us in education, that can be trusted, schooled in its many professions. Its many representatives created their own images and symbols. In a sense, its unique character will utilize all of the joyful, poignant, and devastating experiences of historical man to stay with the task of improving the human abode.

439

The symbol from the agonized experience of his own time may be that of Zorba,[5] after all.

Disillusioned past the need for more illusion, modern man may still, like Zorba, assert his stubborn zest for life. Our cities pose the eternal trial assigned to Sisyphus. They may never be redeemed, but the shoulder must return to the rock. Remember that a truly modern man (Albert Camus) has said, "We must imagine Sisyphus happy." Every school man, every teacher knows the reality: if he must have the satisfaction of surely defined accomplishment there is nothing in the school for him but cynicism and despair. But there is always the need for another day of a man's work, largely defined.

We all mean well, and because we are no such fools after all, we may yet build well, although like Zorba's feat of engineering, our fondest efforts of mind and back may come tumbling down. Our works are the *investments* of ourselves, not ourselves. Unless the symbol of Zorba acquires a general meaning modern man can have his spirit crushed. Anyone can be reduced and conquered if he identifies himself with the failure or the success of any of his works.

The school will be humanized, the city remade by a population that has discovered and asserted its own worth. The educator will play a man's role in this future, will be identified with the student with whom he enters the school as psychic peer. Either will be fit company when he finds himself alone with the other; both will be capable of community; neither will need to push the other; and both will be very difficult to push. They will plan solid constructions, dream good dreams, and love life together. And when constructions crumble and dreams fade, they will persist undismayed. With no need for self-delusion, they will abjure the game—so common to generals, bureaucrats, and politicians—of verbalizing obvious defeats into victories. They will stand in the ruins of their temporary hopes and look with horror; then in the company of the gods and wiser men, they will laugh at it all and at themselves, rebuild the fire, have a barbecue and turn again to the sources that will renew them.

5 Nikos Kazantzakis, *Zorba the Greek*, trans. by Carl Wildman (New York: Simon and Schuster, 1959). Zorba is an epic individual and an existential man. He knows much of agony but admits no dismay.

Chapter XIV

Since 1967–The Urban Effort Reconsidered

In an atmosphere of hostility between the community and the schools, education cannot flourish. A basic problem stems from the other social forces influencing youth. Changes in society— mass media, family structure, religion—have radically altered the role of the school. New links must be built between the schools and the communities they serve. The schools must be related to the broader system which influences and educates ghetto youth.[1]

Of Time and the Schoolbell

The educator must entertain all the possibilities within man's fate. At the dictate of this premise, the gloomiest of all alternatives must be considered: *Man may not make it.* This is not a reiteration of the known, that man has unmistakably in his hands the instruments of a general and total self-destruction. Throughout time the person has had means of suicide at his hands' disposal, but this did not mean that he was necessarily disposed to use them.

[1] *Report of the National Advisory Commission on Civil Disorders* (New York: Bantam, 1968), p. 440.

The question is whether the human spirit, the will to live, sufficiently endures and whether man's intelligence is undamaged enough to let him use all that he knows which might save him.

Many thoughtful men surveyed the disintegration of the Western community brought about by World War I and speculated that civilization might not endure a second world war. The proposition was put to test. It is presumed that civilization did indeed endure its second and more general agony within the century. But did it, indeed?

Between the world wars, Webb Miller wrote of his reporting in the truce interval and named his summation, *I Found No Peace.*[2] Now again, years of peace marred by the cold war, the hydrogen bomb, the arms race, and conflicts in Korea, the Middle East, the Congo, and Vietnam, to name a few intrusions. What does it signify? It could signify that the distrusts, the hatreds, the fears are so far out of hand that the civilized hopes and the capacity for building institutions to contain greed and terror may be inadequate to create the conditions for survival.

If this is not reality, but only a threat of it, then the job for education in the most profound sense must be morale building. Morale cannot be built on vain hopefulness. It must be based on the capacity and the desire of the free, willed intelligence to make its way through large dilemmas and to create enduring fabrics of opportunity and peace.

The inclination to short-cut solutions and to avoidance of the central dilemmas is a large potential of the creature. Eric Hoffer has limned well the disposition of the regressive and frightened mind in *The True Believer.*[3] It is a good summation of what education is up against. In a zany and horrifying novel called *Mother Night,* Kurt Vonnegut, Jr., comes to the very heart of the matter:

> The dismaying thing about the classic totalitarian mind is that any given gear, though mutilated, will have at its circumference unbroken sequences of teeth that are immaculately maintained, that are exquisitely machined.

[2] Webb Miller, *I Found No Peace* (New York: Simon and Schuster, 1936).
[3] Eric Hoffer, *The True Believer* (New York: New American Library, 1962).

442

Hence the cuckoo clock in Hell—keeping perfect time for eight minutes and twenty-three seconds, jumping ahead fourteen minutes, keeping perfect time for six seconds, jumping ahead two seconds, keeping perfect time for two hours and one second, then jumping ahead a year.

The missing teeth, of course, are simple, obvious truths, truths available and comprehensible even to ten-year-olds, in most cases.

The willful filing off of gear teeth, the willful doing without certain obvious pieces of information . . .[4]

The school can only keep time with human survival if it relentlessly seeks all the evidence, allows no relevant knowledge to be censored from the inquiry. It cannot serve unless it is committed without reservation to the discipline on evidence: "the truth, the whole truth, and nothing but the truth." And having studied the subject profoundly, and having confidence in its methods of intelligence, of *objectivity* and *science*, it will not be obstructed or dismayed by Pilate's niggling question.

If its curriculum is not so conceived and dedicated, all its schoolbells will march to the tempo of the cuckoo clock in Hell.

The Great High School Idea

The very large high school, with student populations as large as 6,000 students, is nothing new. Many high schools were intended to be "big," but they became "overgrown" as a result of expanding population and underbuilding. No great merit was usually ascribed to their size, and sometimes considerable regret was expressed.

Educators comparatively recently have enunciated rules of thumb with respect to minimum size for the high school that could possess all the attributes of modern education. Among the numbers arbitrarily suggested for this minimum have been 500, 800, or 1,000 students. Surely there must be a point below which the school will lack certain appurtenances of modernity—varied laboratory facil-

---

[4] Kurt Vonnegut, Jr., *Mother Night* (Greenwich, Conn.: Gold Medal Books, 1961) , p. 145.

ities, broad programing, extensive library, audio-visual and other technological resources, guidance and other pupil personnel services. The smaller school must often either deny itself these basic necessities or achieve them at a very considerable per pupil cost.

Optimum sizes have been more cautiously prescribed. Educators, perhaps responding nostalgically to a small-school bias, have somewhat inarticulately subscribed to a notion that a school could be too big. At some point it has been felt that "the bigger, the better" concept must encounter the principle of diminishing returns. The hypothesis in this position might be expressed thus: *At a point, the number of problems solved by an increase in size is met and begins to be exceeded by the numbers of problems caused by this increase in size.* No precise investigation of this broad hypothesis has been conducted. Factors that could be assessed relevant to the proposition are transportation and traffic problems, logistical matters, management costs, and disciplinary and control issues. In addition, more subtle factors such as depersonalization and bureaucratization are involved and deserve some assessment.

The point may be illustrated both at the practical and the psychological levels. If the school is relatively small, but above the necessary minimum, luncheon places may be simple, limited, and even provide dual space. Food services will not of necessity be formidable. In the arena of mass feeding the edible evidence seldom suggests the axiom that the larger the numbers fed, the higher will be the quality of the cuisine. The same necessity in a very large institution will require elaborate facilities and a formal food service, and it is not unlikely that a point of sharply increased costs will be reached. However, we will not make a large issue over this particular here.

In the psychic dimension the illustration may be drawn in more profound educational terms. In the relatively small school the administration and the faculty may know and to some degree relate themselves to the identities of all the students. Achievements, abilities, backgrounds, aspirations of students will not be merely recorded but known. The culture of the school will include a fabric of knowing communication about persons and events that reaches and helps to sustain the identities of almost all present. A single overworked guidance person may do an adequate educational job in this context. In the very large school persons are likely to be identified from rosters; major achievers in any field are likely to be as remote from the common body of their fellow students as are the big men on large campuses, chiefly known to their fellows by their names in the college paper. Within this circumstance of small acquaintance and large anonymity, the staff requirements for guidance, counseling, and pupil personnel services may increase in greater than arithmetic proportions. Professional services in this and other areas will now be required to deal with problems that are a function of size and that seldom even appear in the reduced context.

Despite the logic within the foregoing, the American educational culture is experimenting with an articulate confidence in a new concept of institutional largeness, the "great high school" idea.[5] In Pittsburgh, for instance, the plan, as of 1968, was to build perhaps five new supersecondary schools each with a population of 5,000 or more students. This could represent the American preoccupation with bigness gone berserk in educational terms. It could simply mean grandiose "thinking big" standing in counterfeit of genuine educational vision. It could but need not necessarily mean these things.

As a matter of fact, the cultural determinants of the "great high school" idea are formidable. The intent to keep the adolescent in school through all his teen-age years is very largely achieved. The secondary school plant of most cities is worn, overcrowded, and outmoded; the school must be rebuilt. Its new structure must be flexible and responsive to the best in new, research-vindicated practice. Special problems of urban life, long neglected, must find an educational response. For example, the viability of the city as a desirable abode is currently very much in question. Among other things the city no doubt needs symbols of its intent toward revitalization; a couple of luxury hotels, a big-league franchise, and a

5 See S. P. Marland, Jr. (Pittsburgh Superintendent of Schools), "The Education Park Concept in Pittsburgh," *Phi Delta Kappan*, March 1967.

new stadium scarcely fill the bill. Perhaps the great high school can extend and elevate somewhat the symbolism of urban renaissance. Probably more important is the fact that this idea is responsive to a large and demonstrated urban necessity—to make the school a place for the children of all the groups and cultures within the city to draw together in common respect and common purpose. In the city as it is, clustered into class and ethnic ghettoes, the culture of the neighborhood school does tend to be relatively simplistic in a pluralistic society.

Plans for the superschools are, of course, weighted with attention to "the new technology of education." However, a smaller school can be modern in this respect. Size may indeed impose new communication necessities, but these should not be confused with educational needs or with economies effected.

The major hope would be that any educational experiment would work out for the student's very large advantage. No other hope is tolerable to the educator. Any aim or hope for educational progress predicated largely on size is likely to be a vain one. Educational imagination must go beyond this, as beyond coping imaginatively with problems newly created by size, to qualify as vision.

The urban dilemma must be comprehended in its most profound terms. The school will not serve to unify an atomized urban culture if it simply stands as a lighthouse of integration in a sea of segregations and biases. The waves of societal divisiveness will then pound upon and erode the foundational integrity of the school. For instance, the superschool will surely be multiverse in program. This is a two-edged potential. Through its extended comprehensiveness the school can serve to widen its reach to a large range of student interests, motivations, and aspirations. On the other hand, the particularist divisions within the smaller school stand in danger of being accentuated. If snobbery toward the vocational, neglect of the general, and special favor to the college-bound continue to characterize the institution as today they so largely do, the *great school* will find itself torn by an internal disintegration that will make mockery of its high purposes.

The plans for some of these schools include subdividing into smaller integral units. This is a dramatic instance of coping with difficulties specially created to be coped with. The progeny of Parkinson's Law should be numerous in this context. In this device, as with programing, as with the devices of academic grouping, the possibilities for class, status, and ethnic divisions come to school in aggravated divisiveness.

To predict that the new schools of the cities will be less than educational Utopias is of itself no indulgence in pessimism. The schools of the future can be less than perfect and still measure much progress beyond the present dismal mediocrity. Beyond quietly expressing the belief that the best education of the future will be found where schools are inevitably or intentionally kept smaller, the effort now must be toward constructively analyzing the pitfalls that must be avoided. Again, to say that these schools can become educational monstrosities is not to say that they must. We shall discuss the directions and the critical decisions that must be made if the hazards in the design are not to be institutionalized into destructive practice.

It must be resolved and acted upon that a school can only be as good as the sum total of the learning situations within its classrooms. Although this is not an especially fresh phrasing of what can be simply a tired old cliché, every educator will bow piously to these good words. But the good teaching that is the first requirement for a great school is deeply seasoned professional teaching, meeting the austere but by no means impossible requisites set forth throughout this work. Neither good intentions nor good press releases will qualify instruction in the conventional or duffer's model as good teaching. Furthermore, a school administration will not be capable of building a real educational institution unless it fully comprehends, accepts, and feels viscerally the primacy of this criterion. It has to know not the easy words but the basic reality that a fully professionalized teaching force is by far the most important factor in determining the quality of education.

If an administration digests and acts upon this fact, then it can live comfortably and well with certain corollary implications that sometimes cause administrators the same redness of countenance

447

and shortness of breath associated with the wearing of tight collars. The most binding of implications are these:

1. That faculty are equal colleagues in the educational enterprise, not by courteous phrasing but by actual qualification.

2. That for a school to be well or wisely run it must involve faculty actively, not perfunctorily, in the decision-making process.

3. That the assessment of staffing needs for auxiliary personnel and for special nonteaching personnel must await experience and testing within the school. That is, the table of organization must be drawn up, except for initial necessities, after the faculty has found out what it can do and what it needs to have done for it. In a revolutionary and essential reconceptualization of the table of organization, this means that most of the professional nonteaching force will stand in a staff relationship not to administration but to faculty. By direct connection this implies that administration itself, educationally perceived, belongs in exactly this same relationship.

4. That the gauge of how seriously the school takes education must be the degree to which it mobilizes professional strength to affect the education of students. This is measured in class load, in teacher–student ratios. Furthermore, the teacher–student ratio is to be found by counting students in classrooms, not by dividing the number of students by the number of people in the school bearing college degrees.

Everything within the educational competence and vision of the staff must be mobilized toward the one largest source of the urban trouble, which is the central dilemma of modern man. This again and always is the problem of developing an adequate and secure self-definition in every person. If the school is to be very big, the magnitude of the task must be recognized in scale. No easy evasions can be tolerated. The new structure of the school will be impressive, even magnificent. These adjectives will be used proudly when ground is broken, when inaugural ceremonies are held, and at a good many commencements thereafter. They will perhaps deservedly swell community pride and surely swell the self-esteem of those whose names appear on the bronze plaque in the foyer. But as far as the students are concerned, this pride is neither edible nor sustaining. No evidence exists that magnificence of edifice translates itself into an enhancement of self on the part of those who labor therein. Physical structures do communicate, but it is nonverbal stuff like the threatening overtones of a Kafka nightmare. The only speech within the school, the only human meaning, will be what persons say to one another.

This big, big school will have to democratize itself studiously and consciously. The possibility is not so much that it will become undemocratic through tyrannical intent, but that it will become so through witless bureaucratization. This works in subtle ways at the student level. An elite few, for example, may become the agents for general expression in such fields as varsity athletics and dramatics. The status of the few will be enhanced, perhaps out of perspective, while the general will be forced willy-nilly into making virtue of vicarious identification with the prowess or talent of the chosen. If in the small school problems of cliques, of restricted clubs, of secret societies (forbidden or sanctioned), and of social-class snobberies affect the attaining of a cohesive community, how much aggravated will these same problems be in the phenomenally enlarged institution! The magnitude of plant expansion must be more than matched by the expansion of opportunity for every student to participate in every activity. This participation must be available to all who seek it, not to those who prove themselves to have special merit in a kind of academic elimination contest.

This school must take its measure of student potential from its grand view of the school and of the urban challenge. The great thing about the concept of the new big school is the courage and the confidence it reflects. The schoolteacherish distrust of self and life that expresses itself in fear and distrust of students must not be permitted to roam the school corridors. There will be an abundance of young humanity within these corridors. The temptation of the schoolteacherish will be to attempt to meet this challenge by a proportionate increase in the volume of the schoolbells. These can be the corridors in which freedom and responsibility are developed, or they can provide ample galleries for the aimless shuffling of many feet. This school will have to deny itself frightened thoughts about its police problems and hall traffic control and put its confidence in the things that bring out responsible human behavior. None of them are new and untried, although this school should dare even to be experimental in exploring the frontiers of freedom. The instruments that should be studied and used more than ever before include individual study programs; free time within the schedules and an abundance of attractive places for its exercise; responsible student government with clearly defined though limited areas of real authority; general expectation and a general press toward reasonable behavior rather than strict codification and legislative enforcement of a welter of schoolteacherish rules and regulations; an in-service program of education that bears down not on an assortment of pedagogical odds and ends but on a continuing, thoughtful inquiry as to the real meaning and function of this school in the troubled urban life of modern America.

Thus, if there is some hazard in great size, it is possible to turn it into an optimistic prospect. If the new school matches the exuberant confidence of its blueprinting with a studied confidence in good education, it may overcome the hazards with something to spare. Indolent education can turn even the easiest situation into a bad school. It would be great to see education vindicate itself in the most contrary of environments. It might just be possible that a profound dedication to make the urban school a great educational institution would work. In its school America might begin to take the measure of the grave malaise that afflicts it and thus a true American renaissance might begin to take place.

The Crisis of the Late 1960s

In these paragraphs written in 1968, it is clear that the educator must look at the task of urban education with a redoubled sense of urgency and an awareness of the profound inadequacy of educational vision and action up to this time.

Good education can come toward the heart of the problem of unrest in the cities. But before education can effect its really saving works upon the cities, the public will have to find out what modern

450

education is all about. To assist in that task, this work will make serious effort to bring its weight to bear.

Newark, Detroit, Milwaukee: these names mark a frightful reckoning brought about by complacency and half-measures and the ignoring of the inevitable consequences of the long storing up of the "grapes of wrath" in the American community. For those caught by surprise in 1967, the devastation in the cities served only as an excuse for pronunciamentos of outrage and moral smugness. The disposition to relate to these events in terms of preconception is not amazing. However, the abundant evidence of a willingness to shape the interpretation of this national crisis to the uses of low-grade partisan politics has been one of the least edifying spectacles on the public scene within our recent history. The response in terms of constructive words and actions has not been altogether lacking. The fundamental rebuilding of the American city will not take place, however, if the enterprise be conceived or motivated simply as a well-calculated holding action against disaster.

Fears and angers brought about the riots, the burnings, and the lootings of 1967. This knowledge should be sufficient to make it clear that fear and anger should be excised from the motivations of public response. When an arsonist cries "burn, baby, burn," on the eve of riot and again on the morning after, both emotions rise easily, but such hysteria is at least as old as Nero.

The educator will begin to make the necessary basic sense of these issues when he cuts through to the realization that human conduct never seems outlandish if its roots are understood. In this special danger-charged context, it is to the point to reassert some reality that earlier we have insisted be recognized with something like life-or-death intensity.

The Kerner Report

On July 28, 1967 the President of the United States established the National Advisory Commission on Civil Disorders. Its membership was comprised of moderate minded men and women, both black

451

and white. Its composition was notably lacking in militant reputation; this fact caused some apprehension that its ultimate report might lack in vigor or fundamental analysis. Such did not turn out to be the case.

Chairman of the commission was Governor Otto Kerner of Illinois; Vice Chairman was Mayor John V. Lindsay of New York City. The other members were Senator Fred R. Harris, Oklahoma; Senator Edward W. Brooke, Massachusetts; Congressman James C. Corman, California; Congressman William M. McCulloch, Ohio; I. W. Abel, President of the United Steelworkers of America; Charles B. Thornton, Chairman of the Board, Litton Industries; Roy Wilkins, Executive Director, National Association for the Advancement of Colored People; Katherine Graham Peden, Commissioner of Commerce, State of Kentucky; and Herbert Jenkins, Chief of Police, Atlanta, Georgia.

The Report of the National Advisory Commission on Civil Disorders (which became generally known as the "Kerner Report") was made public March 1, 1968. It proved to be a penetrating and thoroughgoing inquiry directed sharply toward three fundamental questions with respect to the disorders of the preceding summer. The three questions were: What happened? Why did it happen? What can be done to prevent it from happening again? This excerpt from the summary of the report suggests its tone and impact:

> This is our basic conclusion: Our nation is moving toward two societies, one black, one white—separate and unequal.
>
> Reaction to last summer's disorders has quickened the movement and deepened the division. Discrimination and segregation have long permeated much of American life; they now threaten the future of every American.
>
> This deepening racial division is not inevitable. The movement apart can be reversed. Choice is still possible. Our principal task is to define that choice and to press for a national resolution.
>
> To pursue our present course will involve the continuing polarization of the American community and, ultimately, the destruction of basic democratic values.
>
> The alternative is not blind repression or capitulation to lawlessness. It is the realization of common opportunities for all within a single society.

The alternative will require a commitment to national action—compassionate, massive and sustained, backed by the resources of the most powerful and the richest nation on this earth. From every American it will require new attitudes, new understanding, and, above all, new will.

The vital needs of the nation must be met; hard choices must be made, and, if necessary, new taxes enacted.

Violence cannot build a better society. Disruption and disorder nourish repression, not justice. They strike at the freedom of every citizen. The community cannot—it will not—tolerate coercion and mob rule.

Segregation and poverty have created in the racial ghetto a destructive environment totally unknown to most white Americans. *What white Americans have never fully understood—but what the Negro can never forget—is that white society is deeply implicated in the ghetto. White institutions created it, white institutions maintain it, and white society condones it.*[6]

The immediate consequence of the report, after an initial editorial flurry, was to produce no significant action and some continuing talk. In the main, it tended to fade from public consideration.

But events brought it back to central consideration. On April 4, 1968 in Memphis, Tennessee, Dr. Martin Luther King, Jr. was the victim of a well-plotted assassination. In its wake, the nation experienced a weekend compounded of grief, of conscience seeking, and of tension. Not surprisingly, the murder of Dr. King triggered new violence in Chicago, large-scale burnings in Washington, D.C., in heretofore peaceful Pittsburgh, and elsewhere. The violent potential in white racism scarcely needed this tragic demonstration to prove itself, but a new dimension of its terrible quality was revealed. Dr. King was, of course, a most distinguished American, a winner of the Nobel Peace Prize. He was also the leader of the nonviolent civil-rights movement. He was militant, but he preached a militancy that rested on love and abjured violence. He urged a common human effort in behalf of all the poor and deprived and

6 *Report of the National Advisory Commission, op. cit.,* pp. 1–2. [Emphases added.]

neglected; he fanned no flames of counterracism. Instead, Dr. King had placed militant black striving squarely in the middle of the democratic tradition. The dream he had was the great American dream made accessible to all Americans. And one of the deniers of that dream murdered him.

The shock of the killing and the immediate disorders thereafter brought the Kerner Report back into public attention. "What can we do?" became a new and pressing question. The report, more closely examined, seemed to become real rather than academic. Educators could find a summation of the consequences of discrimination and segregation. The report gave solid evidence, not altogether new to educators, that ghetto schools were academically inferior, racially segregated, relatively poorly staffed, older and overcrowded, and generally starved for funds.

Among basic strategies and other recommendations that the report urged on educators were these:[7]

> To increase efforts to end de facto segregation
>
> To provide bonus support for ghetto schools
>
> To establish exemplary schools in urban settings
>
> To enrich the quality of ghetto schools by offering added teacher incentives, lower class sizes, special education facilities
>
> To broaden the curriculum to include recognition of the history, culture, and contribution of minority groups

That quality education is expensive the report acknowledged. But the urgency behind its recommendations could scarcely be ignored. Whether the American community would move in this area, as in others, with essential speed and commitment, remained a moot question. Surely its conscience had been touched by tragedy, and doubtlessly too some measure of fear affected its judgment. But the spring of 1968 had brought an international dollar crisis; the Vietnam adventure still exacted a thirty billion dollar tariff upon the budget; an income-tax surcharge was imminent. Despite the report's endorsement, for example, of the Teacher Corps, the corps'

[7] *Ibid.,* pp. 424–456.

budget was sharply cut for the ensuing year. American priorities were in contention and deeply mired in doubt and confusion.

Yet amid the confusion, the concluding words of the report set forth its unequivocal mandate: "It is time now to end the destruction and the violence, not only in the streets of the ghetto but in the lives of the people."

The *basic* necessity in the Kerner Report, as far as education is concerned, is to study it. It should become central to the curriculum of American education, especially in these areas:

1. It should be analyzed and studied by every school administrator and every board of education.

2. It should become a basic document for teacher education; it should be required reading for all who will enter the schools in professional roles.

3. It should become a standard textual item in the high-school curriculum, particularly in courses on the problems of democracy and American history.[8]

The Condition of the City

Let us turn again to the city. Just how bad it has become for human habitation has perhaps escaped the notice of those who could immunize themselves from it by commuting, by air conditioning, or by retreat to the quiet corners of its restaurants, theaters, and galleries. Yet even the expense-account transient has had its ugliness brought home on occasion: while he fumed at failure to halt a cab for an hour, when he changed his shirt for the third time in a day to be presentable for a late-afternoon appointment, when the street noises prevented slumber in an expensive hotel, when the frayed nerves of harried folks brought upon him the discourtesies of a maid, a doorman, a cab driver, a waiter, and a policeman—all within two hours of rising. If thus with the transient, what of the

8 *Ibid.,* p. 483.

455

dweller? Noise, air pollution, stacked-up garbage, jam-packed streets, every hour a rush hour, cries, elbows, dirty looks, imprecations. Even the privileged who go to work well-suited and briefcased to offices in Midtown, Loop, or Golden Triangle know these realities. And for them there is both compensation and escape. Yet, even these on occasion must "blow off steam." Sometimes, they drive like maniacs, slash at a golf-ball, read riot to wife and children, and sometimes put a bullet through their brains.

To be alive is a burden, often a weary one, and now and then for some—an intolerable one. In the city the burdens of existence, to say the least, are not lessened. What then of the burden of living in the city upon the poor—despised, housed in squalor amid rats and filth, lacking avenues either of compensation or escape? What will be the likely event if one thus burdened finds a rock in his hand and a sudden overpowering anguish and anger in his spirit? Can we not predict a shattered window?

This exposition is not a sanction for violence, not an apology for looting and burning. It is an explanation to the effect that to regard the urban riots of 1967 and 1968 as extraordinary behavior, something less than human and something inspired of an inexplicable evil, is both unseeing and unthinking.

Children have tantrums, wives throw pots and pans, men in anguish beat an angry fist upon a wall—and nurse their broken knuckles in some rue. These are real and meaningful, and common, human behaviors. They are not rational; they are self-destructive. They often work against the interest of the doer. But again, they are common human deeds; everyone knows of them. No one in good sense writes a person out of the human community because he is capable of such behavior. In truth, under given circumstances and provocations and tensions almost anyone is prone to such conduct.

Newspaper accounts sometimes assessed it as strange that in the urban rioting the initial causes had been small events. No historian would call this remarkable: the Boston Massacre was no great slaughter; Fort Sumter had no considerable strategic value; Archduke Ferdinand was a nonentity and Sarajevo, a provincial town. Chance sparks run fast and far in dry tinder.

Nor is the meaning of the urban disorders diminished by the

sure and certain knowledge that many Negroes did not approve or participate. The point is that conditions were so incendiary that enough persons did approve and participate to cause a very terrible toll of death and damage. When things come to this pass, the passions of men move without reason; consequence is forgotten; the innocent get hurt. That is simply the nature of riot and of war.

The Reality of the Black American

To put things in manageable proportions, we shall review the simple realities about the Negro in the American community:

1. His immigration constituted a general exception to all of the conditions that made America something of a promised land for all others who came here.

2. Even after release from slavery, his fundamental equality was effectively denied in economic, social, political, and educational spheres.

3. His every gain was achieved against stubborn resistance from the white population.

4. His many efforts to achieve recognition by legal and nonviolent means, though responsible for very real gains, were often rebuffed and scorned. Legal efforts have been countered with flagrant unconstitutional subterfuge; nonviolence has been countered by bullets and bombs, even upon the bodies of little children.

5. In an affluent society the Negro lives far beyond statistical probabilities within the margins of the poor.

6. In his efforts to achieve recognition the Negro has had to provide proofs where others were taken on faith; where merit was demanded, he has had to put forth seven talents when the going price was one. His recognition "at face value," because his color was different, has often meant an invitation to disdain, insult, and injury.

These are realities. Being altogether as other men are, these things bred a deep fear and hatred in the black American, who could not escape being instructed by reality. In some, these emo-

457

tions could not be contained. Hence, the consequence; hence, the nights of agony in the great cities.

A Matter of Values Reconsidered

When men turn to violence, whether blinded by bitterness engendered by their unsolved problems or acting in the vain hope of thus solving them, it must be that their scale of values has been distorted, neglected, or betrayed. A scale of values is important to a civilization, and it has become common to speak of American civilization. Somewhere in the American value pattern resides a commitment to certain elements contrasted with antivalue commitments.

Values	Antivalues
Human dignity	Self-preferment and ethnocentrism
Constitutional guarantees; the rule of law	Legalistic evasion of civic obligations; the rule of power and influence
Respect for property rights	Relentless addiction to acquisition
Peaceful solutions through the rule of reason	Solutions through force and manipulation

In general, these value-loaded concepts represent a very large verbal consensus. In the main, though some dilemmas of resolution exist among them, the positive values constitute a considerable consonance through mutually supportive interactions. If the consensus in practice were as considerable as the verbal assent to these principles, the tensions and struggles of American public life would be less intense and acrid. What goes wrong when such a splendid value system is expressed amid such pervasive disorders?

The root of the trouble is painfully apparent. A spurious value system, or rather an antivalue system, contests for the real domination of the American mind. Each element of it offers a counterfeit of the true substance. The antivalue commitments are *not* the other side of the coin of the real values of American civilization. They are counterfeit stuff, and to whatever degree they gain acceptance they drive the genuine out of circulation. We shall take each of these fundamental value conflicts into consideration, shall show their bearing upon our civic tensions and struggles, and in each case shall relate the matter to the fundamental choices within the school.

Human dignity versus self-preferment and ethnocentrism. Teachers used to appeal heavily to the notion of *teacher dignity.* It was as though dignity were acquired ex officio, somewhat as naval officers are constituted gentlemen by an act of Congress. But man possesses a dignity that no fiats of position or legislation can enhance. He is the creature who conceives himself to be born in the image of God. It is immaterial here whether this conception be harbored as a living reality or a comforting illusion. The fact remains that man can invent no more sustaining myth than this. With only lesser alternatives at man's disposal, all of them comparatively damaging to his self-esteem and some of them downright degrading to it, the best that man can take pride and stock in is his "humanness." This he shares with every other person. If he seeks status by denying his common human inheritance, how then does he glorify himself? The best image that man has ever conceived of himself has been his common sharing in his own best perception of the divine.

The school then must teach and be built upon the premise that all the devices of self-preferment are vain and self-defeating. The school in which the dignity of each individual is secure is the school that is matter of fact and universal in its recognition of human dignity. This involves very practical and day-to-day realities for the school. For example, in the school where individual dignity is secure, marks will be taken as relatively unimportant measures of achievement. They will never be distorted into meaningful stratifications of human worth.

If the opportunities for self-expression and for special development in the school are in any sense scarcity items, it is certain that special preferment will ordinarily be accorded to those who need these opportunities the least. Special programs for "the gifted" have consistently been of this order. It has been poignantly amusing to hear the case made that the academically talented have somehow been neglected by the school. In point of fact the school has been

459

too often mobilized only for these. The fact that "the gifted" have sometimes been harassed by their peers, even induced to camouflage their abilities on occasion (though this phenomenon has been greatly exaggerated), has been attributed to vulgar anti-intellectualism. More often the real reasoning has been a defensive reaction, a deep exasperation with having the institution geared to the motivations and interests of an academic elite. People do not resent the special achievements of those with whom they participate in common pursuits, in common purposes. It is lack of common purpose that divides the school and that divides the students within it against itself.

Constitutional guarantees and the rule of law versus legalistic evasion of civic obligations and the rule of power and influence. The school errs fundamentally (though not as greatly as some would urge it to do) in teaching the American constitutional system as a government perfected. To teach that American political science has at its disposal a practically perfect instrument for adapting to societal needs constitutes no major perpetration of hokum.

The frightened and defensive fringes within the community often feel that the school somehow instructs in disloyalty when it penetrates the dark corners of public and private corruption and dereliction. This fear is real enough, but the hypocrisy it urges upon the school must be ignored. The same standards must be applied when the public is cheated in governmental contracts and when the school makes curriculum the stuff of such derelictions. When public officials, corporation executives, or union officials lie, their acts constitute betrayal; when the school holds up the truth beside such misstatement, it refuses the sanction of its silence to betrayal.

The value conflict in American life is real. The school need not be torn in its loyalties; it belongs only to the real value system, not to its counterfeit competitor. But if the school fails to recognize this reality it can scarcely hope to make a value impact on youth. The school is not the only source of evidence upon reality accessible to youth. If youth finds that the school has made its peace with corruption and public dereliction, will it not hold the school itself to be a betrayer?

Respect for property rights versus the relentless addiction to acquisition. Our society is built upon the conviction that a person's human and property rights, while not identical, are basically and humanely interconnected. "A man's home is his castle" is a common assertion implying sanction of the home as a private refuge with large guarantees against intrusion. The right to acquire title to goods and properties somewhat in proportion to the effort required in the process is basic to the theory of economic motivation. The product of the society is an impressive witness to its efficacy as incentive. Contracts are granted a basic legal sanction, and while these agreements should be carefully written and carefully read before signing, the force of contract has about it a certain moral idealism. "His word is as good as his bond" is a phrase that elevates a man in the common esteem to a veritable model of probity.

Although property rights and human rights are related, they are not identical. In the institution of slavery they were dead set, one against the other. Before workmen allied themselves in protection against coercive aggregates of economic power, the ability of a man to turn his efforts, the power of his mind and muscle, into his own collection of useful goods was severely limited. Unions and the hard-won right of collective bargaining have gone far to produce certain equities in the struggle for economic equality. The social process has been markedly improved and refined. Nevertheless, the struggle is sometimes raw and hurtful; the inequities are not all erased, and the benefits of concerted orderly process remain far from universal.

Productivity and acquisitiveness are not the same. Neither are they all that life is governed by. They are not the total goals of a *good* society. Economic man is not the full measure of human capacity. Thorstein Veblen, indeed, set productivity and acquisitiveness quite at odds with one another. He saw the "instinct for workmanship," the basic productive motivation, often being thwarted and exploited by predatory and acquisitive motivations. It is within everyone's range of experience and powers of observation to note that the willingness to work and the pleasure of building something useful and creditable to self and species is not necessarily the same as to gain enormous edifices of property and power.

461

The school has to take thought and stock of itself with regard to the motivations and aspirations that it sanctions and reinforces. The fact of education is not merely an economic asset, though this is the factor that educational propaganda so often stresses. More important, education is an ethical asset. Instruction in ethics may indeed restrain pure acquisitiveness and will surely insist on the existence of other virtues.

Peaceful solutions through the rule of reason versus force and manipulation. The chips are pretty well down on this contest. The school is in its hardest bind at this point because in this value contest "good" and "bad" in any societal consensus are meaningless terms. Conscience condemns force and manipulation; yet conscience gives force and manipulation its highest honors—and even employs them to its uses. The division of the American mind on the Vietnam excursion is the proof. The school has no allowable foundation for a value commitment here. That does not mean that it must be utterly paralyzed, but it cannot go far beyond the utter contradiction of its most profound codes in this arena.

However, it can keep its forum free. Both consciences must be allowed the floor, both must essay their persuasiveness. Beyond this the school has a limited alternative. It can ever so tentatively build on the belief that there is a slight human bias in favor of peace. The evidence is far from conclusive, but let the school push this hope a little. The curriculum is good on wars, not necessarily in the chauvinistic sense. It explains well the roots and causes; it is learned as to the techniques and instruments of war; it is affectively competent in reconstructing the imagery and the emotions of bellicose endeavors. This should not be censored.

But let the range of its scholarly and technical competence be extended. Too often the curriculum is abominably dull and tedious when it dutifully deals with the United Nations and its agencies. It simply does not create any impression that peace has any moral or emotional equivalents to war. If the society cannot decide which is better, war or peace, the school can scarcely make up its mind. But the school, if it must equivocate, might at least do so fairly. The techniques of peace-making are as vigorously intellectual as any lessons Karl von Clausewitz penned, and the emotions of man are as live in other arenas as in battle. In a world hesitant to choose between life or death, the modest plea of the curriculum-maker perhaps must be: *equal time for peace.* Whatever more the schools will risk for peace and reason in solving mortal issues will have to derive from the courage and conscience of those who teach in them. The value structure lends nothing but its contradictions to guide them.

The Students Reconsidered

The school works out its total effect in the developing of five discernible types of students, whom we have somewhat arbitrarily classified and designated as the alienated student, the "hipster," the cynic, the successnik, and the *person.*

First, because he has called himself so dramatically to attention, is the *almost utterly alienated student.* To take the extreme examples, whether he is cutting a wide swath of murder from Nebraska to points West, practicing marksmanship on living targets from a university tower in Texas, or achieving holocaust within a neighborhood, this "student" has obviously been endowed with a richly negative view of life and social relationship. A good deal of such views must needs come from the impact of social institutions. Since those on whom we focus are young, the principal social institution outside the home from which they derived such large negative impact must have been the school. This was surely not the intention of the school, nor is it the charge that the school lies exclusively blameworthy. Because our competence lies in the field of educational responsibility and not in examining the consequences of religious dogma, it is with the influences of the school that we must concern ourselves. If the alienated were only an aberrant few, merely an insignificant minority rendered savage perhaps by psychotic personality, it might be possible to shrug off such consequence as statistically negligible. But other phenomena in the world of youth call themselves into the reckoning.

The *hipsters* intrude themselves as a comparatively recent entry

463

into categories of educational analysis. A monologue, constructed as a composite from conversations with assorted "hippies" (and freely translated into more conventional English) renders its own judgment, somewhat peculiar and fearfully telling, upon the institution of our concern:

> The school—the school is all hung up. It's all a big game—I don't mean football—it's the game the teachers play, the game the students play to make it easy, or make it big for that matter. It's the big game the principal is playing, and the game the little cats play with the big cats that goes on all the time. Man, that school was full of hate. The teachers hated each other, the man in the office hated the teachers, everybody hated the students, and a lot of the students, all of them who didn't like the game, hated the whole works. Seems to me the studies were built on hate. Oh, sure, they've got a lot of love: love the flag, love your country, love law and order, love free enterprise. You boil that down, brother, it still says hate: you hate Russia, you hate the Viet Cong (you love General Ky naturally), you hate those dirty . . . [censored] that go tearing up the towns, you hate those noisy picketing troublemakers with long hair and guitars that go picketing and making trouble and talking and singing about love, love, love. Man, it's all one big game of hate, and we're not playing. We don't want to get at anybody's guts, we've got love, love in the heart and love in the soul. We're going to talk, and let me tell you, baby, we're going to live it.

The hipsters have a lot more to say, and some of it is a good deal harder to take than this. We hope that their perceptions are wrong. What is relevant here is that all should be aware that this is a second body of response to the school that has become visible and significant. Note that in the hipster view the school is totally the captive of a games-playing establishment. That establishment it perceives to be rooted entirely in the specious aspect of the value system, which we have set forth as counterfeit coin.

Both the alienated and the hippie hold a negative relationship to the value structure of the school as they perceive it. The alienated perceive the sum total value structure to be the cluster that we have designated counterfeit. This is not to say that the alienated perceive self-seeking, sanctified materialism, to be false coin. The deprivation in their eyes is not to be able to lay hold of it. The hippie, on the other hand, sees clearly the worthlessness of this currency. However, because his instruction has been naïve in respect to values, he perceives the bad stuff to be the only circulating medium. Therefore, he opts out. He thinks that he must coin his own values because he has so seldom been offered anything other than depreciated currency.

The *cynic* commutes between conformity and alienation. He may even wear his hair at medium length to assure acceptance as he changes costumes at the end of the line. He is fairly certain that the price he pays for goods required to attain status is an exorbitant one. He is also fairly certain that there is no way to arrive but to play the game hard in public and to seek to develop an authentic self in private or in anonymity. He is an inviting prospect for schizophrenia. Operationally the cynic is willing to defraud; he passes bad coin understanding full well its nature. He easily turns counterfeiter.

The *successnik* fills his time accumulating junk and stocks his treasure house with lead. He is the cultural counterpart to the alienated. Both trust the bad coin as legal tender. Only the successnik is born handy to it or to the acquisition of the necessary skills to acquire it. Since reality threatens this system of security, the successnik builds elaborate defenses around himself. The suggestion that it might make sense to weigh the dross against the gold can excite him to fury. He sometimes keeps his fictional edifices intact a long while, though seldom for a lifetime. Floods have a rude way with sandcastles.

The other student is simply *the person.* He is the one who has escaped cultural damage to the degree that he must be called by name and will not fit another category. Strangely enough, he is any of the foregoing or all of them—alienated, hipster, cynic, successnik. At one time these all bore names that some used with warmth and intimacy. If they have now become types (and undesirable ones at that), perhaps it was partly because the school so seldom addressed them by a name that they recognized.

The school when it clearly sees its human function admits no categories among its graduates: it wants to see only persons passing

465

through. Each of the first four groups has somehow lost significant holds upon identity. The forces that affected them affect all in some manner or degree.

Let us now come to the larger point. Each classification is but a description of behaviors all traceable to hurts and fears, to damage and neglect, to a failure of love.

The relation of the school's human purpose to the value structure, the value content as it were, becomes evident. The school must clearly state what the value structure is and assure the student that it is not neutral with respect to its desires for him. It must teach responsibility and choice, and it must make clear that there is a basis for responsible choice. But how does the school hold those persons who in various manners stand ready to opt out? How does the school retain them in human community? It does so by seeking each one out, over and over, addressing him by name; it recognizes his identity; it authenticates his selfhood repeatedly and consistently; it delivers messages to him that it verifies, guarantees, acknowledges, and stands behind. In a word, the school accepts the student in life and lives that life with him.

Concluding Commentary: Stone Age Man in the Space Age

The world indeed does move. The children born in 1969 will, if they survive, be only 31 years old in the year 2000. The twenty-first century is near at hand.

And already, as well we know, it is the Space Age. Phineas Fogg's record is shattered—and not to a mere 79 or even 78 days. It is now a matter of how many times the earth is orbited in a *single* day. And we are confidently told it will not be long before man will take a trip to the moon and come back to tell us about it—of what kind of cheese it is made, perhaps.

There is no question of man's abilities to travel. But how much better? Now, there is a question for us. For man to travel in space:

466

what liberation our achievements already signify! Man has conquered tremendous fears: fears of the unknown, fears of terrible altitudes, fears of intruding upon the realms of the gods themselves. How much more daring even than Prometheus is modern man! What doubts of self the spaceman has conquered, or sternly beaten down. And he has escaped from normal views of time and distance—even challenged the view that humanity is forever earthbound. To ride at heights that make Everest a little lump of rock, at speeds to make millponds of the seven seas—what a glorious perspective for the mind of man! How much of the petty, the trivial, the molehills made mountains, he is able to leave behind. So this is the Space Age—an era of mortal glory.

Consider the man of the Stone Age, the limits that encompassed him, the terrors that beset him. Did he not dread the forces of nature, even when fearfully he took fire for his own use or wrestled certain beasts to submission? How terrible to him were the reaches of the other valleys, how awful the faces of the strangers who dwelt beyond the hills. Quick to the club or spear when new faces trespassed within the tribal realm! Beards or skins of other colors, surely these were the signs of danger, of evils, of enemies—or of inferiors to be caught and set to drudgery. How frightened was Stone Age man, and how dangerous in his fear. So many things to be afraid of: nature, plagues (the long nights without TV), and other men—other frightened men. The world was big, broad, *and scary*.

Now we know that the world is not so big a place as we whip around it at 17,000 miles an hour and more. We live on a small planet inhabited by one kind of man: human kind. But we knew that before the Space Age. Wendell Willkie, in the 1940s, flew around it at less than 300 miles an hour and pronounced the reality: *one world*. And the atomic scientists extended the insight: *one world—or none*.

To what spacious insights man has grown!

Today, tomorrow, or in ten years man will set forth on his journey to the moon. He may travel alone, or with a few, but the efforts of tens of millions will be used to launch him—and prayers in a hundred tongues will attend him.

467

Who will be left behind? Modern men to be sure will see him off. There will be men fit for the Space Age viewing his trip. They will be well nourished in mind and body, dedicated to intelligence and inquiry, devoted to human welfare beyond little matters. Fear in them will be diminished to natural proportions. They will be clean of hate, bias, and chauvinism. Man in space will be the product of the genius of the human spirit's liberation, and these attributes are also products of the same genius.

But others will also be left behind. It is the Space Age, but it is historical man who inhabits the earth. Off to the moon, but on earth there are many millions scarcely rid of the dreadful heritage of the Stone Age. Of the men behind, ninety of a hundred will still be uncertain of their next day's food; millions will be dying of ills that other men have already learned to cure; a great fraction will not yet have crossed the threshold of literacy. And in the most enlightened lands, perhaps the lands of the astronauts themselves, men of Stone Age postures will recite the old fears, look alarmed at strangers, panic at differently colored beards or skins, yell gibberish of clubs and spears at the thought of other tribes. Yes, time is relative, and the fearful Stone Age types still skulk and cower among us.

Would it not be a monstrous irony if on the day of the moon launch, children should again be murdered by Stone Age men in the basement of some church? It must not be. We must somehow transform *historical man* into *modern man*, a species fit to survive in the Space Age.

Franklin A. Lindsay said it succinctly:

> The dramatic success of the Mercury program, where we elevated man into space, must be balanced against our failure to elevate large segments of our own society to the level of equal opportunity. Certainly we could not solve our earthly problems by turning our backs on space, but we should be very careful before we turn our backs on earth.[9]

[9] Franklin A. Lindsay, "Our Gamble in Space: The Costs and the Choices," *Atlantic Monthly* (August 1963), p. 54.

There is well-founded talk of an "explosion of knowledge." However, it might be more becoming to let later generations praise us for a second golden age or a new renaissance. To contain our new knowledge we must have an explosion of responsibility or an explosion of conscience.

At this point education might employ a different approach to youth. It might assert that its generation must be more responsible than its parents' generation had been. The parental generation is rightly and sorrowfully aware of the limitations of its accomplishments. However, it is not insignificant achievements with which youth may be confronted as a challenge. The parental generation has done these things:

1. Encountered and endured the Great Depression, and beat it back without scrapping the basic democratic framework. Indeed, by inventive legislation it built in safeguards against the recurrence of such deadly economic paralysis.

2. Built schools and put more children to school and college than any people in history.

3. Went to war and beat to unconditional surrender some of the meanest men and basest ideas in human history.

4. Built a large though insecure edifice for world order. Fought in Korea a true police action somewhat successfully in its name. Gave aggressors a warning and gave peace another chance.

5. Lessened through its efforts dread of polio and other plagues.

The elders will not quit their efforts, but they must have youth with them. And youth must go well beyond its heritage.

A lot of confidence in youth is well grounded—and so is some worry. It is sound to worry when polls of college youth indicate that majorities would give up the several guarantees of the Bill of Rights without objection. This is frightening. Our rights might better be lost by cowardice than by ignorance: that way they might at least be regretted. Our first responsibility is to learn in depth the meaning and necessity of our freedoms and to defend them. If the school would help to create an explosion of responsibility, there are plenty of places to start.

Educators can purge themselves of offensive, fearful Stone Age postures and walk upright in the company of modern men. Educators can become insistent toward home and neighborhood that Stone Age attitudes about creeds and races shall cease to be of consequence in decision-making.

They can make their schedules a time of learning. This learning can educate youth to scorn the silly pastimes of the bored and wretched and put off the ridiculous togs of fleeting fashion. It can raise them to leave off the games of childhood and become responsible. It can help them to grow up.

Schools can develop citizens who confront and expel officials who scorn their oaths and neglect their offices. Low-level politics can be driven out of the schools. Responsible educators can help to advertise the qualities of responsible school board members and the deficiencies of the low-grade ones.

The meaning of human concern can become a central study; the central discipline can be taught as being *good to all men,* who, after all, are brothers.

The school can put man back to work in his own behalf. The merit of youth, even in rebellion, can be both reproach and challenge to the society. If youth lends its effort and discontent to remaking society and not to abandoning it, we may yet make this terrible century the best and not the last for modern man.

On
Extended
Readings

To study the school in order to attempt to understand some of the meaning, the rigor, the joy, and the agony of education is a necessary purpose for some to undertake and is a commendable one for those who undertake it. To set limits on the study is an exercise in futility. The school may be narrowly defined, so narrowly, in fact, that it becomes scarcely worth study, except as a strange institutional phenomenon. Education is potentially as large as life and as involved; it asks of its serious student only what life demands, a lifetime of observation and study.

As teachers, we have often presented reading lists as "reading programs for a lifetime." In education this may contain an element of bad advice, as its reading lists are extremely perishable. Bad books, nothing books abound. But the number and quality of books on education, on the school, on the student increases. It is one of the few solidly hopeful signs, even though the best books, no doubt, lie ahead.

This then is intended as a guide to significantly related reading that is supplementary to the text in either support or contradiction of the author's premises. It is necessarily selective and limited; an ambitious student in the course of a year might make a substantial dent in it. It is not intended, in the main, as an acknowledgment of

471

the author's indebtedness. Such indebtedness is either made explicitly or is visible within the work. As a matter of fact, the obligation of the writer runs far beyond the notations in the work, to the inspiration and teaching of dozens of colleagues, thousands of readings, and innumerable observations and experiences within the school. The conceptualization of the work is the author's. It is hoped that it will be found original and creative; at the same time, it is intended to have been centrally relevant to contemporary educational problems and dilemmas and responsible to the finest commitments of American democracy and universal education.

General Background

Let us first suggest a number of works, none of which we have particularly leaned on, but which furnish, as we see it, friendly and supportive company for our text. The reading of any or all of these would extend and no doubt clarify the context of this work.

First, one should read Michael Young, *The Rise of the Meritocracy* (New York: Random House, 1958), because of its penetration of the fundamental issue: Shall the potential for democratic achievement be subverted by modern conceptions of governing elites? Readers are warned to finish this rather brief work before drawing conclusions. At least one reviewer has made himself ridiculous by a short and fast scanning of this beautifully misleading construction. After this, if the reader were starting from "scratch" his readings about education (which is an unlikely assumption), we would recommend A. S. Neill, *Summerhill* (New York: Hart Publishing Co., 1960), because it presents a devastating psychic shock to conventional views and expectations of schools, parents, and students. It may safely be assumed that a large modern school system will not be built on Neill's blueprint, but before anything new and vital is built, a lot of the rubble of conventional nonsense will have to be cleared away. Neill has been a help in this regard. And so, too, have been Paul Goodman and Edgar Friedenburg; thus, we recommend their respective works, *Growing Up Absurd* (New York: Knopf, 1956) and *The Vanishing Adolescent* (Boston: Beacon Press, 1959). Their continuing output tends to refresh the stream of American educational thought with most essential additives.

The reader is next directed to Lawrence A. Cremin's, *The Transformation of the School* (New York: Knopf, 1961). This book is a change of pace to solid, responsible, sound interpretative history. It is a comprehensive treatment of the emphases in American education from 1876 to 1957. Do not anticipate that the solid quality of Cremin's work means dull writing: far from it. Raymond Callahan, *Education and the Cult of Efficiency* (Chicago: University of Chicago Press, 1962), with great precision limns the cause and technique of administrative straitjacketing in the schools. He does not exaggerate; his scholarly restraint and the enormity of the phenomena he reports tend to assure this. But to read Callahan without the refreshment of perspective afforded by William H. Whyte, Jr., *The Organization Man* (New York: Simon and Schuster, 1956), or G. Northcote Parkinson, *Parkinson's Law and Other Studies in Administration* (Boston: Houghton Mifflin, 1957), is to miss much of the irony and comedy in his data, which indeed Callahan in his admirable crusading intensity seems himself somewhat to have missed.

Then Earl C. Kelley, *In Defense of Youth* (Englewood Cliffs, N.J.: Prentice-Hall, 1962), should be read largely because youth deserves and needs its defense. Daniel Schreiber (ed.), *The School Dropout* (Washington, D.C.: National Education Association, 1964), has compiled one of the few pieces of "official educational literature" ever to justify its printing cost. It is an excellent symposium, focusing attention at the point where education must prove itself—on the difficult cases. For those who want to learn what it really means to take a long, cool, detached, critical view at familiar institutions, the Veblenian model is best; therefore, we highly recommend Thorstein Veblen, *The Theory of the Leisure Class* (New York: Macmillan, 1898).

Three items of "professional literature" stand together in a large measure of mutual compatibility and considerable consonance with our work. These are Association for Supervision and Curriculum Development, *Perceiving, Behaving, Becoming: A New Focus for Education* (Washington, D.C.: National Education Association, 1962); H. Gordon Hullfish and Philip G. Smith, *Reflective Thinking: The Method of Education* (New York: Dodd, Mead, 1961); and Arthur W. Combs and Donald Snygg, *Individual Behavior*, rev. ed. (New York: Harper & Row, 1959).

Among books we would recommend as basic back-up works are Robert W. Heath (ed.), *New Curricula* (New York: Harper & Row, 1964), for its clear-cut reporting of such developments as the "new mathematics," The CHEM Study, PSSC physics, Project English, and others; James B. Conant, *The American High School Today* (New York: McGraw-Hill, 1959), and James Gardner, *Excellence: Can We Be Equal and Excellent Too?* (New York: Harper & Row, 1961), not so much because of intrinsic merit, but because of the effect of their prestigious weight upon the dialogue—in a word, because they are documents of some small historical significance. Similarly, we recommend Jerome S. Bruner, *The Process of Education* (Cambridge: Harvard University Press, 1961). This work had an undeniable seminal effect, but beyond that, acquaintance with it is simply an essential hallmark of conversance with the field. Solon T. Kimball and James E. McClelland, *Education and the New America* (New York: Random House, 1962), with which this text takes some issue, belongs among these works.

For accurate and objective reporting on a lively area of controversy, the reader cannot find better than Morris L. Bigge, *Learning Theories for Teachers* (New York: Harper & Row, 1964). It is a beautiful piece of educational exposition, not in our style but altogether to our liking.

Other important books to bulwark the reader's general view of the educational scene are Martin Mayer, *The Schools* (New York: Harper & Row, 1961), the best journalistic examination of education to date; and Philip H. Phenix, *Education and the Common Good* (New York: Harper & Row, 1961), a provocative effort, even though it reduces (or elevates, as the case may be) the school to a moral abstraction.

For further reading in historical and social foundations, priority is given to these basic works on American civilization: Merle Curti, *Growth of American Thought,* 3rd ed. (New York: Harper & Row, 1964), and Max Lerner, *America As a Civilization* (New York: Simon and Schuster, 1957). Each of these furnishes a fine springboard to the subject, and either will provide rich bibliographical resources for years of pertinent study. W. J. Cash, *The Mind of the South* (New York: Knopf, 1941), is intrinsically meritorious, but beyond this it illustrates the meaning of a profound regional analysis in ultimate terms. It is doubtful that any work on any aspect of the American scene comes even close to this one in its consistently hard-working intelligence and the quality and fabric of insights produced and sustained by it.

The pertinence of the foregoing especially to Parts One and Three of the text is general and pervasive. In addition, conceptual depth in these dimensions is well forwarded in a number of issues of *Daedalus* (Journal of the American Academy of Arts and Sciences), especially these: *Quantity and Quality* (Fall 1959) ; *The Professions* (Fall 1963); *The Visual Arts Today* (Winter 1960); *Excellence and Leadership in a Democracy* (Fall 1961) ; *Science and Technology in Contemporary Society* (Spring 1962) ; and *Creativity and Learning* (Summer 1965).

Educational Philosophy

When it comes to philosophy of education no one is competently studied or equipped to speak with understanding who is not deeply grounded in the pragmatic-progressive analysis. This means that he should have read most of what John Dewey has written and a good deal of William James and Charles Peirce. He will have studied widely and well in the works of John Child, William Heard Kilpatrick, Sidney Hook, and Boyd Bode. This statement asserts that there has indeed been an authentic philosophical undergirding of the democratic educational enterprise and that in the works of these men it has had its exposition and delineation.

475

For a short reading list on philosophy of education, these works have particular relevance to themes in this text:

Brameld, Theodore. *Education as Power.* New York: Holt, Rinehart, and Winston, 1965.

————. *Education for the Emerging Age.* New York: Harper & Row, 1965.

————. *Philosophies of Education in Cultural Perspective.* New York: Dryden, 1955.

Hook, Sidney. *Education for Modern Man.* New York: Knopf, 1963.

Kneller, George F. *Existentialism and Education.* New York: Wiley, 1958.

Nash, Paul. *Authority and Freedom in Education.* New York: Wiley, 1966.

Phenix, Philip H. (ed.). *Philosophies of Education.* New York: Wiley, 1961. A very convenient little reader.

Soderquist, Harold O. *The Person and Education.* Columbus, Ohio: Merrill, 1964.

Methods and Practices

Certain works elaborate instructional practices, pose models, and push enthusiasms that have excited some interest, even of a bandwagon order. Many of these are centrally important. In our view, others are marginal to the real necessities of our time; some are, we think, utterly irrelevant. But they relate, even if negatively, to the matters emphasized especially in Chapters IV, VI, VII, and XII. It is hoped that the reader may appraise them in clearer perspective in the context of this book.

Beggs, David W., and Edward G. Buffie. *Independent Study.* Bloomington: Indiana University Press, 1965.

Brameld, Theodore. *The Use of Explosive Ideas in Education.* Pittsburgh: University of Pittsburgh Press, 1965.

Brown, Clarence W., and Edwin E. Ghiselli. *Scientific Method in Psychology.* New York: McGraw-Hill, 1955.

476

A Climate for Individuality. Joint Project on the Individual and the School. Washington, American Association of School Administrators, Association for Supervision and Curriculum Development, National Association of Secondary-School Principals, and Department of Rural Education of the National Education Association, 1965.

Corey, Stephan M. *Action Research to Improve School Practices.* New York: Bureau of Publications, Teachers College, Columbia University, 1953.

Doll, Ronald C. *Curriculum Improvement: Decision Making and Process.* Boston: Allyn and Bacon, 1964.

Flanders, Ned A. "Teacher Influence, Pupil Attitudes, and Achievement," in Bruce J. Biddle and William J. Ellena (eds.), *Contemporary Research on Teacher Effectiveness.* New York: Holt, Rinehart, and Winston, 1964.

Glaser, Robert. *Newer Educational Media.* University Park: Pennsylvania State University, 1961.

Goodlad, John I., and Robert H. Anderson. *The Nongraded Elementary School,* rev. ed. New York: Harcourt, Brace & World, 1963.

Grambs, Jean D., Clarence G. Noyce, Franklin Patterson, and John C. Robertson. *The Junior High School We Need.* Washington, D.C.: Association for Supervision and Curriculum Development, 1961.

Griffin, William M. "The Wayland, Massachusetts High School Program for Individual Differences," *N.A.S.S.P. Bulletin,* 47 (March 1963), 118–127.

Hovey, Donald E., Howard E. Gruber, and Glenn Terrell. "Effects of Self-Directed Study on Course Achievement, Retention, and Curiosity," *Journal of Educational Research,* 56 (March 1963), 346–351.

Kingsley, Howard L. *The Nature and Conditions of Learning.* Revised by Ralph Garry. Englewood Cliffs, N.J.: Prentice-Hall, 1957.

Manolakes, George. *The Elementary School We Need.* Washington, D.C.: Association for Supervision and Curriculum Development, 1965.

McJackson, David M., W. L. Shoemaker, and Paul Westmeyer. "Experiments with Independent Study," *N.A.S.S.P. Bulletin,* 45 (January 1961), 198–208.

McKeachie, W. J. "The Improvement of Instruction," *Review of Educational Research,* XXX, 4 (October 1960), 351–359.

Morrison, Henry C. *The Practices of Teaching in the Secondary School,* rev. ed. Chicago: University of Chicago Press, 1931.

Shumsky, Abraham. "The Subjective Experience of the Researcher," *The Journal of Educational Sociology,* 36 (November 1962), 134–138.

————. "Learning About Learning from Action Research," in *Learning and the Teacher.* Yearbook. Washington, D.C.: Association for Supervision and Curriculum Development, 1959. Chapter 10.

Smith, Wendell, and J. William Moore. *Programmed Learning: Theory and Research.* Princeton: Van Nostrand, 1962.

Strang, Ruth. *Guided Study and Homework, What Research Says to the Teacher.* Washington, D.C.: Department of Classroom Teachers, American Educational Research Association of the National Education Association, 1955.

Wiles, Kimball, and Franklin Patterson. *The High School We Need.* Washington, D.C.: Association for Supervision and Curriculum Development, 1959.

Wrightstone, J. Wayne. *Class Organization for Instruction, What Research Says to the Teacher.* Washington, D.C.: Department of Classroom Teachers, American Educational Research Association of the National Education Association, 1957.

Technology and the Media

The plans, the speculations, and the aspirations of the educational technologists are represented in symposia in two special issues of major professional journals: "Big Business Discovers the Education Market," *Phi Delta Kappan,* XLVIII, 5 (January 1967); and "Computers and the Schools," *NEA Journal,* LVI, 2 (February 1967), 15–32. These furnish good cross-section views.

The following titles afford an exploratory reading program on developments of which modern educators should be critically aware:

Bushnell, Donald D., and Dwight W. Allen (eds.). *The Computer in Education.* New York: Wiley, 1967.

Goodlad, John I., John F. O'Toole, Jr., and Louise L. Tyler. *Computers and Information Systems in Education.* New York: Harcourt, Brace & World, 1962.

Loughary, John W. *Man-Machine Systems in Education.* New York: Harper & Row, 1966.

Lumsdaine, A. A., and Robert Glaser (eds.). *Teaching Machines and Programmed Learning.* Washington, D.C.: National Education Association, 1960.

Trow, William C. *Teacher and Technology: New Designs for Learning.* New York: Appleton-Century-Crofts, 1963.

Among substantial works on the media (chiefly television) and children are these:

Himmelweit, Hilde T., A. N. Oppenheim, and Pamela Vince. *Television and the Child.* London: Oxford University Press, 1958.

Schramm, Wilbur, Jack Lyle, and Edwin B. Parker. *Television in the Lives of Our Children.* Stanford: Stanford University Press, 1961.

Education in the Cities

To search for definitive work on the problem of urban education is fruitless, for the city is undefined, not so much undefinable as constantly redefining itself. To make sense urban education must attach itself to urban reality. Thus, urban education must become rooted in the winds of change. Whatever the result of the social forces tugging and hauling within the city, they will somewhat affect the direction of the urban school. And, at the same time, the school—the force of education, as it were—will become a signal force in shaping the direction and velocity of urban change.

If the literature has been less than definitive, it is, nonetheless, helpful and often vital. First, a few books that cut through apathy and content to get at something like the raw nature of the problem: Michael Harrington, *The Other America* (New York: Macmillan, 1963), had much to do with dispelling the myth of a comprehensive affluence in this nation; Claude Brown, *Manchild in the Promised Land* (New York: Macmillan, 1965), and *The Autobiography of Malcolm X* (New York: Grove, 1965) picture the conditions of the contemporary black American, his views of it, and the distance traveled since the time of Booker T. Washington, in whose image many men of good will but antique social thought would like to see the shaping of Negro leadership. Harvey Cox, *The Secular City* (New York: Macmillan, 1965), is strongly representative of the growing view within the churches that religion must come to man "where the action is," and the action is in the troubled city.

The student should not minimize the service performed by the compilers of good anthologies. Two of these commend themselves especially: Everett T. Keach, Jr., Robert Fulton, and William E. Gardner (eds.), *Education and Social Crisis* (New York: Wiley, 1967); and A. Harry Passow, Miriam Goldberg, and Abraham J. Tannenbaum (eds.), *Education of the Disadvantaged* (New York: Holt, Rinehart, and Winston, 1967). A useful symposium on "The Future Metropolis" that neglects *only* the educational sector appears in *Daedalus* (Winter 1961).

If the question in anyone's mind is "What's Wrong with City Schools?" some of the answers are to be found in Martin Mayer's graphic report under that title in *The Saturday Evening Post,* September 9, 1967. Edgar Z. Friedenberg finds the evidence so gloomy that he penned "Requiem for the Urban School" in the November 18, 1967, issue of *Saturday Review;* in the same issue, Susan L. Jacoby wrote a report on the schools of the nation's capital under the title "Education in Washington: National Monument to Failure." Books expand the evidence: Jonathan Kozol, *Death at an Early Age* (Boston: Houghton Mifflin, 1967); Herbert Kohl, *36 Children* (New York: New American Library, 1967); Peter Schrag, *Village School Downtown* (Boston: Beacon Press, 1967). All are written with deep tones of urgency. The best attention yet paid this subject in any professional educational journal is the March 1967 issue of *Phi Delta Kappan* devoted to "Problems of Urban Education."

The issues of urban education include, of course, the central problem of integration. The following works, among many others, provide solid evidence and much reassuring data as to the feasibility and the constructive educational effects of integration in the schools.

Coleman, James S., and others. *Equality of Educational Opportunity.* Washington, D. C.: U. S. Government Printing Office, 1966.

Commission on School Integration, National Association of Intergroup Relations Officials, *Public School Segregation and Integration in the North.* Washington, D. C.: NAIRO, 1963.

Giles, H. H. *The Integrated Classroom.* New York: Basic Books, 1959.

Katz, Irwin. "Review of Evidence Relating to Effects of Desegregation on the Intellectual Performance of Negroes," *American Psychologist,* 19, 6 (1964), 381–399.

U. S. Commission on Civil Rights. *Racial Isolation in the Public Schools.* Washington, D. C.: U. S. Government Printing Office, 1967.

Weinberg, Meyer. *Research on School Desegregation: Review and Prospect.* Chicago: Integrated Education Associates, 1965.

Williams, Jr., R. M., and M. W. Ryan (eds.). *Schools in Transition: Community Experiences in Desegregation.* Chapel Hill: University of North Carolina Press, 1954.

Subject Index

Name Index

ABOUT THE AUTHOR

Ryland W. Crary was born in Astoria, Oregon in 1913. He received his B.A., M.A., and Ph.D. from the State University of Iowa. He subsequently taught and/or participated in educational projects in thirty states, as well as four foreign countries on three continents. He taught eight years in junior and senior high schools, served on the faculties of Teachers College (Columbia University) and Washington University (St. Louis). He has held a staff position at NEA Headquarters, and served as Director of Research for the National Educational Television Center. His publications include: *Latin America and World Struggle for Freedom* (Boston: Ginn, 1943); *America's Stake in Human Rights*, coauthored with John Robinson (Washington, D.C.: National Council for Social Studies, 1948); *Challenge of Atomic Energy*, coauthored with Hubert Evans and others (New York: Teachers College Publications, 1948); and *How to Teach About Communism*, coauthored with Gerald Steibel (New York: Anti-Defamation League, 1949). He also served as editor of *Education for Democratic Citizenship* (Washington, D.C.: National Council for Social Studies Yearbook, 1951), as well as the *History of Education Quarterly*, 1961–1965.

A NOTE ON THE TYPE

This book was set on the Linotype in "Baskerville," a facsimile of the type designed, in 1754, by John Baskerville, a writing-master of Birmingham, England. This type was one of the forerunners of the "modern" style of type faces. The Linotype copy was cut under the supervision of George W. Jones of London.

Composed, printed, and bound by American Book–Stratford Press, Inc., New York, New York. Typography by Bob Freese.